The Net-Zero Transitions in Energy and Finance

Since the United States hosted the Leaders' Summit on Climate in 2021, numerous countries have committed to net-zero emissions targets. Given the sizes of their economies, populations, and greenhouse gas emissions, emerging markets and developing economies in South, East, and Southeast Asia will play a key role in determining whether or not these targets are achieved. *The Net-Zero Transitions in Energy and Finance* focuses on net-zero transitions in Southeast Asia and applies the lessons learned to other major emerging markets and developing economies. The book argues that net-zero emissions targets require synchronised changes not only in complementary elements in energy systems but also in the financial institutions that fund and invest in facilitating system transitions. Proposing novel frameworks for analysing electricity system transitions using empirical evidence, this book identifies enabling factors, drivers, and barriers, and suggests solutions for overcoming the challenges of multi-sector transitions.

AKIHISA MORI is an associate professor of global environmental economics and leads Team Sustainability Transitions at Kyoto University, Japan. He served as vice president of the Asian Association of Environmental and Resource Economics in 2019–2021. He has published research on sustainable energy transitions in journals including *Environmental Innovation and Societal Transitions*, *Energy Research & Social Science*, and *Energy Policy*.

NUR FIRDAUS is a researcher at the National Research and Innovation Agency, Indonesia, and a PhD student in Team Sustainability Transitions at Kyoto University, Japan.

YASUHIRO OGURA is a senior research fellow at the National Institute of Science and Technology Policy, Japan. He is engaged in government foresight activity for science, technology, and innovation policies in Japan, having obtained a PhD in global environmental studies at Kyoto University.

The Net-Zero Transitions in Energy and Finance

Southeast Asia and Beyond

AKIHISA MORI
Kyoto University

NUR FIRDAUS
National Research and Innovation Agency

YASUHIRO OGURA
National Institute of Science and Technology Policy

CAMBRIDGE
UNIVERSITY PRESS

CAMBRIDGE
UNIVERSITY PRESS

Shaftesbury Road, Cambridge CB2 8EA, United Kingdom

One Liberty Plaza, 20th Floor, New York, NY 10006, USA

477 Williamstown Road, Port Melbourne, VIC 3207, Australia

314–321, 3rd Floor, Plot 3, Splendor Forum, Jasola District Centre, New Delhi – 110025, India

103 Penang Road, #05–06/07, Visioncrest Commercial, Singapore 238467

Cambridge University Press is part of Cambridge University Press & Assessment, a department of the University of Cambridge.

We share the University's mission to contribute to society through the pursuit of education, learning and research at the highest international levels of excellence.

www.cambridge.org
Information on this title: www.cambridge.org/9781009689427

DOI: 10.1017/9781009689410

When citing this work, please include a reference to the DOI 10.1017/9781009689410

First published 2026

Cover image: Hoa Binh offshore wind power plants in Vietnam, January 2025

A coal power plant near Ho Chi Minh City in Vietnam, November 2008

Photos taken by Akihisa Mori

A catalogue record for this publication is available from the British Library

A Cataloging-in-Publication data record for this book is available from the Library of Congress

ISBN 978-1-009-68942-7 Hardback

Contents

Preface

This book is the outcome of two research projects led by the Team Sustainability Transitions, Kyoto University: Stranded Assets and Energy Transitions in Southeast Asia, and Coal Divestment and Sustainability Transitions in Asia.

Stranded Assets and Energy Transitions in Southeast Asia was launched in July 2022 against the backdrop of increasing concerns about switching from coal to natural gas in power generation. The Organisation for Economic Co-operation and Development and the G20 agreed on ending official export credit for unabated coal-fired power plants in 2021. Natural gas is regarded as a 'bridge technology' in the energy transition from fossil fuels (coal and oil) and nuclear towards renewables. The European Union classifies natural gas and nuclear as transits in the taxonomy for sustainable activities, and the Association of Southeast Asian Nations (ASEAN) as amber in the taxonomy for sustainable finance. However, natural gas can generate the locking in of large-scale, carbon-intensive infrastructure, which could undermine the transitions to net zero energy systems. Natural gas has similar complementarity elements along the value chain as coal, ranging from upstream (exploitation and refinery) and middle stream (storage, processing, and transport of products), to downstream (power generation, fertiliser and petrochemical production, as well as distribution, logistics, and last-mile delivery). The system is supported by infrastructure elements, such as liquidation, transport (carriers and pipelines), ports, terminals, and storage tanks. In addition, constructing new infrastructure can generate detrimental ecological and social impacts. Furthermore, new gas power plants and supporting infrastructure can be stranded in the net zero transitions. These concerns prompted us to estimate stranded investments in gas power and supporting infrastructure vis-à-vis coal power and the development costs of newly installed non-hydropower renewable power.

Coal Divestment and Sustainability Transitions in Asia was launched in April 2021, amid the storm of the COVID-19 pandemic. The research project explores how Asian countries should address trade-offs between the net zero climate target and economic and social agenda, typically, national energy security, energy for all, and business sustainability, particularly in energy industry and financial institutions, amid the growing demand for electricity. Although central banks share the climate change transition risks, many young coal fossil-fuel power plants hold back local banks and investors from divestment. Foreign investors increased perceived profitability and lowered financial risk to new gas projects, motivating them to co-finance natural gas assets. In this context, the Energy Transition Platform (ETM) and Just Energy Transition Partnership (JETP) are expected to be game changers that can redirect the transition pathway from natural gas-sourced electricity systems to renewable energy-sourced ones. This expectation motivated us to investigate the novel contributions of ETM and JETP to existing global climate finance on the ground.

We named this book *The Net-Zero Transitions in Energy and Finance: Southeast Asia and Beyond* in the expectation that it would have global implications. Southeast Asia is not the only region struggling to reconcile economic growth with overcoming coal lock-ins. Many emerging markets and developing economies outside Southeast Asia face the same challenges as they rely heavily on coal and have many young coal power plants. South Africa is one such country and launched the Just Transition Transaction before JETP. The book covers the South African case and equips the audience beyond Southeast Asia with strategies to navigate the complexities of achieving net zero energy transitions through innovative financial mechanisms.

The analyses and interpretations presented in this book are those of the authors and do not necessarily reflect the views of their affiliated institutions.

Acknowledgements

The authors would like to thank the Singapore-based Climate Foundation for research funding. This funding helped in the development of the idea of analysing the energy transition in Asia from the viewpoint of stranded assets. The research results constitute the core element of the book. They also express their gratitude to the Japan Society for the Promotion of Science (grant number 21H04941) for funding the financial chapters of the book.

The authors thank the Vietnamese Institute of Energy, the ASEAN Centre for Energy, the Sustainable Development Solution Network (at Sunway University, Malaysia), and the Council on Energy, Environment and Water for hosting seminars and giving invaluable feedback. They also thank Dr Vo Thang of the Australian National University for his invaluable inputs. Coupled with feedback from anonymous reviewers on the book proposal, the feedback enhanced the quality of the chapters and the book.

The authors also appreciate Philip Good and Chris Harrison at Cambridge University Press for their constructive relationship and invaluable support. Finally, they thank Eri Miyazawa and Miki Yoshikawa, managing staff of the Team Sustainability Transitions, Kyoto University, for managing the research projects.

Figures

Tables

Abbreviations

AC	alternating current
ADB	Asian Development Bank
AF	Adaptation Fund
BAU	business-as-usual
BECCS	bioenergy with carbon capture and storage
BESS	battery energy storage systems
BEV	battery electric vehicle
CBDR-RC	common but differentiated responsibility and respective capabilities
CCGT	combined cycle gas turbine
CCS	carbon capture and storage
CCUS	carbon capture, utilisation, and storage
CDP	Carbon Disclosure Project
CEED	Centre for Energy, Ecology, and Development
CIF	Climate Investment Fund
CIF-ACT	Climate Investment Fund–Accelerating Coal Transition
CIPP	Comprehensive Investment and Policy Plan
CREZ	Competitive Renewable Energy Zones
CSP	competitive selection process
DC	direct current
DCCEEW	Department of Climate Change, Energy, the Environment and Water (Australia)
DER	distributed energy resources
DOE	Department of Energy (Philippines)
DPPA	direct power purchase agreement
DSO	distribution systems operators
DUs	distribution utilities (Philippines)
EHV	extra-high voltage

EJ	exajoule
EMDEs	emerging markets and developing economies
EPC	engineering, procurement, and construction
ERC	Energy Regulatory Commission (Philippines)
ESCO	energy service company
ESG	environment, social, and governance
ESS	energy storage system
ETM	Energy Transition Mechanism
EVN	Electricity Vietnam
FiT	feed-in tariff
FOM-ESS	front-of-meter energy storage system
GCAM	Global Change Analysis Model
GCF	Green Climate Fund
GDP	Gross Domestic Product
GEF	Global Environment Facility
GEOP	Green Energy Option Program
GFANZ	Glasgow Financial Alliance for Net Zero
GHG	greenhouse gas
GW	gigawatt
IAM(s)	Integrated Assessment Model(s)
IEA	International Energy Agency
IFC	International Finance Corporation
IPCC	Intergovernmental Panel on Climate Change
IPG	International Partners' Group
IPP	independent power producer
IRENA	International Renewable Energy Agency
ISSB	International Sustainability Standard Board
JET IP	Just Energy Transition Investment Plan
JETP	Just Energy Transition Partnership
kW	kilowatt
LDCs	Least Developed Countries
LNG	liquefied natural gas
MDB(s)	Multilateral Development Bank(s)
MPs	mandated participants (Philippines)

MUFG	Mitsubishi UFJ Financial Group
MW	megawatt
NDC(s)	Nationally Determined Contribution(s)
NGCP	National Grid Corporation of the Philippines
NGFS	Network of Central Banks and Supervisors for Greening the Financial System
NPV	net present value
NZE	Net Zero Emissions
O&M	operation and maintenance
OECD	Organisation for Economic Co-operation and Development
PDP8	Eighth Power Development Plan
PLN	Perusahaan Listrik Negara (Indonesia)
PPA	power purchase agreement
PV	photovoltaic
RES-E	renewable energy source-based electricity
RET	renewable energy technology
RMP	Resource Mobilisation Plan
RPS	renewable portfolio standard
SEA	Southeast Asia
SIDS	Small Island Developing States
SLB	sustainability-link bond
SSPs	shared-socioeconomic pathways
TCFD	Task Force on Climate-Related Financial Disclosures
TDP	Transmission Development Plan
TSO	transmission system operators
TWh	terawatt hour
UHV	ultra-high voltage
UNFCCC	United Nations Framework Convention on Climate Change
USD	US dollar
WESM	wholesale electricity spot market

Recommended Citations for Chapters

CHAPTER 1

Mori, A. (2026). The net-zero transitions in energy and finance: An introduction. In: Mori, A., Firdaus, N., and Ogura, Y. *The Net-Zero Transitions in Energy and Finance: Southeast Asia and Beyond*. Cambridge University Press, 1–32.

CHAPTER 2

Mori, A. (2026). Propagation of climate-related transition risks between the financial and electricity sectors. In: Mori, A., Firdaus, N., and Ogura, Y. *The Net-Zero Transitions in Energy and Finance: Southeast Asia and Beyond*. Cambridge University Press, 33–56.

CHAPTER 3

Mori, A. (2026). Determinants of the direction and speed of electricity system transition: An analytical framework. In: Mori, A., Firdaus, N., and Ogura, Y. *The Net-Zero Transitions in Energy and Finance: Southeast Asia and Beyond*. Cambridge University Press, 57–81.

CHAPTER 4

Firdaus, N., Ogura, Y., Mori, A. (2026). Estimated stranded assets in the electricity sector in the Southeast Asian region. In: Mori, A., Firdaus, N., and Ogura, Y. *The Net-Zero Transitions in Energy and Finance: Southeast Asia and Beyond*. Cambridge University Press, 82–129.

CHAPTER 5

Mori, A. (2026). Reconciling net-zero emissions and growing electricity demand: Electricity system transitions in Vietnam. In: Mori, A., Firdaus, N., and Ogura, Y. *The Net-Zero Transitions in Energy and Finance: Southeast Asia and Beyond*. Cambridge University Press, 130–158.

CHAPTER 6

Mori, A. (2026). Moving towards a natural-gas-based electricity system: Electricity system transitions in the Philippines. In: Mori, A., Firdaus, N., and Ogura, Y. *The Net-Zero Transitions in Energy and Finance: Southeast Asia and Beyond.* Cambridge University Press, 159–188.

CHAPTER 7

Firdaus, N., Mori, A. (2026). How has global net-zero finance advanced net-zero electricity system transitions? The cases of ETM and JETP. In: Mori, A., Firdaus, N., and Ogura, Y. *The Net-Zero Transitions in Energy and Finance: Southeast Asia and Beyond.* Cambridge University Press, 189–217.

CHAPTER 8

Mori, A., Firdaus, N. (2026). Making financial systems work for net-zero transitions in electricity systems. In: Mori, A., Firdaus, N., and Ogura, Y. *The Net-Zero Transitions in Energy and Finance: Southeast Asia and Beyond.* Cambridge University Press, 218–246.

1 The Net-Zero Transitions in Energy and Finance

An Introduction

1.1 BACKGROUND

In December 2015, at the twenty-first session of the Conference of the Parties to the United Nations Framework Convention on Climate Change (COP 21) in Paris, parties to the convention from 195 countries reached an agreement to combat climate change. The resulting Paris Agreement reaffirmed the goal of limiting the global temperature increase in the twenty-first century to well below 2°C compared to pre-industrial levels, limiting the temperature rise to 1.5°C. To ensure their best efforts, the agreement required all parties to submit nationally determined contributions (NDCs) that would aim beyond previous goals and to regularly report on their emissions and their implementation efforts, subject to international technical expert reviews.

Subsequently, a special report from the Intergovernmental Panel on Climate Change (IPCC, 2018) and its Sixth Assessment Report confirmed that rapid and deep reductions in CO_2 emissions were necessary to limit the temperature rise to 1.5°C (IPCC, 2021). The IPCC's scenario analyses show that net emissions of greenhouse gases (GHGs) must be reduced by 43% by 2030 compared with 2019 levels, and those of CO_2 should reach zero by around 2050 (IPCC, 2022b).

Since the United States rejoined the Paris Agreement and hosted the Leaders' Summit on Climate in 2021, numerous countries have committed to net-zero emissions targets. As of November 2022, around 140 countries had announced or were considering net-zero targets, covering approximately 90% of global emissions (Climate Action Tracker, 2022). Many emerging markets and developing economies (EMDEs) have gone beyond their NDCs to pledge future net-zero emissions, with varying deadlines: for example, Malaysia, Thailand, and Vietnam by 2050; China and Indonesia by 2060; and India by 2070. These pledges resulted in the Glasgow Climate Pact, proposing to limit the rise in the global average temperature to 1.5°C around 2050 and phasing down unabated coal power and inefficient subsidies for fossil fuels (UNFCCC, 2021).

To achieve the net-zero emissions target, the global energy mix must go through a profound transformation with a dramatic increase in energy efficiency and low-emission sources and the replacement of unabated fossil-fuel-based energy sources across the energy sector. Coal demand must decline by 90%, oil by approximately 80%, and natural gas by more than 70% in 2021–2050. In addition, by 2050, 65% of natural gas and 90% of coal must be consumed in facilities equipped with carbon capture, utilisation, and storage (CCUS) and co-fired with ammonia or green hydrogen. Carbon sequestration in the agriculture and forest sectors, bioenergy carbon capture and storage (BECCS), and direct air carbon capture and storage from ambient air will be used to offset the emissions from the remaining few sources that will be operated without CCUS. Immediate and massive deployment of all available clean and efficient energy technologies, particularly existing and proven ones such as wind, solar power, and battery electric vehicles, is required by 2030 to achieve the 2050 net-zero targets (IEA, 2022).

However, the net-zero energy transition is more complex than simply applying low-carbon energy transitions (Markard & Rosenbloom, 2023). This transition is not limited to whole systems changing and declining within a single energy or electricity sector. It is a paradigm shift that entails multiple, partly simultaneous transitions of different sociotechnical systems in almost all economic sectors, ranging from energy, mobility, building, manufacturing, and mining to financial sectors. The transition will require the scope to address difficult-to-decarbonise sub-sectors and regions because of the challenges facing low-carbon electrification and the lack of access to cost-effective technologies to achieve it. Fierce scrambles for critical minerals and metals such as lithium, cobalt, nickel, copper, and rare earth materials must be incorporated because complementary technologies such as batteries and storage are emerging as domains (Fornillo & Lampis, 2023; Scholten et al., 2020), and sector coupling through vehicle-to-grid is becoming a viable option. The financial sector must change its institutions and business models to direct finance and investments towards net-zero emissions.

The transition is demanding. It must be swift, radical, and actively pushed forward by many key societal actors, together with a stronger role for governments in cross-sectoral policy coordination. It must address disruptive impacts such as declines in incumbent technologies and established business models, industrial decline, and job losses. It will intensify the economic and political struggles of regime actors and newcomers (Johnstone & Hielscher, 2017; Markard, 2018). The transition should also mitigate large amounts of toxic waste (Maulia, 2022) and the distributive, recognition, and procedural injustices that extractive activities in fragile states and communities of marginalised people may generate or reproduce (Canelas & Carvalho, 2023). Furthermore, it must address large-scale land acquisitions and land-use changes associated with fossil-fuel-free agriculture (Neville, 2020). The financial sector is expected to accelerate radical shifts by redirecting the flow of financial resources.

Against this backdrop, this book tackles multiple transitions in the finance and electricity systems to investigate how they overcome coal lock-ins to advance the pathway towards the net-zero emissions target.

The remainder of this chapter is organised as follows. Sections 1.2 and 1.3 elaborate on how the financial, energy, and electricity sectors have responded to the commitments to low and net-zero carbon emissions so far and present the remaining challenges. Sections 1.4 and 1.5 discuss the opportunities and risks of two bridging technologies – natural gas and transition finance – to raise research questions for this book. Finally, Section 1.6 describes the structure of the book and concludes with an overview of its scholarly contributions to the field.

1.2 RESPONSES IN THE FINANCIAL SECTOR

Since the turn of the millennium, the global financial sector has gradually enhanced commitments to reducing the emissions impact of its financing and investing. On the one hand, this sector has increased fiduciary responsibility for finance and investment associated with emissions, transparently estimating and reducing them. On the other hand, the sector has increased sustainable finance to help its clients reduce emissions through green investments and business model innovation. The chronology since 2000 includes the following initiatives.

2000
: Foundation of the Carbon Disclosure Project (CDP)

2003
: Launch of the Equator Principles

2005
: Publication by the United Nations Environmental Programme Financial Initiative (UNEP FI) of a legal framework for the integration of environmental, social, and governance (ESG) issues into institutional investment

2006
: Publication of the Principles for Responsible Investment (PRI) by UNEP FI

2012
: Launch of the Principles for Sustainable Insurance by UNEP FI

2014
: Launch of the Green Bond Principles by the International Capital Market Association (ICMA) (updated in 2021)

2015
: Publication of the Prudential Regulation Authority report on climate change and the insurance sector by the Bank of England
: Organisation of the Task Force for Climate-related Financial Disclosure (TCFD)
: Paris Climate Agreement

2017
: Publication of framework and recommendation by TCFD

Launch of the Network of Central Banks and Supervisors for Greening the Financial System (NGFS)

2018

Laying down voluntary principles for those issuing green bonds by the ICMA

2019

Publication of the Principles of Responsible Banking by UNEP FI

2020

Launch of Net-Zero Asset Managers Initiative

2021

Launch of UN PRI-convened Net-Zero Asset Owner Alliance, Net-Zero Banking Alliance, Net-Zero Insurance Alliance, Net-Zero Financial Service Providers Alliance, Net-Zero Investment Consultants Initiative, and Glasgow Financial Alliance for Net Zero (GFANZ)

Launch of the International Sustainability Standards Board (ISSB)

Glasgow Climate Pact

1.2.1 *Fiduciary Responsibility*

In the 2000s, the financial sector and the United Nations developed voluntary guidelines to incorporate finance and investments' environmental and social impacts into decision-making. The Equator Principles were adopted in 2003 to serve as a common baseline and risk management framework for financial institutions to identify, assess, and manage environmental and social risks when financing projects, particularly large-scale infrastructural and industrial ones. In 2006, United Nations Secretary-General Kofi Annan invited a group of the world's largest institutional investors to join a process to develop the Principles for Responsible Investment. In parallel, the United Nations Environmental Programme Financial Initiative (UNEP FI) has published several reports that define environmental, social, and governance (ESG) investments as the fiduciary responsibility of institutional investments and that legitimise these investments (UNEP FI, 2005; 2009; 2015). In response, the United States revised the Employee Retirement Income Security Act of 1974 (ERISA) to allow consideration of the expected return on alternative investments with similar risks, including ESG investments (Employee Benefits Security Administration, 2015).[1]

In the meantime, fossil-fuel divestment movements have emerged and spread worldwide. The landmark article by the co-founder of 350.org, McKibben (2012), helped crystallise the core logic of divestment, and Carbon Tracker (2011) fuelled the student-led divestment movement across universities in North America and Australia. They attracted academic attention, leading to an increase in the analysis of campus-based campaigns. The concepts of the carbon budget and stranded resources and assets provided a scientific rationale for fiduciary duty in divestment (Caldecott, 2017). Some activists have organised advocacy networks to bring cases against universities managing funds and pension funds, seeking fossil fuel divestment (Franta, 2017; Bousso, 2021). Pension funds and export credit agencies are large global investors that have invested heavily in fossil fuels (Gupta et al., 2020). Others have mobilised movements to nurture, gain attention for, and institutionalise new norms (Blondeel et al., 2019; Gunningham, 2017).

Divestment movements have shown mixed results so far. On the one hand, well-known institutional investors and asset managers such as the Rockefeller Foundation, the Norway Pension Fund, and New York City's pension funds announced that they would divest from coal and the fossil fuel sector to balance their financial and moral responsibilities (Hunt & Weber, 2019) and protect their share prices (Bassen et al., 2021). Others shifted their portfolios away from high-carbon-emitting industries to reduce the carbon exposure of their investment portfolios. On the other hand, divestment did not significantly change the return or the risk of a globally well-diversified portfolio of industry indexes nor influence total financial risk for the investor (Plantinga & Scholtens, 2021). Divestment even

[1] While the interpretive bulletin was repealed in the Trump administration, the Labor Department reversed the repeal to issue new rules to allow fiduciaries to consider ESG factors when electing 401(k) investments and exercising shareholder rights in 2022 (Stern, 2023).

ended up transferring fossil fuel assets and carbon dependency to EMDEs (Gupta et al., 2020).

1.2.2 *The Paris–Glasgow Financial Regime*

The Paris Climate Agreement has enhanced the financial sector's concerns about climate-related risks and stranded assets for financial stability. These are conceptualised in the Bank of England's 2015 report and the subsequent governor's speech, which called for their financial supervision (Carney, 2015; Prudential Regulation Authority, 2015).

Since then, a variety of multilateral initiatives and networks have been organised to manage the risk and make orderly transitions. The Network of Central Banks and Supervisors for Greening the Financial System (NGFS) was established to enhance the role of the financial system in managing risks and mobilising capital for green and low-carbon investment. The NGFS defined and promoted best practices for financial supervisors and central banks so that they could help improve the solvency of individual financial institutions and enhance the resilience of the financial system (NGFS, 2019). The Task Force on Climate-related Financial Disclosures (TCFD) was organised in 2015 and published a framework and set of recommendations in 2017 to help companies and financial institutions consistently measure, manage, and report their climate-related risk exposures (TCFD, 2017). Investors, companies, cities, states, and regions have increasingly employed the reporting system of the Carbon Disclosure Project (CDP) since 2018, when the CDP aligned with the disclosure platform of the TCFD.[2] The UNEP FI and 130 founding banks officially launched the Principles for Responsible Banking in 2019 to encourage signatory banks to take action to align their core strategies, decision-making, lending, and investment with the UN Sustainable Development Goals and the Paris Climate Agreement.

[2] With more than 18,700 companies worth over half of the global market capitalisation disclosed through the CDP in 2022 (CDP, 2023).

The Glasgow COP 26 in 2021 reinforced the momentum for climate action in the financial sector. The Glasgow Financial Alliance for Net Zero (GFANZ) was founded to mobilise the entire financial sector to achieve the investment levels required for a net-zero transition. The Net-Zero Banking Alliance was organised under the GFANZ, requiring would-be signatory members to set and publicly disclose long-term and intermediate targets based on accepted science-based decarbonisation scenarios and to regularly review them to ensure consistency (UNEP FI, 2021). To increase the number of net-zero-committed financial institutions, the GFANZ has developed the tools, data, and methods needed to turn signatories' commitments into action. It also gives guidance on the net-zero transition plans needed to demonstrate accountability for net-zero targets, phase out stranded assets, capitalise on emerging opportunities, reduce the risk to businesses and society of a disorderly transition (GFANZ, 2022b), and enhance microprudential regulations and supervision (NGFS, 2023).

Furthermore, the alliance has supported the G7 and G20 in launching and scaling up the Just Energy Transition Partnership (JETP) to accelerate capital mobilisation in support of a net-zero transition in EMDEs through private-sector leadership and public–private collaboration (GFANZ, 2022a). The JETP was established as an additional funding channel to the Green Climate Fund (GCF), that has mobilised a significant portion of climate finance since the COP 15 Copenhagen in 2009. The GCF is supported from a wide variety of sources, including public, private, bilateral, and multilateral ones. It takes a bottom-up approach that emphasises country ownership, employs a direct-access modality to provide funding through accredited implementing entities satisfying fiduciary standards, and uses results-based management to address criticisms directed at the Global Environment Facility and multilateral financial institutions (Mori et al., 2019). However, implementation has fallen short of commitment. Approved projects amounted to US$48 billion from 2015 to September 2023, including GCF financing and co-financing.

Private finance accounts for 35% of the total funding (Green Climate Fund, 2023). In contrast, the JETP has committed to providing a larger amount of blended finance than provided by the GCF, exclusively for decarbonising the electricity sector: US$8.5 billion to South Africa, US$20 billion to Indonesia, and US$15 billion to Vietnam (Farand, 2023). Such initiatives can be a showcase of blended finance for climate change mitigation in other sectors and regions for rolling out and scaling, if they prove to deliver high performance.

1.2.3 *Sustainable Finance*

In the meantime, sustainable finance has been boosted. Sustainable investing assets – including impact/community investing, positive/best-in-class screening, sustainability-themed investing, norm-based screening, corporate engagement and shareholder action, negative/exclusionary screening, and ESG integration – increased from US$23 trillion in 2016 to US$35 trillion in 2020 in the United States, Canada, Japan, Australasia, and Europe (Global Sustainable Investment Alliance, 2021). Such assets accounted for 36% of total assets under management, going beyond niche investments.

The issue of five types of climate bond – green, social, sustainability, sustainability-linked, and transition bonds – has grown rapidly. It increased to surpass US$1 trillion in 2021 from less than US$100 billion in 2016. Among them, green bonds account for 58% of the cumulative amount, followed by social and sustainability bonds. While the United States issued the largest financial value of green bonds early in this period, China surpassed it in 2022. The Bank of China issued the largest financial value of green bonds for renewable energy, low-carbon transport, waste recycling, and water projects. The China Development Bank issued the largest value of certified new climate bonds for the use of low-carbon transport. China Three Gorges Corporation has emerged as the top non-financial corporate issuer in the world (Climate Bonds Initiative, 2023c; 2023d).

Green bonds are regarded as a short-term solution to the main barriers to low-carbon energy infrastructure – policy uncertainty and short-termism in the financial system (Hafner et al., 2020). The Green Bond Principles' recommendations for reporting the use of green bond proceeds by issues helped stakeholders understand the information by enhancing transparency, accuracy, and integrity, spurring issuance.

However, green bonds have shown mixed results in terms of carbon reduction. They have reduced emissions from issuer companies in the post-issuance period and increased ownership by long-term and green investors (Flammer, 2021). In contrast, they have not always unlocked new sources of capital for green investment or made green investments financially viable by themselves (Maltais & Nykvist, 2020). While these financial benefits depend critically upon how proceeds are used to generate climate and financial impacts, green bond issuers have shown little incentive to use their proceeds to achieve ambitious science-based targets (Tuhkanen & Vulturius, 2022).

In addition, the issuance of green bonds raised concerns about greenwashing and threatened the credibility of the whole market for sustainable finance. 'Greenwashing' refers to the selective disclosure, exaggeration, or concealment of environmental performance (Li et al., 2025), misleading consumers about a firm's environmental performance or the environmental benefits of a product or service (Delmas & Burbano, 2011). There were no standards for defining what 'green' was, nor were there selection criteria or frameworks providing transparency on the use of proceeds, external validation, or reporting to investors within capital markets (Alfsen et al., 2018; Sangiorgi & Schopohl, 2021).

In response, the Green Bond Principles were updated in 2021 to recommend transparency and disclosure and promote integrity in developing green bond markets (ICMA, 2022). A green taxonomy was developed as a classification system for sustainable activities and greener investment choices. The European Union implemented a green taxonomy in 2020 as part of the European Green Deal initiative. The Association of Southeast Asian Nations (ASEAN) published a taxonomy for sustainable finance to enable member states to implement an orderly transition and adopt sustainable finance. The International Sustainability Standards Board (ISSB) was organised according to the principles of International Financial Reporting Standards and backed by the G7 and the G20 to develop standards for a global baseline of sustainability and climate disclosures. By building on the work of market-led investor-focused reporting initiatives, including the Climate Disclosure Standards Board and TCFD, ISSB's report aims to facilitate interoperability with disclosures that are jurisdiction-specific and/or aimed at broader stakeholder groups (IFRS Foundation, 2023).

1.3 RESPONSES IN THE ENERGY AND ELECTRICITY SECTORS

1.3.1 Transformation of Investments

The Paris Climate Agreement and subsequent stringent climate policy have decreased capital expenditure on unabated fossil fuels (Figure 1.1a). Advanced economies and EMDEs had reduced such expenditure by US$200 billion by 2015, and China by US$40 billion by 2020. Upstream oil and natural gas investments account for 70% of the global decrease and 84% of that of EMDEs (Figure 1.1b). The decrease in investments in upstream oil and natural gas was statistically significant between 2016 and 2019, even after controlling for oil market tightness, global factors, and other typical firm-level control variables (Bogman et al., 2023).

Clean energy investments have steadily grown since the Paris Climate Agreement. Investments in renewables and energy efficiency in end-use increased by US$270 billion and US$60 billion from 2015 to 2022, respectively. However, these changes have not sufficiently offset the decrease in unabated fossil fuels (Figure 1.1a).

Abrupt divestment and reduction of fossil fuel investment ahead of a ramp-up of clean energy technologies hiked fossil fuel prices, causing a rebound effect and deterring a zero-carbon transition

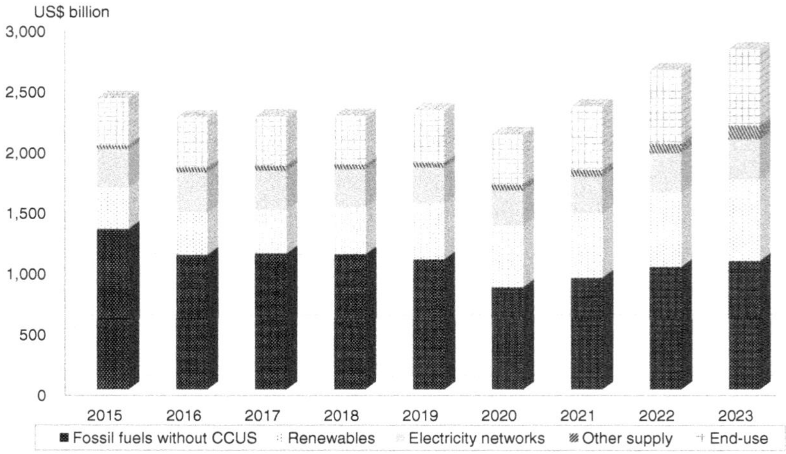

FIGURE 1.1(A) Global energy investment by type of energy, 2015–2023.
Source: Compiled by the authors based on data from the IEA (2024k).

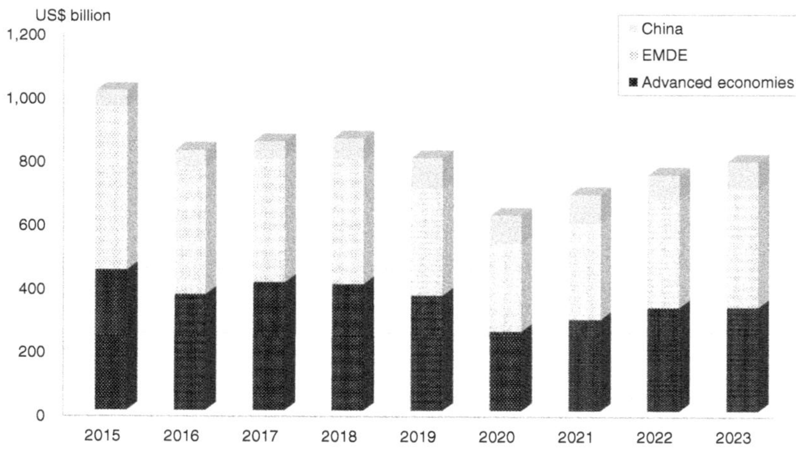

FIGURE 1.1(B) Global oil and gas upstream investment by economic category, 2015–2023.
Source: Same as Figure 1.1a.

in the short term. The energy shift from fossil fuels to renewable energy sources increased electricity consumption in high- and upper-middle-income countries, whereas middle- and lower-middle-income

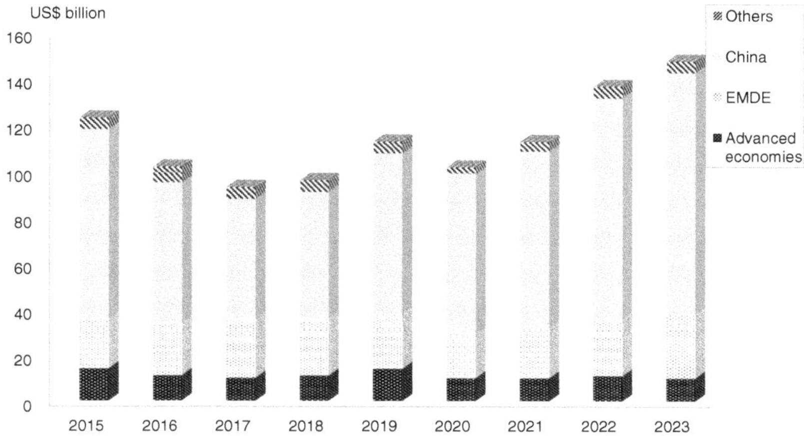

FIGURE 1.1(C) Global coal investment by economic category, 2015–2023.
Source: Same as Figure 1.1a.

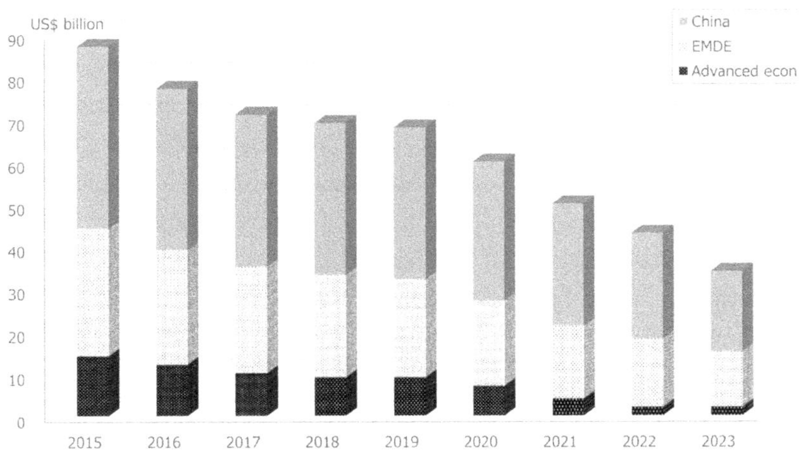

FIGURE 1.1(D) Global coal power investment by economic category, 2015–2023.
Source: Same as Figure 1.1a.

countries were more sensitive to inflation, electricity pricing, and population growth induced by increasing electricity consumption. Abrupt divestment and reduction also made the electricity system

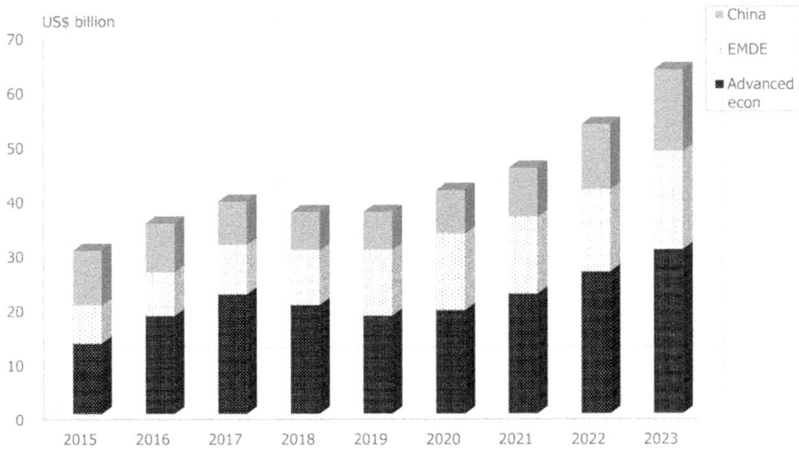

FIGURE 1.1(E) Global nuclear power investment by economic category, 2015–2023.
Source: Same as Figure 1.1a.

vulnerable to climate change, as seen in the global heatwave- and drought-induced electricity crises in 2022 (Murtaugh & Ding, 2022). Russia's war in Ukraine spurred energy price hikes, raising energy security concerns in energy-importing countries and triggering changes in energy and climate policies. The resultant windfall gains and energy security concerns encouraged fossil fuel producers to invest in oil and gas again. The rebound was remarkable in China, which invested more in oil and natural gas upstream and in coal in 2022 than in 2015 (Figures 1.1b and 1.1c). As a result, the European Parliament decided on the inclusion of natural gas and nuclear as transitional activities in the EU taxonomy (European Commission, 2022).

1.3.2 *EMDEs and China*

Ramping up clean energy technologies requires the transformation of the electricity model and whole-system changes for large-scale integration of intermittent renewable-energy-sourced electricity (RES-E). An RES-based electricity system is consistent with the liberalised model, which is constituted by vertical unbundling, wholesale markets, retail competition, decentralised prosumers, and network-based governance (Mori, 2022). The model allows private participation and ownership in generation even under the dominance of state-owned utilities in the grid, thus incentivising developers to invest in RES-E projects (Geddes et al., 2020). The model also accepts flexibility in supply through flexible generation, storage, demand response, and interconnection through markets, thus satisfying the technical prerequisites for large-scale intermittent RES-E integration (Iychettira, 2021).

In contrast, the electricity system in many EMDEs and China is characterised by a state monopoly or a hybrid model (Urpelainen & Yang, 2019), which is consistent with the conventional fossil-fuel-based, vertically integrated, and hierarchical electricity supply system. Only 32% systems undertook full vertical unbundling and 18% went through both vertical and horizontal unbundling in developing countries in 2015, against 69% and 43% respectively in developed countries (Foster et al., 2017). State-owned electric utilities play a dominant role in these systems, along with independent power producers. The systems have no or limited wholesale markets or space for choosing retail suppliers (Gratwick & Eberhard, 2008).

In addition, many EMDEs and China will suffer from large amounts of stranded costs if they encounter abrupt divestment and smaller investments in generation capacities. They have regarded coal power as the baseload generation, developing capacities to supply electricity for all at an affordable price and to satisfy growing demand. This is why they have so many relatively new coal power plants.

Perceived high risks of stranded assets and energy security concerns have motivated EMDEs to prioritise policies to improve economic sustainability and resilience ahead of those switching from fossil fuel to green energy policies and technological efficiency in power generation (Taghizadeh-Hesary et al., 2021). The requirement for electricity sector reform imposes an additional political bottleneck in these regimes' resistance to the transition to RES-based electricity systems, making governments hesitant to advance changes in the complementary elements. This situation prolongs fossil fuel lock-ins, making it more difficult for renewable investments to gain higher economic returns than fossil fuel ones (Firdaus & Mori, 2023). This is why investment patterns have been kept intact instead of using divest–invest strategies (Rosenbloom & Rinscheid, 2020).

The dual challenges accrued to the hybrid model and high stranded costs have reinforced the barriers to decarbonising the electricity sector. Setting aside the unfavourable and uncertain policy environment, the dominance of state-owned utilities having a large portion of coal power generation in their portfolios and their poor creditworthiness as off-takers squeeze the space for private and international developers to gain profits from renewable energy investments, shrinking demand for renewable energy financing (Liebman et al., 2019). State-owned utilities are reluctant to develop, or incapable of developing, renewable energy projects that would leave their coal assets stranded. Underdevelopment of the capital market makes it difficult to provide and access long-term financing. Due in part to banks' perception of renewable investments as risky, short debt tenures and high debt-financing costs make renewable energy developers reluctant to access bank loans (Nguyen et al., 2019). The limited availability of non-recourse financing deters investments (Sarangi, 2019).

The OECD and G20 agreement on ending official export credit for unabated coal power plants (OECD, 2021a) posed an additional challenge. The official export credit has supported EMDEs to build new coal power capacity and thus has been criticised as a source of coal lock-in (Davidson, 2023; Sauer et al., 2022). Subsequently, over 200 globally significant financial institutions established coal exclusion policies and accelerated coal divestment (Trivedi & Srivastava, 2023). The agreement and policies force EMDEs to give up new coal power projects so long as they depend on international finance. While the amount of coal power investment has decreased since 2015, the decrease was accelerated in 2023 (Figure 1.1d).

GFANZ's JETP and ADB's Energy Transition Mechanism (ETM) were launched to address these triple challenges. JETP deals have been announced for South Africa, Indonesia, and Vietnam and are under negotiation with India. The ETM agreed to provide finance to Indonesia, the Philippines, and Vietnam. These partner countries have vertically bundled hybrid electricity models but with varied extents of private participation, wholesale market development, and retail competition (Figure 1.2). One extreme is South Africa, where state-owned utility companies dominate the whole system. The other extreme is India, where private participation is widely accepted in generation, and various types of privatisation have been undertaken in distribution with varying performance (Dubash et al., 2018). State-owned utilities become less dominant in generation as private developers increase RES-E supply (Figures 1.3a and 1.3b). Others fall in between. The Philippines is an exception; the country has undergone vertical unbundling, developed a nationwide wholesale spot market, and increased retail competition to a limited extent.

The extent of coal lock-in also varies among them. Coal-abundant economies such as India have historically used coal as the primary source of power generation. Long-term coal supply contracts with coal-mining and transport companies (Carl, 2015), long-term power purchase agreements with large industrial and commercial customers (Kumar & Chatterjee, 2012; Rose et al., 2016), and cross-subsidy for residential use and agricultural irrigation (Rahman et al., 2022) have reinforced infrastructural, institutional, and social lock-ins (Mori, 2024). In addition to the lock-ins, these economies have piled up new coal power plants. Although rapid increases in RES-based electricity have gradually reduced the proportion of coal power used in India and South Africa, the lock-ins block rapid shifts in the energy mix compared with China (Figure 1.4).

Oil- and natural-gas-abundant economies such as Indonesia shifted their primary energy source towards coal in the 2000s and 2010s to address future depletion, mostly financially backed by China (Mori, 2020). The Philippines and Vietnam have increased coal

	China	India	Indonesia	Philippines	South Africa	Vietnam
Regulation	Independent regulator (National Electricity Commission)	Independent regulator (Central Electricity Regulatory Commission)	Ministry of Energy and Mineral Resources	Independent regulator (Energy Regulatory Commission)	Some regulatory functions performed by the utility and energy ministries	Ministry of Industry and Trade (MOIT), with influence from Vietnam Electricity (EVN) in the policy-making process
Generation	Quasi-competitive without a wholesale spot market	Competitive (central- and state-government-owned and private)	Dominance of regulated national monopoly (PLN) with competitive bidding by independent power producers (IPPs)	Competitive (National Power Corporation [NPC] and IPPs) with wholesale spot market	Dominance of Eskom and IPPs	Dominance of EVN and IPPs
Transmission	Regulated quasi-single buyer(SGCC, CSG)	Regulated national monopoly(POWERGRID)	Regulated national monopoly (PLN) with a government-determined tariff	Regulated national monopoly (Transco, NGCP)	Regulated national monopoly (NTC)	Regulated national monopoly (EVN-NPT)
Distribution	Regulated local monopoly with government-determined tariff	Regulated provincial monopoly (discom) with a government-determined tariff		Regulated franchises (NPC-SPUG, private distribution utilities, and cooperatives)	Regulated local monopolies (Eskom and municipalities) with government-determined tariffs	Regulated regional monopolies (EVN-NPC, EVN-CPC, EVN-SPC, EVN-Hanoi, and EVN-HCMC) with government-determined tariffs
Supply				Partially competitive (NPC-SPUG, private distribution utilities, cooperatives, and suppliers)		

FIGURE 1.2 Electricity systems in selected emerging markets and developing economies.
Source: Compiled by the authors based on Comins (2023), Dubash et al. (2018), EVN (2023), Geddes et al. (2020), Iychettira (2021), Lin et al. (2019), and Zissler (2023).

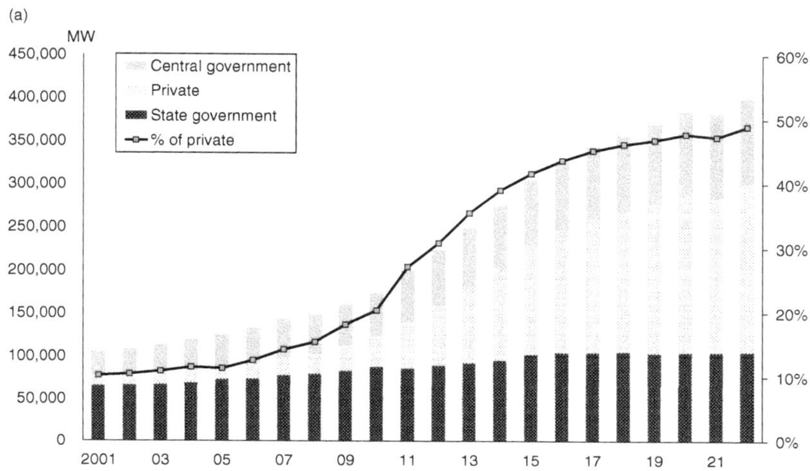

FIGURE 1.3(A) Percentage of installed power generation capacity by ownership in India, 2001–2022.
Source: Compiled by the authors based on data from the Central Electricity Authority, India (2022; 2023).

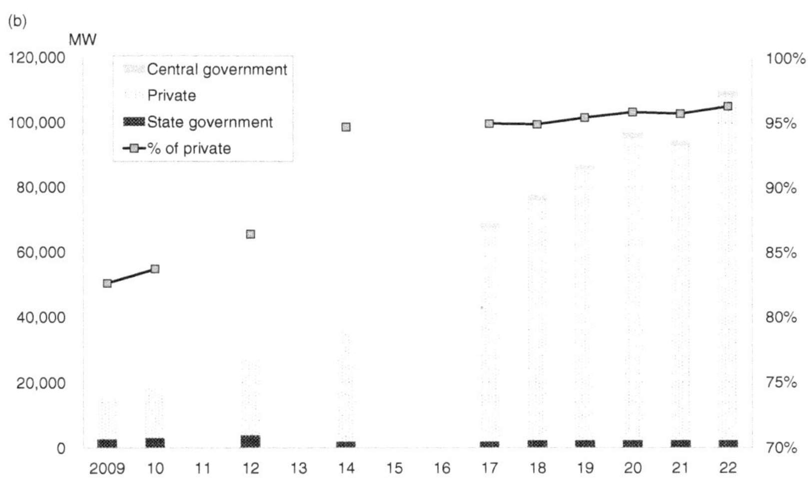

FIGURE 1.3(B) Percentage of installed RES-E capacity by ownership in India, 2001–2022.
Source: Compiled by the authors based on data from the Central Electricity Authority, India (2022; 2023); data is missing for 2011, 2013, 2015, and 2016.

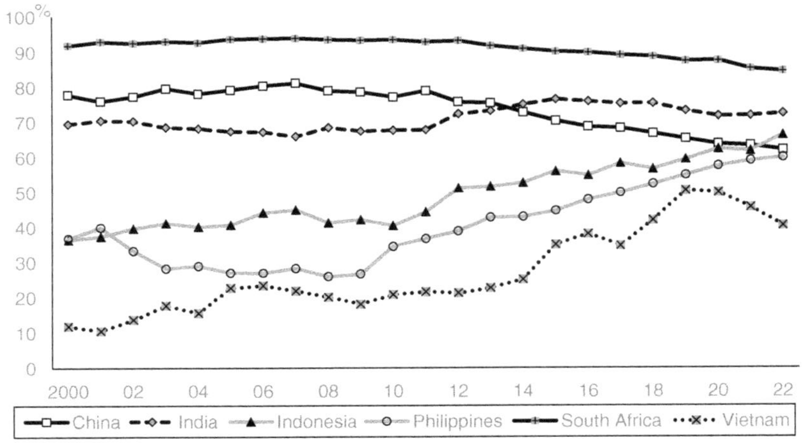

FIGURE 1.4 Percentage of coal in the energy mix of power generation in ETM and JETP countries and China, 2000–2022.
Source: Compiled by the authors based on data from the International Energy Agency (IEA, 2024h; 2024i; 2024d; 2024a; 2024j; 2024b).

imports to increase coal power generation. These young coal power plants and supporting infrastructure discourage governments and power producers from retiring their plants much earlier than the natural ends of their lifetimes.

Seeing that the JETP and ETM are small, slow, and demanding, partner countries pay more attention to bridging technologies and transition finance to address the challenges they face. Investments in oil and gas upstream and power generation capacities have rebounded in EMDEs since 2021 (Figure 1.1c). EMDEs and China have noticeably increased nuclear power investments since 2022 (Figure 1.1e). ASEAN adopted the category of 'Amber' in its taxonomy to denote activities that contribute to sustainability but that require remedial measures to transition (ASEAN Taxonomy Board, 2021; 2023).

1.4 NATURAL GAS DEBATES

In this context, natural gas is framed as a bridge technology or transition fuel necessary for a smooth global energy transition, despite a lack of clarity on the time horizon and the target system (Kemfert et al., 2022).

Natural gas has sparked controversy in arguments over sustainable energy transitions. It is argued that it can play a supporting role in reducing CO_2 emissions and bridging the gap between coal and renewable energy technologies (RET) in the short term. Natural gas is advocated as the cleanest fossil fuel and a climate-friendly alternative to coal and oil, even though its expansion alone will not sufficiently attain global climate targets (IEA, 2011).

Many scenario-based analyses have supported the positive role of natural gas in decarbonising the electricity sector. These analyses predict that natural gas will exceed coal as a major source of power generation under the 2050 net-zero CO_2 emissions scenario. This particularly holds when CCUS technologies are available. It can lower the cost of electric sector decarbonisation and make a significant contribution to decarbonisation under the coal phase-out in the US by 2035 if a net-zero GHG emissions policy allows the operation of carbon removal technologies such as bioenergy with carbon capture and storage and direct air capture (Bistline & Young, 2022). More than 80% of reliance on non-dispatchable renewables substantially increases the system cost, leading to higher curtailment and overbuilding total installed capacity (Jenkins et al., 2018).

In addition, natural gas consumption increases with the diffusion of renewables (Guidolin & Alpcan, 2019). It can balance out the variability of RES-E supply across weeks and seasons with consumption. In such scenarios, the value of natural gas shifts from providing energy to providing capacity, which ensures a larger integration of RES-E into grids (Bistline & Young, 2022).

From another perspective, however, natural gas development is regarded as a dead-end pathway (Markard & Rosenbloom, 2023). It is seen as a trajectory that seems to make sense in the short run but would be incapable of delivering over the longer term. Natural gas does not contribute to more fundamental system reconfiguration and thus creates further delays in transitions (Meadowcroft et al., 2019). Its use causes and reinforces carbon and natural gas lock-ins (Cabico, 2022), crowding out investments in RET and delaying transitions to RES-based electricity systems for substantial periods (Gürsan & de Gooyert, 2021). Strict enforcement of the carbon neutrality targets reduces fossil fuel consumption and demands earlier decommissioning of existing fossil fuel assets. Their long technical lifespans and amortisation periods generate infrastructural and behavioural lock-in effects (Brauers, 2022), strand the assets, and impose financial losses on asset owners, investors, and operators (Mercury et al., 2018). Stranded costs can be substantial because natural gas power requires a series of investments ranging from exploitation fields and power plants to related infrastructure such as pipelines, storage tanks, loading and unloading facilities, and import terminals for liquefied natural gas (LNG). The infrastructure may motivate host country governments to develop petrochemical industries, as seen in Map Ta Phut in eastern Thailand and as planned in southern Thailand (Mori, 2003).

The perception of high stranded costs prompts governments and power and gas industries to organise coalitions to resist the transition or to seek proliferation through transformation into a hydrogen economy (Dickel, 2020). This reinforces discursive lock-ins (Brauers, 2022) and legitimises investments in natural gas assets and usage (Janzwood & Millar, 2022).

In addition, natural gas may be seen to have much higher climate impacts when assessments incorporate full-lifecycle GHG emissions and updated warming potentials of methane (Kemfert et al., 2022). The operation of gas plants can spill fuel and chemicals that contaminate soil, degrade water quality, and threaten the abundance of coral reefs, fish, and other marine organisms. It also discharges emissions that can deteriorate air quality (Linseed Field Power Corporation, 2021; Wagas & Andres, 2022).

Batteries and hydrogen generated from renewable sources can mitigate the controversy as an alternative bridging energy in the future, when their levelised costs of electricity decrease substantially (Schmidt et al., 2019). However, current batteries cannot provide large-scale, long-term storage solutions and thus do not fundamentally overcome the challenge associated with the high penetration of renewables, even though they do provide short-term solutions. Current hydrogen production plants cannot supply hydrogen commercially due to low capacity (Tordoir, 2022). In addition, hydrogen production from methane increases methane leakage from natural gas production and other GHG emissions, such as ozone (Kemfert et al., 2022).

Furthermore, the narrative of stranded natural gas assets is criticised from the point of view of just energy transition. Criticism comes from sub-Saharan Africa, where millions of people suffer from limited or unreliable electricity, and economic development depends on energy access and consumption (Bugaje et al., 2022). It argues that maximising the full value of the abundant natural gas available in resource-rich countries can contribute to a just global energy transition so long as it does not generate new forms of social exclusion, human rights violations, energy poverty, or inequality. These conditions would be satisfied if ESG risks in production and distribution were fully addressed through dynamic technologies and policy innovation, enabling legal and policy frameworks to be established that create green economic opportunities and sustain investments in these technologies and clean, smart infrastructure (Olawuyi, 2022). Governance structures and smart information technologies are also called for to promote coordination, interoperability, and multi-stakeholder partnerships among various stakeholders in the natural gas industry, especially among regulatory institutions, to enhance synergies among different stakeholders (Pereira & Olawuyi, 2022).

Empirical studies have shown mixed effects of natural gas in sustainable energy transitions. On the one hand, Denmark, Japan, India, and Turkey exhibit increasing competitive pressures from RET on natural gas and thus show the bridging effect of natural gas (Bessi et al., 2021). On the other hand, natural gas crowds out RET and delays the bridging process under persisting coal dominance in China. Heavy reliance on natural gas from the US has prompted Mexico to intensify its co-dependence on electricity and natural gas systems and has strengthened carbon lock-in (Vera et al., 2023). In

Poland, poor forecasts and highly uncertain and speculative estimates of future demand caused a long-term lock-in to gas imports from Russia and increased the risks of supply-side security in the transition from a coal-based energy system (Kuchler & Höök, 2020). In Germany, gas lock-ins were reinforced by a number of factors: the geopolitical influence of the US, security of supply concerns due to the planned coal and nuclear phase-out, pressures from a wide variety of actors, and investments in Nord Stream, a network of offshore natural gas pipelines that run under the Baltic Sea from Russia to Germany. These natural gas lock-ins led to construction plans for three large-scale LNG import terminals (Brauers et al., 2021), with operations due to start by 2025 (Cavcic, 2025). German investors and electricity generators worked with the government to create a capacity market to compensate for losses in the form of capacity payments (Gawel et al., 2022; Sen & von Schickfus, 2020).

1.5 RESEARCH GAP

1.5.1 Multiple System Transitions

We can understand these necessary synchronised system transitions as multiple transitions of different sociotechnical systems. They can be defined as the third phase of net-zero energy transitions (Markard & Rosenbloom, 2023).

Phase I: Emergence and adoption of niche technologies such as wind and solar powers
Phase II: Whole-system change and decline within a single energy or electricity sector
Phase III: Multiple transitions of different sociotechnical systems
Phase IV: Transitions in hard-to-abate and carbon-intensive sectors

Attention to financial system transitions may potentially overcome the limitations of the traditional financial risk–return thinking in finance theory. Financial risk–return thinking can be expanded to argue that changes in capital costs induced by climate-related transition costs will be propagated to the financial and real sectors and will eventually advance system transitions towards net zero. However, the geographical concentration of sustainable finance and the slow implementation of the Paris–Glasgow financial regime raise concerns about the speed of behavioural changes that changes in capital costs will generate in electricity systems.

Previous research has investigated a variety of aspects of financial system transitions. These include the effects of green bonds on corporate net-zero emissions and sustainable development (Bhutta et al., 2022), sustainable business model innovation in the banking sector (Yip & Bocken, 2018), macroprudential policies such as climate-related stress tests (Dunz et al., 2021; Monasterolo et al., 2018), and microprudential policies such as disclosure requirements and environmental and social risk management standards (Cato, 2022).

Recent publications have begun to cover the impacts and responses of the energy and financial sectors (Claeys et al., 2024). Researchers have proposed causal mechanisms for the propagation of climate-related risks and have investigated changes in capital costs and their impacts through scenario analyses, from the real to the financial sector (Campiglio et al., 2022; Daumas, 2023).

However, all of these studies are based on traditional financial risk–return thinking and optimal risk–return investments in the mainstream finance theory. They have not provided the theoretical foundation, analytical frameworks, or empirical evidence that support transformative finance or finance for electricity system transitions.

Multi-sector transition research has been growing within sustainability transition research to unpack the complexity of multi-system interactions (Ohlendorf et al., 2023). However, the field is still small and niche and focuses mostly on transitions of upstream and downstream sectors of the supply chain, such as automobile and battery manufacturing, mineral-extractive sectors, and electricity generation and abatement technology manufacturing sectors (Finstad & Andersen, 2023). While analytical frameworks have been developed to understand why ongoing multi-system interactions among upstream and downstream sectors have not evolved into cross-system coupling (Andersen & Geels, 2023) current multi-sector transition research has not recognised transitions in financial systems, and thus has not observed synchronised changes in the financial and energy sectors as such.

1.5.2 *Financial System Transitions*

Transformative finance or finance for transformative changes is presented as a counterargument to traditional financial risk–return thinking and optimal risk–return investments. It includes exploration of the shift of capital allocation towards long-term sustainability investments and priority on financial return from investing in system change, performance evaluation of clients from financial value towards integrated value (Schoenmaker & Schramade, 2021), and fostering in-house skillsets and mindsets to map out unquantifiable systemic uncertainties and maximise system change impact focusing on long-term benefits (Loorbach et al., 2020). Transformative finance may be an element of financial system transition that would accelerate net-zero real-sector transitions and overcome the short-termism that has blocked the financing of long-term sustainability investments. Newell (2021) goes further to require greater social and democratic control over the ownership, direction, regulation, production, consumption, and financing of energy.

However, these proposed financial system transitions demand changes that may be too radical for incumbent financial actors to accept under current institutional and organisational arrangements.

1.5.3 *Multiple System Transitions in Highly Coal-Dependent Small EMDEs*

In addition, little research has paid attention to small EMDEs that are highly dependent on coal and on international finance. They were hit hardest by the OECD and G20 agreements on the end of official export credit for unabated coal power because most of their energy production capacity development has relied on international finance.

There is much research on highly coal-dependent large EMDEs such as China and India, which are far less dependent on international finance. These economies can mobilise domestic finance to increase coal power and ensure national energy security, energy for all, and international finance to increase RES-E and mitigate increases in CO_2 emissions. In contrast, small EMDEs have less domestic financial capital and thus cannot mobilise finance to take the same energy transition strategy as China and India.

Apart from the studies initiated by the Economic Research Institute for ASEAN and East Asia (ERIA), few practical financing and energy transition strategies have been argued for so far. ERIA has published collections of papers on the role of finance in low-carbon energy systems (Anbumozhi et al., 2016), low-carbon energy transitions (Anbumozhi et al., 2018), and renewable energy (Phoumin et al., 2023) in Southeast and Northeast Asia. These books have explored how green finance has induced energy efficiency and increased the use of renewables in energy production and consumption. However, most of them did not focus on the gap between the achieved reduction in fossil fuel consumption and carbon emissions, and the reduction required to achieve the net-zero target. Few have gone beyond the changes in the energy mix to give insights for overcoming the dual challenges of the hybrid electricity model and coal lock-ins and reconciling international coal divestment, net-zero targets, and national energy security.

1.6 THE BOOK

1.6.1 Aims, Scope, Research Questions, and Structure

The book fills these three research gaps on the multiple-system transitions of finance and energy systems, practical strategies for financial system transitions, and their applicability in EMDEs. The book assumes the 2050 net-zero emissions target as given and limits the scope to the Paris–Glasgow financial regime, which we define as the financial regime associated with the goals of the Paris Agreement and reinforced in the process for the Glasgow COP 26. The book also covers net-zero transitions in the financial sector that are involved in electricity system transitions towards net zero in EMDEs.

For this purpose, the book raises two research questions:

(1) Why has the Paris–Glasgow financial regime and financing net zero been slow in progress?
(2) Why are highly coal-dependent small EMDEs attracted to the shift to natural-gas-based electricity systems instead of RES-based ones?

To answer the first question, we identify possible underlying factors and mechanisms in both the financial sector and the electricity sector that would retard the Paris–Glasgow financial regime and the financing of net zero. Then we employ a simplified cost–benefit framework to illustrate the cost–benefit schedules associated with net-zero transitions and demonstrate how the underlying factors and mechanisms that we have identified here can change transition costs and benefits.

To illustrate the cost–benefit schedules, we employ the Global Change Analysis Model (GCAM) to estimate the cost of technological changes and assess the costs and benefits of changes in other complementary elements in an electricity system through empirical case studies. The illustration answers the second research question.

Based on these answers, the book proposes practical net-zero finance and electricity system transition strategies that are suitable for highly coal-dependent EMDEs.

The remainder of the book is organised as follows. Chapter 2 develops a framework that explains plausible causal mechanisms for the propagation of climate-related transition risks between the financial and electricity sectors, based on a literature review. The framework may help readers to understand how the financial and real sectors react to climate-related transition risks, and what underlying factors play key roles in their behavioural changes.

Chapter 3 builds an analytical framework that illustrates different pathways towards RES-based electricity systems by grid paradigm – the super-grid, distributed smart-grid, and flexible grid paradigms – by developing from the work of Fox-Penner (2020), Markard and Hoffmann (2016), and Mori (2021b). The framework enables us to identify different sets of changes that are required in the transitions by grid paradigm. The framework suggests that the financial sector must go beyond financing technological and organisational changes at the company level to induce changes in infrastructural and institutional elements to advance electricity system transitions towards net zero.

Chapter 4 estimates the technological costs of electricity system transitions towards net zero in Southeast Asia. By conducting several scenario analyses with different combinations of technological applications using the GCAM, the chapter suggests that heavy technological transition costs give additional stimulus to the energy switch from coal to gas for power rather than to transitions to an RES-based electricity system. Net-zero emissions targets will impose substantially heavier technological transition costs in the Southeast Asian region (except Indonesia): more than 10% of annual GDP for new installation of RES-E capacity and 2–3% for stranded costs owning to the early retirement of fossil fuel power plants in 2026–2035. The availability of CCUS mitigates the transition costs by 3% in 2031–2035 but increases it by 1% in 2036–2040, while a global gas price hike reduces the transition costs by 1.5–2% of GDP annually in 2021–2050.

Chapters 5 and 6 employ the analytical framework built in Chapter 3 in empirical country case studies with inductive, longitudinal multi-case designs to assess the costs and benefits of infrastructural, institutional, and organisational changes associated with electricity system transitions towards net zero in Vietnam (Chapter 5) and in the Philippines (Chapter 6).

We take Vietnam and the Philippines as empirical case studies for two reasons. First, the Southeast Asia region rapidly increased installed coal power capacity in the 2010s and thus has many young coal power assets that will incur higher costs to asset owners if stranded.

The region is likely to choose natural gas as the primary response to credit rationing and deter the net-zero energy transition. Particularly, Vietnam and the Philippines perceive natural gas and LNG power generation as bridging technology and have begun LNG imports on a large scale (Nitta & Shiga, 2023) despite suspicion of underutilisation of LNG infrastructure (as expressed by Take, 2023). The Philippines regards natural gas as a clean and indigenous source of energy and a balancing energy that can satisfy the grid's intermediate or mid-merit supply requirements (Philippines Department of Energy, 2021a).

Second, the two countries exhibit a sharp contrast in the electricity model: in Vietnam, there is vertically integrated, centralised, monopolistic supply by state-owned electricity utilities (Electricity Vietnam, EVN) with partial liberation of generation; in the Philippines, there is unbundled, market-based supply by oligopolistic generators, single private system operators, and regionally monopolised distribution units with hundreds of distributed energy resources and microgrids. An in-depth comparative analysis of the two countries can provide valuable implications for countries struggling with transitions from coal-based electricity systems to other electricity models.[3]

Chapters 5 and 6 reveal that high transition costs associated with infrastructural and institutional changes prolong the transition process, causing a loss of momentum for the transition to RES-based electricity systems. Coupled with predicted growing electricity demand, these factors prompt the two countries to choose a fuel switch from coal to LNG to immediately respond to credit rationing rather than transitioning to RES-based electricity systems.

Chapter 7 explores how the Paris–Glasgow financial regime rebalances the cost–benefit schedules associated with electricity system transitions towards net zero; the chapter focuses on the JETP and ETM, comparing them with GCF. We find that the current

[3] For instance, India regards natural gas as one of the prominent alternative energies to coal (Yergin, 2020).

commitment to ETM and JETP has not yet filled the financial gap for net zero, either quantitatively or qualitatively. Few programmes have been specified for disbursement. The long procedural process and institutional reform requirements delay actual disbursements, posing challenges for private financing and scaling.

Finally, Chapter 8 discusses why the JETP and ETM and the Paris–Glasgow financial regime have not generated transformative changes in electricity systems in highly coal-dependent small EMDEs, using the research results presented in Chapters 3–7. We find that in these cases the benefit of electricity system transitions towards net zero is substantially smaller than the cost, and the ETM and JETP have only marginally filled the gap quantitatively and qualitatively. Transition and transformative finance may facilitate transformative changes in incumbent electricity companies and move electricity systems towards net zero, but traditional financial risk–return thinking, optimal risk–return investments, and short-termism must be overcome to make transition and transformative finance work.

1.6.2 Scholarly Contributions

We highlight three scholarly contributions of this book. First, the book provides a novel analytical viewpoint of net-zero finance. Net-zero finance is different from divestment and renewable energy finance (Donovan, 2020; Raikar & Adamson, 2019), not to mention the incorporation of social and environmental concerns into energy systems (Dorsman et al., 2016). It proposes the facilitation of transformative changes in systems, and synchronised changes in the complementarity elements of systems, in the move towards net-zero GHG emissions. It goes beyond technological fixes or product-and-process changes at the company level (Clayton et al., 1999). This is why net-zero finance must be analysed and evaluated from the viewpoints of system transformation or sustainability transition. The book takes electricity systems as a case to evaluate net-zero financial mechanisms under the Paris–Glasgow financial regime and identify underlying factors and cruxes that can make them work effectively.

Second, the book argues for finance system transitions and explores their interaction with electricity systems transitions. Traditional financial risk–return thinking and optimal risk–return investments in mainstream finance theory assume that changes in the cost of capital, triggered by changes in technology, policy, and perception, are propagated into the real sector, eventually generating behavioural changes and changes in the economic structure. In contrast, the financial sector is assumed to maintain the current investment rules: maximising financial returns instead of the integrated value that incorporates environmental and social ones, abiding by fiduciary duties that focus only on financial return, managing quantifiable risks instead of creating and capturing integrated value, and short-termism instead of long-term return.

The book presents a counterargument to these implicit assumptions based on the cost–benefit schedule of electricity system transitions towards net zero and proposes practical strategies for finance system transitions. Then it argues that net-zero finance system transitions can rebalance the costs and benefits of electricity system transitions towards net zero, expanding net-zero transitions economy-wide.

Third, the book provides novel empirical findings on the costs and benefits of electricity system transitions towards net zero in Southeast Asia, particularly in highly coal-dependent small EMDEs. It employs mixed methods: quantitative scenario-based analysis and empirical case studies of Vietnam and the Philippines. The former estimates the cost of technological changes in Southeast Asia, whereas the latter investigates the costs and benefits of the changes in other complementarity elements and combines the results. The latter approach also tests the validity of the proposed analytical framework for electricity system transitions and indicates elements that should be counted on to investigate the costs and benefits.

While our empirical case studies do not quantitatively estimate costs and benefits, their basis on empirical evidence makes the results convincing and applicable to coal-dependent small EMDEs in other Southeast Asian countries and beyond the Southeast Asian region.

2 Propagation of Climate-Related Transition Risks between the Financial and Electricity Sectors

2.1 INTRODUCTION

Climate-related stranded assets have attracted attention owing to growing concerns over the negative impacts of the transition to a low/net-zero-carbon economy on the value of assets of carbon-intensive industries and the economy-wide knock-on effects of massive value destruction within the fossil fuel industry (Shimbar, 2021a). Climate-related stranded assets are generated when any of the three categories of climate-related risks materialises: physical, transition, and liability risks. Physical risks are damages to physical assets, natural capital, and human lives resulting in losses of productive capacity, output, and value of financial assets arising from climate-related weather events. Transition risks are rooted in a reassessment of the value of an extensive range of assets by transitioning towards a lower-carbon economy through disruptive innovation, such as renewable energy and battery storage (Green & Newman, 2017), regulatory and policy changes, and sudden changes in the climate preferences and risk perception of financial actors and consumers. Liability risks are the potential effects (especially for the insurance industry) that may arise if people and organisations demand compensation from carbon extractors and emitters for damage or loss suffered. Liability risks have the potential to be both a driver and a consequence of the physical impacts of the transition to a net-zero economy (Caldecott et al., 2021).

Climate-related stranded assets may be classified into three categories: stranded resources or unburned fossils, stranded capital or unusable capacity, and financially stranded assets (Daumas, 2023). About 80% of coal, 50% of gas, and 33% of oil must be left underground to improve prospects of limiting average global warming to at most

2°C above pre-industrial levels (McGlade & Ekins, 2015). Limiting the global temperature increase to 1.5°C further drops the value of fossil reserves and the stock market value of the fossil fuel industry compared with a no-climate-policy world and limiting the increase to 2°C (Edenhofer et al., 2020). The stranding of these sizable resources will cause many oil, gas, and coal companies to suffer from diminishing asset values, which may lead to bankruptcy and default without a reorientation of their business models (Chevallier et al., 2021).

Stranded resources are likely to be generated in countries that concentratedly export a few low-complexity carbon-intensive products, such as oil and gas. Such countries have relatively few nearby diversification opportunities (Andres et al., 2023; van de Graaf, 2018). As such, a unilateral transformation away from fuel exports is likely to be economically harmful in the short term (Ansari & Holz, 2020). The corporate value of oil and gas companies that are not members of the Organisation of the Petroleum Exporting Countries (OPEC) will also be hit because their export costs are higher than those of OPEC companies, and government policies to boost domestic demand or maintain high prices may not be sufficient to compensate for declining exports (Mercure et al., 2018). Early closures of coal mines would also severely hit workers and local communities (Hauenstein, 2023).

Electric utilities are likewise anticipated to suffer from stranded capital or unusable capacity. Stranded fossil fuel resources will force such utilities to reduce the operation of generation capacity. Shifting towards renewable-energy-sourced electricity (RES-E) accelerates the under-utilisation of fossil fuel power plants and infrastructure (Löffler et al., 2019). The nature of irreversible investment may prompt the premature decommissioning of existing generation capacities when a carbon price is suddenly implemented (Rozenberg et al., 2020). Electric utilities will bear the costs linked to retrofitting when reducing the carbon footprint of electricity generation.

Research has estimated the stranded costs of existing and planned generation capacities of electric utilities. Immense transition and litigation risks can induce profound structural changes and reorganisation in financial and market power worldwide if economic diversification and divestment away from fossil fuels are not quickly pursued (Mercure et al., 2021). This holds for electric utilities in Japan (Caldecott et al., 2016), China (Caldecott et al., 2017), and European countries (Caldecott & McDaniels, 2014). Estimations of the impacts of stranded resources on reduced utilisation revealed that a reduction in fossil fuel production in export countries would hit the US, China, and Japan hardest by cascading losses (Cahen-Fourot et al., 2021). Investigations of the responses of electric utilities to stranded assets have identified concerns about transition costs, energy security, and social and ecological impacts of transitions as factors affecting the direction and speed of changes in the energy mix in electricity generation (Firdaus & Mori, 2023).

Meanwhile, the propagation of climate-related risks through financial and non-financial networks has remained understudied (Campiglio et al., 2022). The financial sector has supported investments in coal power capacities (Mori, 2020; Mori, 2022; Sauer et al., 2022). Conversely, they may place pressure on energy companies and electric utilities in their portfolio to reduce their carbon footprint and stranded asset risks (Van Benthem et al., 2022). Nonetheless, past research has concentrated on the impacts on financially stranded assets (Campiglio et al., 2022) and has not investigated climate-related risks as drivers for behavioural changes to mitigate the risk in the production and financial sectors. Daumas (2023) conducted a literature review to map out the transmission channels in the financial sector and the drivers for systemic risk but paid scant attention to the production sector.

Against this backdrop, this chapter presents a literature review to comprehensively identify the causal channels of transmission of climate-related transition risk to the electricity sector. The channels entail different types of transition risk drivers, direct and indirect impacts through the financial sector, and second-round effects through responses by the financial and electricity sectors.

The chapter also presents a literature review of empirical analyses to identify bottlenecks that block the channels from generating and reinforcing behavioural changes.

The remainder of this chapter is organised as follows. Section 2.2 presents the direct and indirect causal transmission channels to the electricity sector, based on a literature review. Section 2.3 reviews the empirical evidence on the effectiveness of transmission channels, and Section 2.4 discusses them to illustrate modifications of transmission channels. Section 2.5 concludes by highlighting the remaining challenges, such as the link between transition risk and electricity system transitions, which will be explored in greater detail in Chapter 3.

2.2 CAUSAL TRANSMISSION CHANNELS BETWEEN FINANCIAL AND PRODUCTION SECTORS

2.2.1 Transmission Channels between Production and Banking Sectors

Dunz et al. (2021) identified two transmission channels of climate-related transition risks. The first channel begins with regulatory changes that directly affect the cost of capital for the banking sector, represented as green supporting factors. They entail a reduced risk weight for the banking sector's green assets, which reduces the overall interest rate setting for the banking sector, and lower liquidity requirements for green loans, which reduce the interest rate for the green capital goods production sector. The regulatory change makes green finance more attractive for the banking sector, particularly where financial arrangements – such as project financing arrangements specifically targeting green investments – and green bonds allow the banking sector to separate the financing of low-carbon energy projects from their traditional businesses. To attract the green capital goods production sector, the banking sector offers favourable terms of lending conditions, which can stimulate investments, increase productivity, and reduce prices. In turn, better economic performance in the green capital goods production sector further incentivises the banking sector to increase credit exposure but may generate green bubbles, leading to green asset stranding. Conversely, green supporting factors make the brown capital goods production sector less profitable, increasing the banking sector's non-performing loan ratio and decreasing its capital adequacy ratio.

The second channel begins with stringent climate policies that directly affect the production sector, represented as carbon pricing. Carbon pricing will increase the price competitiveness, demand, and profits of green capital goods against brown ones. However, the green capital goods production sector does not fully compensate for the reduced consumption owing to the resultant tighter budget constraints and lower GDP. This holds particularly for economy-wide uniform carbon pricing because it greatly reduces demand compared with piecemeal, sector-focused pricing. Uniform pricing gives a systematic shock affecting all companies with large carbon emissions (Bolton & Kacperczyk, 2021b). In response, the banking sector offers unfavourable terms of borrowing conditions to the production sector to cover the higher risk of loan default or credit rationing, ultimately to minimise default risk. While the green capital goods production sector can partially offset the unfavourable conditions owing to relatively better economic performance, the brown capital goods production sector cannot. In the electricity sector, fossil-fuel-based power generators would increase wholesale electricity prices to compensate for the faster depreciation rates of assets, thereby amplifying concerns about the security and reliability of electricity supplies.

Carbon pricing may also increase sovereign risk in fossil-fuel-exporting countries with high state ownership. These countries tend to allow fossil fuel companies to continue exploiting their reserves without regard for climate impacts owing to a high economic and budget dependency on fossil fuel reserves (Shimbar, 2021b) and formidable political resistance from state-owned companies (Hansen, 2022). The remaining market value destruction and transition risks are turned into sovereign risks (Jaffe, 2020b). This holds particularly true for newly developed reserves because they are likely to be stranded (Heede & Oreskes, 2016). They will impact sovereign fiscal revenues and refinancing conditions on the international market, affecting the probability of default on sovereign bonds (Battiston et al., 2019). Stranded resources will hit the banking sector because sovereign bonds comprise a large portion of the holdings of banks and investment funds (Roncoroni et al., 2021).

By anticipating future regulatory changes and the resultant impacts on profits, the banking sector may change the terms of lending conditions or impose a credit ceiling before governments take any action. The changed conditions transfer into prices, demand, and profits in both sectors, which decreases the market share of brown capital products and the banking sector's exposure to the brown capital goods production sector. Prior adjustments can mitigate the macroeconomic impacts, resource and asset stranding, and financial system instability that can accompany regulatory changes.

2.2.2 *Transmission Channels via Investors*

Asset owners, managers, and institutional investors, such as pension and investment funds, play key but varied roles in the propagation of transition risk. They suffer larger negative portfolio effects from the revaluation of assets (Campiglio et al., 2022) owing to high exposure to high-carbon emissions sectors in their equity portfolios (Monasterolo et al., 2017). They also suffer second-round effects or indirect losses from the devaluation of production sectors' debt obligations on the interbank market owing to mutual exposures (Battiston et al., 2017). In addition, contagion via common exposures occurs when investment funds seek to restore their value-at-risk level of the same asset classes before the shock (Roncoroni et al., 2021).

Asset owners, managers, and institutional investors may employ a variety of tools to manage the transition risk, ranging from divestment to engagement, management of financed emissions, and investment in 'green' alternatives. Divestment enables investors to reduce the sensitivity of portfolio returns deriving from transition and litigation risks. Institutional investors expect divestment to incentivise carbon-intensive production sectors to reduce investment projects and to offer higher rates of return to attract investment. However, divestment imposes financial constraints on companies with high exposure to climate risk, making them incapable of retrofitting. In the case of toxic releases in the US, relaxing financial constraints has reduced releases from public firms (Xu & Kim, 2022).

In addition, divestment may cause emissions or ownership leakage – that is, reducing climate-related risks for one actor at the expense of others. Original owners may sell their fossil fuel assets to new owners who have less concern about climate change than the original owners and who will increase emissions (French & Resnick-Ault, 2021). While such sales enable new owners to reconcile requirements for decarbonisation with their current core business, it can generate cross-border reallocation of the social and economic risks of stranded assets from the Global North to the Global South, increasing fossil fuel asset stranding in the latter (Gupta et al., 2020).

For this reason, shareholder engagement is regarded as a sound hedging strategy to foster decarbonisation. Engagement – direct dialogue, proxy voting, and legal actions – influences the corporate governance and business practices of the firms in their portfolios and mitigates transition and litigation risk. The selective retention of stakes in carbon-intensive production sectors committed to emissions reduction and improvement of the diversification of their portfolios can reconcile engagement with transition risk reduction (van Benthem et al., 2022).

Disclosures of climate-related financial risks have been employed as a form of engagement. Institutional investors require companies to disclose such risks in their portfolios. To maximise their leverage over the sectors, they join existing coalition platforms or organise new ones, such as the Task Force on Climate-Related Financial Disclosure (TCFD) and Climate Action 100+ (Gupta et al., 2020). They also use their materials and guidelines for disclosure to develop strategic climate plans that make their investments align with the Paris Agreement (TCFD, 2017). The plans are typically composed of forward-looking targets for emissions reduction, timelines for the retirement of fossil assets, and investments in renewable energies.

Institutional investors are also required to disclose climate-related risks associated with investments in fossil fuel companies as prime owners of fossil fuel assets. Most of the transition risk associated with stranded oil and gas assets falls on private investors, overwhelmingly in OECD countries, including substantial exposure through pension funds and financial markets (Semieniuk et al., 2022). Disclosure enables other stakeholders to accurately price risk exposures and fosters a smooth and efficient transition of financial markets towards decarbonisation, while avoiding divestment and transfer of ownership to less accountable parties that may generate ownership leakage (Mercure et al., 2021).

However, stakeholder engagement alone, particularly voluntary disclosure, has shown limited impacts on behavioural changes in companies in the portfolio. Direct engagement changes corporate behaviours only when implemented in tandem with a distinct and explicit divestment scheme (Dawkins, 2018).

2.2.3 *Amplifiers and Mitigators*

The aforementioned impacts can be amplified through multiple factors. First, interconnected industrial networks transform simple transition shocks into complex dynamics that bring about economy-wide output reduction. They can generate cascading losses in the value of assets in other sectors that use fossil fuel energy as a production input or are involved in the economic value chains of companies that do so. These include high-carbon energy utilities, energy-intensive industries (steel, cement, petrochemicals), housing, and transportation (Battiston et al., 2019; IRENA, 2017). They can also cause demand loss in both fossil-intensive and non-fossil-intensive sectors and then impose a higher risk of loan default on financial market participants (Vermeulen et al., 2021). In South Africa, the transport, electric utility, and auxiliary financial sectors exhibit vulnerability to the loss of coal exports, and the metal ores, basic iron and steel, glass, and electric utility sectors show vulnerability to the export loss of internal combustion engine vehicles (Godin & Hadji-Lazaro, 2020).

Second, financial interconnectedness and the characteristics of the financial network could amplify initial direct losses incurred owing to assets' vulnerability to climate-related risks via the reverberation of gains and losses (Monasterolo, 2020). The frequency of banking crises can be increased by 26% to 248%, and rescuing insolvent banks will cause an additional fiscal burden of approximately 5% to 15% of GDP per year (Lamperti et al., 2019).

Third, a lack of information on climate-related impacts could trigger a system-wide reassessment of losses from climate change by herd behaviour in finance. The reassessment and consequent loss of finance and access to business insurance can prevent fossil fuel businesses from operating, and a country from securing a stable energy supply (Jaffe, 2020a).

Conversely, a policy that protects investors' balance sheets can mitigate macroeconomic downturn and lead to higher investment in green productive capacity (Comerford & Spiganti, 2022). A credible financial market with sound supervision can also mitigate losses and asset stranding associated with disorderly transitions. These markets can mitigate asset price volatility and help the endogenous recovery of interbank assets (Roncoroni et al., 2021). For example, the Network of Central Banks and Supervisors for Greening the Financial System (NGFS) was established in 2017 to provide a high-level framework for the integration of climate-related factors in prudential supervision (NGFS, 2019).

2.2.4 *Disruptive, Abrupt, and Disorderly Transitions*

Disruptive, abrupt, and disorderly transitions can also amplify changes in the cost of capital, financial risks, and asset prices. Disruptive transitions occur when there is a gap in the technological trajectory between rising and sunset industries. Investments in sunset industries are supported by uneven and erratic climate policies, highly publicised setbacks in low-carbon technology, vested interests in high-carbon sectors, and biased information provided by prominent forecasters and scenarios (Semieniuk, 2021). Political activism and rent-seeking by specific societal interest groups can increase stranded assets if such activities make policy implementation delayed and uncertain (Bretschger & Soretz, 2022; Kalkuhl et al., 2020).

Uncertainty about policy interventions makes fossil fuel extraction more voracious, causes discrete jumps in capital valuation (van der Ploeg & Rezai, 2020), and increases stranded assets (van der Ploeg, 2020). Unanticipated policy events can trigger legal claims to compensate for losses. Litigations by activists and court decisions requiring alignment with the 1.5°C target materialise litigation risks. Liability risk can freeze current policies that support incumbent high-carbon technologies, further increasing the discrepancy in technological trajectories; under the existing bilateral investment treaties to protect foreign investors, host country governments may be held liable for stranded contracts and must compensate international companies for their stranded assets associated with unanticipated climate policies (Bos & Gupta, 2018).

Delayed policy actions would generate significantly greater asset stranding than accelerated deployment (IRENA, 2017). A higher proportion of European electric utilities will downgrade their credit ratings to 'speculative' if they delay the replacement of obsolete generation capacity (Hickey et al., 2021). Emerging economies will suffer from rapid and significant asset stranding after 2030 if they increase installed coal power capacity to satisfy growing electricity demand (Saygin et al., 2019).

Abrupt and disorderly transitions are triggered by disruptive events affecting transition drivers, such as stringent climate policies, low-carbon technologies, preferences, or a widespread change in expectations of their impacts (Semieniuk, 2021). They generate sudden devaluations of assets in some sectors, impose significant risks for portfolio losses and debt default on some financial actors, generate credit rationing, and erode confidence, which has direct impacts on macroeconomics and financial system stability (Papandreou, 2021).

2.2.5 Responses in the Energy and Electricity Sectors

Early cancellation of *new* fossil fuel capacity can mitigate the transition risk. Premature retirements of power generation capacity and new capacity installation after 2030 would be nearly half of new capacity installation if currently announced nationally determined contributions (NDCs) were strengthened to achieve greater near-term emissions mitigation (Iyer et al., 2015). Suspending new additions to coal power capacity will save annual power generation by 44% in 2030–2050 in China (Wang et al., 2020a). A policy limiting the new construction of coal plants combined with higher renewable energy targets could be politically feasible and would allow higher mitigation ambition in the future (Malik et al., 2020). Early cancellation can be associated with the suspension of ancillary infrastructure development, which further reduces asset stranding.

In contrast, early policy intervention for the early retirement of *existing* capacity does not always mitigate stranded costs. China and, to a much lesser extent, South Korea, Japan, and Turkey are required to drop installed coal capacity significantly by 2030 in low-carbon technology pathways towards staying below the 2°C limit. They will face much higher stranded costs than in the delayed policy intervention scenario, which aligns with national energy plans for 2030 (Saygin et al., 2019). In contrast, stranded coal power asset value is lower in the delayed policy action scenario than in IRENA's REmap case, which assumes that RES-E accounts for 85% in power generation (IRENA, 2018). The lower stranded costs of delayed policy intervention incentivise coal power generators to lobby to delay policy intervention or to skew interventions to proliferate existing installed capacity and technologies. Retrofitting with carbon dioxide capture, utilisation, and storage (CCUS) and bio-energy with carbon dioxide capture and storage (BECCS) and repowering by co-firing ammonia can make up the bulk of capacity reduction by early retirement, so long as these options become commercially available at an affordable cost on a large scale and are operated in an ecologically and socially sustainable manner. Deployment of the full potential of CCUS and BECCS would reduce stranded generation by 69% and 45% on average, respectively (Lu et al., 2022).

Prior announcements of policy interventions may also not motivate incumbent companies to change their behaviours. It could be rational for them to invest in fossil energy production if overall costs are lower than those of clean alternatives and if capital depreciation rates are lower than carbon taxes (Baldwin et al., 2020), so long as initial returns are sufficiently larger than the anticipated stranded costs.

Nonetheless, some incumbent companies may reorient their business and foster business model innovation for sustainability to seek new profit opportunities as well as to mitigate profit losses and asset stranding (Berggren et al., 2015; Mori, 2021a). They can leverage their resources and capabilities to reorient for innovation in order to capture value in new niche sectors in domestic and international markets (Steen & Weaver, 2017). They can also foster organisational innovations that are intertwined with technology and complemental product and process innovation (Zott et al., 2011) through transformation, diversification (Andersen & Gulbrandsen, 2020), acquisition, merger, joint venture (Ruggiero et al., 2021), and strategic alliances with niche innovations (Hess, 2014). By spreading out sustainable business model innovation throughout economic value chains and with multiple actors, some incumbent companies create standards for compatible technology development, change legislation, shift the perceptions of users or potential users, pool knowledge and resources to co-create new products and services, develop them to be commercially viable, share infrastructure, embrace collective marketing, and bundle forces to compete against other technologies (Planko et al., 2019; Planko & Cramer, 2021). They may apply internal carbon pricing to full supply-chain emissions or Scope 3 emissions to reduce the risk of stranded fossil assets in expected carbon regulation, and then spread out the innovation throughout their value chains.[1]

2.3 EMPIRICAL EVIDENCE ON RISK TRANSMISSION AND SECTORAL RESPONSES

2.3.1 *Risk Transmission*

Exposure to climate risks in terms of carbon emissions and intensity affects the creditworthiness of loans and bonds issued by the production sector (Capasso et al., 2020). However, such exposure is not yet fully priced in the value of financial contracts and investor risk management strategies (Monasterolo, 2020). While climate-related physical risk is not priced, the risks stemming from the US climate policy debate had been priced in 2012–2018; investors hedged against the imminent transition risks (Faccini et al., 2023). Investors react to a series of negative news reports about climate change to hedge against short-term risks and to improve their environmental profiles (Giglio et al., 2021). Prior findings suggest that climate-related transition risk is not recognised as a powerful driver that induces long-term changes in the production and financial systems towards decarbonisation.

Nonetheless, the occurrence of limited, short-sighted impacts does not mean that the financial and production sectors have not responded to long-term climate-related transition risks and generated behavioural changes in incumbent production and financial sectors at the sectoral and individual levels.

2.3.2 *Banking Sector*

The banking sector has priced climate-related physical risks into their loans. Firms with higher exposure to a long-run drought risk pay significantly higher spreads on their bank loans since the publication

[1] 'Scope 3 emissions' refers to greenhouse gas emissions discharged from activities from assets not owned or controlled by the reporting organization but that indirectly affect organizations in its value chain.

of the Stern Review (Javadi & Masum, 2021). In the US from 2007 to 2014, climate-related physical risk resulted in unfavourable corporate financing terms related to bank loans, such as higher interest paid, higher likelihood of being required to collateralise the loan, and a greater number of covenant constraints (Huang et al., 2022). Such risk also significantly negatively impacts bank loan supply in China, particularly loans supplied by banks with fewer deposits and located in coastal areas (Li & Wu, 2023).

The banking sector started to price climate-related transition risks in credit ratings and yield spreads after the Paris Agreement (Seltzer et al., 2022). Banks in the Euro area reduced the share of loans to firms with higher carbon emissions compared with those with lower emissions (Reghezza et al., 2022). Banks supplying syndicated loans to emerging markets have started pricing climate-related transition risks for loans to emissions-intensive sectors (Ho & Wong, 2023). Some major banks employ more stringent non-pricing contractual terms, such as shortening loan tenors and imposing collateral requirements. As of June 2021, 29 out of the world's 56 banks that had supplied nearly 70% of loans and 41% of underwriting services for coal power plants had already stopped financing new plants. Of these 29, 18 banks have gone further, imposing restrictions on customers' coal revenues and setting a target year for phasing out banking services to businesses related to coal power generation. Conversely, eight major commercial banks have not committed to such schemes, of which five are Chinese (Chan et al., 2022).

The OECD and G20 agreement on officially supported export credit to end support for unabated coal power plants (OECD, 2021a) is expected to stop additional carbon risk exposures in the banking sector, particularly those in China's two policy banks – the Chinese Development Bank and Export-Import Bank of China. The carbon risk exposures of overseas energy infrastructure projects amount to between 4% and 22% of the portfolio's value (Monasterolo et al., 2018). The high transition risk will make them encounter financial distress even with an average shock of 10%.

2.3.3 *Institutional Investors*

Institutional investors have also recognised that climate-related transition risks have started to materialise. They began to mitigate the risks to protect their reputations, moral/legal considerations, and expected impacts on portfolio risk and returns (Krueger et al., 2020). The Big Three index funds – BlackRock, Vanguard, and State Street Global Advisors – have focused their engagements on companies in which they have substantial stakes. Their higher stockholding is associated with companies' smaller carbon emissions. The association has becomes stronger in more recent years, when they publicly committed to tackling environmental, social, and governance issues (Azar et al., 2021).

However, institutional investors are not always seriously and comprehensively committed to reducing fossil fuel production to stay below the 2°C limit (Rempel & Gupta, 2020). They exit fossil fuel companies altogether only when other energy sources become relatively and reliably less costly and capable of being invested in at a sufficient scale (Christophers, 2019). They concentrate on divestment and exclusionary screening in industries with high Scope 1 emission intensity or emission per sale (Bolton & Kacperczyk, 2021) and with sufficiently scalable and profitable alternatives, such as the oil, gas, electric utilities, and automobile industries.[2] Institutional investors' threats of future exits and divestitures can improve the environmental and social policies of companies in their portfolios if they are environmentally and socially conscious and the company managers' compensation is linked to the stock price (Gantchev et al., 2022).

In addition, divestment and engagement have not shown significant differences in terms of risk and return from unrestricted portfolios (Plantingaa & Scholtens, 2021). The insignificant difference may accrue for smaller stockholding by individual investors, investment

[2] 'Scope 1 emissions' refers to carbon or greenhouse gas emissions that come from sources that are controlled or owned by an organisation.

advisors, and mutual funds; they avoid holding stakes in fossil fuel companies, thus revealing only a moderate exposure of their assets to carbon risk (Benz et al., 2021). Disclosures of Scope 1 emissions even lead to lower returns and divestments, despite the positive association of the climate-conscious institutional investors' ownership with better CDP-based measures of climate risk (Ilhan et al., 2023).

For other industries, institutional investors have most frequently employed discussions with management, subsequently proposing specific actions to management on climate risk, submitting shareholder proposals, and voting against management on proposals. Less than half of institutional investors assess carbon footprints and stranded asset risks – the two most common approaches within the first steps towards managing climate risk. Most have refrained from further actions, such as more engagement, climate risk hedges, or divestment, even if portfolio companies have not responded to engagement or have showed resistance (Krueger et al., 2020). In India, few financial institutions assess physical and transition risks, and even fewer quantify and use the information to guide financial decisions systematically. Instead, they integrate risks into their business strategy to seek opportunities for green finance (Colenbrander et al., 2023).

Participation in climate-oriented coalitions and partnerships has filled limited gaps in financial institutions' capacity to achieve ambitious climate actions. While investor initiatives such as Climate Action 100+ are gathering huge amounts of capital, a lack of internal accountability, minimal transparency into their goals and timelines, and limited ambition have restricted their influence over investors' actions, particularly in the oil and gas industries (McDonnell et al., 2022).

2.3.4 *Energy Sector*

In the face of transition risks, major investor-owned energy companies have made varied responses. Most European-integrated oil companies have capitalised on their abundant capital, transferable skills, synergies with existing operations, and market positions to generate value and diversify into new energy sectors, such as wind, solar, storage, electric vehicle charging, and biofuels. While diversification enables them to be less exposed to carbon risks (Curtin et al., 2019), it does not require the full replacement of existing infrastructure, expertise, and staff; it can include modest investments in renewable energy, improved energy efficiency, and capacity expansion (Herzog-Hawelka & Gupta, 2023).

Conversely, US-integrated oil companies remain focused on their current core business of production, processing, storage, and sale of fossil fuels, and seek to maximise returns to shareholders for as long as demand for their products lasts. Privately held independent exploration and production companies have low management capacity and low financial flexibility to pursue diversification and have fewer opportunities to transfer skills or find synergies. Moreover, they have less pressure from activists and equity investors and fewer reputational concerns over climate strategies (van Benthem et al., 2022).

2.3.5 *Electricity Sector*

Electricity system inertia prevails globally, which risks utility-driven carbon lock-in and asset stranding. Particularly, inertia and carbon lock-in prevail in Asia. Electricity utilities in China, India, Vietnam, Indonesia, and the Philippines prioritised the expansion of coal-based capacity in the 2010s (Mori, 2021b), and thus have many young coal power plants. China and India will bear disproportionally significant stranded costs because coal plants built within five years will have to be retired, equivalent to only half their technical or nominal operating lifetime (Cui et al., 2019). Of 300 GW of would-be stranded coal power assets that were built by 2014, 59% are in China and 22% in India (Farfan & Bayer, 2017). Stranded investments were projected to be around 7.5% of the 2016 GDP in India and 3% in China, against less than 0.1% in the EU and the US combined, and the loss of revenue would be 42% in India, 60% in China, 35% in the EU, and 15% in the US (Kefford et al., 2018).

The Paris Agreement and the reduction of levelised costs of intermittent RES-E unlocked this inertia. Among over 3,311 utilities worldwide identified for the period 2011–2018, 14% prioritise renewables, of which only 15% reduced both coal and gas capacities. However, most of them continued to grow their gas or coal portfolio or reduced either their coal or gas capacity, but not both. This implies that even renewables-prioritising utilities add low-carbon fossil fuel assets to their growing core business rather than replace fossil fuel capacity with renewables (Alova, 2020).

The OECD and G20 agreement on ending official support to export credit for unabated coal power plants and subsequent credit constraints persuaded some countries to decide on the early retirement of *new* coal power capacity. However, these agreements are not so powerful as to scrap all new coal power projects, not to mention to enforce early retirement of existing capacity. China has bypassed the agreement to finance *new* coal power capacity in existing industrial projects under the Belt and Road Initiative represented by industrial nickel and steel developments in Indonesia, and to gain equipment supply contracts for the expansion of existing coal power plants and the revival of previously shelved projects in Laos (Suarez, 2022). China has gone further to reverse the decrease in domestic net coal power capacity, adding 29.8 GW of net coal power capacity and commissioning another 38.4 GW in 2020, against a net capacity decrease of 17.2 GW in the rest of the world (Global Energy Monitor and Centre for Research on Energy and Clean Air, 2021). Nationwide power blackouts and electricity rationing in 2021 accelerated investments in new coal power, with China granting permits for 106 GW of capacity across 82 locations in 2022, compared to new installations of wind and solar capacity of 125 GW (Shepherd, 2023). China has justified this on the basis of supporting grid stability and mitigating the intermittent nature of renewables (Senlen et al., 2023). The carbon intensity target in China's NDC also justifies an increase in coal power capacity before 2030.

In the same vein, international credit rationing does not always induce the early retirement of *existing* coal power capacity and replacement with RES-E. In the US, risk-averse investors and lenders have chosen to extend the physical life of *existing* coal power plants and avoid investments in new plants to minimise asset stranding (Rode et al., 2017). Meanwhile, the Philippines and Vietnam abandoned new coal power projects and instead initiated new gas power projects to satisfy growing electricity demand while initiating large-scale wind projects (see Chapters 4 and 5). A Thai power generator has reconciled the decarbonisation requirement and profitability by acquiring a portion of stakes in existing coal power with an integrated gasification combined cycle system in Japan; this helps reduce the company's carbon footprint in its portfolio (Banpu Power, 2021).

2.4 DISCUSSION

Figures 2.1 and 2.2 illustrate the theoretical causal transmission channels of the two types of transition risks – green supporting factors and stringent climate policies – based on our literature review.

Transition risk directly affecting the financial sector, such as green supporting factors, influences the production sector, including,

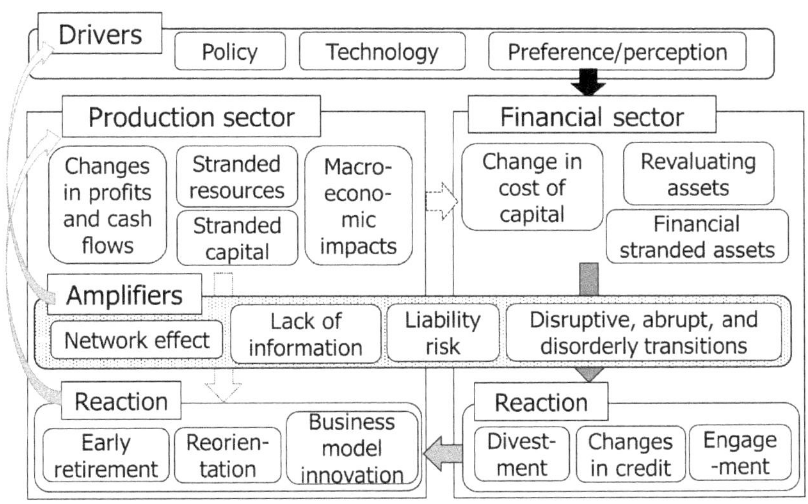

FIGURE 2.1 Propagation of transition risk (theoretical) when green finance policy and technology are the drivers.
Source: Authors.

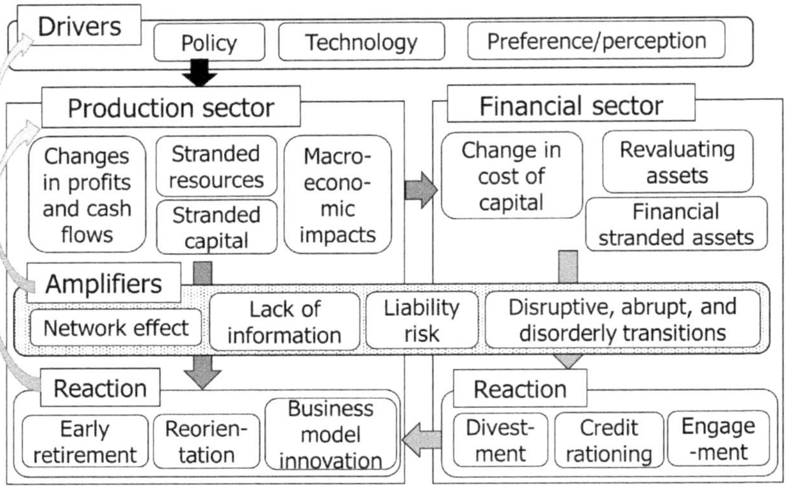

FIGURE 2.2 Propagation of transition risk (theoretical) when carbon pricing and deployment of renewable energy technologies are the drivers. Source: Authors.

indirectly, the electricity sector. The financial sector incorporates the changes in the cost of capital and revalued resources and assets into financing decisions and reallocates financial resources through changes in the terms of lending and ceilings, engagement, and divestment. To increase profits and enhance competitiveness, the production sector may respond to the changes in terms of financing to change their technologies and business models.

Transition risk that directly hits the production sector, in the form of stringent climate policies and deployment of green technologies, also affects the production sector through macroeconomic impacts and the financial sector. The production sector faces changes in profits and in the value of resources and assets, along with economy-wide, macroeconomic changes in terms of production output, unemployment, current account, and sovereign risks. The financial sector responds to changes in the production sector by revaluing the cost of capital and financial assets. The sector reduces transition risks by employing divestment, engagement, credit ceilings, and updated terms of finance. Notably, reactions to the changed financial terms may generate a second-round effect on the financial sector. Orderly, anticipated, and smooth transitions not only reduce the amplification of the initial effects and repercussions in the transition risk drivers but also create room for the production sector to adapt to the new normal along value chains. The financial sector can thus revisit investment decisions to minimise asset stranding. These prior behavioural changes could reduce transition costs and thus prevent system risks from being materialised.

However, empirical analyses suggest that the transmission channels have not worked effectively in changing corporate behaviour in the production sector owing to recognition gaps between and within the production and financial sectors. Whereas major global private banks and institutional investors with long-term perspectives are aware of the transition risk and have started to integrate climate risks into decisions, many investors still do not consider the basic approaches to identifying and managing carbon and stranded asset risks (Krueger et al., 2020). Whereas energy and electricity companies in Europe have started to incorporate these risks into their investment processes, those with vertically integrated structures or that are exempted from reputation and litigation risks have ignored the transition risk.

The latter's ignorance of the risk is due partly to their perception that the early retirement of *existing* capacity has had little or no mitigation effect on stranded costs. The supposition is that climate warming will not exceed the 2°C limit in the Paris Agreement so long as the largest investor-owned energy companies use their existing proved reserves (Heede & Oreskes, 2016). Institutional investors tend to take a conservative stance on committing seriously and comprehensively to reducing fossil fuel production so long as energy and electricity companies generate profits (Rempel & Gupta, 2020).

Blended finance can potentially unlock institutional investment for development purposes in developing countries (OECD, 2021b). With this expectation, the Just Energy Transition Partnership was established to fund coal-dependent developing countries to support coal phase-out and transitions towards clean energy while addressing the social consequences. However, blended finance is too small and weak to go beyond an increase in RES-E capacity to a large-scale integration into grids. Holistic system change is required to integrate RES-E into grids on a large scale and ensure system stability and reliability. In addition, whole-system changes or electricity system transitions lead to surges in demand for flexible and dispatchable generation capacity, such as battery energy storage systems, and in demand the critical minerals and metals for the mass production of these technologies (Scholten et al., 2020). Financial approaches to individual energy and electric companies may induce behavioural changes, but the reactions of these companies are constrained by the infrastructure and institutions of the system and accessibility to the minerals, metals, and technologies that ensure flexibility.

These pieces of empirical evidence require updates on the theoretical causal transmission channels of the transition risk shown

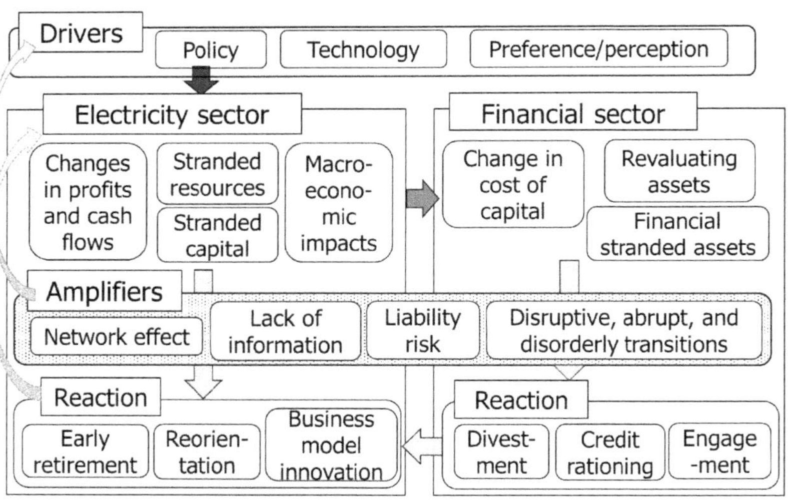

FIGURE 2.3 Propagation of transition risk in practice when carbon pricing and deployment of renewable energy technologies are the drivers. Source: Authors.

in Figure 2.2 on three points. First, direct impacts are not sufficiently strong to change corporate behaviours in the electricity sector. Second, indirect impacts are much less strong than direct ones because the financial sector does not always incorporate changes in the cost of capital and financial assets in financing decisions, and it hesitates to explicitly combine engagement with a distinct and explicit divestment. Third, voluntary and heterogenous responses in the electricity sector have marginal second-round effects on the propagation of the transition risk. The updated channels are illustrated in Figure 2.3.

2.5 CONCLUSION

Climate-related stranded assets have attracted attention amid growing concerns over the negative impacts of the transition to a low/net-zero-carbon economy on the value of assets of carbon-intensive industries and the economy-wide knock-on effects of massive value destruction within the fossil fuel industry. However, the propagation of climate-related transition risk to the electricity sector through financial and non-financial networks has been under-investigated. Against this backdrop, this chapter has presented a literature review to elucidate the theoretical direct and indirect causal channels of climate-related transition risk and has reviewed empirical analyses of such risk's effect on behavioural changes.

We have illustrated how transition risk is transmitted and generates behavioural changes in the electricity sector in theory. The financial sector revalues the costs of capital and financial assets and transmits the risk by divestment, engagement, credit rationing, and changes in financing terms. The risk is amplified by network effect, lack of information, liability risk, and disruptive, abrupt, and disorderly transitions. Lack of mitigation effect on stranded costs makes energy and electricity companies hesitant to commit to the early retirement of *existing* capacity even though major global private banks, institutional investors, and export credit agencies are changing engagement with them. Chinese state banks' continuous financing of coal power remains a barrier to the early retirement of *new* capacity globally. Corporate behaviours in financial approaches to individual energy and electricity companies can change only when synchronised with changes in the electricity system. Another important aspect is when accessibility to critical minerals, metals, and technologies for flexible and dispatchable generation capacity can be ensured.

3 Determinants of the Direction and Speed of Electricity System Transition

An Analytical Framework

3.1 INTRODUCTION

Sociotechnical systems are constituted by complementarities in terms of technology, infrastructure, organisations, and institutions that play critical functions or criticality affect performance (Markard & Hoffmann, 2016). Technological complementarities are created to engineer design, procure technologies, and construct, operate, and maintain plants and grids. Infrastructure complementarities can generate positive effects for a broad range of technologies. Institutional complementarities are created to secure financial capital for investments in electricity systems (Lehr, 2013). Organisational complementarities are created to ensure efficient systems operation (IEA, 2016), minimise operation costs and commercial risks, and avoid sunk-cost investments for the individual actor. Organisational assets, competencies, and services positively affect the focal technology. Organisational changes can be closely associated with institutional changes. Notably, organisations seek legitimacy for their activities in their institutional environments. The emergence of new forms of organisation can bring about simultaneous de-institutionalisation and new institutionalisation (Strambach & Pflitsch, 2020).

A strong complementarity slows or impedes transitions because each complemental element has its own dynamics, time horizon, and development speed. Intangible institutions tend to show faster transitions than technologies, markets, consumption patterns, infrastructures, production facilities, and supply and distribution chains

(Sovacool & Geels, 2016). Asynchronous development and technological limitations can create bottlenecks, giving transitions diverging logic in terms of goals pursued, decision-making style, and scale of operations (Markard et al., 2016).

Thermal and RES-based electricity systems are constituted by different competition and complementarity elements within and across the sector (Mori, 2021b). In thermal electricity systems, the business model takes advantage of the scale of the economy to generate revenue through selling electricity to end-consumers. The model has a value proposition centered on electricity generation and supply that emphasises affordability, efficiency, and reliability (Bryant et al., 2018). A network infrastructure is developed to satisfy individual interconnection requests from centralised utility-scale generation plants and secure the stability and reliability of fuel transportation and grid operation. Fossil fuel power generation is a proven, standardised technology that does not require much in the way of testing, qualifying processes (Tushman & Rosenkopf, 1992), or site-specific activities (Steffen et al., 2018). Meanwhile, investments in thermal electricity supply systems are perceived as highly risky because of sunk investments, high entry barriers, long operating lifetimes, and complementary capital investments (Schmidt et al., 2017). Network regulations that allow vertically integrated monopolistic or oligopolistic supply and cost-of-service regulations that secure a stable revenue stream over the years are employed as institutional complementarities to attract financial capital. Organisational complementarities, such as a long-term fuel supply, a transportation contract, and a power purchase agreement, are also created to minimise commercial risks and sunk investments (Mori, 2020).

Transitions to RES-based electricity systems call for a whole-system change towards capital-intensive distributed local electricity production (Newbery et al., 2018). RES-E generators are modular, small, distributed, location-constrained, and non-synchronous, and they have low short-run costs. RES-E generator output also varies owing to the variability and unpredictability of its primary resource. These different technical characteristics cause operational challenges: controllability of distributed generation, short-term adequacy, over-generation, ramp requirements, forecast errors, and network congestion (IEA, 2016: 74).

These challenges can be effectively addressed by enhancing the system's flexibility, defined as the ability of the grid and the generation fleet to balance supply and demand over multiple time-scales. Several flexibility options have been implemented, including changes in grid dispatch rules; flexible generation, reserve, and stability services from RES-E; transmission and coordination; demand response; and energy storage connected to the grid or to generation plants (Denholm et al., 2016). These options differ not only in cost and cost-effectiveness but also in paradigms for the grids towards which electricity systems move.

Against this backdrop, this chapter identifies the changes in the elements of complementarity in electricity systems that must be associated with the transition from fuel-based to RES-based electricity systems, showing how these changes affect the direction and speed of the transition and presenting an analytical framework for this. We include gas as a type of flexible generation in the first stage of transitions, considering the contexts of Southeast Asian countries: high political priority on energy for all and perceived substantial increase in electricity consumption by 2050, namely by three to five times higher than the 2020 level.

The remainder of this chapter is organised as follows. Section 3.2 reviews the literature to identify the required changes in the elements of complementarity in electricity systems. Section 3.3 discusses how these changes affect the direction and speed of the transition in the context of emerging markets and developing economies. Section 3.4 provides the hypothetical determinants of the direction and speed of transition of electricity systems. Section 3.5 summarizes the chapter and looks ahead to its applications in later chapters.

3.2 CHANGES IN THE ELEMENTS OF COMPLEMENTARITY BY GRID PARADIGM

RES-based electricity systems have different grid paradigms. These can be classified as super-grid, distributed smart-grid, and flexible grid paradigms. Elements of complementarity differ by paradigm.

3.2.1 Super-Grid Paradigm

The super-grid paradigm assumes large-scale integration of utility-scale RES-E in grid systems and grid operators by incumbent utilities, keeping hierarchical and centrally controlled electricity distribution networks intact. Efficient network capacity, stronger transmission grids, greater storage capacity, and flexible responses for system balancing must be put in place to integrate RES-E into grids on a large scale (Gulagi et al., 2018; Mueller et al., 2014; Newbery et al., 2018).

High-voltage (HV) and ultra-high-voltage (UHV) direct current (DC) transmissions are core technology and infrastructure elements of complementarity. These technologies enable long-distance electricity transmission on a large scale with lower transmission loss and land resources than conventional extra-high voltage systems (Zhou, 2018).These technologies can significantly reduce renewable curtailment (Burgholzer & Auer, 2016) and make investments in utility-scale RES-E located far away from the centre of consumption commercially viable. Such systems also enable large-scale pumped storage hydropower located in wide geographical areas to secure stability and reliability of grid operation. Incumbent utilities can keep hierarchical and centrally controlled electricity distribution networks and may shift the business model towards system integration in case of unbundling (Fox-Penner, 2020). As single buyers in regions, incumbent utilities tend to uptake most of the electricity from independent power generators by power purchase agreements with take-or-pay clauses, and the rest from wholesale energy spot markets (WESM), if they are developed.

Transmission cost-recovery regulations should be revisited to recoup connection and network costs through tariffs. Tariff regulations that ensure a reasonable rate of return incentivise incumbent utilities to make grid investments. However, such investments carry over the excess capacity of traditional networks (ten Heuvelhof & Weijnen, 2013) and the inefficient utilisation of transmission and distribution network assets (IEA, 2016), and they impose the heavy burden of connection and network costs on RES-E providers and consumers. The lowest overall generation and transmission costs can be achieved through anticipatory planning for designing transmission solutions for sets of projects in various geographical areas, and proactive planning that considers the trade-off between spending more on transmission and accessing high-quality resource sites as well as the market value of Renewable Energy Certificate (REC) (Madrigal & Stoft, 2012).

Institutional elements must be developed to integrate RES-E on a large scale and to ensure and enhance flexibility in the electricity system (Table 3.1). WESM – intraday and day-ahead markets – enable maximum use of demand response services supplied by distributed energy resources (DERs) through their trading. Such markets can generate merit order effects and reduce electricity prices when low-cost RES-E is supplied (Lagac & Yap, 2020).

Capacity markets or payment contracts are placed to ensure long-term grid reliability by procuring the appropriate amount of power supply resources when needed, particularly in a grid emergency. In exchange, capacity payments are made to these suppliers, in addition to earnings gained by selling electricity on the energy market. These add to concerns over the insufficient incentives that energy-only markets can give investors to deliver fully renewable, reliable, and affordable energy electricity in liberalised energy markets, even with strong carbon pricing (Kraan et al., 2019).

Incumbent utilities must adjust their business models to a single buyer and be unbundled functionally and legally from generation. This adjustment ensures non-discriminatory grid access and a level playing field for power producers.

Table 3.1 *Changes in elements of complementarity and business models in large-scale RES-E integrated electricity systems, by paradigm*

Elements of complementarity	Super-grid paradigm	Flexible grid paradigm	Distributed smart-grid paradigm
Technological	Long-distance (ultra) high-voltage DC transmission lines	Existing high- and medium-voltage AC transmission	Smart grid: metering, visualisation, real-time data transfer
Infrastructural	Pumped storage hydropower	Front-of-meter energy storage systems (FTM-ESS)	Behind-the-meter energy storage systems (BTM-ESS)
Organisational	Single buyer as a platformer	Industrial users and prosumers	Separated transmission system operator (TSO), distribution system operator (DSO), retailers, energy service companies (ESCO), energy aggregators
Institutional	Wholesale energy spot market (WESM); anticipatory planning; regulated network tariff	Bidding for ancillary service contracts; anticipatory planning	Deregulated wholesale and retail energy and capacity markets; non-discriminatory grid access; independent system operator; anticipatory planning; time- and location-based tariff programmes
Business model	System integrator	Vertically integrated utilities	Energy and data management service supplier

Source: Compiled by the authors based on Eid et al. (2017), Fox-Penner (2020), IEA (2016), Mah et al. (2017), Ricardo Energy & Environment (2018), and ten Heuvelhof & Weijnen (2013).

However, incumbent utilities can keep the traditional hierarchical and centrally controlled electricity distribution networks and supplier-oriented business models. Feed-in tariffs and net metering boost RES-E, leading to loss of customer bases and difficulties in financing grid development (Eberhard & Shkaratan, 2012). To protect their customer bases and avoid financing difficulties, incumbent utilities limit third-party access under build–operate–transfer clauses in long-term power purchase agreements (PPAs) (Antikainen et al., 2011) or prevent third parties from entering the WESM (Lehr, 2013), at the expense of grid efficiency (Yao et al., 2019).

3.2.2 Distributed Smart-Grid Paradigm

In contrast, the distributed smart-grid paradigm assumes a declining availability of conventional large power plants and their potential as reactive power owing to the large-scale integration of RES-E in grids (Weber et al., 2022). Large-scale integration of small, distributed, location-constrained, and non-synchronous RES-E calls for properly managing unforeseen peaks of distributed local electricity production and uncertainty (Abrishambaf et al., 2019).

Smart grids or advanced metering infrastructure are key infrastructural elements in this paradigm. They allow for two-way communication between utilities and their customers, thus facilitating the development of a market platform that enables large-scale integration of various types of DERs, such as RES-E, energy storage, electric vehicles, demand response, and virtual power plants, in grid systems and better management of DERs (Bistline & Young, 2022). They also allow behind-the-meter energy storage systems (BTM-ESS) to supply ancillary and system-balancing services, thus improving grid stability and reliability, making efficient use of infrastructure, and reducing the need for investment in transmission networks (World Bank Group, 2016).

Demand-side management has gained attention as a means of reconciling large-scale integration with grid reliability. It can potentially reduce peak generation capacity requirements, function as a reserve, and improve the utilisation of generating units and network assets by modifying consumption patterns. In particular, demand response can provide flexibility to the electricity system through temporal reductions or increases in energy consumption. Demand response can benefit consumers by offering low tariffs in periods of off-peak demand, and can benefit renewable producers by increasing off-peak demand and tariffs (O'Connell et al., 2014).

The optimal use of demand response requires reliable control strategies and market frameworks (O'Connell et al., 2014). Time-based tariff programmes can incentivise small owner-consumers to be price-responsive and supply ancillary services and demand response (Weber et al., 2022), effectively managing distribution congestion. They help transmission system operators (TSOs) enhance reliability and flexibility by peak shaving, valley filling, and ramp reduction to electricity systems (Uribe-Perez et al., 2016). Locational marginal prices and strategic siting of RES-E generators also help mitigate network congestion and renewable curtailment (Mueller et al., 2014). Remuneration above the weighted average cost of capital is desirable to incentivise DER suppliers to modernise distribution networks and deploy charging systems for electric vehicles (Eid et al., 2017). Network charges increase the value of small-scale solar photovoltaic battery ESS for the customer and the market, stimulating investments in and operation of distributed RES-E and storage resources (Thomsen & Weber, 2021). A green energy tariff will also empower owner-consumers to actively choose electricity suppliers with decarbonised electricity and thus incentivise suppliers to minimise the costs of decarbonisation if a regulatory framework ensures transparency of the carbon content of energy products and prevents greenwashing (UK Department for Business, Energy & Industrial Strategy, 2021).

However, small owner-consumers, as well as commercial and industrial consumers, are directly exposed to the variability and volatility in the WESM unless critical peak pricing, real-time pricing, and locational marginal pricing are implemented to use demand response to supplement generation resources and resolve system and/or local capacity constraints. All such consumers must change consumption in response to frequency changes during a specified commitment period. Ancillary services such as regulation reserves, spinning reserves, and supplementary services supplying reactive power as primary and secondary reserves can fill a demand–supply gap in a short time (Morales-España et al., 2022). To effectively change consumption patterns, consumers must be aware of the time and locational price, comprehend its features, and understand how behaviour influences costs. A survey in Sweden showed that the majority of electricity consumers are unaware of the differences between energy and demand response prices (El Gohaly et al., 2022) and thus do not satisfy the preconditions for the optimal use of demand response (El Gohaly et al., 2023).

Third-party energy resource aggregators and energy service companies (ESCOs) help electricity systems manage the uncertain behaviour of many small and distributed RES-E in real-time operation (Burger et al., 2017; IRENA, 2020). They provide services differentiated by quality and value by adopting new data analysis techniques (IEA, 2016). They make use of these differentiated retail services to close information gaps, coordinate distributed resource operations, and pool the generation and/or consumption flexibility of small, distributed customers/prosumers at a low voltage level (Lipari et al., 2018). They individually aggregate small ancillary, system-balancing, and demand response service supplies to provide sufficient, reliable, and flexible electricity that is tradable in markets. For this to work, ancillary service markets or procurement agreements must be implemented. These ensure that third-party aggregators and ESCOs supply ancillary services on behalf of small owner-consumers. Balancing service markets or mechanisms must be arranged longer before real-time than ancillary services and must allow aggregated short-term flexibility resources.

Third-party energy aggregators and ESCOs may help the rapid deployment of BTM-ESS by offering them solar photovoltaic (PV),

BTM battery ESS, smart meters, displays, and home energy management systems without upfront costs and risks of imbalance exposure and fluctuations in prices (Yamashiro & Mori, 2023). In exchange, individual small owner-consumers must comply with the submitted plans to charge and discharge batteries or dispatch outputs of DERs as suppliers; they must also control their power consumption for a short period as consumers (VIET, 2021b) for the benefit of congestion management and system reliability. Government-initiated support programmes can redirect them towards smart meters and distribution networks (Mah et al., 2017; Sovacool et al., 2021).

Nonetheless, these novel institutions and organisations may not make the distributed smart-grid paradigm work effectively so long as incumbent utilities work as system integrators. Incumbent utilities exercise market power to restrict grid access and a level playing field to DER and ancillary and system-balancing services suppliers under ownership bundling. Incumbent utilities may use their flexible resources and accept supplies from DER and ancillary and system-balancing services, but only to the extent they can manage the stability and reliability of grid operation, to prevent big consumers and prosumers from discontinuing service contracts. Big customers create their microgrids and urge direct access to the grid, and some prosumers require direct PPAs with customers and peer-to-peer trading without a wiring grid. Incumbent utilities suffer from declining output of traditional power plants that have long brought higher economic values. They may compensate for the resultant revenue reduction by transforming into system integrators to create smart, controllable, information-rich sales platforms of localised markets and procurement.

When perceiving the transition of end-users from passive energy consumers to active prosumers, and regulatory changes to support the transition, such as the Electricity Market Directive (European Union, 2022), incumbent utilities may enhance their function as distribution systems operators (DSOs) and reorient themselves towards energy service units (Fox-Penner, 2020) to compensate for the downward pressure on profit margin and the loss of revenue from power generation. They can capitalise on the increasing proportion of distributed and customer-driven power production and demand to provide energy efficiency solutions (Frei, et al., 2018) and comprehensive energy solutions. These services include personalised customer engagement services, consultant services for energy market design, advanced forecasting services that help prosumers avoid the risk of punishment, and flexible capacity forecasting potential services that enable ancillary service suppliers to determine the most appropriate control strategy for market participation and portfolio building (Rossi et al., 2022). They may also supply energy as a service in monthly flat-fee service contracts. This service enables customers to receive all the power they require, along with RES-E capacity, without spiking power bills in exchange for energy efficiency and energy-saving measures (Bryant et al., 2018). Utilities may exploit big data from their customer base to provide media and entertainment, home automation, building security, energy saving, and data aggregation (Nillessen & Pollitt, 2016). The transition from a traditional product-oriented, capital-intensive business model based on tangible assets towards a service-oriented, expense-intensive business model based on intangible assets may present a great managerial and organisational challenge (Helms, 2016), particularly for incumbent utilities with large assets specific to the existing model. Nonetheless, pursuing the aforementioned new model via alliances can help mitigate transition costs (Eklund & Kapoor, 2019) and allow DSOs low-cost options by either avoiding or postponing any investment in low-voltage cables (Proka et al., 2020).

To foster business model innovations, system operators must be unbundled and independent, which can ensure non-discriminatory grid access, provide a level playing field for DERs and ancillary service suppliers, and enhance reliability and flexibility for system balancing at distribution levels. The unbundling of electricity rates can provide transparency and enable consumers to be more aware of how much they are paying, specifically the fees that go to the distribution utilities and fees considered as pass-through charges collected by distribution utilities for the government and for power generation companies (Philippines Department of Energy, 2019a). The latter includes distribution wheeling charges that independent power producers (IPPs) and prosumers pay for using transmission and distribution systems and associated facilities under direct PPA and peer-to-peer trading.

3.2.3 *Flexible Grid Paradigm*

Transitions towards the super-grid and distributed smart-grid paradigms impose different challenges on incumbent utilities. The super-grid padigm assumes the management of generation, transmission, and distribution across broad geographical areas. The paradigm requires high upfront costs and technological capabilities for investing and operating UHV DC transmission lines. Operations in wide geographical areas involve forecast errors, along with vulnerability to disaster- and weather-related events and cyber-attacks (Fox-Penner, 2020). Lack of mutual trust, incompatible markets and regulations, and unenforceable agreements emerge as barriers to cross-border grid interconnection (Delina, 2021; Scholten et al., 2020). The paradigm may raise concerns over the specialisation of fossil fuel power generation in some regions (Resousudarmo & Effendi, 2022; Tan et al., 2022). Incumbent utilities and regulators must address these challenges to advance transitions to the super-grid paradigm.

Meanwhile, the distributed smart-grid paradigm assumes competition among incumbent utilities and RES-E generators, DER suppliers, and ancillary service suppliers in the deregulated WESM, ancillary and system-balancing service market, and retail market. Retail competition and open access policy allows qualified electricity end-users and contestable customers to choose their electricity supplier at an agreed contract price if this is operated in tandem with other regulatory reforms. These reforms include unbundling of transmission and distribution wheeling charges, removal of cross-subsidy within incumbent utilities (Philippines Department of Energy, 2021a), reduction of excessive loyalty penalty charging through opt-in and opt-out switching, and removal of obligation thresholds for energy suppliers (UK Department for Business, Energy & Industrial Strategy, 2021). The policy also enhances transparency in the power industry and empowers consumers (Philippines Department of Energy, 2021a). However, the policy can aggravate a death spiral of higher tariffs and smaller customer bases because incumbent utilities are often incapable of adopting new business models that increase customer and prosumer bases, including digital experience, customised services, third-party aggregation, and third-party ownership (Ode & Wadin, 2019).

Notably, microgrids and net metering accelerate the utility death spiral because they facilitate uneconomic bypass. Microgrids allow customers to pay lower electricity bills by avoiding transmission and distribution charges. Net metering allows DERs to sell excess generated electricity at a retail rate that is higher than the wholesale price that utility-scale generators set for utilities. Both undermine the economic viability of utilities (Rochlin, 2016). To prevent this death spiral, incumbent utilities may merge and acquire distributed energy companies to diversify their service offerings (Pereira et al., 2022), as well as start in-house business units, fund external incubators, and form investment funds and coalitions (Fox-Penner, 2020).

The flexible grid paradigm is between the super-grid and distributed smart-grid paradigms. The flexible paradigm assumes flexible dispatchable generation as the main technology for grid stability and reliability. Incumbent utilities may invest in flexible generation technologies to adjust their generation level to cope with load variations and to start at short notice (Müller et al., 2014). These technologies include fossil-fuel-based ones, such as combustion engines, aeroderivative gas turbines with very low additional operational cost, flexible combined-cycle gas turbines (CCGT), and flexible coal; as well as non-fossil-fuel-based ones, such as hydro reservoir, biomass, biogas, and concentrated solar power that operates as mid-merit plants.

Large-scale front-of-the-meter electrical energy storage systems (FTM-ESS) can reduce levelised costs of electricity, installed capacity, and spilled energy with large-scale integration of RES-E in grids (Keck et al., 2019).

The paradigm also assumes high- and medium-voltage alternating current (AC) transmission and FTM-ESS, such as electric batteries and hydrogen, as complemental infrastructural elements. High- and medium-voltage AC transmission lines are low-cost alternatives to high-voltage and ultra-high-voltage (UHV) direct current (DC) ones. Utility-scale FTM-ESS helps incumbent utilities secure the stability and reliability of grid operation by themselves because they can develop the storage in the form of grid energy storage.

Changes in institutional complementarities are incremental. Instead of deregulated wholesale and ancillary service markets, bidding for demand response and ancillary service contracts is institutionalised. Qualifications are often imposed to restrict bidders to large industrial users, prosumers, DER suppliers, and ancillary service suppliers. Where retail markets are deregulated and gas suppliers provide demand response, the same institutional arrangements can be applied for RES-E DER suppliers. The qualifications of suppliers and terms of the conditions of service contracts affect how market-based institutions, such as time-based tariff programmes and locational marginal prices, make small consumers price-responsive and stimulate ancillary service suppliers to develop smart grids and distribution networks and use demand-side options.

The flexible paradigm requires the least adjustment in business models to incumbent utilities. Incumbent utilities can keep their hierarchical, centrally controlled electricity distribution networks by adding medium-voltage AC transmission and replacing inflexible generation with flexible generation technologies and grid energy storage. They may accept RES-E, demand response, and ancillary services to the extent that they can manage the stability and reliability of grid operation by using their flexible resources. However, the replacement may lock in CO_2 emissions for 25 to 30 years or proliferate obsolete and inefficient fossil generation if incumbent utilities choose new or renovated fossil generation as a flexibility option (Müller et al., 2014).

3.2.4 Required Changes in Elements of the Electricity System and Grid Paradigm

Table 3.1 (see Section 3.2.1) sorts the changes we have presented by elements of complementarity and by grid paradigm. In the technological and infrastructural elements, the super-grid paradigm requires large investments in the development of (U)HV DC transmission lines and a variety of large-scale generations, such as pumped storage hydropower and ancillary service markets or agreements, while the distributed smart-grid paradigm requires the smart grid and BTM-ESS. The flexible grid paradigm requires the development of extra-high-voltage (EHV) DC transmission lines and FTM-ESS; it can save investment costs by accepting fossil-fuel-based flexible dispatchable generation in the transition period.

The distributed smart-grid paradigm demands substantial changes in institutional and organisational elements. More than creating deregulated wholesale and retail energy and capacity markets, institutional and organisational elements must be associated with the development of network governance that ensures non-discriminatory third-party grid access, time- and location-based tariff programmes that incentivise small DERs to participate in demand response, and ESCO or energy resource aggregators that work towards the effective use of small-scale DERs. These changes can generate a utility death spiral, prompting incumbent utilities to change their value propositions to energy and data management and service supply. The super-grid and flexible grid paradigms require development of wholesale markets or bidding to procure RES-E and ancillary services, but they may promote reliance on conventional anticipatory planning. Incumbent utilities may retain their vertical integration and regionally monopolistic supply wherever allowable, and capitalise on them to enhance their system integration.

3.3 DETERMINANTS OF DIRECTION AND SPEED OF TRANSITION

The results of our review have led us to formulate a hypothetical framework that explains the direction and speed of electricity system transitions (Figure 3.1). The framework is composed of decisive and enabling factors and barriers. The geographical location of major power generation plants and centres of consumption, as well as the distribution of utility-scale RES-E and DERs, are assumed to be potential decisive factors. Space availability and constraints vary significantly by country. Some countries have suitable places for utility-scale wind and solar power. These countries may designate them as wind and solar parks, purchase lands, develop infrastructure, give preferential measures to attract investments (Burke et al., 2019), and export RES-E through (U)HV DC transmission lines. Other countries may self-consume RES-E generated at wind farms and rooftop solar near communities and buildings. This variety generates differences in the distribution of utility-scale RES-E and DERs by countries (Figure 3.2) and can affect the choice of the RES-E grid paradigm.

The super-grid paradigm fits well with countries with relatively large utility-scale RES-E generation and pump-up storage capacities in wide geographical areas. Networks of long-distance UHV transmission lines connecting utility-scale RES-E, pump-up storage, and centres of consumption generate scale economy and reduce renewable curtailment, bringing benefits that exceed high investment costs. Given that UHV transmission lines accept electricity from whatever source, they can be used to reconcile the large-scale integration of RES-E – particularly energy generated from large-scale hydropower and utility-scale RES-E plants – and the vested interests of incumbent power producers that have relied mostly on coal power in the transition (Global Energy Interconnection Development and Cooperation Organization, 2019).

The distributed smart-grid paradigm is appropriate for countries with a comparably large amount of small-scale DER and electricity-isolated regions with off-grid or limited grid connections

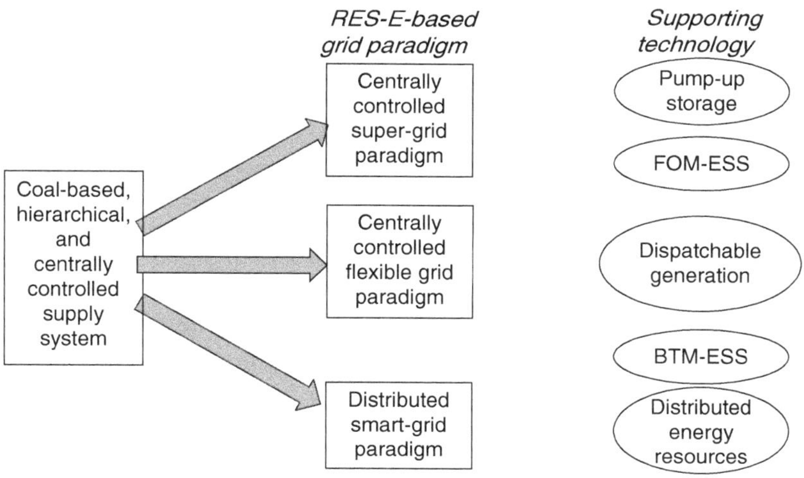

FIGURE 3.1 Hypothetical analytical framework for electricity system transitions through grid paradigms.
Source: Authors.

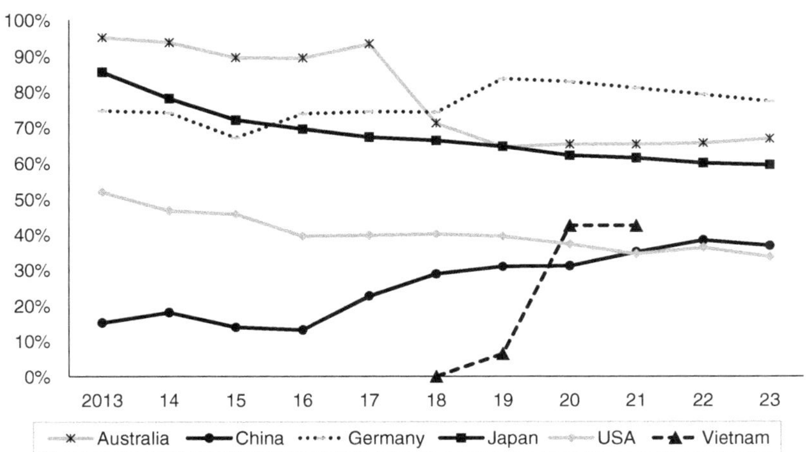

FIGURE 3.2 International comparison of the ratio of distributed solar to total installed solar capacity, 2013–2023.
Note: Rooftop only for Vietnam.
Source: Compiled by the authors based on data from IEA, *PVPS Trends Report* 2014–2024, and Vietnam Electricity (2021).

without stable supply. Combined with BTM-ESS, small-scale DER helps these regions achieve 100% electrification and stable supply with microgrids. This also creates a large potential for demand-side options and makes demand-side integration cost-effective, particularly where distribution systems are modernised and electricity tariffs are not heavily subsidised.

Countries without advantages in either super-grid or distributed smart-grid paradigms may adopt the flexible grid paradigm. Developing several long-distance (U)HV transmission lines and smart grids requires huge amounts of investment that exceed governments' technological and financial capabilities. Commercial, industrial, and rich residential consumers may be able to afford to pay, but most individual residential consumers and residents in tall buildings may not. The flexible grid paradigm allows these countries to extend the period of investment and thus mitigates transition costs in the short term.

3.4 DISCUSSION

3.4.1 Energy Narratives

The three compelling narratives of 'energy for development', 'energy for RES industry development', and 'energy for all' work as both enabling factors and barriers to electricity system transitions (Mori, 2021b). This holds particularly true for emerging markets and developing economies (EMDEs) that simultaneously encounter the challenges of satisfying growing demand, accelerating sustainability transition, and supplying electricity at an affordable price for all (Dutt & Ranjan, 2022).

The 'energy for development' narrative privileges energy as critical to economic growth and long-term strategic security. The narrative supports transitioning to RES-based systems so long as stakeholders can enjoy decreases in capital cost and improvements in operation and maintenance. However, changing the infrastructure and institutional elements to realise either the super-grid or the decentralised smart-grid paradigm would take several years or decades. RES-E developments and uptakes are further delayed where the 'energy for industrial development' narrative prevails. High local content requirements and restrictive foreign ownership are implemented to foster renewable energy industries as a new engine of industrial development (PwC, 2018). Meanwhile, investors become hesitant over new fossil fuel power projects and even divest from them. The hesitation over investments in RES-E capacity and divestments from fossil fuel power causes frequent and severe power crises amid growing electricity demand and raises conflicts with the 'energy for all' narrative, which prioritises the role of energy in meeting basic human needs and ending poverty.

These compelling narratives may prompt policymakers and incumbent utilities to choose natural gas as a bridge technology or transition fuel to move towards the flexible grid paradigm. The paradigm accepts large-scale fossil-fuel-based generation as dispatchable flexible generation and system balancing technologies. It requires relatively few radical changes in, or add-ons to, existing organisational and institutional elements and only minor changes in the business models of incumbent utilities. Incumbent utilities and suppliers can avoid or at least postpone the utility death spiral associated with the transition to the distributed smart-grid paradigm: that is, when declining demand for their output with high economic value forces them to raise tariffs to help recover the cost of operating the grid system, which further loses customers and deviates from the traditional business model that relies on only power generation and supply (Castaneda et al., 2017). In the meantime, local commercial and industrial gas suppliers may emerge as suppliers of DER and flexible dispatchable generation (Uhde & Malima, 2020), helping incumbent utilities to reconcile large-scale integration of RES-E and grid reliability. The 'indigenous or domestic energy resource' narrative is also both an enabling factor and a barrier to transitions in electricity systems. Fossil-fuel-abundant countries are motivated to exploit and consume domestic fuel, driving the system towards fossil-fuel-based systems, whereas renewable-energy-abundant countries move towards RES-based electricity systems.

3.4.2 *Decarbonising Dispatchable Flexible Generation*

Decarbonising dispatchable flexible generation is indispensable for RES-based electricity systems, particularly those with flexible grid paradigms, in the aim to achieve net zero. However, investments in clean dispatchable capacity such as pump-up hydro, biomass, and geothermal are insufficient and delayed due to policy uncertainty, coordination failure between demand and supply, and implementation and geopolitical risks (DCCEEW, 2024a, 2024b).

Capacity markets, certificate schemes, and revenue underwriting are proposed as institutions to address these uncertainties and risks. Capacity markets have already been implemented in several countries, such as Germany and Japan; they can proliferate the full depreciation of hydropower and fossil fuel power plants to avoid their stranding (Gawel et al., 2022). However, they would not accelerate investment in lower-emissions technologies or the attainment of net-zero targets. In addition, building new fossil-fuel-based plants for strategic reserves is not economically justifiable, and existing plants close to the end of life may not be sufficiently reliable (DCCEEW, 2023).

Certificate schemes coupled with large-scale RES-E targets have also been implemented. They include REC in the United States and Canada, green certificates and a Guarantee of Origin in the European Union, and non-fossil-fuel certificates and green electricity certificates in Japan. However, these schemes lack the flexibility to incorporate energy mix and geographic considerations and do not ensure that the right types and amounts of generation are provided in the right places at the right times (DCCEEW, 2023). In addition, regulatory uncertainty strongly affects certificate market volatility and price risk, harming certificate markets (Fagiani & Hakvoort, 2014). Corporate REC purchases would not increase RES-E generation and would even value the effectiveness of mitigation efforts so excessively as to skew decisions (Bjørn et al., 2022). However, no certificate scheme is applied for clean dispatchable capacity (DCCEEW, 2024a).

Revenue underwriting such as Australia's capacity investment scheme (CIS) is proposed as an alternative to increasing clean dispatchable capacity in the flexible grid paradigm (DCCEEW, 2023, 2024a, 2024b). The scheme involves competitive bidding for RES-E generation and storage projects that can fill expected reliability gaps. Long-term revenue support through an agreed revenue 'floor' and 'ceiling' would decrease financial risks for investors, encouraging investments in clean dispatchable capacity. In addition, yearly flexible adjustments to tender targets, assessment criteria, and location enable the government to address the inherent uncertainty associated with energy transitions (Table 3.2).

Table 3.2 *Institutions supporting clean dispatchable capacity for the flexible grid paradigm*

	Capacity market (e.g., strategic reserve)	Certificate scheme for RES-E (e.g., expanded large-scale RES-E targets)	Revenue underwriting (e.g., capacity investment scheme)
Accelerated VRE investment	N/A	No	✓
Long-term investment certainty	N/A	✓	✓
Reduced emissions	No	✓	✓
Wholesale and retail price	N/A	Lower than BAU	Lower than BAU
Costs to government	N/A	Significantly high	Significantly low
Wholesale price volatility	Low	Low	Low
Timely implementation	✓	Depends on legislation	✓
Flexibility to target gaps	No	Limited	✓
Effective implementation	N/A	Simple and familiar	Requires capacity

Source: Compiled by the authors from DCCEEW (2023, 2024a, 2024b).

However, decarbonising dispatchable capacity generates a trilemma among net-zero energy transition, the 'energy for development' narrative, and asset stranding. Successful CIS can reconcile net-zero energy transition with energy security but makes natural gas assets stranded. Long-term operation of natural gas power may unfold the 'energy for development' narrative and avoid asset stranding. Still, it may move the electricity system towards being gas-based, perpetuating a hierarchical and centrally controlled supply system and reinforcing a technological, institutional, and social lock-in. It becomes more challenging to reconcile vested interests with decarbonising dispatchable capacity and thus retard net-zero energy transitions. Avoiding investments in and operation of natural gas power may prompt decarbonising dispatchable capacity but does not unfold the 'energy for development' narrative.

3.4.3 Contexts in Emerging Markets and Developing Economies

Electricity systems in EMDEs are far from the standard market model. They are characterised by the hybrid market model, which consists of the dominance of state-owned utilities with IPPs, the absence of competitive wholesale and retail markets, and a lack of granular price signals (Gratwick & Eberhard, 2008).

In these contexts, influential political and economic actors often intervene to block the transition to an economic dispatch and nationwide WESM. First, incumbent state-owned utilities oppose open and unbiased access to grid networks to protect their vested interests. Second, incumbent state-owned utilities and the government offer favourable, long-term PPAs and credit guarantees to ensure the cost recovery of IPPs and to attract their investments under retail price regulations and uncertain future demand, which disincentivises IPPs from selling their electricity in the WESM. Third, distributive consideration pressures the government to offer subsidised tariffs to consumers and allow cross-subsidisation to distribution utilities. Finally, local utilities and governments protect their local vested interests (Mori, 2018).

The absence of competitive wholesale and retail markets and lack of granular price signals critically affect the direction and speed of electricity system transitions. First, the electricity system can hardly uptake ancillary services for grid stability. Large-scale FTM-ESSs are of no use to support the super-grid paradigm even with the development of (U)HV transmission lines, and a hundred BTM-ESSs are likewise of no use to the distributed smart-grid paradigm even with the development of a smart-grid network. Second, resultant longer dispatch before real-time dispatch increases renewable curtailment (Iychettira, 2021). Economic development, development of state capacity, and moving towards democratic political institutions are expected to induce a transition towards an electricity model with vertical unbundling, competitive wholesale and retail markets, and temporally and spatially granular pricing (Urpelainen & Yang, 2019).

3.4.4 Updated Analytical Framework

Figure 3.3 provides an updated analytical framework that incorporates the energy narratives we have discussed and the contexts of EMDEs. It

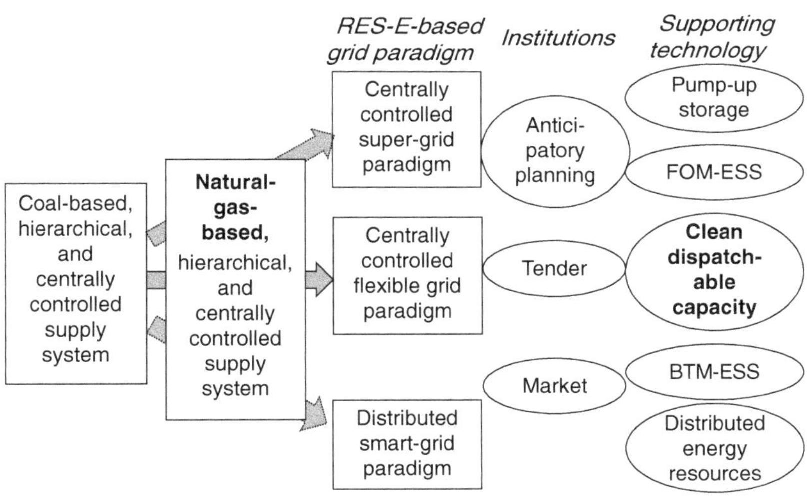

FIGURE 3.3 Proposed analytical framework for electricity system transitions through grid paradigms.
Source: Authors.

revises the hypothetical framework in Figure 3.1 at three points. First, electricity systems are supposed to shift to a natural-gas-based, hierarchical, and centrally controlled supply system before transitioning to RES-based electricity systems to unfold the three narratives. Second, clean dispatchable capacity is in place to move RES-based electricity systems, particularly those with a flexible grid paradigm, towards net zero. Third, the hybrid market model and limited granular price signals are explicitly incorporated as complementary elements that substantially affect the directions and speed of transitions in electricity systems and the grid paradigms they move towards.

3.5 CONCLUSIONS

In this chapter, we identified changes in the elements of complementarity in electricity systems in the transition towards different grid paradigms of RES-based electricity systems and presented an analytical framework. For this purpose, we conducted a literature survey to define three grid paradigms in RES-based electricity systems and investigated the required changes in the elements of complementarity.

The super-grid paradigm requires developments in large-scale RES-E generation, large-scale pump-up storages, (U)HV backbone transmission and many connecting lines, and ancillary service markets or agreements. This paradigm allows vertically integrated systems to remain intact. The distributed smart-grid paradigm requires smart grids, BTM-ESS, effective wholesale and retail energy and capacity markets, and vertical ownership unbundling. These two paradigms can coexist technologically, but substantial differences in their institutional and organisational elements generate conflicts of interest among the main actors. A country must choose either one as its main grid paradigm.

Meanwhile, the flexible grid paradigm requires the development of (E)HV DC transmission lines and FTM-ESS. Notably, it can minimise transition costs and changes in institutional, infrastructural, and organisational elements by accepting fossil-fuel-based power as flexible dispatchable generation. These intermediary characteristics enable the paradigm to address the three compelling narratives of 'energy for development', 'energy for RES industry development', and 'energy for all' that EMDEs encounter, prompting them to choose the paradigm as a transitional one. However, decarbonising dispatchable capacity can generate a trilemma among net-zero energy transition, the 'energy for development' narrative, and asset stranding, perpetuating and even reinforcing lock-ins in gas-based electricity systems. Specific contexts in EMDEs, particularly reconciling investors' cost recovery and distributive pressures from society, further prolong institutional development and transitions to RES-based electricity systems.

Based on these findings, we have built an analytical framework for electricity system transitions through grid paradigms. We will employ it in the case studies of transitions in electricity systems in Chapters 5 and 6.

4 Estimated Stranded Assets in the Electricity Sector in the Southeast Asian Region

4.1 INTRODUCTION

In contrast to the rapid and wide deployment of renewable energy in China and India since the late 1990s, transitions to renewable energy in Southeast Asia have been relatively stagnant despite rich renewable energy sources (Erdiwansyah et al., 2019a). The slower shift in electricity generation in Southeast Asian countries (excluding Singapore) indicates that they have relied on and invested mainly in fossil fuels for electricity generation (Clark et al., 2020).

Notably, investment in electricity generation from fossil-fuel-based energy might affect future costs by 'stranding' polluting assets to achieve the Paris Agreement's Nationally Determined Contributions (NDCs) and net-zero emissions (NZE). After 2017, new investment in fossil electricity may not be feasible to continue due to high emissions unless it is combined with carbon capture: the emissions from such assets needs to be minimised, and power plants have to be shut down to achieve emissions reduction targets even if they have not reached the end of life (Pfeiffer et al., 2016). Although carbon capture and storage (CCS) technology can simultaneously minimise stranded assets and help to achieve climate targets (Budinis et al., 2018; Pfeiffer, 2018), the costs remain high.

The risk of stranded assets owing to a shift away from fossil fuels to renewable energy has been a critical concern for countries that have abundant fossil fuel resources and rely heavily on fossil fuels to generate electricity. Stranded assets may pose significant economic and policy challenges, affecting all stakeholders in the energy sector, such as policymakers, regulators, companies, investors, and lenders.

The stranding of assets may counter the deployment of renewable energy (Kefford et al., 2018). Those benefiting from fossil fuel assets tend to take measures to avoid losses, as they believe that stranded assets cause adverse economic effects. Early retirement of coal power plants, for example, not only leaves facilities abandoned but also drains revenues, as the owners cannot monetise their assets. Stranded costs may also be distributed across actors related to the business chain, and the losses depend on how significantly they own and rely on the asset for rent-seeking (Firdaus & Mori, 2023). Thus, stranded asset risk may discourage incumbents from transitioning unless they receive compensation or financial support to finance the transition.

Several empirical studies have performed regional and global analyses of the stranding of assets to meet global climate targets through energy transitions. Caldecott et al. (2015, 2016, 2017) analysed stranded assets in thermal power plants in Australia, China, and Japan. Malik et al. (2020) and Cui et al. (2022) estimated stranded assets in the power generation sector in India and Indonesia, respectively, countries heavily relying on coal for powering the economy. In the context of Japan, Oshiro and Fujimori (2021) included both the energy supply and energy demand sectors in their analysis. Binsted et al. (2020) focused on Latin America. Other studies have global coverage, such as Curtin et al. (2019), Edwards et al. (2022), Fofrich et al. (2020), IRENA (2017), Iyer et al. (2017), Johnson et al. (2015), Kefford et al. (2018), Mercure et al. (2018), Pfeiffer et al. (2018), and Saygin et al. (2019). These studies considered near- and long-term climate targets (i.e., NDCs and net-zero emissions, respectively) and highlighted how international efforts could achieve climate goals by the significant and rapid reduction of fossil fuel CO_2 emissions.

However, scenario analysis specific to the Southeast Asian region has been lacking. Achieving climate targets requires early retirements of coal and gas power plants and rapid installation of low- and non-carbon-emitting technologies. Notably, the region has relied heavily on fossil-fuel-based electricity, and an increasing number of countries in the region have been investing in them. This continued investment may undermine the commitment to reduce emissions and achieve climate goals (Chen & Mauzerall, 2021). Thus, studies simulating and analysing the shift in the energy mix and stranded investment in Southeast Asia in the context of climate policy and technology scenarios are becoming increasingly important.

In addition, previous research has not considered the uncertainty and volatility of natural gas prices. Pressure for fossil fuel divestment has discouraged oil and gas companies, particularly global oil companies, from investing in new natural gas projects (French & Resnickault, 2021) and stepping into phase-out (Trencher et al., 2022). The Ukraine war and subsequent economic sanctions on Russia and the counter-embargo by Russia changed the global oil and gas trade flow. These landscape changes may affect oil and gas prices, the direction and speed of energy transition, and stranded costs.

Against this backdrop, this chapter analyses the impact of climate policy and technology application on the energy mix and stranded assets in the Southeast Asian region using simulation with an integrated assessment model (IAM).

4.2 LITERATURE REVIEW

4.2.1 The Concept

Caldecott et al. (2013) proposed a 'meta' definition of 'stranded assets' as assets losing value due to unanticipated or premature write-downs, devaluations, or conversion to liabilities. Researchers in various fields have put forth different definitions of stranded assets, including 'economic loss' for economists, 'impairment' for accountants, 'stranded cost' for regulators, and 'financial loss' for investors (Caldecott, 2018). From the perspective of investment, the International Energy Agency (IEA, 2013) defines stranded assets as 'those investments which have already been made but which, at some time before the end of their economic life (as assumed at the investment decision point), are no longer able to earn an economic return, as a result of changes in the market and regulatory environment brought about by climate policy'. Similar definitions of stranded assets refer to economic loss from assets or investments affected by changes in the market and regulatory environment, disruptive innovation, societal norms, or environmental shocks associated with climate policy (CTI, 2011; Generation Foundation, 2013; Jackson, 2018). These definitions emphasise the impact of unanticipated events related to addressing climate change on assets that may no longer be used (i.e., their lifetimes are shortened), causing economic losses. An analysis of the costs associated with premature retirements and new installations (i.e., capital investments for future energy systems, including the cost of technologies) can provide an overview of the economic implications of climate change mitigation (see Binsted et al., 2020; Way et al., 2020). This also can be considered as representing transition costs from a technical perspective (Köberle et al., 2021).

Asset stranding is not a novel phenomenon; the term originally refers to Schumpeter's concept of creative destruction (Caldecott, 2018). However, owing to climate policy, stranded assets in the energy sector have received significant global attention as a transition risk. Climate policy requires a fundamental structural transformation of the incumbent energy regime. This leads to fossil fuels being more or less phased out (depending on the role of carbon capture and storage) and replaced by cleaner energy sources (e.g., nuclear and renewable energy) (Zenghelis et al., 2018). Consequently, stranded assets have significant adverse implications for a variety of stakeholders: these include unemployment, lost revenue, lost profit, and reduced tax income for governments (Caldecott, 2017). The repercussions may vary in magnitude depending on the stringency of the climate policy implemented.

Meanwhile, efforts to address climate change need to consider additional costs on top of stranded costs and investment costs in new installations. From the government's perspective, policy cost, as one of the concerns in emissions reduction efforts, is also critical in the decision to adopt early actions to decarbonise the power sector. Policy costs represent climate mitigation options, which carry potential economic impacts for policymakers aiming to achieve climate goals. These can be measured by various indicators, such as the price of carbon required to achieve a desired emission mitigation goal, mitigation effect on GDP, reduction of GDP, consumption loss, and deadweight loss (JGCRI, 2023). Policymakers may assess whether the option taken to address climate change is costly (Köberle et al., 2021).

4.2.2 Methodology and Coverage

Stranded assets have been a much-discussed topic in research since the early 2010s, mainly in that related to energy transitions. Studies have quantified the value of stranded assets from different energy sectors. In the upstream sector, several studies have used a forward-looking approach to estimate stranded assets. CTI (2011, 2013) focused on assessing so-called unburnable fossil fuels in the context of staying below the 2°C warming limit. McGlade and Ekins (2015) used a single IAM to estimate the remaining fossil fuel reserves and resources to be compatible with a warming limit of 2°C from 2010 to 2050. Auger et al. (2021) explored the broader impacts of rapid decarbonisation, which include investment in new mines, market prices, international coal trade, stranded assets, and employment at the global level, using various scenarios. Semieniuk et al. (2022) further calculated global stranded assets in the upstream oil and gas sector. This calculation includes the distribution of ownership of transition risk associated with stranded assets.

In the mid- and downstream sector, previous studies have mainly paid attention to coal power plants, considering the rapid growth of new investments in coal power plants, particularly in emerging markets and developing economies. Stranded asset risk in this sector attracts attention from various stakeholders concerning the Paris Agreement and sustainable development goals (Bos & Gupta, 2019). Studies in the power generation sector vary in terms of coverage, methods, and scenario settings (see the list in Table A4.1). These works have attempted to explore and prepare for multiple possible futures, enriching the analysis of energy transitions and of the implications of stranded assets.

Studies quantifying stranded assets have employed different methods for the upstream and power generation sectors (Curtin et al., 2019). These studies have frequently employed IAMs (e.g., Binsted et al., 2020; Cui et al., 2022; Fofrich et al., 2020; Iyer et al., 2017; Malik et al., 2020; Oshiro & Fujimori, 2021), which make them relatively comprehensive in elucidating the cross-linkages and interactions between social, economic, environmental, and institutional dimensions. Although these studies have used different methods, they set relatively similar scenarios (i.e., a combination of an emissions constraint with economic, technological, political, and regulatory factors) (Curtin et al., 2019). These studies generally show that stranded assets become more significant if climate actions are delayed (Binsted et al., 2020; Johnson et al., 2015; Malik et al., 2020; Oshiro & Fujimori, 2021), and that building new fossil fuel power plants can lead to more asset stranding (Pfeiffer, 2018; Pfeiffer et al., 2018). Meanwhile, stranded assets will be less significant if advanced technologies for fossil fuels, such as CCS, are available (Binsted et al., 2020; Johnson et al., 2015; Pfeiffer, 2018). The magnitude of the effects of stranded assets can be influenced by the timing of climate policy implementation. Hence, enhancing near-term climate mitigation targets and reducing or even stopping new construction of fossil fuel capacity, particularly coal power plants, can be critical measures to minimise stranded assets (Binsted et al., 2020; Johnson et al., 2015). Alternatively, new investments in clean and low-carbon technologies can to compensate for the early retirement of fossil fuel power plants.

Given various perspectives on stranded assets, we have followed a simplified definition of stranded assets as the forgone value of a prematurely retired power plant. This definition emphasises that electricity generation assets become stranded because of the requirement to reduce fossil fuel use towards decarbonisation. As in previous studies, we also employed IAMs to track investments in each technology in the power generation sector, considering its lifetime. For scenario settings, we combined emissions reduction targets and mitigation technologies.

4.3 METHODOLOGY

4.3.1 Model Description

IAMs have increasingly become the tool to serve as a bridge between scientists and policymakers to answer central questions on climate change dynamics (Rotmans & van Asselt, 2001). IAMs can be used to answer a series of 'what if' questions, including quantifying the implications of possible future projections. Although the models look holistic and apt for comprehending various dimensions, they have several limitations (Clarke et al., 2014). For example, IAMs tend to simplify assumptions while representing complex, co-evolving physical and social systems. In this regard, they may fail to capture detailed underlying conditions and factors in the systems. Thus, the results should not be interpreted as a single answer to solve the problem; rather, they should be used as a guide for policymaking.

Regardless of their limitations, IAMs are still useful and offer valuable insights to address the climate challenge. In this study, we employed the GCAM (jgcri.github.io/gcam-doc/), one of the available IAMs, to analyse future electricity generation scenarios that align with climate targets. As with other IAMs, GCAM represents the behaviour of and interactions between the energy system, water, agriculture, land use, the economy, and the climate (Calvin et al., 2019). GCAM generates outputs that are not predictions of the future but potential impacts of different scenarios based on various assumptions about future conditions. The model has also been widely used to produce global emissions scenarios, including the Intergovernmental Panel on Climate Change (IPCC) Special Reports (IPCC, 2007, 2014), the Representative Concentration Pathways (Thomson et al., 2011), and the Shared Socioeconomic Pathways (Calvin et al., 2017).

We used GCAM v6.0 in our analysis. In this version, the world economy and energy systems operate across 32 geopolitical regions, and land systems and water supplies are modelled across 384 subregions and 235 hydrologic basins. While the model operates five-year time steps from 2015 (the latest energy calibration year based on IEA energy balances) to 2100, it is relatively flexible for operating at different temporal resolutions through user-defined parameters. Moreover, the model's results are based on an iterative scheme that ensures convergence to final equilibrium prices. As such, supplies and demands are balanced in all markets across the model.

Regarding the energy system, GCAM offers detailed representations of the source of energy supplies, modes of energy transformation, and energy service demands. The supply sector includes depletable primary energy resources, such as coal, natural gas, oil, and uranium, and RES, such as bioenergy, hydro, solar, wind, and geothermal. The modes of energy transformation involve secondary energy carriers – such as refined liquids, refined gas, coal, commercial bioenergy, hydrogen, and electricity – that are then used in the construction, industrial, and transport sectors.

GCAM further considers the evolution of exogenously given technologies.[1] Individual technologies compete for market share based on their technology characteristics (e.g., efficiency), cost of input, and price of output. The costs of each technology depend on (i) its exogenously specified non-energy cost (i.e., fixed and variable operating and maintenance costs incurred over the lifetime of the equipment, except for fuel and electricity costs), (ii) its endogenously calculated fuel cost, and (iii) any cost of emissions, as determined by climate policy. When the costs of technology decline, its use will increase. This, however, is based on an implicit probabilistic (logit) model of market competition.

4.3.2 *Data, Assumptions, and Scenarios*

GCAM is a dynamic recursive model, meaning that the future is unknown for decision-making. This distinguishes it from intertemporal optimisation models that assume agents know the entire future with certainty when they make decisions. Given that

[1] Details of the assumptions used in GCAM are documented in Muratori et al. (2017).

GCAM operates with five-year time steps, the result of each period is used for the next period, including the consequences of events and decisions made in that period, such as resource depletion, capital stock retirements and installations, and changes to the landscape. Decision-makers may consider future profit streams for long-lived investments, but the estimates would be based on current prices.

In GCAM, several key scenario assumptions are taken into account, such as socioeconomics (e.g., population, labour participation, and labour productivity), energy technology characteristics (e.g., costs, performance, water requirements), agricultural technology characteristics (e.g., crop yield, costs, carbon contents, water requirements, fertiliser requirements), energy and other resources (e.g., fossil fuels, wind, solar, uranium, groundwater), and policies (e.g., emission constraints, renewable portfolio standards). From these scenario assumptions, key scenario results include effects on energy systems (e.g., energy demands, flows, technology deployment, and price throughout the energy system), agricultural and land use (e.g., prices and supplies of all agricultural and forest products, land use change), water systems (e.g., water demands and supplies for all agricultural, energy, and household use), and emissions (e.g., greenhouse gases and short-lived species).

Regarding assumptions for the Reference scenario, we followed the shared socioeconomic pathways (SSPs) developed by climate research modellers and widely used in climate research. The SSPs, consisting of five components, are Reference scenarios for climate change modelling studies that assume no additional policies and measures explicitly designed to reduce greenhouse gas emissions. The five SSPs are defined along two axes: challenges to mitigation and adaptation. Each SSP can be paired with a set of emissions mitigation assumptions (e.g., 2.6, 4.5, or 6.0 scenarios). Our study adopted the SSP2 'middle of the road' pathway (O'Neill et al., 2017) as a moderate scenario for future projection (jgcri.github.io/gcam-doc/ssp).

In this study, we selected the Southeast Asian (SEA) region. Given the different emissions reduction targets pledged by different countries (listed in Table A4.2), we set the unified emission target of a 20% reduction from the Reference scenario as the NDC by 2030 and NZE by 2050. In the Reference scenario, we considered no additional coal power plants after 2030. This assumption is based on the 2023 Global Power Plant Tracker report, which collected data on the progress of coal-fired power plant projects in which no new projects will be proposed after 2030 in the SEA region in response to the urge to phase out coal (Global Energy Monitor, 2023).

We also employed four assumptions on available technologies: all technologies are available (FullTech), CCS technology is not available (NoCCS), nuclear is not available (NoNuclear), and both CCS and nuclear are not available (NoCCSNuclear) (Tables 4.1 and 4.2). These assumptions are based on the current situation, in which CCS technology is not commercially available and is still uncertain. Nuclear technology may be less likely to be adopted in the future

Table 4.1 *Scenario setup*

Scenario name	Climate policy	Technology
Reference	None	All technologies are available except nuclear (no more new coal power plants after 2030)
FullTech	NDC (2030) and near- or net-zero emissions (2050)	All technologies are available (no more diesel power plants after 2030)
NoCCS	NDC (2030) and near- or net-zero emissions (2050)	All technologies are available except CCS
NoNuclear	NDC (2030) and near- or net-zero emissions (2050)	All technologies are available except nuclear
NoCCSNuclear	NDC (2030) and near- or net-zero emissions (2050)	All technologies are available except CCS and nuclear

Note: CCS and nuclear will phase in by 2040. In the scenario with high gas prices (HGP), we name the scenarios as follows: FullTechHGP, NoCCSHGP, NoNuclearHGP, and NoCCSNuclearHGP.

Table 4.2 *General assumptions for the NDC 2020–2030 period and the net-zero 2030–2060 period*

CO_2 emission target date	Explanation
2020	GHG emissions follow the Reference scenario
2025	Linear interpolation between 2025 and 2030 levels
2030	20% reduction from BAU
2030–2045	Linear interpolation between 2030 and 2050 levels
2050	Zero emissions

Note: Outside the SEA region, GHG emissions reductions are represented as single emissions constraints that are shared among the remainder of the world.

than other technologies, owing to limited sociopolitical acceptability. Also, countries in SEA regions have gradually reduced diesel power plants. NoCCSNuclear assumes that emissions reductions from the power generation sector are mainly achieved through the addition of renewables (Iyer et al., 2017) and can be offset by technological and natural carbon sequestration, such as direct air CCS, bioenergy with CCS, and terrestrial carbon uptake. For the technical aspects, such as capacity factor, technology costs, and efficiency, we adopted GCAM core assumptions, but we adjusted the timing of the technology phase-in for CCS and nuclear to 2040.[2]

We also considered energy market dynamics, particularly fossil fuel prices. We set high prices for gas owing to recent global tensions (e.g., the Russia–Ukraine war) to assess sensitivity and impact on asset stranding. Our analysis also addressed whether gas should be considered a 'bridge' fuel for the energy transition. We assumed natural gas prices would increase by 10% from the Reference case.

[2] Given that the quantity of hydropower produced in each region and year is exogenous, prescribed as a 'fixed output' in GCAM, we assumed that hydropower capacity will increase by around 7% CAGR until 2040 and keep increasing by 5% and 1% thereafter. This assumption refers to the optimistic scenario of the growing deployment of hydropower in the Southeast Asian region.

4.3.3 Estimation of Stranded Assets

GCAM produces results on electricity generation (shown in EJ) by technology, vintage of the technology, and period. Iyer et al. (2017) calculated new and additional generation from technology in each period and capital investments using the GCAM output (Equations 4.1 and 4.2). The estimated capital investment represents investments over five years following the time step of the model. We used a simple average of the capital investment during the respective period to obtain the average annual investments.

$$\text{Capacity} = \frac{\text{Generation in EJ} \times \left(2.78 \times 10^{5}\right)}{\text{Capacity Factor} \times 8760} \tag{4.1}$$

$$\text{Capital Investment} = \text{Capacity in GW} \times 10^{6} \times \text{Overnight Capital Costs}\left(\text{USD / kW}\right) \tag{4.2}$$

GCAM assumes that power plant capital can be tracked by technology and vintage over the lifetime of the technology. It presumes natural and profit-induced retirement processes, following the S-curve retirement function with several assumptions, such as the median and steepness coefficient and mid-life and variable cost of operation. For example, the default value of –0.1 in the retirement assumptions means that when the value of electricity produced is 10% lower than the variable costs of power production, then 50% of the cohort will not operate in the given period. Moreover, a climate policy, such as a carbon tax, will shut down some portion of the capital stock.[3]

We estimated stranded assets based on the difference between the capacity needed to generate the projected output under the scenario settings and the total installed capacity in the energy system under the business-as-usual (BAU) scenario (Johnson et al., 2015). To quantify the value of stranded assets in monetary terms, we calculated the forgone value of a power plant that had been prematurely

[3] Details of the assumptions related to the retirement of power plants can be found in Binsted et al. (2020).

retired to achieve climate targets as the total overnight capital cost of the assets multiplied by the fraction of the expected (physical) lifetime because of premature retirement (Binsted et al., 2020). This quantification takes depreciation value into account, considering the vintage of the technology, and is expressed as

$$SV = OCC^{\star}\left(\frac{EL - AL}{EL}\right) \quad (4.3)$$

where:

SV = stranded value,
OCC = overnight capital costs,
EL = expected lifetime, and
AL = actual lifetime.

Technologies that are retired before the end of their useful lifetime but after their full 30-year financial lifetime, in this study, are assumed to have zero value and, thus, do not contribute to stranded costs.

4.3.4 Policy Cost

GCAM employs the 'deadweight loss' approach to measuring welfare loss from emissions mitigation efforts, for three reasons. First, the deadweight loss approach is a straightforward way to calculate in GCAM. Second, the approach provides a computationally tractable method for measuring the change in welfare, although it is only an estimation. Third, the deadweight approach takes advantage of GCAM's detailed technological characterisation.

$$c = \int p_y \times \Delta A_y \quad (4.4)$$

$$c_y^n = \frac{c_y}{(1+r)^t}, \text{ where } t = y - 2025 \quad (4.5)$$

where:

c = cost of CO_2 mitigation
y = five-year time period
p = carbon price
ΔA = emissions abated
c^n = net present value (NPV)
r = discount rate

Employing the deadweight loss approach, GCAM calculates the cost of emissions mitigation (policy cost) at each GCAM time step (Equation 4.4). The associated emissions are recorded for each carbon tax, and costs occurring between time steps are inferred by interpolation, which can then be summed with or without discounting (Equation 4.5). Carbon prices are estimated and set by GCAM to achieve the climate target. In this case, GCAM determines the feasible value of carbon prices to achieve emissions reduction (area under the marginal abatement cost curve). The value will differ depending on the scenario, as different energy mixes generate different emissions levels. The deadweight loss approach is a simple method and has no direct link to the macroeconomy. Nonetheless, the costs can be viewed as a proportion of GDP to represent the magnitude of mitigation consequences. From the economic perspective, climate change mitigation costs represent emissions reduction efforts that are crucial for policymakers (Fujimori et al., 2023). To estimate mitigation costs, GCAM can also consider a discount rate, as estimations would need to value the benefits of mitigation measures to achieve cost-effective solutions in decarbonisation. The use of discount rates is useful for comparing costs and benefits over time, which can show how significant future benefits are to justifying each dollar spent today for mitigation actions. Our estimation employed a 5% discount rate, commonly used in climate models (2–7% is the common range) (see Newell & Pizer, 2001).

4.4 RESULTS

4.4.1 CO_2 Emission Pathways and Energy Mix by Scenario

In the Reference scenario driven by energy generation from fossil fuels (Figure 4.1), total CO_2 emissions will continue to rise until 2030 and will keep increasing. To achieve the NDC target by 2030 and NZE by 2050, actions to reduce emissions from the power sector are critical after 2025, as seen from the NDC-to-NZE scenario. Delaying actions may decelerate energy transition and adversely affect climate goals.

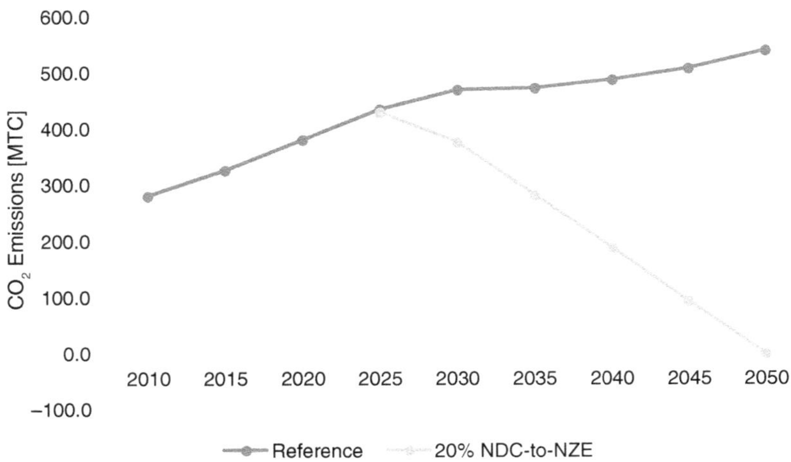

FIGURE 4.1 Changes in total CO_2 emissions in Reference scenario and the nationally determined contributions to net-zero emissions (NDC-to-NZE) scenario.

In the Reference scenario, gas power plants produced 45.8% of the electricity supplied, equivalent to 1.43 EJ, whereas coal power plants contributed 33.2% (1.0 EJ) in 2020 (Figure 4.2). The percentage of renewable energy (geothermal, hydro, wind, solar, and biomass) was 19.6% (0.61 EJ). Since there will not be newly built CFPPs after 2030, gas power plants will dominate electricity generation, accounting for 47.7% (4.8 EJ), while coal power plants will only generate 2.1% (0.21 EJ) of total electricity generation in 2050. Renewables will produce more electricity at 4.9 EJ (47.8%).

In the FullTech scenario, nuclear and CCS technology will phase in by 2040. Renewables, such as geothermal (2.1%), hydro (24.8%), wind (18.9%), solar (19%), and biomass (10.3%), will significantly contribute to the electricity supply by 2050. These proportions are not substantially different from those in the NoNuclear scenario (Figure 4.3). Although the proportion of fossil fuels decreases significantly to achieve the emissions reduction target, CCS technology can perpetuate fossil fuel power plants and save a small portion of them. Compared with coal, the percentage of gas remains relatively

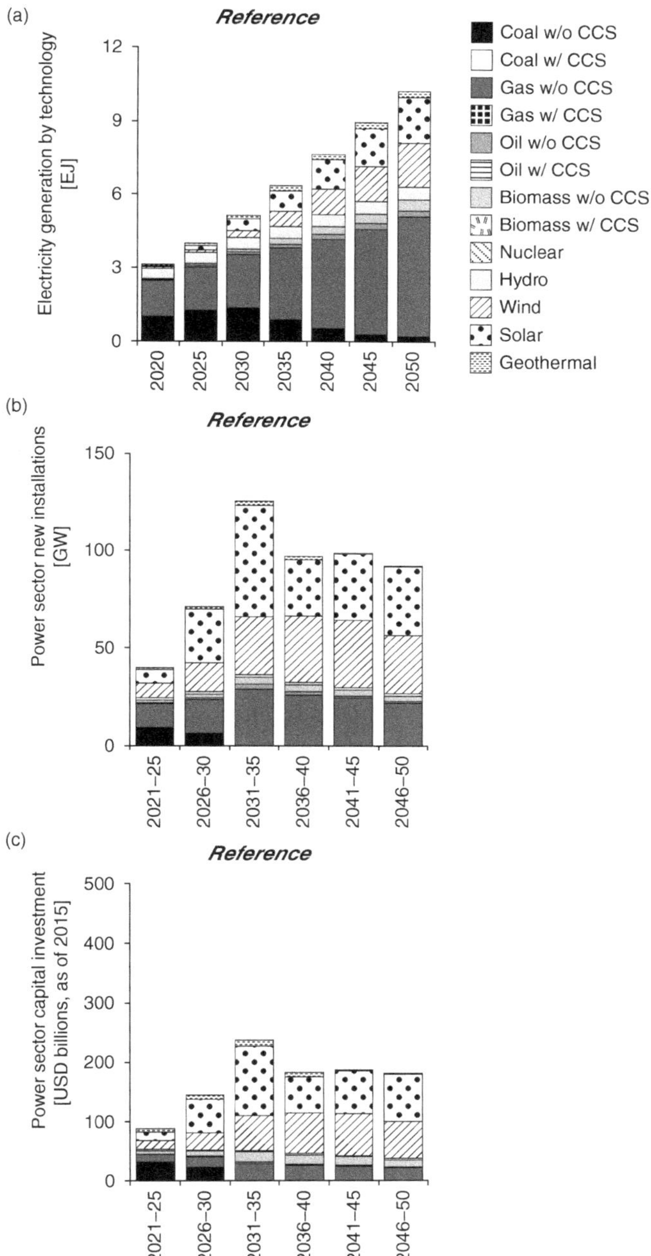

FIGURE 4.2 (a) Estimated energy generation and energy mix in the Reference scenario; (b) estimated new capacity additions in the Reference scenario; (c) estimated new capital investment cost in the Reference scenario.

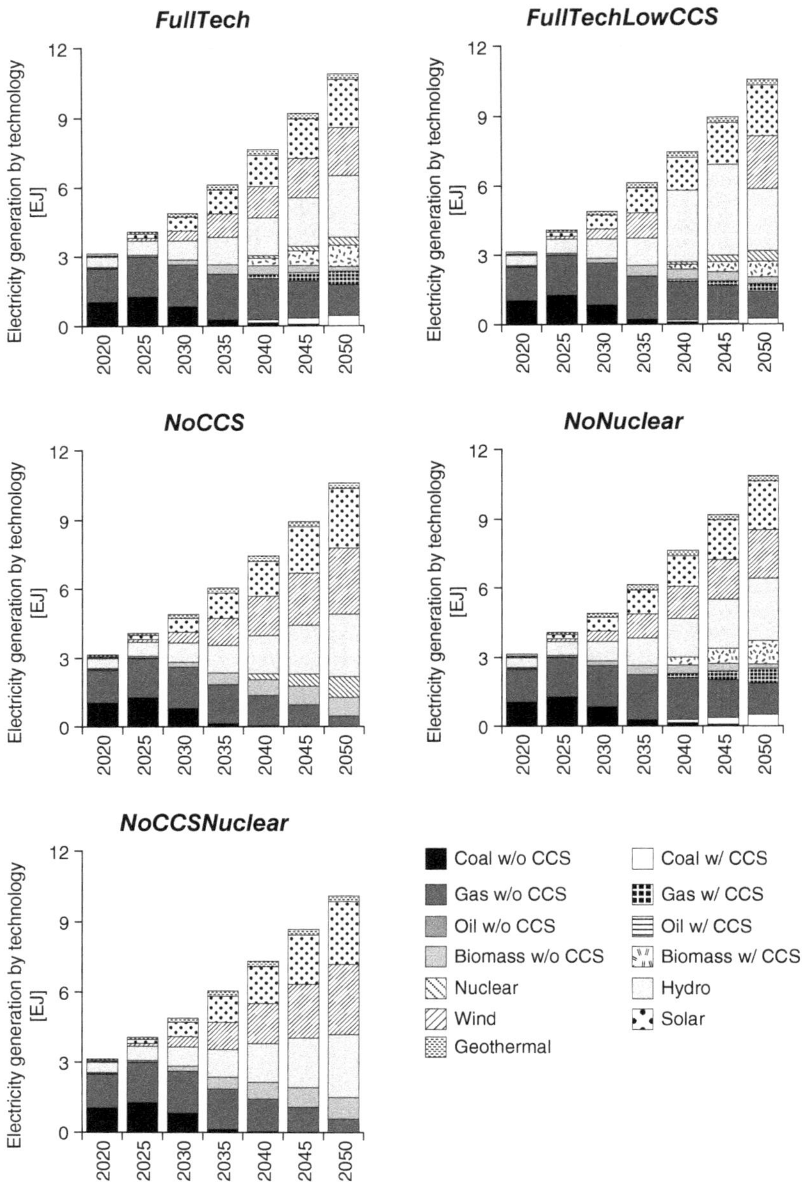

FIGURE 4.3 Energy mix by scenario.

large (17.6% in 2050). Because gas is cleaner than coal in terms of emissions, coal power plants are prioritised in the phase-out.

Meanwhile, when CCS is entirely unavailable, as in the NoCCS and NoCCSNuclear scenarios, electricity generation will become slightly lower because the unavailability of CCS technology becomes a pressure for fossil fuel power plants, mainly coal power plants, requiring a significant reduction in electricity production. However, gas power plants will also suffer from stranded asset risk hereafter. In these two scenarios, renewables, mainly solar and wind, will grow considerably to generate electricity. Moreover, biomass will be more needed when CCS technology and nuclear are unavailable, starting from the period in which the aim is to achieve the near-term target. Thus, more significant deployment of non-emitting technologies, such as solar and wind (and nuclear, if available and cost-effective), is required.

4.4.2 *Stranded Capacity and New Capital Investment*

Changes in the energy mix are associated with new investments and stranded assets. In the Reference scenario, investments in all technologies are critical to providing sufficient electricity. Capacity additions are predominantly in clean technologies, particularly solar, wind, and hydro, while new additional capacities of fossil fuels, mainly gas, are relatively small. This is because fossil fuel technologies have high-capacity factors such that they can produce large amounts of electricity. Moreover, intermittent renewables with lower capacity factors require more capacity per unit of electricity generated compared with other technologies (Iyer et al., 2017). New capacity of 524 GW will be installed during the 30 years from 2021 to 2050 to meet growing electricity demand. These capacity additions amount to roughly 3.6 times the total installed capacity in 2020 (Figure 4.4).

New capacity additions are more significant in scenarios other than in the Reference case. These additions are driven by a decline in fossil-fuel-based power generation owing to premature retirement, requiring a large proportion of renewables to meet the electricity

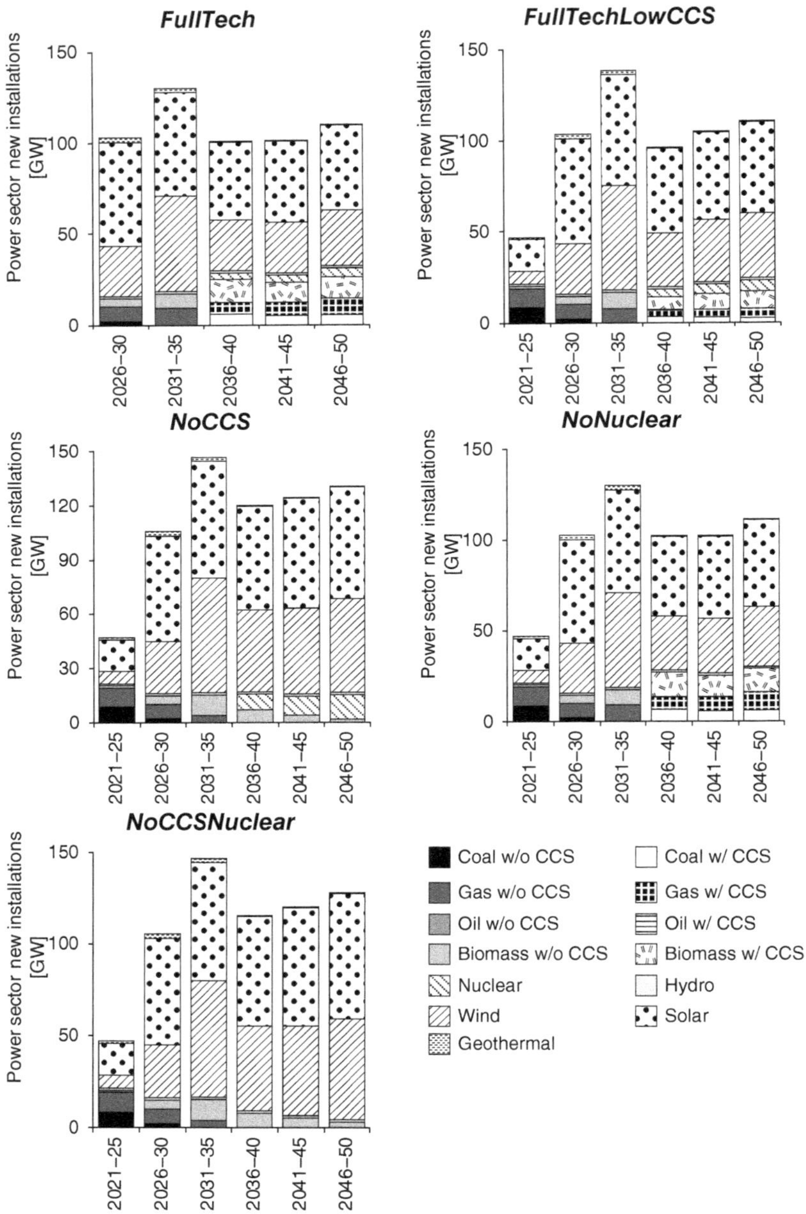

FIGURE 4.4 New capacity additions by scenario.

demand and achieve both NDC and NZE (Binsted et al., 2020). In the FullTech scenario, for instance, 590 GW will be added from 2021 to 2050, and 63.9 GW of fossil fuel power plant capacity becomes stranded (Figure 4.5). Additions are primarily from hydro, solar, and wind. New additions of renewables, however, are less for the FullTech and NoNuclear scenarios than the other two scenarios. The NoCCS and NoCCSNuclear scenarios lead to more asset stranding of fossil fuel power plants, requiring significant additions from renewables. For the NoCCS and NoCCSNuclear scenarios, 672.9 GW and 661.8 GW of new capacity will be added, and 93.2 GW and 87.9 GW of fossil fuel power plant capacity will be stranded, respectively.

New capacity additions, mainly from renewables, offset the retired capacity of fossil fuel power plants. Particularly, coal power plants will significantly undergo early retirement, followed by gas power plants. This holds for the NoCCS and NoCCSNuclear scenarios, which involve more considerable stranding of coal power plants (Figure 4.5). When gas prices increase, gas power plants will become less efficient, slowing down new installations and leading to stranded assets for the existing plants. The stranded capacity will be slightly higher in the NoCCS and NoCCSNuclear scenarios because CCS technology is unavailable.

The availability of CCS technology significantly changes the future fuel mix. Addressing the 2050 target with CCS in the portfolio will allow the Southeast Asian region to continue using fossil fuels, mainly gas, to provide a significant share of the electricity supply. However, even if CCS technology is available, stranded capacity is inevitable for fossil fuel power plants, and the electricity supply will potentially be low, considering the problems with renewable energy.

4.4.3 New Investment and Premature Retirement Costs

In the Reference scenario, around USD 1 trillion is needed between 2021 and 2050 to install new capacities (Figure 4.2). The proportion

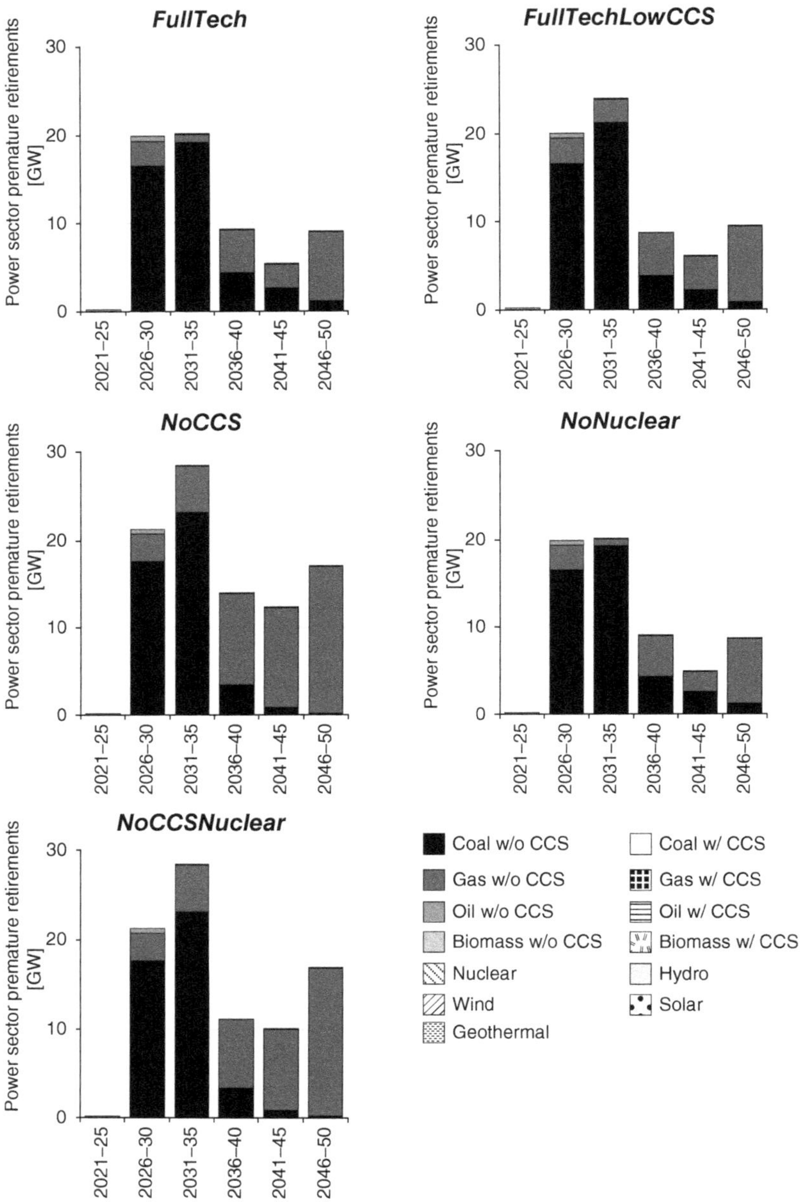

FIGURE 4.5 Premature electricity retirement capacity by scenario.

of new installation costs of renewables is more significant than that of fossil fuel power plants.

In contrast, investment costs for new capacity addition are higher in all five scenarios. Among them, the NoCCS scenario requires the highest cost, amounting to USD 2 trillion between 2021 and 2050 (Figure 4.6), or 7.98% of the Southeast Asian region's GDP. Investment costs will increase as climate goals approach, along with a significant decline in fossil fuel capacity. The NoNuclear scenario requires the lowest cost, around USD 1.93 trillion or 7.44% of GDP. High investment costs of nuclear power plants generate differences in both scenarios.

The NoCCS scenario requires more new investment costs to install capacity additions because of significant early retirement in fossil fuel power plants. In this scenario, the cumulative stranded costs will be the highest amount, around USD 272 billion, between 2021 and 2050. By contrast, the stranded costs of the NoNuclear scenario are the lowest (USD 224 billion), indicating that CCS technology can avoid stranded costs. Figure 4.7 shows that stranded costs will peak in 2035 across the five scenarios. This suggests that near-term mitigation action is critical, affecting the magnitude of stranded costs, to achieve deeper emissions reductions in the long term.

The results showed that the proportion of stranded costs of coal technologies is larger than that of oil and gas power plants. Coal power plants are more capital-intensive than gas and oil plants and have longer lifetimes (60 years for coal power plants against 45 years for oil and gas plants); the economic value of coal power plants depreciates more slowly (Binsted et al., 2020). Moreover, the stranded costs of gas power plants will be more considerable in 2050, showing that they are used to bridge the transition but then should be retired to achieve the NZE target. In other words, gas plants will be potentially stranded in the Southeast Asian region because of continued gas infrastructure investment (e.g., plants, pipelines, terminals, and storage tanks) followed by retirement.

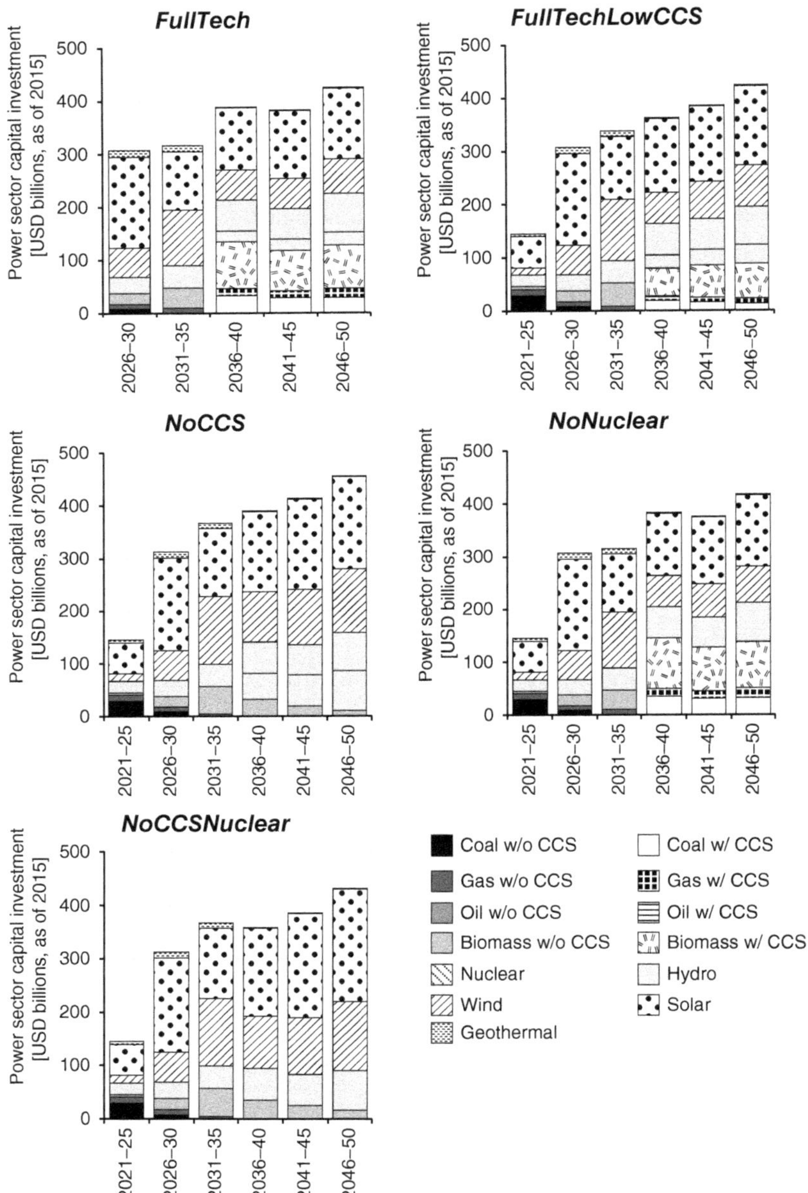

FIGURE 4.6 New installation costs by scenario.

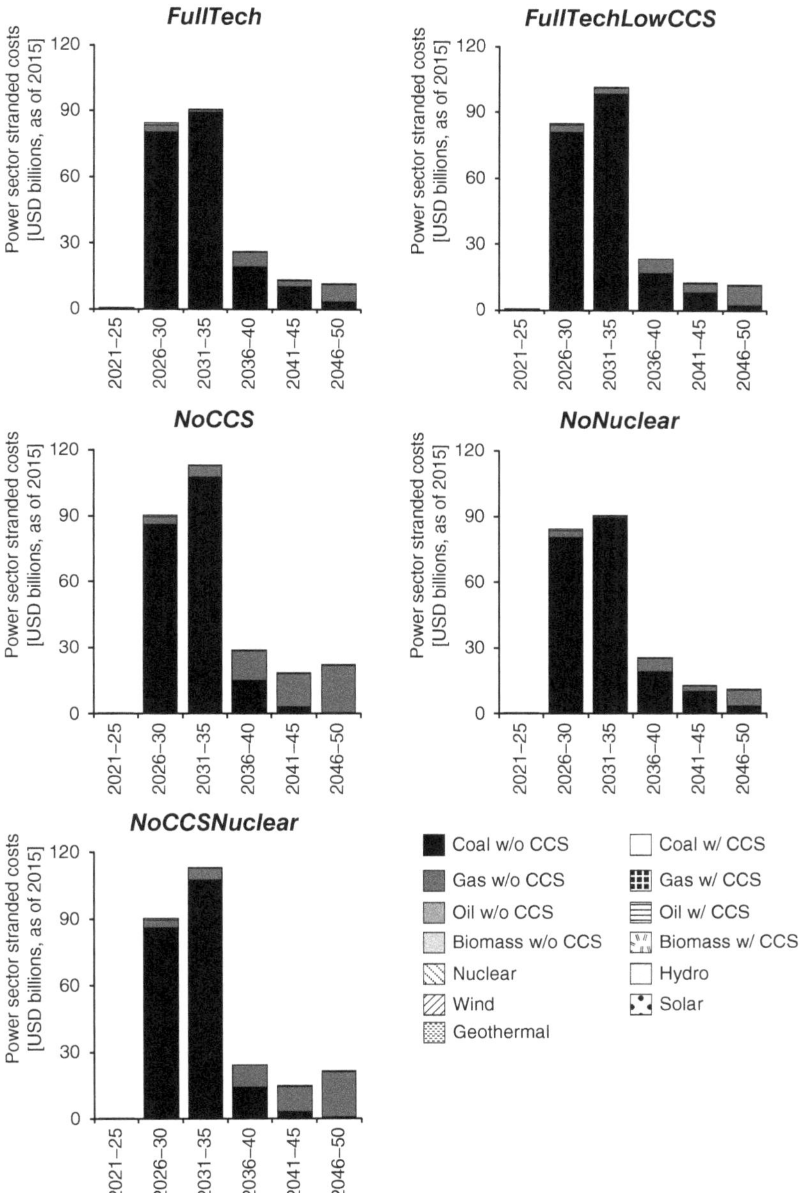

FIGURE 4.7 Premature electricity retirement costs by scenario.

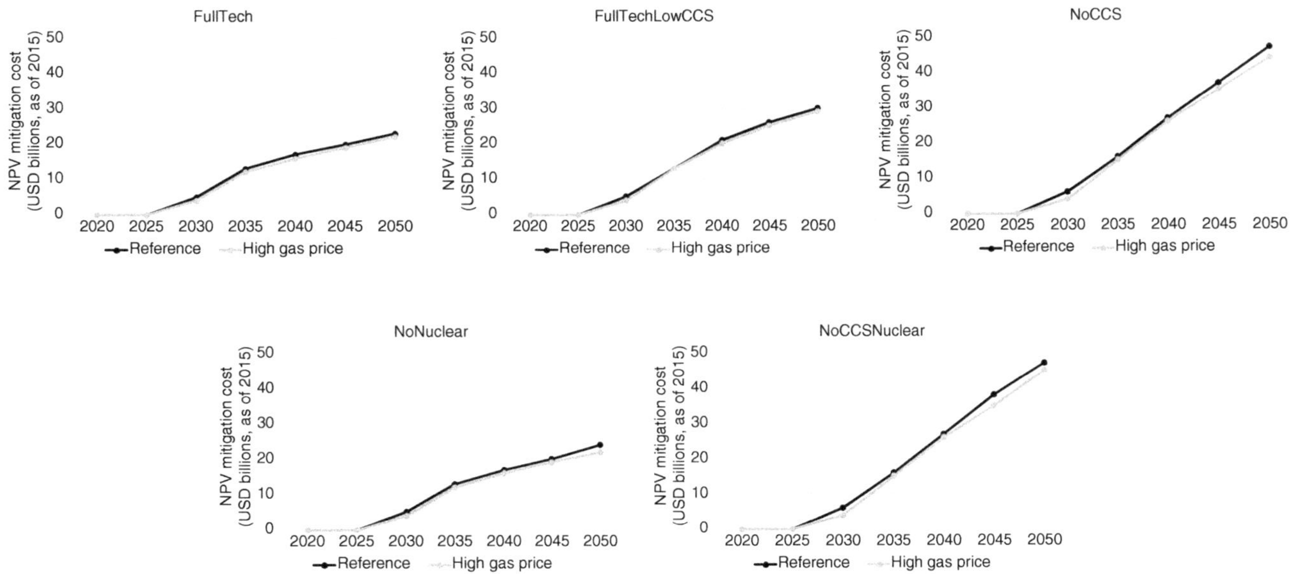

FIGURE 4.8 NPV policy costs by scenario (5% discount rate).

4.4.4 Policy Cost

Across the scenarios, the cumulative costs of achieving the climate target increase over time (2021–2050), reaching USD 78–134 billion (net present value, NPV, constant 2015 USD, or 0.28–0.48% of the estimated GDP of the region) (Figure 4.8). The highest policy costs come from the NoCCS and NoCCSNuclear scenarios, implying that deploying CCS in combination with renewables and nuclear can minimise policy costs to reach the NZE target by 2050. This result aligns with Fujimori et al. (2023), who argue that renewable energy and CCS can reduce loss in GDP.

4.4.5 Sensitivity Analysis of High Gas Prices

A 10% increase in gas price reduces the amount of electricity produced from traditional gas (Figure 4.9). In the FullTech scenario, total electricity generation from gas will decrease by 11.3% from 2021 to 2050, and installed gas capacities will drop by 32.6% (Figure 4.10). This situation also applies to gas with CCS, in which new additions will decline by 19% (from 23.1 GW to 19.4 GW). This difference is caused by less new installation of gas power plants, both with and without CCS. Since high gas prices reduce new additions to gas power capacity (both traditional gas power plants and those with CCS), stranded assets and costs from gas power plants are smaller by 1% (Figure 4.11) and by 6.9% (Figure 4.12), respectively. On the other hand, a slightly higher nuclear power capacity is required, from 32.5 GW to 32.9 GW, but it increases new installation costs in the NoCCS scenario (NoCCSHGP) (Figure 4.13).

Gas power plant stranding will be significant in the later period as the long-term climate target approaches. However, gas power plants with CCS are required to provide sufficient electricity supply (base load). High gas prices will lower policy costs because only a limited number of gas power plants are installed, resulting in lower emissions and reduced mitigation costs. In this regard, higher gas prices make gas power plants uneconomic, and reducing new fleets

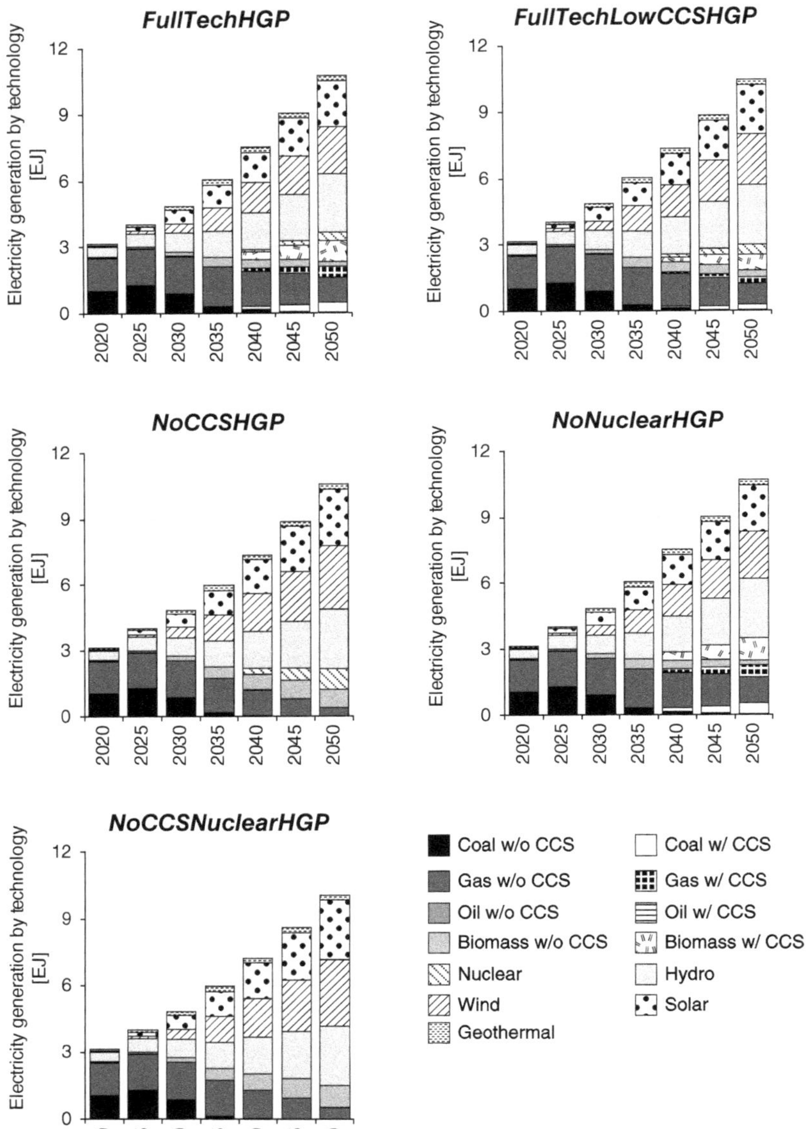

FIGURE 4.9 Energy mix by scenario (high gas prices).

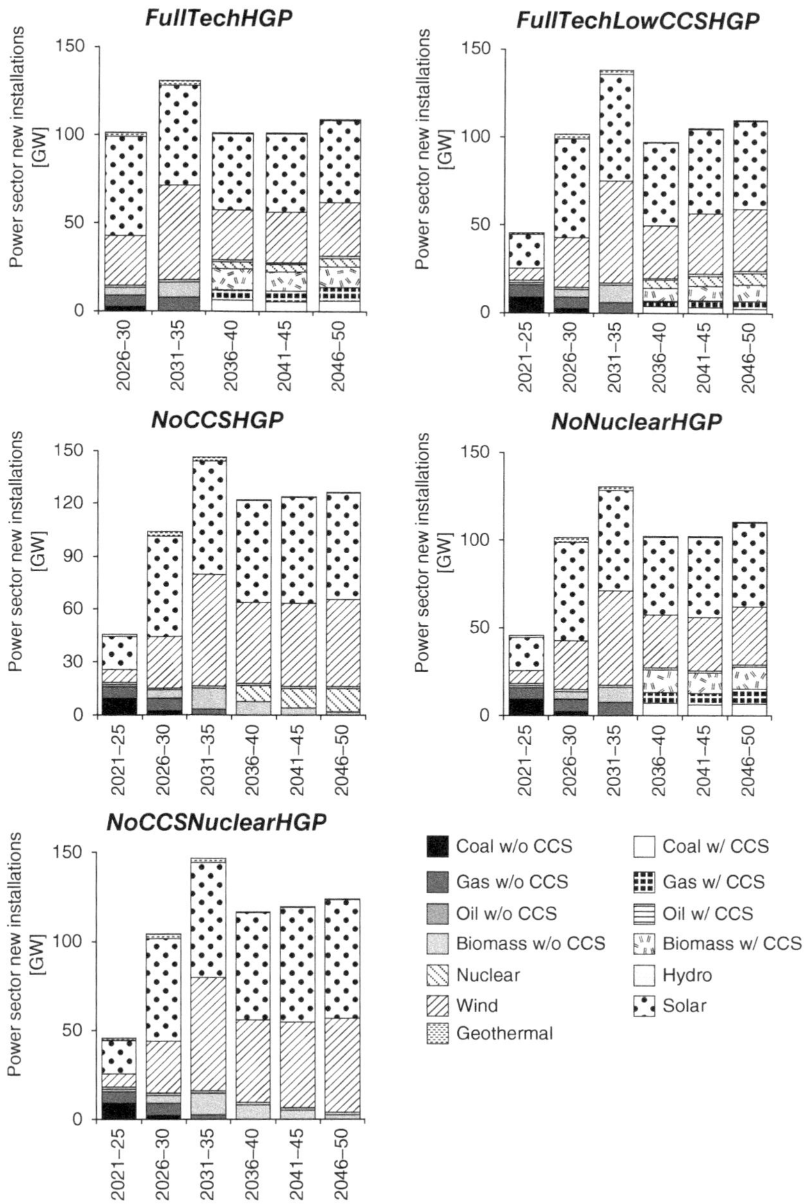

FIGURE 4.10 New capacity additions by scenario (high gas prices).

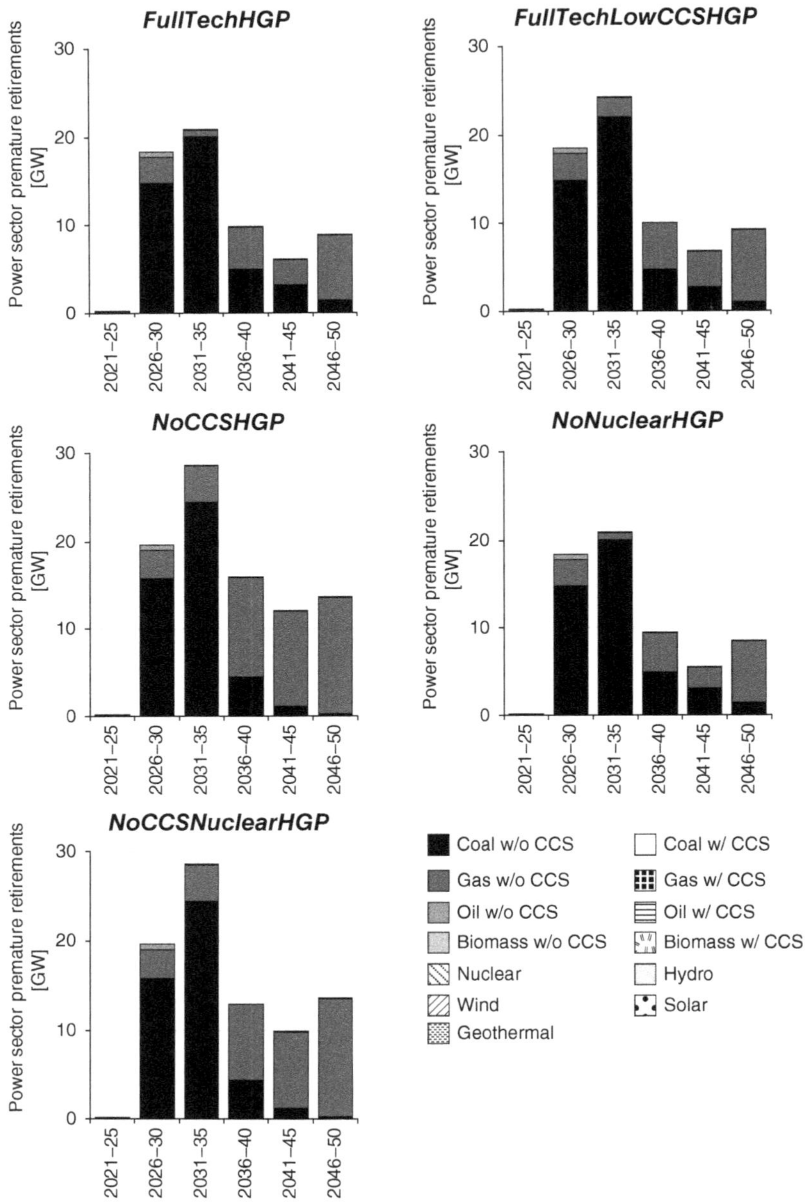

FIGURE 4.11 Premature electricity retirement capacity by scenario (high gas prices).

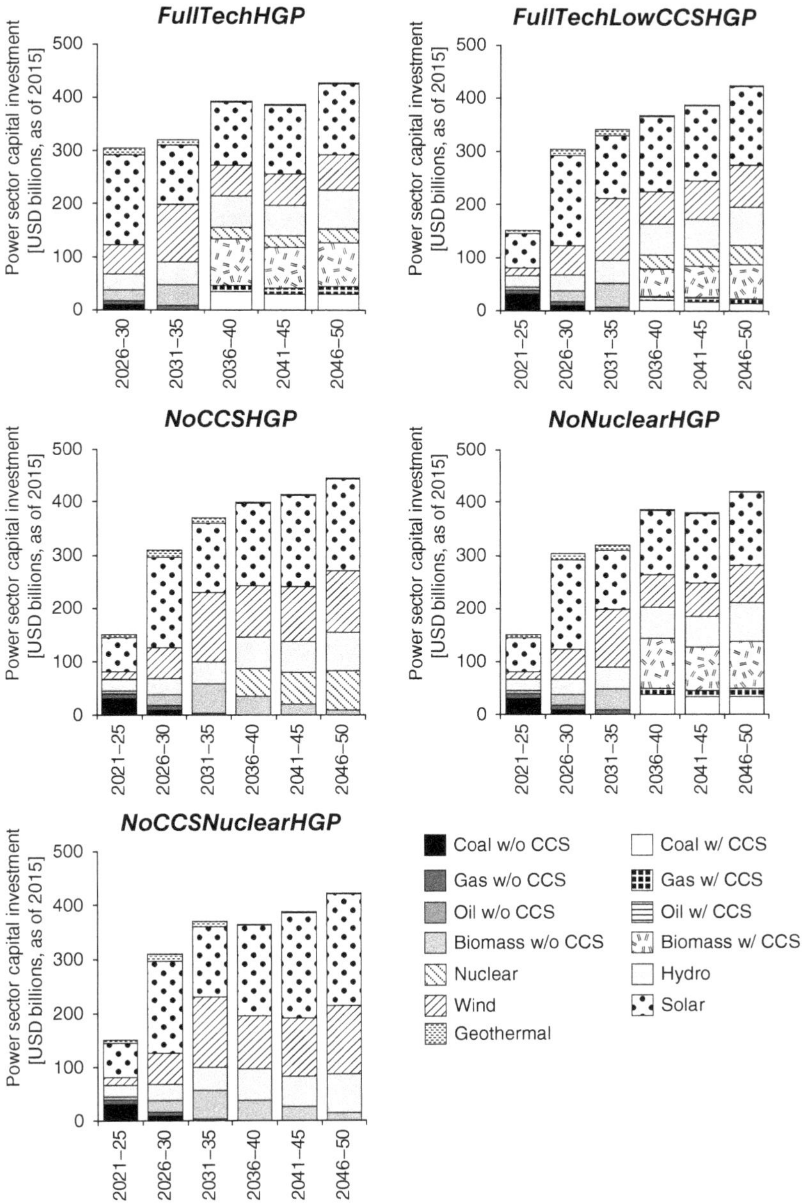

FIGURE 4.12 Premature electricity retirement costs by scenario (high gas prices).

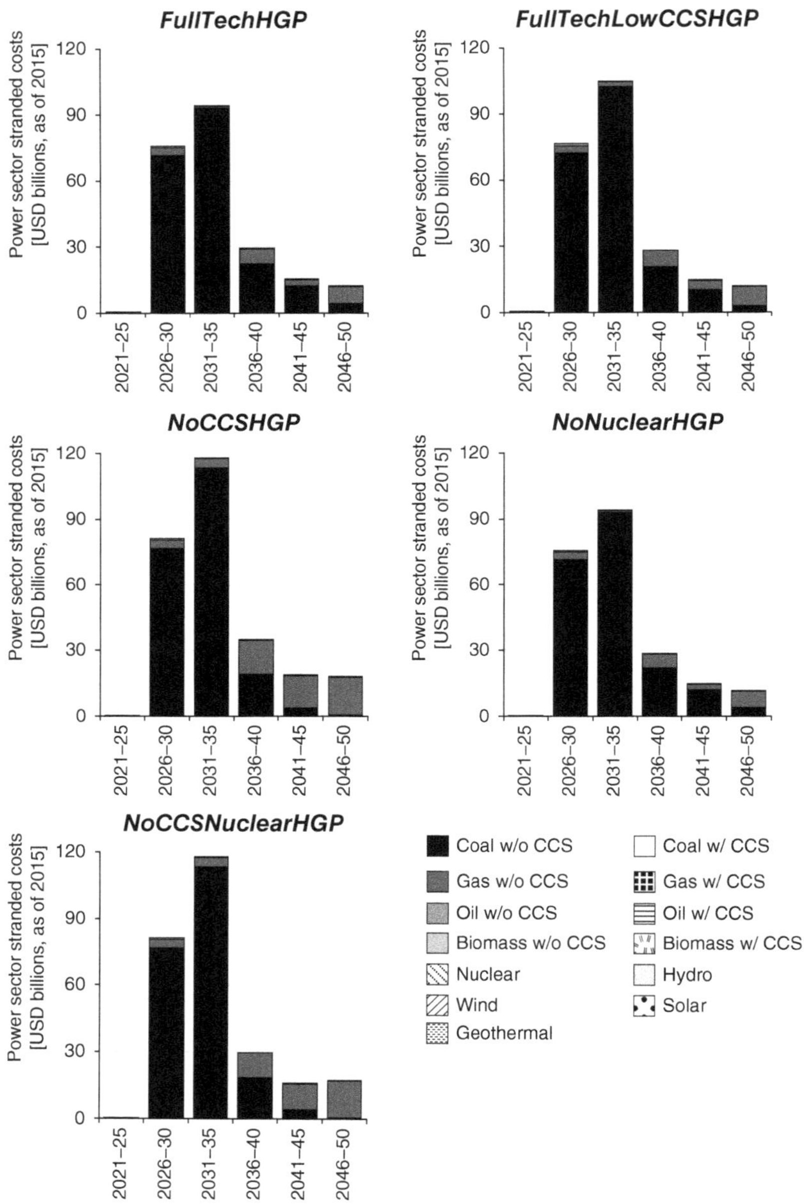

FIGURE 4.13 New installation costs by scenario (high gas prices).

can minimise policy costs. Thus, increasing gas prices indirectly links to mitigation efforts to reduce emissions from gas power plants so that the costs will decline.

4.5 DISCUSSION

Our simulation results found that the SEA region must bear the sum of new installation and stranded costs by 8.3–9% of GDP cumulatively during 2021–2050 (Table 4.3). If using NPV, the total costs are mitigated to 3.5–3.8% of GDP. These findings imply that countries in the region must reallocate substantial portions of investments into energy transitions, mostly renewable energy. In addition, stranded costs accounted for only 0.8–1% of GDP, and stranded costs for coal power are 4–10 times higher than those for gas in all scenarios. The difference is larger in the NoNuclear scenario than the FullTech one because the stranding of gas capacity will be slightly less, supported by gas with CCS and a large share of RES-E, but the stranding capacity rate of coal power is the same. These results imply that stranded costs are less likely to discourage SEA countries from investing in gas power capacity. Rather, they are likely to be motivated to use gas power as a bridging technology and to wait for declining investment costs despite the predicted suffering from more considerable stranded costs of gas power plants in the future.

CCS can mitigate new installation costs and stranded costs, as existing fossil fuel power plants can keep operating with low emissions (Table 4.3). Our analysis found that CCS technology can save USD 45 billion from potential stranded and new investment costs between 2021 and 2050 (FullTech vs. NoCCS). This is reasonable, given that Southeast Asia has relied mostly on coal and gas power plants to satisfy growing electricity demand. In the NoCCS scenario, capital and stranded costs will be more significant. In addition, overcoming limitations in technological capability (IRENA, 2022) and increasing the political and social acceptance of nuclear power generation (Iyer et al., 2017) have become far more critical.

Table 4.3 *Summary of total estimated costs per GDP, 2021–2050*

	Cost % of GDP		NPV % of GDP	
Scenario	Reference	High gas price	Reference	High gas price
FullTech				
New installation costs	7.509%	7.588%	3.105%	3.141%
Stranded costs	0.865%	0.868%	0.429%	0.423%
Policy costs	0.951%	0.894%	0.299%	0.280%
NoCCS				
New installation costs	7.976%	7.992%	3.279%	3.299%
Stranded costs	1.044%	1.037%	0.503%	0.497%
Policy costs	1.695%	1.603%	0.509%	0.480%
NoNuclear				
New installation costs	7.440%	7.507%	3.084%	3.116%
Stranded costs	0.860%	0.861%	0.427%	0.421%
Policy costs	0.951%	0.894%	0.298%	0.280%
NoCCSNuclear				
New installation costs	7.668%	7.672%	3.184%	3.200%
Stranded costs	1.012%	1.005%	0.493%	0.486%
Policy costs	1.711%	1.619%	0.513%	0.483%

Furthermore, our simulation results imply that it is more reasonable to maintain the existing power plants and retrofit with CCS in the future to supply electricity when gas prices increase because this reduces the need for new investments in gas power plants, assuming that new additions will lead to additional costs and make gas power plants inefficient because of high fuel costs. Since there will not be significant additions to gas power plant capacity, the energy system needs new installations from other technologies, particularly renewables, to meet electricity demand after 2030 and achieve the NZE target. As a result, new installation costs become higher when gas prices increase (see Table 4.3). This is in line with Bistline and Young's (2022) findings that natural-gas-fired power generation can lower the costs of electric sector decarbonisation. Another implication is that stranded costs will increase in response to higher gas prices, new installation of renewables, and required emissions reductions to meet long-term climate goals. These costs will be more significant under the NoCCS scenario, requiring rapid phase-out of fossil fuel power plants.

4.6 CONCLUSION AND REMAINING CHALLENGES

The Southeast Asian region has relied heavily on fossil fuels for their increasing needs since the early 1990s, while the proportion of renewable energy has been increasing. Continuing investments in fossil-fuel-based electricity generation can leave these investments stranded in the effort to achieve NDCs and NZE. This concern raises a question on how large the stranded investments and costs are, on the one hand, and the required investments and costs for transition to the NDCs and NZE, on the other. However, area-specific scenario analysis has been lacking.

To fill this research gap, we applied GCAM to estimate the potential effect of climate policies and technology applications on future energy mix and stranded assets in Southeast Asia. Our simulation results showed that in the aim to achieve NDC and NZE targets, additional capacity is covered mainly by renewables (i.e., hydro, wind, and solar power) and partly by fossil fuels with CCS, if available. This result highlights the urgent need for a drastic shift to renewable energy and wider application of CCS, given that the peak of stranded assets by fossil-fuel-based (mainly coal) electricity will come in the relatively near term (2030–2035). Coal power accounts for more than 80% of stranded costs in 2021–2040, but gas power accounts for the majority thereafter.

However, a shift to renewable energy requires high costs: the SEA region needs investments in new installation capacity by 7.4–8% of GDP from 2021 to 2050, which is 8.7 times higher than stranded costs. The new installation costs will be lower if they are discounted, although still relatively high. The required installation costs will be lower if CCS is commercially available. In the case of high gas prices, stranded costs from gas will decrease 22–25%, but new installation costs, mainly from renewables, will increase by 0.2–1.5% to compensate for a decrease in gas capacity.

Countries in the region have stated ambitious near-term renewables targets, aiming to have 35% of primary energy from renewable sources by 2025 (IRENA, 2022). The deployment of renewables has been increasing, albeit at a snail's pace owing to social, economic, and political barriers to low-carbon energy transitions (Erdiwansyah et al., 2019b). Assuming the OECD and G20 agreement on ending official export credit for unabated coal power plants and the much lower stranded costs of gas assets than coal assets as given, our results imply that it is more cost-effective for policymakers in the region to switch the energy for electricity generation from coal to renewables and natural gas, waiting for CCS be commercially available at a large scale in the near term, than to invest a large amount in renewables at the sacrifice of GDP. Our findings confirm findings in the previous literature, such as Bistline and Young (2022), that lowering gas capacity (due to either high gas prices or phase-out) will tend to increase transition costs as more renewable capacities are needed. Thus, our research contributes to the current discourse on gas power as a bridging technology.

Table A4.1 *Selected studies on stranded assets reviewed in the power generation*

Authors and year	Coverage	Methodology, tools, and assumptions/scenarios	Stated value of stranded assets
Johnson et al. (2015)	Global	• The total of discounted unrealised annual charges between the time of retirement and the economic lifetime to estimate stranded assets • MESSAGE-MACRO integrated assessment model • Emissions scenarios consistent with a limit at or below a 2°C rise by 2100, including the near-term aims by 2030	USD 165–550 billion over the 2011 to 2050 period
Caldecott et al. (2015)	Australia	• Net present value of profits foregone because of premature retirement of plants • Plant-by-plant analysis	AUD 8.4–18.3 billion (or AUD 560 million – AUD 3.66 billion per year)
Caldecott et al. (2016)	Japan	• The remaining value of prematurely retired plants with a straight-line depreciation method to calculate stranded assets value • Scenarios of stranded assets over 5-year, 10-year, and 15-year periods, considering factors such as falling electricity demand, rapid growth in renewables, and nuclear restarts	5-year scenario: JPY 8,453 billion (USD 76 billion) 10-year scenario: JPY 8,924 billion (USD 80.2 billion), of which JPY 6,223 billion (USD 56 billion) in plants built after 2016 15-year scenario: JPY 6,857 billion (USD 61.6 billion), of which JPY 5,307 billion (USD 47.7 billion) in plants built after 2016: equivalent to 22.6%–29.4% of the current market capitalisation, and 4.5%–5.9% of the total assets, of Japan's power utilities

(continued)

Table A4.1 *(cont.)*

Authors and year	Coverage	Methodology, tools, and assumptions/scenarios	Stated value of stranded assets
IRENA (2017)	19 G20 countries and other European Union countries	• The remaining book value of assets substituted before the end of their anticipated technical lifetime and without recovery of any remaining value to achieve 2050 decarbonisation targets. • Scenarios include (i) accelerated renewables and energy efficiency (REmap), and (ii) business-as-usual (delayed policy action until 2030) • A 27% reduction in the primary use of fossil fuels by 2030 and more than 60% reduction by 2050 compared to 2015 levels	USD 1.9 trillion under delayed policy action – more than twice as much as in REmap, at USD 0.9 trillion
Caldecott et al. (2017)	China	• Straight-line depreciation method to calculate stranded assets value, assuming 40 years of depreciation • Scenarios of stranded assets over 5-year, 10-year, 15-year, and 20-year periods, considering factors such as falling electricity demand, rapid growth in renewables, and nuclear restarts	5-year scenario: CNY 7,201 billion (USD 1,047 billion) 10-year scenario: CNY 5,797 billion (USD 843 billion) 15-year scenario: CNY 4,420 billion (USD 643 billion) 20-year scenario: CNY 3,086 billion (USD 449 billion), equivalent to 4.1–9.5% of China's 2015 GDP

Iyer et al. (2017)	Global	• Power generation capacity of prematurely retired assets
		• Global Change Analysis Model (GCAM)
		• Achieve 80% reductions in economy-wide GHG emissions in 2050 relative to 2005; this includes:
		  • 'Full Tech' scenario: utilise fully available technologies
		  • 'No Nuc' scenario: no new deployment of nuclear technologies, greater deployment of carbon capture and storage (CCS) technologies and renewables
		  • 'No CCS' scenario: no deployment of CCS technologies, greater deployment of nuclear and renewables
		  • 'No Nuc & CCS' scenario: no new deployment of nuclear technologies, all emissions reductions achieved through renewables
			10–15 GW per year between 2016 and 2025 across all scenarios
			5–10 GW per year between 2026 and 2050 across all scenarios

(continued)

Table A4.1 *(cont.)*

Authors and year	Coverage	Methodology, tools, and assumptions/scenarios	Stated value of stranded assets
Pfeiffer et al. (2018)	Global	• Idle capacity running under normal utilisation rate • Capacity running at low utilisation rates would constitute stranding • 1.5°C and 2°C scenarios	51%–58% of all power plants that are operating, planned, and under construction would be stranded If all currently planned projects were cancelled, 10%–20% of existing capacity would be stranded
Kefford et al. (2018)	US, EU, China, and India	• NPV of unearned revenue due to premature retirement of environmentally unsustainable plants • Summing the discounted unrealised annual charges between the time of retirement and the economic lifetime to quantify the value of the stranded assets • IEA 2DS pathway	By 2060, USD 541 billion in the US, EU, China, and India alone, of which 66% and 31% of the costs (USD 358 billion and USD 169 billion) are shared by China and India, respectively Setting a minimum operational capacity factor for the retirement of 40% increases the magnitude of the early retirement problem significantly for unabated coal and increases the value of stranded assets by 43% to USD 773 billion
Mercure et al. (2018)	Global	• The remaining value of prematurely retired plants • E3ME-FTT (Technology Fusion Trajectory) • 'IEA expectations' scenario: fuel use from the IEA's 'new policies scenario' • 2°C scenario: achieves 75% probability of remaining below 2°C while limiting bioenergy use	USD 12 trillion (in 2016 US dollars) under a 2°C limit, which comprises over 15% of global GDP Discounted global wealth loss of USD 1–4 trillion

Saygin et al. (2019)	G20 countries excluding EU countries	• The remaining value of prematurely retired plants • Straight-line depreciation method to calculate stranded assets value, assuming 50-year lifetime and different capital costs in OECD and non-OECD countries • REmap scenario (2°C scenario with 66% probability) • Delayed policy action scenario: BAU until 2030; following 2030, the deployment of renewables and energy efficiency accelerates sufficiently to ensure that the global energy system remains within the same emissions budget by 2050	In G20 countries: by 2050, USD 1,563 billion under delayed policy action; USD 792 billion under the REmap case Globally: by 2050, USD 1,824 billion under delayed policy action; USD 927 billion under the Remap case By 2050, stranded coal assets would represent around 75% of total stranded assets value (USD 695–1,368 billion), and China alone would represent 45% of the total Delaying action to mitigate climate change until 2030 doubles stranded asset value
Cui et al. (2019)	Global	• Compares trajectories against the Paris Pledge scenarios • Incorporates unit-level data into a global integrated assessment model (GCAM) to calculate lifetime limits • Four scenarios: continued coal growth, NDC, well below 2°C, and 1.5°C	320 GW or 16% of global installed capacity is expected to shut down by 2030, counting both announced retirements and plants whose lifetimes would exceed 50 years; Achieving the 2°C goal requires a 720 GW or 36% reduction in capacity by 2030, and achieving the 1.5°C goal requires an 1890 GW or a 94% reduction

(*continued*)

Table A4.1 *(cont.)*

Authors and year	Coverage	Methodology, tools, and assumptions/scenarios	Stated value of stranded assets
Binsted et al. (2020)	Latin America and the Caribbean	• The remaining value of prematurely retired plants (GCAM) • Straight-line depreciation method to calculate stranded assets value, assuming a 60-year lifetime • Scenarios include NDCs-to-2°C, NDCs-to-1.5°C, straight-to-2°C, and straight-to-1.5°C	USD 40–90 billion 60–128 GW of fossil fuel power plants (15–33% of total installed capacity in LAC) stranded between 2021 and 2050, of which natural gas and oil power plants constitute nearly 50%
Fofrich et al. (2020)	Global	• Maximum power plant lifetime (integrated assessment models: GCAM, REMIND, MESSAGE, IMAGE, AIM, WITCH) • Analyse coal and natural gas-fired power plant utilisation rates and lifetimes across 171 scenarios and three levels of emissions mitigation (1.9, 2.6, and 4.5 W/m^2 of radiative forcing, i.e., trajectories likely to avoid 1.5°, 2°, and 3°C of global warming by the end of the century)	Coal-fired power plants: maximum power plant lifetimes of 9, 16, and 19 years for 1.9, 2.6, and 4.5 W/m^2 of radiative forcing, respectively Gas-fired power plants: maximum power plant lifetimes of 12, 17, and 19 years for 1.9, 2.6, and 4.5 W/m^2 of radiative forcing, respectively
Oshiro and Fujimori (2021)	Japan	• The remaining value of prematurely retired assets (AIM/Enduse) • 2030 policy combined with NDC goal (16%, 26%, and 36% reduction) • 2050 policy scenario combined with • MCS goal (70%, 80%, 85%, and 90% reduction)	USD 8–82 billion

Malik et al. (2020)	India	• Power generation capacity of prematurely retired assets • Incorporates unit-level data into global integrated assessment models (i.e., AIM/Enduse, MARKAL, IMAGE, POLES, GEM-E3, REMIND, WITCH) to calculate lifetime limits • Early action scenario with abatement towards a global goal well below 2°C after 2020 • Delayed action scenario follows India's current policies and NDC targets until 2030 and abatement towards a global goal below 2°C thereafter	14–159 GW under early action scenario 133–227 GW under delayed action scenario
Cui et al. (2022)	Indonesia	• The remaining value of prematurely retired plants • A plant-by-plant assessment • A retirement priority ranking system based on multiple technical and environmental criteria • GCAM • The pathway to achieve 1.5°C by 2050	9.2 GW (2030) 21.7 GW (2031–2040) USD 4.6 billion through 2030 and USD 27.5 billion through 2050.

(*continued*)

Table A4.1 *(cont.)*

Authors and year	Coverage	Methodology, tools, and assumptions/scenarios	Stated value of stranded assets
Edwards et al. (2022)	Global	• The remaining value of prematurely retired plants • A plant-by-plant assessment • A retirement priority ranking system based on multiple technical and environmental criteria • GCAM • 1.5°C and 2°C limits (no new coal plants after 2020, coal plants under development come online by 2030, and delayed mitigation from coal power and other sectors)	USD 1.4 trillion (a 1.5°C policy) USD 1 trillion (a 2°C policy).

Table A4.2 *Plans and/or targets regarding nationally determined contributions (NDCs) submitted by countries in Southeastern Asia to UNFCC*

Country[a]	Climate plan and time coverage	Links
Brunei Darussalam	• Reduce GHG emissions by 20% relative to BAU levels by 2030 • Increase the total proportion of renewable energy to at least 30% of total capacity in the power generation mix by 2035	https://unfccc.int/sites/default/files/NDC/2022-06/Brunei%20Darussalam%27s%20NDC%202020.pdf
Cambodia	• The updated NDC seeks to decrease emissions by 41.7% from the business-as-usual scenario by 2030, with half of that reduction concentrated in the Forest and Land Use Sector (FOLU) and the rest primarily in the energy, agriculture, industry, and waste sectors; Cambodia's updated NDC also has a strong adaptation component • 25% of renewable energy in the energy mix (wind, hydro, biomass) by 2030	https://unfccc.int/sites/default/files/NDC/2022-06/20201231_NDC_Update_Cambodia.pdf
Cook Islands	An unconditional emissions reduction target of 38% (conditional: 48%) by 2030 relative to the baseline scenario	https://unfccc.int/sites/default/files/NDC/2022-06/Cook%20Islands%20INDCsFINAL7Nov.pdf
Democratic People's Republic of Korea	An unconditional emissions reduction target of 16.4% (conditional: 36%) by 2030 relative to the baseline scenario	https://unfccc.int/sites/default/files/NDC/2022-06/2019.09.19_DPRK%20letter%20to%20SG%20special%20envoy%20for%20NDC.pdf

Table A4.2 *(cont.)*

Country[a]	Climate plan and time coverage	Links
Federated States of Micronesia	• By 2030, reduce carbon dioxide emissions from electricity generation by more than 65% below 2000 levels • By 2030, increase electricity generation from renewable energy to more than 70% of total generation	https://unfccc.int/sites/default/files/NDC/2022-10/Updated%20NDC%20of%20the%20MICRONESIA.pdf
Fiji	• 30% of BAU CO_2 emissions from the energy sector by 2030 • Of the 30% reduction of BAU baseline CO_2 emissions, 10% will be achieved 'unconditionally' using available resources in the country, and 20% achieved 'conditionally'	https://unfccc.int/sites/default/files/NDC/2022-06/Republic%20of%20Fiji%27s%20Updated%20NDC%2020201.pdf
Kiribati	An unconditional emissions reduction target of 12.8% (conditional: 61.8%) by 2030 relative to the baseline scenario	https://unfccc.int/sites/default/files/NDC/2022-06/INDC_KIRIBATI.pdf
Lao PDR	An unconditional emissions reduction target of 60% by 2030 relative to the baseline scenario	https://unfccc.int/sites/default/files/NDC/2022-06/NDC%202020%20of%20Lao%20PDR%20%28English%29%2C%2009%20April%202021%20%281%29.pdf
Malaysia	An unconditional target to cut carbon intensity against GDP by 45% by 2030 compared to 2005 levels	https://unfccc.int/sites/default/files/NDC/2022-06/Malaysia%20NDC%20Updated%20Submission%20to%20UNFCCC%20July%202021%20final.pdf

Marshall Islands	• Commitment to reduce GHG emissions to at least 32% below 2010 levels by 2025 and to at least 45% below 2010 levels by 2030; net-zero GHG emissions by 2050 at the latest	https://unfccc.int/sites/default/files/NDC/2022-06/RMI%20NDC-UpdateUPDATED_01.20.2021.pdf
Myanmar	• 414.75 MT CO_2e emissions reduction target by 2030 • Increase the total proportion of renewable energy (solar and wind) to 53.5% by 2030	https://unfccc.int/sites/default/files/NDC/2022-06/Myanmar%20Updated%20%20NDC%20July%202021.pdf
Nauru	• Unconditional GHG emissions reduction target from 10% to 14% • A balance between anthropogenic emissions by sources and removals by sinks by 2050	https://unfccc.int/sites/default/files/NDC/2022-06/Nauru%20Updated%20NDC%20pdf.pdf
Palau	• 22% energy sector emissions reductions below 2005 levels by 2025 • 45% renewable energy target by 2025 35% energy efficiency target by 2025	https://unfccc.int/sites/default/files/NDC/2022-06/Palau_INDC.Final%20Copy.pdf
Papua New Guinea	50% carbon-neutral by 2030 and entirely carbon-neutral by 2050	https://unfccc.int/sites/default/files/NDC/2022-06/PNG%20Second%20NDC.pdf

(*continued*)

Table A4.2 *(cont.)*

Country[a]	Climate plan and time coverage	Links
Philippines	• A projected GHG emissions reduction and avoidance of 75%, of which 2.71% is unconditional 9 and 72.29% is conditional	https://unfccc.int/sites/default/files/NDC/2022-06/Philippines%20-%20NDC.pdf
Samoa	• An absolute economy-wide target of reducing total GHG emissions by 26% in 2030 compared to the 2007 level • 100% of electricity from renewable energy by 2025	https://unfccc.int/sites/default/files/NDC/2022-06/Samoa%27s%20Second%20NDC%20for%20UNFCCC%20Submission.pdf
Seychelles	• 26.4% compared to BAU scenario by 2030 • A decarbonised net-zero emissions economy by 2050	https://unfccc.int/sites/default/files/NDC/2022-06/Seychelles%20-%20NDC_Jul30th%202021%20_Final.pdf
Singapore	Enhance 2030 NDC to peak emissions at 65Mt CO_2e around 2030	https://unfccc.int/sites/default/files/NDC/2022-11/Singapore%20Second%20Update%20of%20First%20NDC.pdf
Solomon Islands	• 12% by 2025 and 30% by 2030 compared to BAU projection • with international assistance, 27% by 2025 and 45% by 2030	https://unfccc.int/sites/default/files/NDC/2022-06/NDC%20Report%202021%20Final%20Solomon%20Islands%20%281%29.pdf
Thailand	• 30% from the projected BAU level by 2030 • Continued vigorous efforts to meet the long-term goal of carbon neutrality by 2050 and net-zero GHG emissions by 2065	https://unfccc.int/sites/default/files/NDC/2022-11/Thailand%202nd%20Updated%20NDC.pdf

Tonga	• 13% reduction in GHG emissions from energy by 2030 compared to 2006 • 70% of electricity generated from renewable sources by 2030	https://unfccc.int/sites/default/files/NDC/2022-06/Tonga%27s%20Second%20NDC.pdf
Tuvalu	A reduction in total emissions of GHGs from the entire energy sector to 60% below 2010 levels by 2025	https://unfccc.int/sites/default/files/NDC/2022-06/TUVALU%20INDC.pdf
Vanuatu	• Vanuatu's INDC mitigation contribution would thus reduce BAU emissions in the electricity sub-sector by 100% and in the energy sector by 30% A sector-specific target of transitioning to close to 100% renewable energy in the electricity sector by 2030	https://unfccc.int/sites/default/files/NDC/2022-08/Vanuatu%20NDC%20Revised%20and%20Enhanced.pdf
Viet Nam	An unconditional emissions reduction target of 15.8% (conditional: 43.5%) by 2030 relative to the baseline scenario.	https://unfccc.int/sites/default/files/NDC/2022-11/Viet%20Nam%20NDC%202022%20Update.pdf

[a] Information related to emission reduction targets was not available for American Samoa, Christmas Island, Cocos (Keeling) Islands, French Polynesia, Guam, Mayotte, New Caledonia, Niue, Norfolk Island, Northern Mariana Islands, Pacific Islands Trust Territory, Pitcairn Islands, Timor Leste, or Tokelau.

5 Reconciling Net-Zero Emissions and Growing Electricity Demand

Electricity System Transitions in Vietnam

5.1 INTRODUCTION

Since the early 2000s, Vietnam has increased its power generation capacity to avoid electricity supply crises that could be triggered by its rapid economic growth. Power generation quadrupled from 25 to 100 billion kWh in the 2000s and more than doubled from 100 to 250 billion kWh in the 2010s (Figure 5.1). In March 2020, Vietnam's Politburo, the highest body of the Communist Party of Vietnam, issued Resolution 55 on Strategic Energy Orientation until 2030 with vision 2045, which highlighted an increase in installed capacity of up to 125–130 GW by 2030, about twice the capacity in 2020 (69 GW) (Tran, 2022).

While the short gestation period prompted the country to increase gas power generation in the 2000s, coal power and hydropower increased rapidly and became dominant in the 2010s (Figure 5.1). The percentage of gas in the total power generation went up to 40% in the late 2010s but down to less than 20% in 2020. Hydropower became dominant in 2012–2014 when new plants started operations and gained priority dispatch owing to its low cost. However, it grew slower because the country stopped building big dams (Pham, 2022). With large investments from China, South Korea, and Japan (Mori, 2022), coal power has become dominant since then and became the majority source in 2020.

The rapid growth in coal power generation and subsequent increase in coal consumption have two negative implications. First,

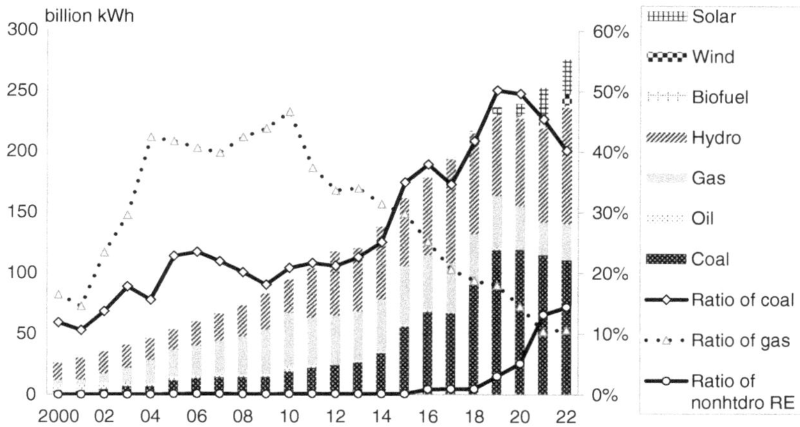

FIGURE 5.1 Power generation by type of energy in Vietnam, 2000–2022.
Source: Compiled by the authors based on data from IEA (2024b).

it turns Vietnam into a net coal importer. The country used to be a net coal exporter and had increased coal exports to China in response to the China-induced coal boost in the 2000s (Mori & Dong, 2018). However, domestic demand for coal power has exceeded domestic supply as new coal power plants started operation. While the price of coal on the international market is less volatile than that of oil or gas, it is highly uncertain. Divestment from the coal industry may accelerate closure, reduce the coal supply, and increase the price. A higher coal price decreases the competitiveness of coal power vis-à-vis renewable-energy-sourced electricity (RES-E), stranding coal power assets and making coal power generators struggle to obtain financing (Minh, 2020). The Vietnamese government perceives that being a net coal importer presents a risk of increased foreign dependency, which has led them to seek alternative sources of domestic energy.

Second, coal power has increased emissions per capita. Greenhouse gas (GHG) emissions more than quadrupled between 2000 and 2020. The increase is associated with toxic air pollution in many cities, adversely impacting human health and labour productivity. According to an estimate, Vietnam lost USD 10 billion or 3.2% of its GDP to climate change impacts in 2020 and will lose 12% to 14.5% of its GDP annually by 2050 without proper mitigation and adaptation measures (World Bank, 2022). Local protests have become so fierce that some new coal power plant projects have been cancelled (Pham, 2022).

In the context of international pressure towards more stringent climate change actions, efforts to attract foreign direct investments, and the aim of showing the prime minister's leadership (Takahashi, 2024), the government has updated its international pledge on GHG emissions. Under nationally determined contributions (NDCs) in 2016, the government pledged a GHG emissions reduction target of 8% relative to a business-as-usual scenario from the reference year 2010 with domestic resources (unconditional) and a reduction targets of 25% conditional on international support through energy-intensity reduction and increase in forest coverage (The Socialist Republic of Vietnam, 2016). It raised the targets to 9% and 27% respectively in the updated NDCs in 2020 (The Socialist Republic of Vietnam, 2020). At the UN climate change conference in Glasgow in 2021 (COP 26), Vietnam's government pledged net-zero GHG emissions by 2050 coupled with stopping deforestation by 2030 and the phase-out of coal power generation by 2040 (Dezan Shira & Associates, 2021). Accordingly, it revised the NDCs in 2022 to raise unconditional emissions targets by 2030 to 15.8% and conditional ones to 43.5%, respectively (The Socialist Republic of Vietnam, 2022). The energy sector is expected to contribute the most, 7% out of 15.8% in the unconditional reduction targets and 24.4% out of 43.5% in the conditional targets. In addition, the OECD and G20 agreed on ending officially supported export credits for unabated coal power plants (OECD, 2021a). The Glasgow Climate Pact agreed to phase down unabated coal power and inefficient subsidies for fossil fuels (UNFCCC, 2021). As such, Vietnam has less access than before to international finance for new coal power plants.

The negative implications of coal power plants, along with Vietnam's pledge to Global Coal to Clean Power Transition Statement and net-zero emissions and international financial restrictions, have led to the cancellation of pipeline coal power projects with a total capacity of 45 GW (Gao et al., 2021; Do & Burke, 2023). The Ministry of Industry and Trade (MOIT) has repeatedly revised the draft Eighth Power Development Plan (PDP8), which covered 2021–2030, seeking government approval to reconcile compelling policy objectives. Accordingly, the planned future energy structure and associated infrastructure requirements were revised for two years pending a cabinet decision in May 2023. Vietnam's the prime minister approved the implementation plan for PDP8 in April 2024. The revisions and the wait for government approval have delayed new investments, resulting in severe power outages that hit multinationals' manufacturing hubs in 2023 (Vu, 2023).

In this chapter, we will analyse how the OECD and G20 agreements on ending officially supported export credits for unabated coal power plants and the pledge to the net-zero GHG emission target have changed the elements of the electricity system in Vietnam; we will aim to elucidate the direction and speed of electricity system transitions up to now and in the future, as represented in the draft and cabinet-approved versions of the PDP8.

The remainder of this chapter is organised as follows. Section 5.2 reviews electricity sector reform and RES-E development to demonstrate past trajectories that may have affected changes in the complementary elements of the electricity system. Section 5.3 presents the methodology and data collection strategy for the case study. Section 5.4 provides the results, organised by grid paradigm and complementary element. Section 5.5 interprets the results and discusses how changes in the complementary elements have affected the direction and speed of electricity system transitions, as represented in the cabinet-approved PDP8. Finally, Section 5.6 concludes the chapter and provides suggestions for future research.

5.2 ELECTRICITY SECTOR REFORM AND RES-E DEVELOPMENT

5.2.1 Electricity Sector Reform

Vietnam's electricity systems are characterised by the monopoly of the state-owned electricity company Vietnam Electricity (EVN) over the transmission, distribution, wholesale, and retail of electricity. EVN was established by merging three existing regional power companies into a single national entity in 1995. It underwent partial ownership that unbundled the generation, transmission, and distribution segments to attract private investments in generation. However, the government was reluctant to shoulder the resultant higher tariffs and the large foreign exchange loss from power purchase contracts denominated in USD and JPY.

This reluctance led to gradual and phased electricity sector reform, moving from a vertically integrated, monopolistic supply system towards a competitive market under the framework of the 2004 Electricity Law and the subsequent 20-year roadmap (Lee & Gerner, 2020). First, state utilities were restructured. In 2003, EVN was partially unbundled into generation and distribution. In 2012, generation was further unbundled to establish three power generation corporations (GENCO 1, 2, 3) under the ownership of EVN, with 11 regional distribution companies.[1] The National Power Transmission Corporation was established in 2018 by reunifying various regional EVN subsidiaries, with monopolistic managing of the transmission network.

Second, private companies were allowed to participate in the sector. In addition to two state-owned companies – Vietnam Oil and Gas Group and Vietnam National Coal-Mineral Industries Holding Corporation Limited (Vinacomin) – private investors were allowed to

[1] In 2010, these distribution companies consolidated into five EVN-owned regionally monopolised power corporations: Northern Power Corporation, Southern Power Corporation, Central Power Corporation, Hanoi Power Corporation, and Ho Chi Minh City Power Corporation.

invest in power generation. International investors were allowed under a build–operate–transfer modality (Koty, 2022). Domestic private companies were onboarded as independent power producers (Le et al., 2022).

Third, competitive power markets were gradually developed (Khoa, 2018). The Vietnam Competitive Generation Market (VCGM) began full operation in 2012 through a bidding mechanism. In an integrated pool, energy is traded through spot and day-ahead markets. All generators must sell all the electricity to the Electricity Power Trading Company, a subsidiary of EVN, and a single buyer through fixed-term contracts. The competitive Vietnam Wholesale Electricity Market (VWEM) succeeded the VCGM in 2015; it allowed large industrial consumers and five regional utilities to negotiate and contract directly with public and private generators. The Vietnam Retail Electricity Market (VREM) was scheduled to start operation in 2022, anticipated to ensure a stable power supply, attract investment from all social sectors, and reduce total operation costs by decreasing CO_2 costs (Lam & Bach, 2023). However, the Electricity Power Trading Company has remained the single buyer in the VWEM (Lam & Bach, 2023), and the operation of the VREM has been postponed.

Good power system planning, government commitment, streamlining of EVN's organisational structure, and improved transmission and distribution loss management have been credited with improvements in the operational efficiency and financial performance of generators (Lee & Gerner, 2020) as well as the security of supply amid rapid growth in electricity demand (Le et al., 2023).

5.2.2 *RES-E Development Policies*

Vietnam's RES-E policy is characterised by uncertain, abrupt, and disordered interventions. On the one hand, generous feed-in tariffs (FiT), income tax exemptions, and land lease payment exemptions have triggered the solar photovoltaic (PV) boom (Do et al., 2020; Do, Burke, Nguyen et al., 2021). The Vietnamese government announced the Revised Seventh Power Development Plan (PDP7) (2016–2020) to encourage renewable energy development. PDP7 was in line with the first national development strategy for renewable energy in 2015, which aimed to increase renewables to around 32% of the total primary supply and non-hydro renewables to 6.5% of electricity generation by 2020 and 10.7% by 2030 (World Bank, 2018). The abandonment of the nuclear power project in 2016 accelerated the shift towards solar and wind power. The government released the solar power development plan in 2017; it stipulated the target of 850 MW of installed solar PV capacity by 2020, 4 GW by 2025, and 12 GW by 2030. The government implemented a FiT at USD 9.35 cents/kWh and allowed independent power producers 20-year power purchase agreements (PPAs) under the FiT that were commissioned before 30 June 2019. It also implemented a FiT for wind power in 2018, at USD 8.5 cents/kWh excluding VAT for onshore, and at USD 9.8 cents/kWh for offshore commissioned before 1 November 2021.

The FiT boosted solar investments, particularly in the central and southern regions. The installed capacity of onshore wind increased from 106 MW in 2017 to 4,784 MW in 2023; for offshore wind, the increase was from 99 MW to 1,104 MW. Solar increased from 8 MW to 17,077 MW in the same period (Figure 5.2). Owing to commercial loans for rooftop solar from banks in Vietnam, such as HSBC Vietnam, BIDV, HDBank, and Oriental Commercial Bank (Nam, 2022), rooftop solar accounted for 43% of the total installed capacity of solar (Figure 5.3), surpassing the percentage in the US and China and in countries where decentralised energy resource (DER) generation isabundant. While the number of installations was much larger in residential than industrial and commercial sectors, the installed capacity was five times higher in the industrial than the residential sector (Viet Nam Energy Partnership Group, 2020).

As such, non-hydro on-grid renewables accounted for 28% of total installed capacity (Figure 5.2) and 14% of total power generation in 2022 (Figure 5.1). Coupled with favourable hydrological conditions for hydropower generation, these conditions have led to a decline in gas power generation, accounting for less than 20% in 2020 (Figure 5.1).

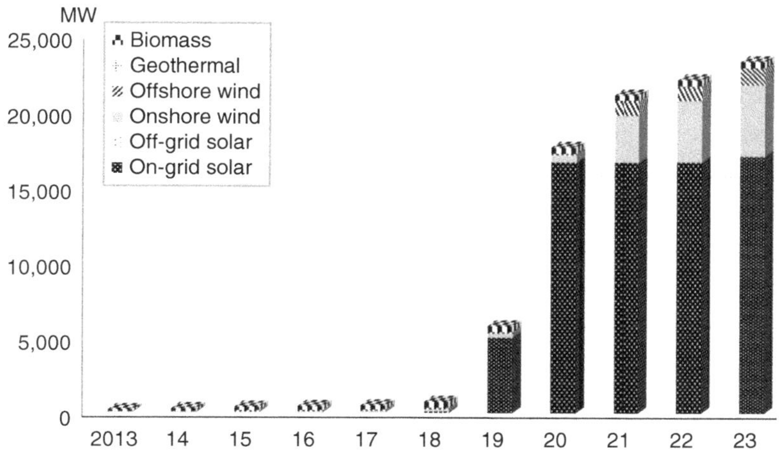

FIGURE 5.2 Installed capacity of non-hydro renewables in Vietnam, 2013–2023.
Source: Compiled by the authors based on data from IRENA (2023; 2024).

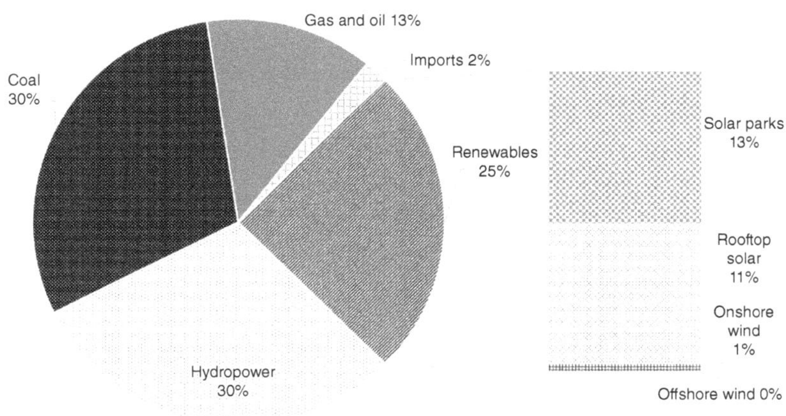

FIGURE 5.3 Installed capacity of power plants by type of energy in Vietnam, 2020.
Source: Compiled by the authors based on data from Nguyen (2021) and the International Trade Administration, US Department of Commerce (n.d.).

The rapid increase in investment is technologically supported by the large domestic production capacity for solar PV cells and modules. PV modules are manufactured in collaboration with Chinese and American manufacturers. Vietnam has increased production capacity in response to ongoing anti-dumping/countervailing duty investigations by the US, and the impetus to capitalise on the US Inflation Reduction Act's tax credits rather than the FiT in Vietnam (Norman, 2023b). Among PV module manufacturers, Vsun increased its installed capacity by 4 GW (Bellini, 2021), JA Solar by 3.5 GW (Oanh, 2022), and AD Green by 2.5 GW (Bellini, 2023). Installed production capacity was increased from 5.2 GW per year in 2017 (Do, Nguyen, & Nguyen, 2021) to 32 GW in 2022, making Vietnam the second largest country for global installed capacity after China (IEA, 2023b).

Key drivers are the same for wind power (Do et al., 2022). An ambitious wind power target and generous FiTs invited a rush to reach the full or partial commercial operation dates (CODs) of 84 wind power projects with a total capacity of 3,980 MW in 2011–2021 (MOIT, 2021). Of these, 20 are nearshore projects with a total capacity of 779 MW that reaches CODs only in 2021 (GWEC, 2022).

However, the government has not launched a new auction programme for solar parks since the previous one expired. This is why the installed capacity of on-grid solar power has increased only marginally since 2020 (Figure 5.2).

5.2.3 RES-E and Grid System Development

Despite the consensus on the urgent need for grid capacity development for large-scale integration of RES-E, studies on electricity system transitions have been relatively limited. Vu (2021) analysed the financial status of EVN and found that its pipeline of large-scale generation projects would constrain grid investments without an increase in tariffs. Based on a survey and semi-structured interviews with energy and marine stakeholders, Do et al. (2022) predicted that PPAs are more likely to be dominant in the trade of offshore wind than in the wholesale market and that developers will be responsible for investing in, constructing, operating, and maintaining transmission connections.

Against this backdrop, the work presented in this chapter expands the scope to include distributed smart-grid and flexible grid paradigms to analyse the changes in the elements of complementarity and explore how they affect the direction and speed of electricity system transition.

5.3 METHODOLOGY AND DATA

5.3.1 Research Design

In the research discussed in this chapter, we employed a case study method with an inductive, longitudinal, single-country case study design. A case study method is suitable for testing internal validity and for affirming the correctness of the inference and rival explanations. It is also relevant in testing external validity and acknowledging analytical generalisations (Yin, 2018). Single-case studies may provide less strong evidence for the relevance of the initial set of propositions compared with multi-case studies, but taking a common or typical case is beneficial in testing hypotheses and providing insights (Sovacool et al., 2018). Through a single-case study of Vietnam, we expected to provide insights into electricity system transitions from the coal-based system in emerging Asian countries.

We employed the framework built in Chapter 3 to analyse the direction and speed of electricity system transitions based on changes in elements of complementarity. We conducted a document-based content analysis, which is appropriate for testing well-structured research questions with a priori analytical categories (Sovacool et al., 2018). As our purpose was to investigate the paradigms relevant to Vietnam's electricity system, we expected the analytical method to yield suitable answers.

5.3.2 Materials

We relied on holistic data collection strategies. We used data from secondary sources, such as academic books, articles, and grey literature published by the Asian Development Bank (ADB), the World Bank, and the Vietnam Initiative for Energy Transition (VIET); and primary sources, such as business journals and daily newspapers. To study incumbent companies, we derived data from annual reports and press releases issued by EVN. We collected documents from online archives using keyword searches.

5.4 RESULTS

5.4.1 Development towards the Super-Grid Paradigm

5.4.1.1 Infrastructure: High-Voltage Backbone Transmission Lines

EVN had developed two circuits of the north–south backbone system of extra-high-voltage (EHV) 500 kV transmission lines by 2005 (EVN, 2018). The National Power Transmission Corporation (EVNNPT) was established in 2008 as a subsidiary of EVN responsible for the investment, operation, and management of the 220 kV to 500 kV transmission systems in the whole country (EVN, 2017). The 500 kV transmission line is considered one of Vietnam's most significant technical achievements and has fundamentally shaped how the power sector has developed.

To improve grid stability and regional balance, the government planned developments of another backbone 500 kV north–south transmission system and upgrades to other transmission lines in the Revised PDP7 (2016–2020). With funding from the ADB, EVN inaugurated the third circuit of the 500 kV transmission line and several 220 kV lines in 2020 (ADB, 2021). Transmission capacity between the north and central regions was expected to increase to 3,600 GW after 2020, and that between the central and the south to 6,500 MW after 2023 (VIET, 2021a). With funding from the World Bank, transmission lines were developed in the Greater Hanoi area, Greater Ho Chi Minh City area, Mekong Delta, and central region. Moreover, five and ten substations at 500 kV and 220 kV levels, respectively, were rehabilitated and upgraded with smart-grid technology. As such, 500 kV and 220 kV transmission lines were extended by more

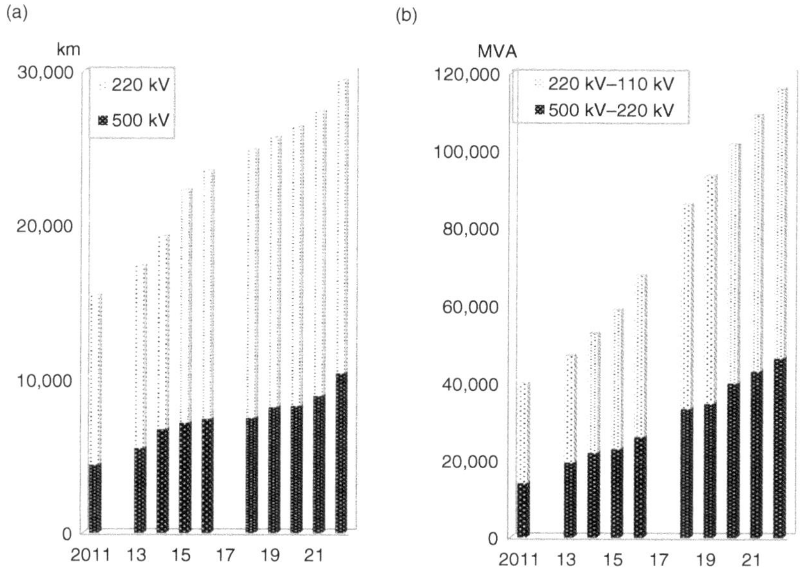

FIGURE 5.4 Grid development in Vietnam, 2011–2022: (a) length of transmission and distribution lines; (b) capacity of transformers/substations.
Note: data is missing for the years 2012 and 2017.
Source: Compiled by the authors based on data from Electricity Vietnam (EVN) Annual Reports for 2010–2011, 2012–2013, 2015, 2016, 2017, 2018, 2021, 2023.

than 1,000 km and 3,000 km, respectively, and 500 kV and 220 kV transformers were expanded by more than 70% in 2015–2020 (Figure 5.4). With joint funding from the Canada Facility and EVN, the National Load Dispatch Center, a subsidiary of EVN responsible for grid operation, has invested in system management infrastructure, such as automatic generation control for frequency and automatic voltage control for voltage management to enhance dispatch management (Rahul, 2021).

EVN has also developed international transmission lines to import electricity from China and Laos to satisfy rapid growth in electricity demand. Cross-border RES-E projects with Laos are ongoing, including the 600 MW Monsoon Wind power project, which is set to sell all its generated electricity to EVN under a 25-year PPA in exchange for limited-recourse project financing from a combination of the Export-Import Bank of Thailand, ADB, and commercial banks. Moreover, the Vietnamese and Lao governments committed to importing 5,000 MW of capacity from Laos by 2030, potentially increasing to 8,000 MW by 2050 (Thompson et al., 2023).

Meanwhile, increasing national security concerns over long-distance EHV transmission lines have driven the government to shift towards upgrading existing regional ones. Transmission development projects can exceed the public debt threshold of 65% of the GDP. However, the fiscal risk discouraged the government from proceeding with tranche 4 of the ADB-funded transmission investment programme (ADB, n.d.). The development of EHV lines is perceived as causing difficulties in voltage regulation, higher power loss, and a greater risk of losing safety and grid stability. Power generation without coordination with urban planning and the economic structure is seen as an underlying cause of the ineffective use of electricity that demands transmission lines (EVN, 2020).

The developments in backbone and cross-border transmission lines have not effectively addressed renewable curtailment. An under-prepared transmission grid, complex administrative procedures, and a high level of policy uncertainty are identified as the underlying causes of such curtailment (Do et al., 2020; Do, Burke, Nguyen, et al., 2021). Insufficient grid capacity increased volatility in the power supply and raised regional imbalance between supply and demand, which threatens grid stability, triggering substantial renewable curtailment. The greatest electricity demand is in the northern and southeastern regions, whereas wind resources are mainly in the southwestern and south-central regions, and solar resources are in the highlands, southeast, and south-central regions (IUCN, 2022a). Between 15% and 25% of existing projects' generation and about 80% of solar capacity in the south are curtailed (Rahul, 2021). Developments in backbone and cross-border transmission lines have helped to mitigate regional imbalance in energy production and consumption. However, solar curtailment has occurred in 110 kV lines in Ninh Thuan, Binh Thuan, and An Giang provinces in the southeastern and south-central regions, and in 220 kV lines in the south-central coast region (Do, Tran & Nguyen, 2021).

The limited effectiveness of backbone transmission lines likewise holds for wind power. The short-term (three-year) FiT eligibility window coupled with case-basis, lengthy, and complex administrative procedures, supply chain issues, and labour disruptions owing to the COVID-19 pandemic made more than 1 GW of registered onshore wind projects and more than 300 MW of nearshore project capacity miss their COD expiration date of 30 October 2021 (IUCN, 2022b; GWEC, 2023). An under-prepared transmission grid and a lack of decisions on the responsibility for transmission connections from offshore wind power project sites to onshore grids have prevented new installations from connecting grids (Do et al., 2022).

5.4.1.2 Infrastructure: Run-of-the-River and Pumped Storage Hydropower

Hydropower imports from Laos have received attention as an alternative to domestic pumped storage hydropower. Laos, Cambodia, and Vietnam adopted transmission grid interconnection technology at the 220 kV voltage level and coordinated in safely operating the regional interconnection grid. This harmonisation constitutes a foundation for developing new interconnecting transmission lines with Laos (EVN, 2021). However, hydropower is not likely to exceed 1.5 GW or 1% of installed capacity in 2030 (MOIT, 2022). Most of the suitable sites for large hydropower plants have already been developed, and the government restricts the development of the remaining potential in consideration of ecological impacts (VietBiz, 2021). In addition, hydropower in Vietnam is substantially affected by seasonal fluctuation and upstream hydropower developments in China and Laos (VietBiz, 2023).

Pumped storage hydropower has long been treated as a priority dispatch owing to its low cost. The draft PDP8 describes an increase in the installed capacity of hydropower by 30% in 2030 and 70% in 2045, of which small hydropower accounts for 55% (VietBiz, 2023). Some existing plants are expanding their scales to serve as pumped storage hydropower (EVN, 2019). With the assistance of Tokyo Electric Power Company, the Bac Ai pumped storage hydropower plant with 1,200 MW capacity will be commissioned by around 2030 (VIET, 2021a). To make it effective as a system-wide front-of-the-meter energy storage system, the country developed transmission lines to connect them, as seen in the Thuong Kon Tum hydropower plant of 22 MW capacity (IEG Review Team, 2022). Nonetheless, ecological limits and seasonal fluctuation hamper the predictability of the extent of the use of pumped storage hydropower as a flexible and dispatchable type of generation.

5.4.1.3 Institution: Procurement of Renewable Energy-Based Electricity and Capacity

The VWEM started operation in 2019, and the schedule for dispatching energy was converted from 60 to 30 minutes to better reflect the system's actual mobilisation of marginal price signals. Large industrial consumers and distribution companies are allowed to negotiate and contract directly with generators. In addition, the government mandated all generators larger than 30 MW, including plants under the build–operate–transfer modality, to sell their electricity in the market and all distribution companies to buy from the market to meet the demand. As of 2022, 108 power plants with a combined capacity of 30.8 GW or 38.8% of total capacity participated in the VWEM (EVN, 2022d), compared with 31 plants with a combined capacity of 9.2 GW in 2012 (EVN, 2022a). RES-E generators with a capacity exceeding 30 MW have a de facto priority to accept and dispatch under cost-based bidding because RES-E is sold at the FiT rate and thus presented in the day-ahead market with submitted price equal to zero (Lam & Bach, 2023).

However, the VWEM has not effectively worked to integrate RES-E in grids on a large scale. The market does not ensure a level playing field among generators. It allows EVN to exercise strong bargaining power for prices, volumes, and grid-connection conditions through its five subsidiary power companies, which are responsible for the grid up to 110 kV and are dominant in distribution (Lee & Gerner, 2020), despite their declining share in generation capacity (Tran, 2022). Ownership bundling allows EVN to cross-subsidise subsidiary companies and exempts subsidiary distribution companies from participating in the wholesale market as retailers and making commercial decisions on the purchase of electricity (Lam & Bach, 2023). The system operator, National Load Dispatch Center, remains a subsidiary of EVN, although the plan has been for it to be independent of EVN by 2025 (Lee & Gerner, 2020). This unbalanced bargaining power has prolonged negotiations over the rate between EVN and RES-E developers,[2] blocking 85 wind and solar projects with a combined capacity of nearly 5,000 MW from connecting to the grid and starting operations. RES-E developers and industrial consumers have shouldered additional costs (Saigon Times, 2023).

5.4.2 Development towards the Distributed Smart-Grid Paradigm

5.4.2.1 Infrastructure: Smart Grid

The installation of smart meters was accelerated after the MOIT initiated the overall roadmap to develop a smart-grid concept in 2016. Demand-side management targets, roadmaps, and implementation plans also pushed the uptake. Smart meters accounted for about 43% of total installed meters by 2019 (VIET, 2021b). However, by 2020 the installation of smart meters had been completed in only one area, Da Nang City (Viet Nam News, 2020). As such, smart grids continue to play a marginal role in integrating distributed energy resources (Vu, 2022).

[2] EVN proposed half of the government-released FiT ceiling rates to developers in April 2023, but developers angrily refused them (Saigon Times, 2023).

5.4.2.2 *Institution: Demand-Side Integration*

The government has gradually developed a legal framework for connecting rooftop solar power systems to the grid. It has not provided third parties access to the transmission and distribution network (Lee & Gerner, 2020). This inaccessibility blocked energy aggregators from emerging; these might have aggregated small DERs to supply demand response and ancillary services and effectively used RES-E. However, the government launched a pilot direct power purchase agreement (PPA) scheme between solar power generators and large consumers in 2020, with a limit of 1,000 MW (Minh, 2023), followed by a full-fledged direct PPA in 2024 (Bellini, 2024a). Direct PPAs enable RES-E generators to sell electricity directly to private off-takers under virtual or synthetic deals, thus allowing them to put the risk of tariff fluctuation on the off-taker in exchange for network cost payment (Santos, 2022b).

The nationally determined retail tariff remains low to recover the cost of solar PV through bill saving without FiT, not to mention behind-the-meter energy storage systems (BTM-ESS). The average residential retail tariff has been high since 2013, when the government formulated retail tariff adjustment rules to keep pace with rising costs and inflation to address the serious financial deficit of EVN and EVNNPT (ADB, 2015). The percent of gross household income spent on electricity has increased for low-income groups, exceeding 10%, and is considered to be at the high end of affordability (Lee & Gerner, 2020). Time-of-use tariffs have been implemented for industrial and commercial customers, as well as retailers of electricity in industrial zones (EVN, 2016). Yet the residential block tariff becomes relatively low for households with higher consumption. Grid-connected BTM-ESS will be compensated only for energy delivered to the grid as virtual ESS, even if it benefits grid operators (VIET, 2021a). On average, the tariff for industrial consumers is lower than for households and is the lowest in Asia (Lee & Gerner, 2020). However, a net metering scheme for rooftop PV installations was implemented in 2024, coupled with the ceiling of electricity that can be sold to the grid being raised from 10% to 20% of the power generated by a rooftop PV installation (Bellini, 2024b).

5.4.3 Development towards the Flexible Grid Paradigm

5.4.3.1 Infrastructure: Battery Energy Storage Systems

The government has perceived no urgent need for installing battery ESS. The cabinet-approved PDP8 (Decision No. 893/QD-TTg) paid scant attention to solar power combined with battery ESS except for the 300 MW installation target by 2030 (Thompson et al., 2023). An EVN feasibility study shows that battery ESS is not economically justified without supplying ancillary services, such as operating reserves (frequency control, spinning reserves, and contingency reserves), voltage support, and peak shifting (General Electric, 2019). Reducing renewable curtailment does not generate significant value (USAID, 2021), particularly amid the expansion of backbone transmission capacity (VIET, 2021a). Even if market-based mechanisms were created to enable payment for ancillary services, the current MOIT decision qualifies ESS as eligible to participate in wholesale energy spot markets, and thus battery ESS will not be supplied in ancillary service markets. Local transmission and distribution lines should be upgraded to scale ESS and to make it technically feasible to charge/discharge within optimal ESS operating parameters (VIET, 2021a).

As such, only one 15 MW utility-scale battery ESS pilot project is ongoing, in Ho Chi Minh City, and it is implemented as a key element of the Just Energy Transition Partnership (US Mission in Vietnam, 2023). The project is co-funded by the US Mission and operated as a joint venture between Vietnamese renewables development platform company AMI Renewables and Philippines-based AC Energy, which has developed 80 MW of solar at two sites and is constructing a 252 MW wind farm nearby the battery ESS (Colthorpe, 2021).

5.4.3.2 Institutions: Bidding for Ancillary Service Contracts

No bidding mechanism has been put in place for procuring ancillary services. The lack of a competitive retail market disincentivises providers from differentiating their services, including supplying ancillary services gain competitive advantage.

5.5 DISCUSSION

5.5.1 Unsynchronised Developments in Infrastructural, Institutional, and Organisational Elements

Table 5.1 summarises the results of our analysis. Underdeveloped infrastructure, institutions, and organisations have impeded transitions towards RES-based electricity systems, particularly under the super- and smart-grid paradigms. Funding from the World Bank and ADB has enabled the development of long-distance EHV transmission lines, but it has not been sufficient to fully address the solar curtailment triggered by the abrupt surge in RES-E. The negative implications of coal power plants, the pledges to the Global Coal to Clean Power Transition Statement and net-zero emissions, and international credit restrictions have worked as drivers to phase out unabated coal power. Electricity sector reform and institutional development have been implemented smoothly. Nonetheless, institutional developments are insufficient for large-scale integration of utility-scale RES-E and demand-side integration in grids.

Uncertain, abrupt, and disorderly policy interventions have interrupted the emergence and development of organisations initiating and financing RES-E deployment and thus the transition to RES-based electricity systems. Renewable curtailment and the government's subsequent prolonged decision-making on the post-FiT rate made RES-E developers and operators incapable of repaying bank loans (Nguyen, 2022). EVN does not accept take-or-pay obligations in the PPAs for solar and wind power (Do et al., 2020; GWEC, 2021). The government postponed the release of the new FiT rate that must be applied after 2019 for solar and 2021 for wind power. While it decided on a new lower FiT rate for new solar power projects in 2020 and implemented it for those that entered commercial operation by 31 December 2020, it did not decide on the new FiT

Table 5.1 *Changes in complementarity elements of electricity systems in Vietnam, by paradigm*

Super-grid paradigm	Flexible grid paradigm	Smart-grid paradigm
Infrastructure		
20-year development of extra-high-voltage backbone transmission lines	Battery energy storage system projects	Smart Grid Roadmap (2012)
Cross-border transmission lines		Complete installation of smart meters only in Danang
Lack of transformers		
Ecological limits in new hydropower and pumped storage hydropower		
Organisations		
Strong bargaining power of the state electricity company		No energy aggregators
Institutions		
Wholesale electricity spot market with cross-subsidy	No bidding mechanism for ancillary and system-balancing services	Direct power purchase agreements (pilots: 2021–2023, full-scale: 2024–)
No reverse auction	No reserve market nor capacity payment contracts	Third-party access via Electric Power Trading Company
No renewable energy market		Time-based tariff for industrial and commercial customers
		Demand responses from 2019 (to reduce peak load)
		Retail market scheduled to run in 2024

Note: Light grey colour implies weak barriers to electricity system transition; dark grey, strong; and medium grey, the middle range.
Source: Authors.

rate for RES-E projects that failed to meet the deadlines owing to the prolonged process of land acquisitions and construction delays. The government's pending decision pushed Southern Power Corporation to announce the pausing of payments, suspension of contracts, and disconnection of rooftop solar power projects with incomplete legal documents from the grid (Duc, 2023). Increased revenue uncertainty delayed the operation of 51 out of 175 government-approved solar power projects which would have supplied a total installed capacity of 6.6 GW out of 15.3 GW (MOIT, 2022). It was not until 2023, when serious power shortages were predicted, that the government released a new maximum FiT rate for solar that would reconcile the revenue certainty of RES-E projects with renewable curtailment. The full-fledged direct PPA was implemented after two years of pilot implementation. Moreover, it was not until the decision on the new feed rate in January 2023 that new wind power projects reached COD. Meanwhile, local banks are discouraged from financing solar and onshore wind projects, and non-EVN generators from investing in them.

5.5.2 *Lock-Ins and Path Dependency*

Past commitments to and commissions of fossil fuel power projects restrict transition pathways from redirecting, as represented in a significant increase in coal and gas power capacity in the PDP8. By September 2022, Vietnam had increased coal power by more than 10,000 MW, or 70% of what was represented in the first draft of PDP8, and constructed or prepared seven coal power plants with a combined capacity of 7,000 MW. While the coal power capacity in the cabinet-approved PDP8 was smaller than that in the first draft, this is simply because new coal power projects with a combined capacity of 2,020 MW were scrapped – all the planned coal power capacity that had not been commissioned was dropped owing to difficulties in obtaining financing associated with fierce local opposition (EVN, 2022b).

The country also approved combined-cycle gas turbine plants using domestic gas fields with a combined capacity of 7,900 MW, more than half of which is owned and developed by EVN (Tachev, 2022). Liquefied natural gas (LNG) power plants with a combined capacity of 4,050 MW began construction in 2021 (Table 5.2). While the cabinet-approved PDP8 removed some local-government-approved LNG power plants, such as Long An 2 (initiated by GS Energy) and Hai Phong 1 and 2 (initiated by Exxon Mobil) with a combined capacity of 7,500 MW – both located in the northern region and originally proposed as coal power plants (Quang, 2022) – the PDP8 assumes that gas power capacity in 2030 will be more than five times larger than in 2020. Path dependency made the cabinet-approved PDP8 assume future conversion from coal to ammonia-biomass co-firing power and from natural gas and LNG power to hydrogen co-firing to reconcile with the 2050 net-zero emissions target.

To reconcile past commissions with the net-zero emissions target, the cabinet-approved PDP8 also describes ambitious wind and solar targets. While the first draft shows ambitious targets for total installed capacity, particularly solar and wind power to align with the 2020 update of NDC (Figure 5.5), the second and third drafts highlight the optimal siting of power sources. These drafts involve a shorter development of transmission lines and no new construction of inter-regional lines by 2030 (Minh, 2021), and a more conservative solar and onshore wind capacity and total installed capacity, assuming implementation of net metering or equivalent tariff regimes for distributed generation (Figures 5.6 and 5.7). However, the cabinet-approved PDP8 describes the RES-E capacity target as 30% in 2030 and 68% to 71% in 2050 (Figure 5.8). It highlights self-sufficiency and self-consumption for solar capacity, describing no new developments in high-voltage direct current transmission lines and stations in 2030 (The Socialist Republic of Viet Nam, 2023).

5.5.3 *International Influences*

International factors have affected the direction of system transitions in Vietnam. First, the government imposed a ceiling on LNG imports (Resolution No. 55-NQ/TW) in 2020 for reasons of

Table 5.2 *Natural gas power projects in Vietnam*

Plant	Capacity (MW)	Gas field	Developers/owners
Domestic gas-fired power			
O Mon III, IV	2,100	Block B	EVN
O Mon II	1,050	Block B	Marubeni and WTO
Converting O Mon I	660	Block B	EVN
Dung Quat I, III	1,500	Blue Whale	EVN
Dung Quat II	750	Blue Whale	Sembcorp
Mien Trung I, II	1,500	Blue Whale	PetroVietnam
Quang Tri	340	Bao Vang	Gazprom
Total capacity	7,900		
LNG thermal power			
Quang Tri	1,500		Vietnam's T&T Group, Korea Southern Power, Hanwha Energy, Korea Gas
Nhon Trach III, IV	1,500		Samsung C&T, Lilama Corp
Quang Ninh	1,500		Marubeni, PetroVietnam Power, Tokyo Gas
Total capacity	4,500		

Source: Compiled by the authors based on GCR staff (2021), Hung (2016), Neely (2021), Shoji (2020), Tachev (2022), and Wright (2022).

national energy security (Thompson et al., 2022). The first and second drafts of PDP8 perceived imported LNG as a flexible fuel option (Figures 5.5 and 5.6) and anticipated that natural gas would account for 25% and 28% of the total primary energy supply in 2045, respectively. However, projected LNG imports in the drafts are regarded as exceeding the ceiling on LNG imports. Following the conclusion of the Standing Government (EVN, 2022c), the cabinet-approved PDP8 has no installed capacity for imported LNG in 2050. Nonetheless, the third draft of PDP8 projected a higher proportion of natural gas in

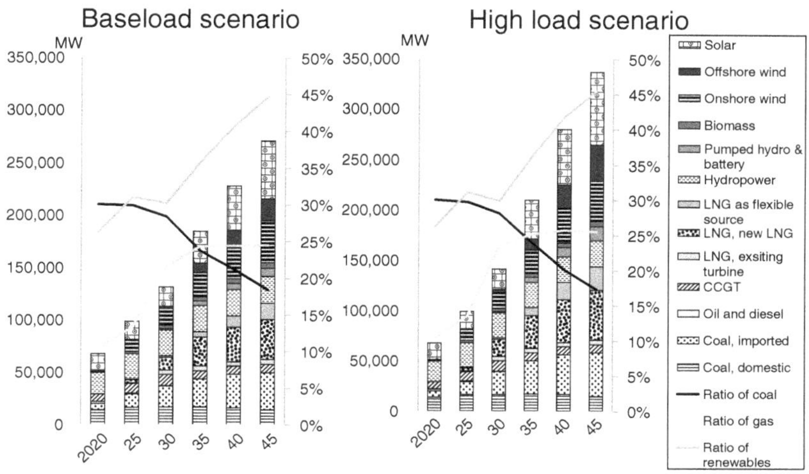

FIGURE 5.5 Energy mix in installed capacity in the first-draft PDP8 (February 2021).

Note: CCGT is a combined cycle gas turbine.

Source: Compiled by the authors based on data from Burke and Nguyen (2021) and Nguyen and Nguyen (2021).

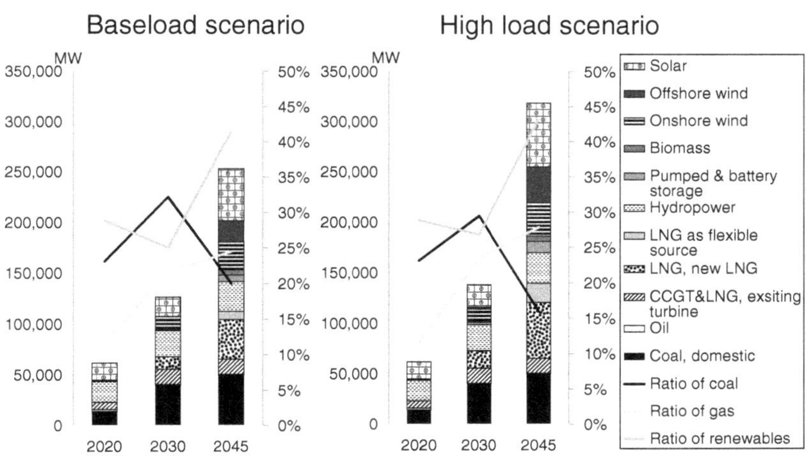

FIGURE 5.6 Energy mix in installed capacity in the second-draft PDP8 (November 2021).

Note: CCGT is a combined cycle gas turbine.

Source: Compiled by the authors based on data from Burke and Nguyen (2021) and Nguyen and Nguyen (2021).

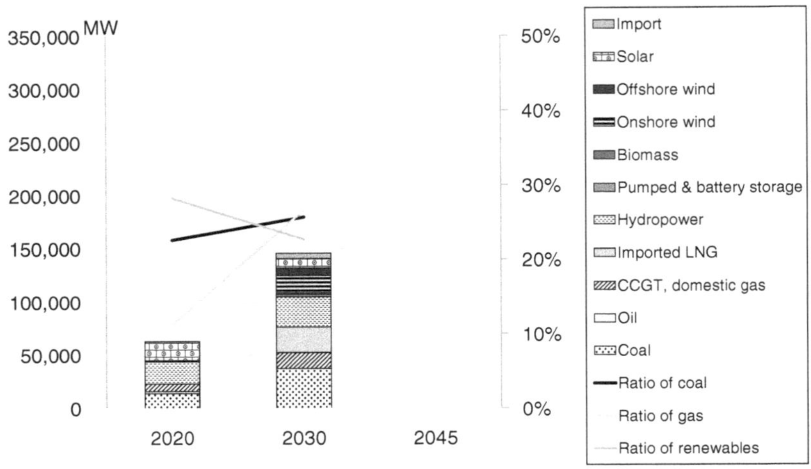

FIGURE 5.7 Energy mix in installed capacity in the high load scenario in the third-draft PDP8 (July 2022).
Notes: Excluding rooftop solar power and co-generation sources; CCGT is a combined cycle gas turbine.
Source: Compiled by the authors based on data from MOIT (2022).

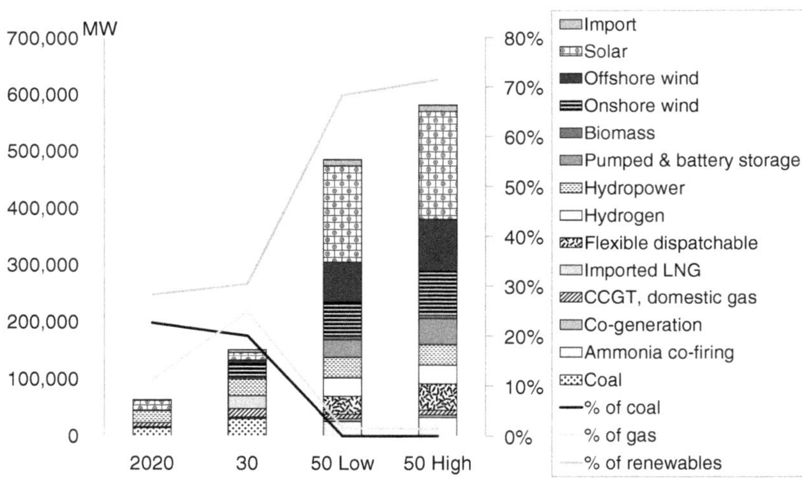

FIGURE 5.8 Energy mix in installed capacity in the cabinet-decided PDP8 (May 2023).
Notes: Excluding rooftop solar power and co-generation sources; CCGT is a combined cycle gas turbine.
Source: Compiled by the authors based on data from the Socialist Republic of Viet Nam (2023).

the energy mix in 2030 than the previous drafts (Figure 5.7). This is because it includes 17,900 MW out of 23,900 MW of installed capacity for LNG power from approved projects in the amended PDP7 and an additional 6,000 MW installed capacity to ensure stable supply in the northern power system (Massmann & Nguyen, 2022). To reconcile project commissions with the ceiling on LNG imports, the cabinet-approved PDP8 assumes that 25,400 MW of installed capacity for LNG power will be converted to hydrogen in 2050; in this setup, the installed LNG power capacity in 2030 in the third draft can be kept intact.

The expectation of attracting international funding pushed the government to redirect the pathway towards an electricity system with large-scale ammonia-biomass co-firing, hydrogen, offshore and onshore wind, and solar combined (Figure 5.8). At COP 26, Vietnam fully endorsed all four clauses of the Global Coal to Clean Power Transition Statement: rapid scaling of clean power generation and energy efficiency measures; rapid ramping-up of technologies and policies to fully move away from unabated coal power generation; ceasing new unabated coal power projects; and a just and inclusive transition from unabated coal power (UN Climate Change Conference UK 2021, 2021). The endorsement opened a window of opportunities to gain international support for energy transitions through the Just Energy Transition Partnership and Asian Zero Emission Community, green credits, climate credits, and green bonds.

5.5.4 Transition to the Flexible Grid Paradigm or Fuel Shift

Our discussion here implies that the cabinet-approved PDP8 regards natural gas and LNG as a bridge fuel between coal and RES-E with rooftop solar and hydrogen combined rather than a flexible dispatchable generation in RES-based electricity systems. The government's pledge to net-zero emissions may result in a mere fuel switch from coal to gas unless ammonia, biomass, and hydrogen become commercially available on a large scale. While the ceiling of

LNG imports restricts imported LNG from being used for power, the government may accelerate the exploitation of domestic natural gas. Nonetheless, continuous external shocks, such as severe power outages in 2022, 2023, and 2024 triggered by heatwave-induced droughts and a reduction in coal imports,[3] destabilised the current regime, leading to institutional changes including the MOIT's approval of the provisional FiT rate for 15 out of 37 RES-E projects with a capacity of 1,200 MW (SGGP, 2023), despite possible harmful effects on vested interests of EVN. The same reason compelled the cabinet to decide on PDP8 with ambitious targets for LNG power and RES-E, followed by the full-fledged direct PPA.

These decisions would direct international investments towards large-scale RES-E generations such as offshore wind, and local banks and investors towards rooftop solar. The acceptance of private investments in the transmission grid and the operation of their invested grid in the 2022 Electricity Law is expected to minimise renewable curtailment (Hawkins, 2022) and move the electricity system towards being RES-based. However, such unpredictable and disorderly policy interventions can impede international green energy financing that is indispensable to moving electricity systems towards the flexible grid paradigm, not to mention the super-grid and the distributed smart-grid paradigms.

5.6 CONCLUSIONS

In this chapter, taking Vietnam as a country case, we analysed how the OECD and G20 agreements on ending officially supported export credits for unabated coal power plants and the pledge to the net-zero GHG emissions target have changed elements of the electricity system and affected the direction and speed of electricity system transitions. We explored how natural gas was considered in the drafting and approval of the PDP8, which has been revised several times to

[3] The risk of such power outages has repeatedly been warned of since 2019 (Bang, 2023).

accommodate the rapidly changing global energy landscape and exert influence on electricity system transitions.

The disorderly and abrupt nature of electricity system reform has critically affected the speed and direction of electricity system transitions. The negative implications of coal power plants, pledges to the Global Coal to Clean Power Transition Statement and net-zero emissions, international credit restrictions, developments of high-voltage backbone transmission grids, and competitive domestic solar PV production capacity worked as enabling factors to mitigate an increase in coal power capacity and generation. However, insufficient developments in infrastructure, institutions, and organisations have not only impeded the transition towards RES-based electricity systems, particularly super- and smart-grid paradigms, but also set up natural gas and LNG as bridge fuels between coal and RES-E with hydrogen combined rather than flexible dispatchable generation in RES-based electricity systems. Uncertain, abrupt, and disorderly policy intervention made RES-E projects less bankable, blocking developers and local banks from emerging and scaling as drivers for the transition. As such, the policy reinforced coal and gas inertia and lock-ins in the electricity system amid growing electricity demand and accelerated the fuel shift to natural gas. Past commissions of coal and gas power may direct the electricity system towards ammonia-biomass co-firing and hydrogen power to mitigate the stranding of fossil fuel assets once these technologies become commercially available on a large scale. It remains unexplored whether the full-fledged direct PPA can be a powerful driver to shift the transition pathway towards the distributed smart-grid paradigm.

These findings indicate the need for further research on this topic. Although our empirical case study showed the decisive enabling factors as well as barriers to the Vietnamese electricity system's transition towards an RES-based electricity system, some are context-specific and less likely to be generalisable for emerging economies and developing countries. Such factors and barriers include long-term planned gradual electricity sector reform, high national security concerns, and competitive domestic solar PV production capacity.

Chapter 6 will focus on the direction and speed of electricity system transitions in the Philippines, a country without context-specific favourable factors for the transition towards an RES-based electricity system.

6 Moving towards a Natural-Gas-Based Electricity System

Electricity System Transitions in the Philippines

6.1 INTRODUCTION

Since the early 2000s, the Philippines has gradually increased its power generation capacity to avoid electricity supply crises that might be triggered by rapid economic growth. Power generation doubled from 45 to 102 billion kWh from 2000 to 2020. Coal accounts for 58% of the energy mix in power generation, followed by natural gas (18%) and renewable energy (14%) as of 2021 (Figure 6.1). Oil is the main energy source in off-grid areas, accounting for 91% of the total supply there.

With the global pressure to reduce greenhouse gas (GHG) emissions, the Philippines submitted its updated nationally determined contribution (NDC) that increased its commitment to GHG emissions reduction from 70% to 75% from the business-as-usual (BAU) scenario in 2030 (Republic of the Philippines, 2015; 2021). In October 2020 the Philippines Department of Energy (DOE) set a moratorium on new coal plants, effectively cancelling, or at least stalling, 10,700 MW of coal power projects in the pipeline. The DOE also updated the Philippine Energy Plan to provide two energy scenarios: 35% renewable energy generation by 2040 (reference scenario) and 50% by 2040 (clean energy scenario).

However, the coal regime is too powerful and locked in for the country to achieve its NDC target. Domestic emitters are exempted from emissions reduction; unconditional contributions (contributions without international assistance) account for only 2.7% against a 75% reduction of the NDC target (Republic of the Philippines, 2021). Incumbent energy oligarchs mobilise political and

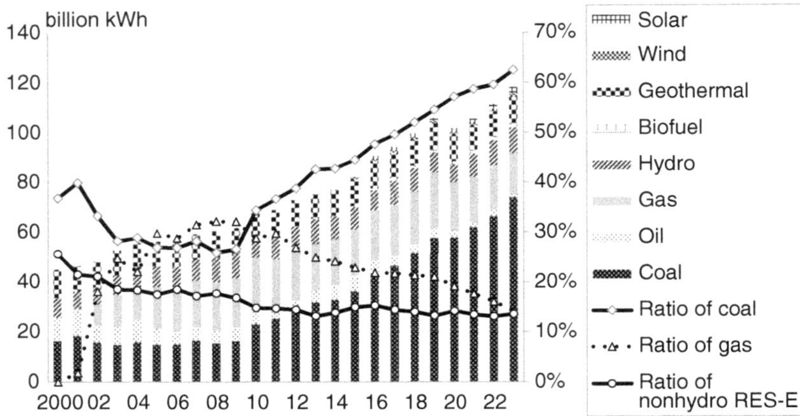

FIGURE 6.1 Power generation by type of energy in the Philippines, 2000–2023.
Source: Compiled by the authors based on data from IEA (2024a) and the Philippines Department of Energy (2024a).

economic resources to resist coal phase-out to avoid their 'young' coal power plants being stranded. Achieving 80% emissions reduction by 2040 would make 11 GW out of 14 GW of coal power assets stranded under the BAU scenario (World Bank Group, 2022). The government has emphasised improved energy security and reliability,[1] energy access, and energy products and services at no additional burden to energy consumers (Philippines Department of Energy, 2021a: 175). In this context, the moratorium on new coal power was implemented after the San Miguel Corporation (SMC) subsidiary Masinloc Power Partners commissioned a new 330 MW supercritical coal power project (Masinloc Power Partners Co Ltd, n.d.) and subsidiaries of Aboitiz and Ayala commissioned GNPower's two new 668 MW supercritical ones (Aboitiz Power, 2023). The moratorium is not applied to existing coal power plants with strong commitments to expansion plans, committed coal power projects, and indicative coal power projects with significant progress in securing the necessary

[1] The Luzon grid was predicted to suffer power outages in 2020 (Marollano, 2020).

permits. The government had not pledged to net-zero GHG emissions at the national level as of September 2023.[2]

In addition, some oligarch power generators have capitalised on the moratorium on new coal power and the depletion of the domestic Malampaya gas field to reorient their business from coal and natural gas to imported liquefied natural gas (LNG) (Table 6.1). Furthermore, the House of Representatives passed the Philippines Downstream Natural Gas Industry Development Act in August 2023 to use gas as a bridging fuel in transitions to an electricity system based on renewable-energy-sourced electricity (RES-E) (CEED Office, 2023).

The incumbent power generators' responses pose two research questions. First, will the Philippines' electricity regime change the energy mix from coal to LNG without transitions towards renewable-energy-based sources? Second, how do power generators and investors consider asset stranding in investing in new and additional gas assets?

Against this backdrop, we aimed to analyse the changes in the complementary elements of the electricity system in the Philippines to elucidate the direction and speed of electricity system transition. We then explored the drivers and barriers that significantly affect such transition. We conducted a document-based content analysis supplemented by semi-structured interviews.

The remainder of this chapter is organised as follows. Section 6.2 reviews electricity sector reform and RES-E development to demonstrate past trajectories that may have affected changes in the complementary elements of the electricity system. Section 6.3 presents the methodology and data collection strategy for this case study. Section 6.4 provides the results of the analysis, organised by grid paradigm and complementary element. Section 6.5 gives our interpretation of the results and a discussion of how changes in the complementary

[2] At the city level, Baguio, Quezon, Dipolog, and Vigan have committed to take part in the Cities Race to Zero campaign and have pledged to achieve net-zero emissions in their localities by 2050 or sooner (ICLEI, 2023).

Table 6.1 *Natural gas power projects in the Philippines as of October 2024*

Year	Plants	Capacity (MW)	Operator
Under operation		3,281	
2000	Santa Rita CCGT	1,043	First Gen
2002	San Lorenzo CCGT	530	First Gen
2002	Ilijan CCGT	1,200	KEPCO, Ilijan Corp/SMC
2016	San Gabriel CCGT	420	First Gen/South Premiere Power Corporation
2016	Avion OCGT	89	First Gen/Prime Meridian Powergen Corporation (PMPC)
Committed[a]		6,070	
2024	Batangas CCGT 1	1,320	Excellent Energy Resources/SMC
2029	Batangas LNG	1,100	Batangas Clean Energy/Ayala
TBD	650MW CCGT	650	Energy World Corporation
TBD	Batangas CCGT 2	440	Excellent Energy Resources/SMC
TBD	Natural Gas CCGT 1 & 2	2,560	Atimonan One Energy Inc./ Meralco Powergen Corp
Indicative[b]		7,146	
2026	San Francisco CCGT	1,200	Quezon Power/EGCO/Thailand, Doosan Enerbility/South Korea
2029	GNPower Sisiman CCGT	1,200	GNPower/Aboitiz
2029	VIRES Gas Floating	450	VIRES Energy/Singapore
2029	Pagbilao 4 & 5 CCGT	1,310	Therma Subic/Abolitz, JERA/ Japan
2029	GNPower Kauswagan LNG	600	GNPower/Aboitiz
TBD	Santa Maria CCGT	1,260	First Gen
TBD	GLEDC Luna LNG CCGT	1,126	Global Luzon Energy Development Corp./EDC

[a] 'Committed' projects are those with service contracts in place, that are in the development/commercial stage and financial closure, and that have been declared as 'committed' by the Department of Energy.

[b] 'Indicative' projects are those with service contracts and that are in the development/commercial stage but without financing closure.

Source: Compiled by the authors based on data from the Philippines Department of Energy (2024c).

elements have affected the direction and speed of electricity system transition. Finally, Section 6.6 concludes the chapter and provides suggestions for future research.

6.2 REVIEW OF THE ELECTRICITY SECTOR AND RES-E DEVELOPMENT

6.2.1 *Electricity Sector Reform*

The Philippines' electricity system has three main grids as well as off-grid electricity networks to supply electricity. Luzon, Visayas, and Mindanao represent the three main grids. While Luzon and Visayas have been interconnected since 1998, Mindanao became interconnected in 2023. Coupled with poor domestic energy resources, the fragmented electricity system has caused frequent unplanned power outages throughout the country. Rural electrification remains the government's top priority in energy policy (Philippines Department of Energy, 2021a).

The country's electricity system has been shaped through responses to crises in the power sector. The state-owned National Power Corporation (NPC) was a monopolised generation company, but severe power crises in 1989–1992 led to private investments in coal power. Gas power used natural gas from the Malampaya gas field under take-or-pay contracts. However, these contracts contributed to the financial crisis of the NPC within the Asian economic crisis of 1997–2001 (ADB, 2018). To address the financial crisis, the government legislated the Electric Power Industry Reform Act to unbundle generation, transmission, and distribution, privatise generation and grid operation, and liberalise generation and supply.

Unbundling and liberalisation shifted the electricity system towards a coal-based, oligopolistic one. In the process of privatisation, privately owned conglomerates took over power generation and joined the electricity market as independent power producers, becoming energy oligarchs. Persistent power crises with unplanned power outages during the 2010s prompted the government to increase the installed generation capacity (de la Cruz, 2014). In response, SMC, Aboitiz, and Ayala built new coal power plants or expanded existing capacity because coal plants were the quickest to build and the cheapest to operate. These coal power projects were delayed owing to fierce environmental opposition and consumers' reluctance to commit to off-take agreements (de la Cruz, 2013). Consumers suspected collusion among major suppliers that created an artificial power shortage and justified a major increase in electricity rates (Viola, 2019). Nonetheless, these investments increased the ratio of coal power to the total installed capacity from 32% in 2015 to 43% in 2021 (Figure 6.1).

Transmission assets are operated by the privately owned National Grid Corporation of the Philippines (NGCP) under a 25-year concession agreement. The distribution sector remains regulated as a public utility. Service providers, called distribution utilities (DUs), consist of private companies and electric cooperatives; they retain licenses and supply customers in franchise areas in a monopolistic manner. Qualified third-party providers are allowed to enter unviable areas to supply electricity. The country has 96 regionally monopolised DUs. Meralco, the Manila-based private-owned electric distribution utility company, is the largest, covering 38 cities and 73 municipalities and representing 75% of the total electricity consumption in Luzon and 55% of the total electricity consumption nationwide (Bacon, 2019). Meralco procures electricity from generation companies through power purchase agreements or from the wholesale electricity spot market (WESM).

6.2.2 *Stagnant RES-E Development Policies*

Under the Renewable Energy Act of 2008, the initial RES-E targets were determined as 800 MW: 50 MW for solar, 200 MW for wind, 250 MW for biomass, and 250 MW for run-of-the-river hydroelectricity. Feed-in tariffs (FiT), priority connections to the grid, priority purchase and transmission, and payment for RES-E were implemented to attain the targets. In 2015, the renewable target was raised to

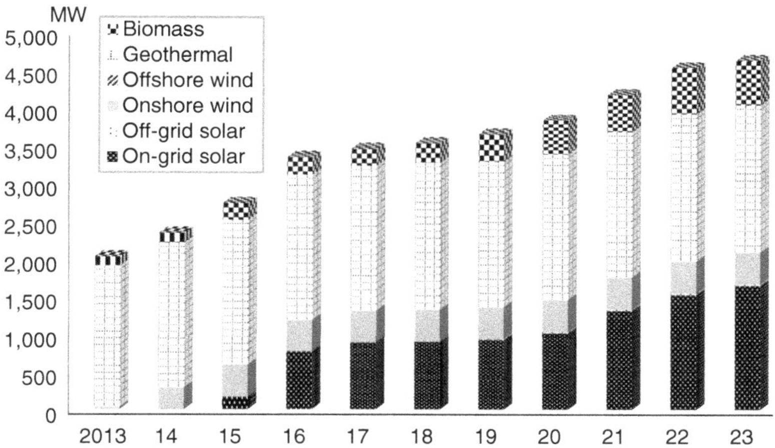

FIGURE 6.2 Installed capacity of renewables in the Philippines, 2013–2023.
Source: Compiled by the authors based on data from IRENA (2023; 2024) and the Philippines Department of Energy (2024b).

1,100 MW, of which 450 MW was to be solar and 150 MW wind. The revision invited a surge in solar and wind power investments. The installed capacity of wind power surged from 33 MW in 2013 to 427 MW in 2016, and that of solar power from 1 MW to 765 MW in the same period (Figure 6.2).

However, the surge in solar and wind capacity triggered curtailment. In Negros Island, the addition of solar power capacity amounted to 88% of peak demand. Combined with the priority dispatch given to solar and other newer forms of renewable energy under the Renewable Energy Act, the surge led to the curtailment of coal and geothermal generating capacity (Lagac & Yap, 2020). Nonetheless, 73% to 80% of the electricity being supplied to captive electricity consumers is sourced from coal and diesel plants, mostly outside Negros Island (Chan et al., 2020). The Dumaguete City government is initiating a big-ticket reclamation project to make effective use of excess capacity (Sorote, 2022).

Subsequently, a renewable portfolio standard (RPS) was implemented, requiring all mandated participants (MPs) to source or produce a specified portion of their electricity requirements from RES-E. The MPs include (i) all DUs for their captive customers; (ii) electricity suppliers for the contestable market; (iii) power-generating companies only to the extent of their actual supply to directly connected customers; and (iv) other electric power industry participants that may be recommended by the National Renewable Energy Board and approved by the DOE. The minimum annual RPS increment was initially set at 1% of the net electricity sales of the MPs for the previous year and raised to 2.52% in 2023 to achieve the country's aspirational target under the National Renewable Energy Program (NREP). The *aspirational* RES-E target under the NREP 2020–2040 is 35% or 15,304 MW by 2030 and 50% or 20 GW by 2040, as defined in the RPS On-Grid Rules (Philippines Department of Energy, 2022a).

The country implemented the Green Energy Tariff Program to replace a FiT to apply competitive auctions for RES-E projects, with 2,000 MW of planned RES-E capacity as the first round (Ahmed, 2020b). The programme enabled independent power suppliers to acquire supply from RES-E projects, making RES-E commercially viable and integrated into the grid (CEED Office, 2020). The renewable energy market also started an interim commercial operation in 2022, in which MPs can buy and sell Renewable Energy Certificates (RECs) to comply with the RPS On-Grid Rules (UNDP Philippines, 2022). The Green Energy Option Program (GEOP) was launched to allow end-users and DUs to procure electricity from their preferred RES-E suppliers. The number of RES-E suppliers under this programme increased from six in December 2020 to 19 in February 2023. Several incumbent power utilities, including Aboitiz, Ayala, and First Gen, are listed as green energy suppliers (Philippines Department of Energy, 2023b).

Furthermore, the 40% foreign ownership threshold for solar and wind projects was removed in 2022 to attract experienced international operators (Maguire, 2023). The removal enabled President Ferdinand Marcos Jr. to persuade nine Chinese firms to commit a collective USD 13.76 billion in renewable investment during his visit to Beijing in 2023 (Norman, 2023a). Foreign investments are expected to increase if Competitive Renewable Energy Zones (CREZ) are built to eliminate regulatory bottlenecks, avoid land permit obstacles, and support efficient, reliable, and resilient power system operation through interconnection (Capongcol et al., 2020).

6.2.3 Impacts of Grid Systems on RES-E Development

The unbundled electricity system allows DUs to pass on the high cost of RES-E procurement to customers. The pass-on has mixed implications in electricity system transition. On the one hand, the government can accelerate RES-E without incurring the high initial capital costs of RES-E generation plants (Guild, 2019), which are relatively high owing to a lack of domestic technology production capacity. On the other hand, consumers may suffer from high electricity tariffs. Replacing coal with RES-E can increase electricity tariffs if the levelised cost of RES-E is higher than that of coal power.

Heavy dependence on international assistance can also have mixed effects. On the one hand, it motivates energy oligarchs to invest in RES-E generation. AC Energy pledged coal divestments by 2030 and increased greenfield and brownfield RES-E investments. Meralco, an energy oligarch with the largest share of electricity sales (38% in February 2022) (Philippines Department of Energy, 2022d), has also installed utility-scale solar and wind power capacity (Philippines Department of Energy, 2023c). The moratorium on new coal power may reinforce the shift in investments. On the other hand, heavy dependence on assistance can impede the transition to RES-based electricity systems for two reasons. First, incumbent utilities are motivated to negotiate *realistic* RES-E targets, considering the perceived intolerable stranded costs derived from the retirement of many 'young' coal power assets. Second, they may seek the borrowing of RECs to minimise the loss of return from early investments. Banking of RECs for two to three years before the starting year of RPS can enable MPs to comply with the annual

RPS requirement by 2022. However, the higher minimum annual RPS increment, coupled with the replacement of FiT with the Green Energy Tariff Program, is predicted to generate a shortfall of RECs from 2024 onwards, because most RECs come from FiT-eligible RES-E plants (Philippines Department of Energy, 2022a). In addition, the cost decline of utility-scale solar PV and battery energy storage systems (ESS) could enable the country to achieve a 100% RES-E system by 2050 with a cost comparable to the energy system in 2015 (Gulagi et al., 2021).

6.3 METHODOLOGY AND DATA

6.3.1 *Research Design*

In this chapter, we employed a case study method with an inductive, longitudinal single-country case study design. This method is suitable for testing internal validity and affirming the correctness of the inference and rival explanations. It is also relevant in testing external validity and acknowledging analytical generalisations (Yin, 2018). Along with the single-case study of Vietnam in Chapter 5, the study in this chapter is thus part of a multi-case study, which can provide stronger evidence for the relevance of the initial set of propositions and the insights into them (Sovacool et al., 2018). A comparative analysis based on the framework in Chapter 3 provides generalised implications on electricity system transitions from the coal-based system in emerging and developing countries. We used the framework built in Chapter 3 to analyse the direction and speed of electricity system transition based on changes in complementary elements. We performed document-based content analysis as it is appropriate for testing well-structured research questions with a priori analytical categories (Sovacool et al., 2018).

6.3.2 *Data Sources*

We relied on holistic data collection strategies. We used data from secondary sources, such as academic books, articles, and grey literature published by the Asian Development Bank (ADB), the World Bank, and the Centre for Energy, Ecology, and Development (CEED); and primary sources, such as government documents, reports and press releases by power companies, business journals, and daily newspapers. To study incumbent companies, we derived data from annual reports and press releases issued by the DOE. We collected documents from online archives by searching for keywords. In addition, we conducted semi-structured interviews with DOE officials, representatives of incumbent generators, and members of research institutions in January 2023 to deepen our understanding of the contexts behind these materials.

6.4 RESULTS

6.4.1 *Transitions towards the Super-Grid Paradigm*

6.4.1.1 *Infrastructure: High-Voltage Backbone Transmission Lines*

Transmission Development Plans (TDPs) have prioritised load growth, generation entry, power quality, system reliability, and island interconnection (NGCP, 2016; 2019; 2020b). Generation entry refers to the accommodation of new power plant connections to the grid and bulk generation capacity additions that drive new transmission backbone development. Generation capacity additions are referred to as conventional large-scale fossil fuel and hydro powers. However, RES-E is explicitly included in the Transmission Development Plan 2022–2040 (NGCP, 2022). Smart grid, grid resiliency, energy storage systems, and CREZ are listed as priority projects for the first time in the plan. TDPs have placed different priorities on transmission developments by grid for intra-grid transmission (NGCP, 2016). This accrues to the differences in transmission bottlenecks by region: persistent power shortage in the Luzon grid, coal and geothermal curtailment in Visayas, and sustained supply deficits in Mindanao.

In Luzon, the initial focus was strengthening the transmission system and improving the reliability and resilience of connections with generation capacities. For this purpose, NGCP invested in extensions of the existing 500 kV transmission backbone and developed a looping of the Northern Luzon 230 kV backbone. NGCP also upgraded the Luzon–Visayas interconnection to high-voltage direct current transmission lines and released a policy framework on ancillary service provision and procurement to attract contracts with ancillary service suppliers when the power shortage became persistent (Marollano, 2020). The Batangas–Mindoro Interconnection was developed to integrate wind power in Mindoro into the Luzon grid (ADB, 2017).

The focus in Visayas has been developing backbone transmission and procuring additional ancillary services, particularly regulating reserves, and frequency response. For the latter's purpose, NGCP is developing the Cebu–Negros–Panay 230 kV backbone transmission project. It has concluded an engineering, procurement, and construction (EPC) contract with Chinese cable producer ZTT Submarine Cable & System to install a subsea cable for the Negros–Panay interconnector as the first stage (Rivera, 2022). Meanwhile, in Mindanao the focus has been on transmission projects that can facilitate investments in new generation capacity. Mindanao has gone through half a century of armed conflict over the right to self-determination of the Muslim population; preventing future bombings of power industry assets, such as transmission towers and substations, is a serious challenge going beyond the scope of the electricity sector (Philippines Department of Energy, 2016).

Mindanao–Visayas interconnections have been developed under the umbrella of the One Grid Philippines Plan (NGCP, 2020a). It was completed in 2023 (NGCP, 2023) after a three-year delay due to the COVID-19 pandemic, right-of-way issues, and damage to a 350 kV high-voltage direct-current submarine fibre-optic cable (Romero, 2016). The completion enables DUs and bulk users to purchase electricity from the WESM and thus use the generating capacity more efficiently through the merit order effect.

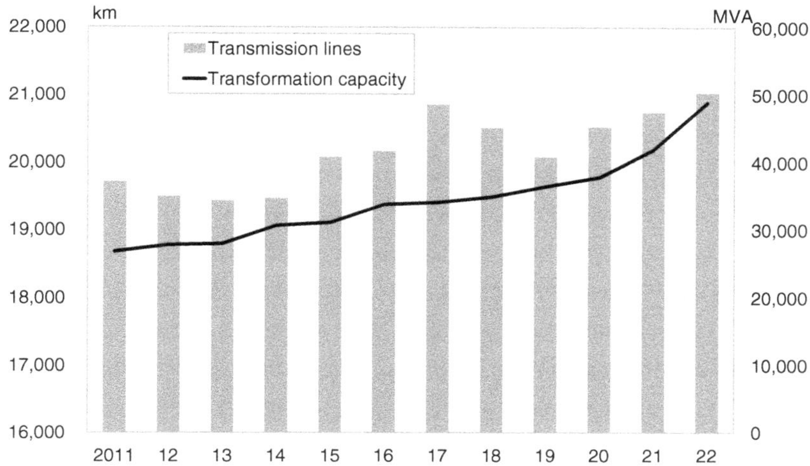

FIGURE 6.3 Development of grid network in the Philippines, 2011–2021.
Source: Compiled by the authors based on data from the Philippines Department of Energy (2022c).

In line with the projected peak demand and generation capacity addition in the TDP, NGCP expanded substation capacity annually by 4.1% from 2011 to 2020. By contrast, the extension of transmission lines is slower, only by 0.2% or 80 km annually (Figure 6.3), owing in part to modernisation and divestments of various sub-transmission assets (NGCP, 2019). Several transmission projects scheduled to be completed in 2020 have been delayed, primarily by the COVID-19 pandemic and prevailing right-of-way issues (Philippines Department of Energy, 2021b).

In addition, small-scale additional capacities are not always associated with transmission development. They are connected to the distribution system and thus are regarded as the responsibility of DUs (NGCP, 2016). Slow progress and uncertain grid accessibility may have slowed or discouraged the installation of new RES-E because new transmission backbone line developments are typically required first for new power plants with large installed capacities (NGCP, 2022).

6.4.1.2 *Infrastructure: Run-of-the-River and Pumped Storage Hydropower*

According to the Energy Plan 2020–2040, which counts on last-minute commitments to new coal power plants,[3] installed capacity of non-hydro RES-E is projected to increase by 10 times to 34 GW (Figure 6.4), and generation to increase by five times to 61 TWh, from 2020 to 2040 in the Reference Scenario (Figure 6.5). In the Clean Energy Scenario, installed capacity would increase by 16 times to account for 52% of the total, and generation by eight times to account for 32%. The plan assumes pumped storage hydropower will be used as a flexible dispatchable fuel to ensure grid reliability. Hydropower is projected to increase by four times in the Reference Scenario, and five times in the Clean Energy Scenario, respectively.

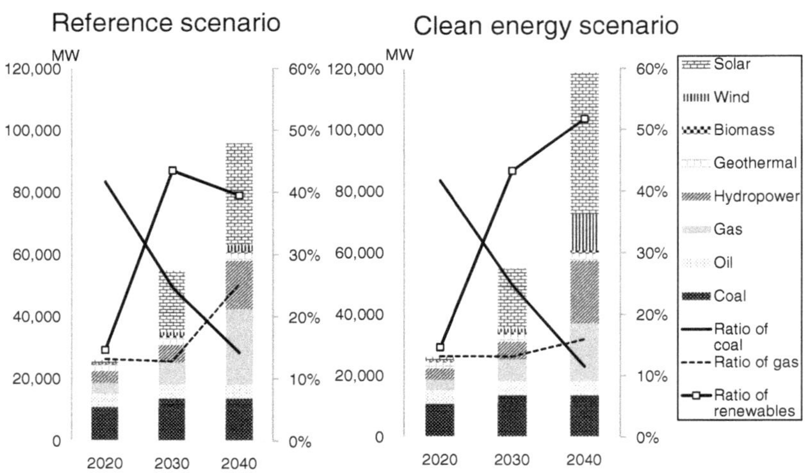

FIGURE 6.4 Energy mix in installed capacity in the Philippines Energy Plan, 2020–2040.
Source: Compiled by the authors based on data from the Philippines Department of Energy (2021a).

[3] The Philippines Energy Plan 2020–2040 updated the previously published Power Development Plan 2020–2040, which had assumed no additional coal power capacity.

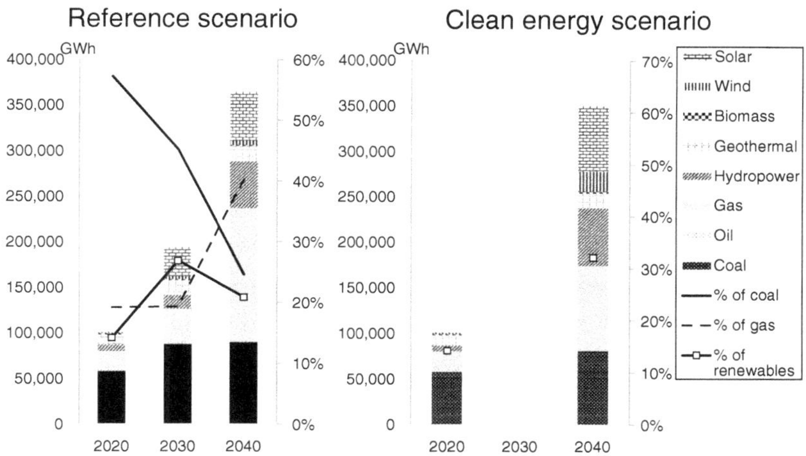

FIGURE 6.5 Energy mix in generation in the Philippines Energy Plan, 2020–2040.
Source: Compiled by the authors based on data from the Philippines Department of Energy (2021a).

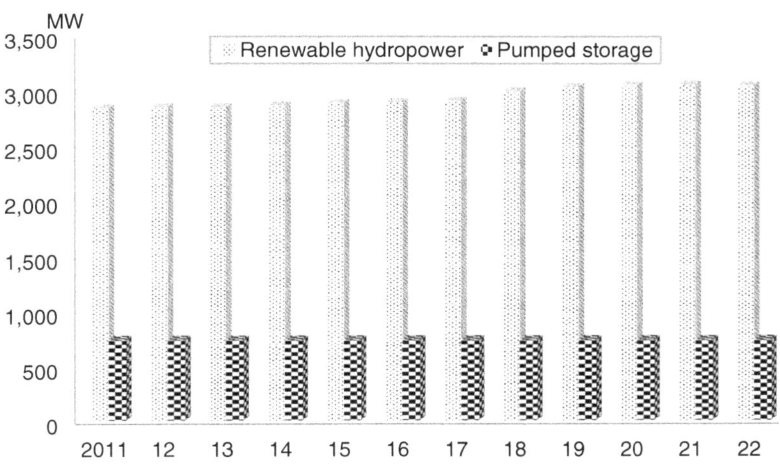

FIGURE 6.6 Breakdown of installed capacity of hydropower in the Philippines, 2011–2022.
Source: Compiled by the authors based on data from IRENA (2021; 2024).

It has become ecologically and socially challenging to develop new large-scale pumped storage hydropower. It took several years for the ongoing 500 MW pumped storage hydropower project to decide on the location and additional years to start commissions (Santos, 2022a). The installed capacity of hydropower has increased by only 200 MW from 2011 to 2022; most additional capacity is small-scale, and none is pumped storage (Figure 6.6). Most of the run-of-the-river hydropower is too small for pumped storage. Moreover, hydropower cannot be exempted from large seasonal fluctuations (ADB, 2018). However, existing hydropower helps generators win bids to supply ancillary services. Incumbent power generators acquire assets of state-owned NPC in the privatisation process and use their old hydropower for ancillary services.

6.4.1.3 Institution: Procurement of Renewable Energy-Based Electricity and Capacity

The Ancillary Services Policy was implemented in 2019 to increase flexibility in clean power generation. The policy mandated NGCP, as system operator, to procure five ancillary service products for grid reliability: three frequency control products (regulating, contingency, and dispatchable reserves), one voltage control product, and one system restoration product. Generating units and qualified reserve-providing facilities were allowed to provide ancillary service products if they met the requirements in the Energy Regulatory Commission's (ERC) Ancillary Services Procurement Plan. The WESM and the Ancillary Services Policy were expected to give additional flexibility to the grid system. A competitive selection process was also instituted to mandate all DUs to secure power supply agreements and provide adequate and proper power supply contracting through a transparent procedure. This was to protect end-users from unnecessary exposure to the volatility of spot prices in the WESM that redounds to the least-cost supply of electricity.

However, the Ancillary Services Policy has failed to attract sufficient frequency control reserves to enhance grid reliability. The standard five-year contract with one-size-fits-all pricing for any type of technology and costs made new investments in technologies, particularly those suitable for grid reliability such as pumped storage hydropower and battery storage systems, financially unviable (Barroco, 2021). Instead, the contract attracted technologies with low fixed costs such as heavy fuel oil, diesel, and fully depreciated hydropower, and energy oligarchs capable of financing power generation with corporate finance (NGCP, 2021).

In response, the DOE issued an advisory for NGCP to convert from non-firm to firm Ancillary Services Procurement Agreements within 30 days and to procure firm ancillary services only through a competitive selection process specific to ancillary services. In addition, it designated all RES-E as preferential dispatch in the WESM (Philippines Department of Energy, 2023b). These adjustments have not shown visible effects in reconciling grid integration of RES-E and grid stability. The NGCP resisted the conversion of all the monthly-based firm agreements and filed a motion for reconsideration (Velasco, 2023). The lack of technical specifications in the Competitive Selection Process (CSP) or RES-E-specific CSP keeps incentivising DUs to procure coal power as the least-cost electricity (CEED Office, 2021). Meralco de facto excludes most RES-E generators from procurement by imposing a minimum capacity offer of 150 MW (net) per bidder; notably, only 12.5% of proposed renewable energy plants have an installed capacity of at least 150 MW (de Torres, 2020).

Consequently, the Luzon grid cannot overcome the persistence of insufficient reserves and power interruptions. The number of alerts warning about possible power interruptions and outages has increased since 2019 (Viola, 2019). While power generators' collusion to create an artificial power shortage and justify a major increase in electricity rates was alleged to have caused the power outage in 2013, inadequacies in the transmission system were seen as the causes in 2019–2023 (Power Philippines News, 2023a). NGCP has delayed at least 71 projects and completed only six of the 16 transmission projects considered nationally significant, causing substantial delays in increasing the installed capacity of both fossil-fuel-based and RES-E (Power Philippines News, 2023b). NGCP is alleged to charge customers for projects even before full completion, undermining the agency's credibility (Power Philippines News, 2023c). These barriers indicate paramount challenges for the Philippines' electricity system to generate co-evolution among infrastructural, institutional, and organisational elements and to transit towards the super-grid paradigm.

6.4.2 Transitions towards the Distributed Smart-Grid Paradigm

6.4.2.1 Infrastructure: Smart Grid

Smart-grid development has also been slow. The instability of the grid system and the resultant power outage in 2016 pushed Meralco to invest in smart grids. The company expected that automated smart meters and an automated metering infrastructure would drive increases in customer base, because such technologies enabled customers to implement energy management and demand response through time-of-use power pricing and to access prepaid electricity services (Nhede, 2016).

To accelerate smart-grid development, the government implemented the National Smart Grid Policy Framework and Roadmap in 2020, showing the steps to achieve the Smart Grid Vision by 2040 and monitoring the progress to push DUs to digitise networks and consumer services (Philippines Department of Energy, 2020). However, Meralco had deployed only 100,000 smart meters by the first half of 2020 compared with its plan of 3.3 million by 2024 (Business World, 2020). The company extended the deadline to 2028 and reset the rollout target to 2 million by 2026 (Velasco, 2022a). Nonetheless, as of November 2022, Meralco is evaluated as the top runner, the only utility that has gone beyond the development of power outage management systems and smart meter reading to install advanced distribution management systems and scale automated metering infrastructure. In contrast, 28% of DUs rely on manually operated network systems and 45% on conventional metering (Freedom of Information Philippines, 2022).

6.4.2.2 *Institution: Demand-Side Integration*

To deploy small-scale (less than 100 kW) distributed energy resources (DERs), the DOE implemented net metering in 2013, with the support of Deutsche Gesellschaft für Internationale Zusammenarbeit. DUs are allowed to use the electricity derived from the net metering programme as the equivalent REC (Philippines Department of Energy, 2022b). However, net metering has had only marginal effects on boosting rooftop solar energy. Rooftop solar amounted to 32 MW out of 1,019 MW, or 3% of solar power capacity, in 2020; notably, 85% of rooftop participants are in metropolitan Manila.[4] Financial barriers, particularly high installation costs, make households hesitant to install rooftop solar (Farias-Rocha et al., 2019).

To address these barriers, several renewable policies have been updated and stipulated (Ahmed, 2018). These include (a) increasing the size limit for the net metering programme from 100 kW to 1 MW to incentivise both large and small commercial and industrial players to adopt solar rooftop systems, (b) setting a clear deadline and standardising the permit process to complete the interconnection process, (c) removing the Distribution Impact Study fee and other related soft costs, (d) allowing remuneration for up to 30% of the surplus power supplied from RES-E generation to the grid (Bellini, 2022; ERC, 2019), and (e) a burden-sharing rule for bi-directional and REC meter installation and wiring costs. DUs are allowed to bank net metering REC in exchange for opening the net metering programme to prospective prosumers in off-grid areas. Qualified net metering end-users are allowed to generate up to 100 kW of electricity from RES-E for their use and sell their excess to the grid.

However, the space for small-scale DERs is limited to off-grid areas. Qualified net metering end-users are prohibited from exporting electricity more than imports at the end of each calendar year (Philippines Department of Energy, 2022b). Grid integration is

[4] The installed capacity of qualified net metering rooftop solar PV increased to 60 MW in 2022 (Bunda et al., 2023).

not permitted to distribute RES-E suppliers and third-party energy aggregators. They are regarded as destabilising grids without REC or aggregated contracting (ADB, 2017).

6.4.3 *Transitions towards the Flexible Grid Paradigm*

6.4.3.1 *Infrastructure: Battery Energy Storage Systems*

SMC Global Power began investing in 31 battery ESS with a combined capacity of 1 GW (Jose, 2022). The company plans to operate over 70 battery ESS with a combined capacity of 2 GW when it has completed all the committed projects (see Table 6.2). Aboitiz has teamed up with Japan's Kawasaki to invest in five battery ESS projects and EDC in four projects (Table 6.2). The Philippines' battery ESS capacity will exceed 4 GW in 2030 if all committed and indicative projects are completed.

In addition, the Philippine government perceives natural gas as a clean and indigenous source of energy and as a balancing energy that satisfies the intermediate or mid-merit supply requirements in the grid (Philippines Department of Energy, 2021a: 84). After the moratorium on new coal power, it sees natural gas as a major alternative to coal for power that satisfies the growing electricity demand. In the Philippines Energy Plan 2020–2040, the installed capacity of natural gas power is projected to increase seven times from 2020 to 2040, accounting for 25% of the total capacity in 2040, and generation is projected to amount to 7.5 times higher and account for 40% of total capacity. In the Clean Energy Scenario, an increase in natural gas power generation will be restricted to less than five times owing to the significant increases in solar, wind, and hydropower. The installed capacity and generation of natural gas power will account for 16% and 27% of the national total.

In line with these energy scenarios, the government has approved investments in floating storage and regasification terminals for imported LNG. Various firms are constructing floating storage and regasification terminals: Linseed Field Power Corporation, a Singapore-based Atlantic Gulf & Pacific Company subsidiary,

Table 6.2 *Private-sector-initiated energy storage system projects in the Philippines as of October 2024*

Year	Operator	Number of projects	Capacity (MW)
Battery ESS under operation		21	599
2018	Masinloc Power Partners/SMC	1	12
2022	SMCGP Philippines Energy Storage/SMC	2	35
2022	Giga Ace 4/Ayala	1	60
2022	Therma Marine/Aboitiz	1	49
2023	SMGP BESS Power Inc/SMC	9	280
2024	SMGP BESS Power Inc/SMC	6	130
2024	SN Aboitiz	1	32
Committed battery ESS projects		62	1,870
2024	SMGP BESS Power Inc/SMC	10	260
2024	EDC	3	90
2024	Fort Pilar Energy	1	20
2025	SMGP BESS Power Inc/SMC	4	110
2025	EDC	1	30
2025	Fort Pilar Energy	3	80
2025	AP Renewables Inc.	1	20
TBD	SMGP BESS Power Inc/SMC	39	1,260
Indicative battery ESS projects		51	1,952
2025	Gritstone Lead Power	1	41
2025	Megawatt Solutions Inc.	6	240
2025	Global Business Power Corporation	4	68
2025	Belgrove Power	1	20
2026	SN Aboitiz	3	96
2026	Megawatt Solutions Inc.	3	120
2026	Helios Energy Storage Corp.	1	200
2026	Global Business Power Corporation	3	60
2026	Therma	2	148
2026	SPC Island Power	2	80
2026	East Asia Utilities	1	30
2027	Helios Energy Storage Corp.	9	500
2027	Global Business Power Corporation	3	48

Table 6.2 *(cont.)*

Year	Operator	Number of projects	Capacity (MW)
TBD	Global Business Power Corporation	1	20
TBD	Cell Power Energy Corporation	10	240
TBD	Therma	1	42
Indicative pumped hydro projects		2	560
2028	San Roque Hydropower Inc.	2	560

Source: Compiled by the authors based on data from the Philippines Department of Energy (2024c).

US-based Excellent Energy with Cebu-based Topline Energy and Power Development, Australia-listed Energy World, Shell, Vires Energy, and Samat (Cabico, 2022). The seven LNG import terminals with a combined capacity of 22 million tons per annum are expected to support LNG imports for gas power plants with a combined capacity of more than 3,000 MW (de la Cruz, 2023; Mercurio, 2023a).

In response, SMC has become proactive in investing in LNG power. Despite being removed from the list of committed and indicative private-sector-initiated power projects, the 1,200 MW Ilijan gas power plant will resume operation once the first LNG import terminal is ready for commissioning (Mercurio, 2023b) and NGCP completes the development of the Balsik-San Jose 500 kV transmission line (Philippines Department of Energy, 2023a). Through its subsidiary Excellent Energy Resources, SMC will start operating three 440 MW combined cycle gas turbines (CCGT) in Batangas and is committed to another 440 MW plant (Table 6.1). First Gen, which has operated gas power plants for decades, will supply LNG for existing and proposed 1,260 MW gas power plants (Power Philippines News, 2022). For this purpose, the company teamed up with Tokyo Gas to develop an interim offshore terminal and a floating storage and regasification unit for imported LNG located at its Clean Energy Complex in Batangas (Pekic, 2022). Meralco is also committed to four 640MW CCGT through its subsidiary of Atimonan One Energy.

These natural gas power and LNG terminal projects have not been without problems. Energy World's planned LNG terminal and 650 MW gas power plant were put on hold after the NGCP claimed that unsecured right-of-way permissions to carry out the transmission installations and upgrades blocked the construction of the necessary local substation (Oxford Business Group, 2021). Phoenix Petroleum Philippines withdrew its application to build an LNG terminal in 2021 despite teaming up with CNOOC Gas and Power and getting notice to proceed from the government in 2018 (Rivera, 2021).

6.4.3.2 Institutions: Bidding for Ancillary Service Contracts

Behind the boost in battery ESS investments is the government's framework for ESS integration in the electricity supply chain to stimulate investments in ESS that supply electricity and ancillary services (Philippines Department of Energy, 2019b). Generation companies, DUs, directly connected customers, end-users winning and operating ESS, qualified third parties, transmission network providers, system operators, and market operators are eligible for granted licenses to provide electricity, ancillary services, and demand and quality management.

6.5 DISCUSSION

6.5.1 Unsynchronised Developments in Infrastructural and Organisational Elements

The results of this analysis are summarised in Table 6.3, which shows that the institutional developments under two decades of electricity sector reform can move the electricity system towards an RES-based one. The system operates the WESM, RES-E market, and bidding mechanism for ancillary and system-balancing services and implements retail competition, which is indispensable for either grid paradigm.

Table 6.3 *Changes in complementarity elements of electricity systems in the Philippines, by paradigm*

Super-grid paradigm	Flexible grid paradigm	Smart-grid paradigm
Infrastructure		
Connecting lines and extra-high-voltage backbone transmission lines		National Smart Grid Policy Framework and Roadmap (2020)
Completed inter-connection of transmission lines (2023)		
Lack of transformers		
Privatisation and renovation of existing hydropower and pumped storager		
Organisations		
Strong bargaining power of incumbent generators and distributors		No energy aggregators
		No local banks to provide loans
Institutions		
Wholesale electricity spot market for Luzon and Visayas in (2010) and nationwide (2023)	Bidding mechanism for ancillary and system-balancing services (2019)	No direct power purchase agreements
Green Energy Tariff Program (2020)	No reserve market or capacity payment contracts	Third-party access in off-grid areas (2019)
Renewable energy market launched interim commercial operation (2022)	Licensing for energy battery system (2019)	Licensing for energy battery system (2019)
		No time-based tariff
		Retail Competition and Open Access (2004)

Note: Light grey colour implies weak barriers; dark grey, strong; and medium grey, the middle range.
Source: Authors.

By contrast, the direction and speed of changes in infrastructure have not been commensurate with institutional developments. NGCP's priority on connecting new large-scale generation plants, lack of credibility (Ahmed, 2020a), and difficulties in private land appropriation have delayed developments of high-voltage backbone and interconnection transmission grids. Delays in backbone and interconnection transmission grids have blocked the efficient trading of electricity across regions in WESM. As such, the electricity system is impeded from moving towards the super-grid paradigm.

The moratorium on new coal power destabilised the electricity regime, prompting all the energy oligarchs to set out RES-E targets to change their electricity portfolios. Ayala has accelerated its divestment of thermal assets and increased investments in RES-E to achieve its commitment to 100% RES-E generation by 2025 and the goal of reaching 20 GW of RES-E capacity by 2030. It has attempted to capitalise on RE100, a global initiative by the world's most influential businesses committed to using 100% renewable electricity in their operations, to switch suppliers through the GEOP and Retail Competition and Open Access (ACEN RES, 2023). EDC has capitalised on its knowledge, prior experience, and organisational culture to accelerate investments in geothermal, hydropower, and LNG power. Similarly, SMC and First Gen are focused on LNG power (First Gen, 2020; San Miguel Global Power, n.d.). Even Aboitiz, which had acquired coal power assets from Ayala shortly before the moratorium (Power Philippines News 2020; 2021), is committed to a half–half portfolio mix of RES-E and thermal capacities by 2030 (Aboitiz, 2023). However, Ayala has invested in international RES-E projects by a much larger amount than in the Philippines, perceiving prolonged renewable curtailment (ACEN, 2023b). Helios and Barracuda decided to invest in solar and wind power and battery ESS combined to reduce curtailment risk (Table 6.2).

Delays in high-voltage transmission line development have also justified the restrictive net metering and smart-grid policy, thus deterring transitions to the distributed smart-grid paradigm. The restrictive net metering policy prevents DER generators, such as rooftop solar, from gaining profits and scaling, and thus restricts renewable energy financing from boosting. Uncertain grid access, tight FiT deadlines, low technology-specific capacity caps, and low supply requirements from RES-E in the RPS additionally increase revenue uncertainty for both DER and utility-scale RES-E generators.[5] These collectively block stakeholders from concluding revenue contracts and discourage local banks from accessing non-recourse financing and providing extended-maturity financing. Local banks adhere to the conventional business model of asset-based commercial loans and collateral requirements, which remain high financial barriers to most RES-E project developers.[6]

While policy banks are proactive in renewable energy financing, the Development Bank of the Philippines is accessible only to large-scale projects that can provide sufficient collateral. The Land Bank of the Philippines is also accessible only to large-scale agriculture-related projects, such as solar sharing. The 40% foreign ownership threshold prevents foreign investors and financial institutions from providing commercial loans and non-recourse financing. These barriers force RES-E generators and project developers to revert to corporate finance as the only available financial source for the best-capitalised providers and most profitable projects (Barroco & Herrera, 2019).

6.5.2 Incumbents' Strong Bargaining Power

Institutional developments in competitive retail and ancillary service procurement have not been powerful enough to redirect incumbent distributors to procure RES-E on a large scale. The fundamental notion of having conventional power plants as baseload generation remains predominant (Gulagi et al., 2021), despite the implementation of

[5] The requirement rate was raised from 1% to 2.5% in 2022, against the target of 35% in 2030 (Asian Power, 2023).

[6] Interview with One Renewable on 18 January 2023.

economic dispatch and procurement of balancing energy with merit order. The captive market and DUs own and build power plants to procure up to 50% of their demand from these plants (Bacon, 2019). Coupled with long-term power purchase contracts with fossil-fuel-sourced electricity, their procurement practices narrow the space for off-taking from RES-E.

Meralco has been criticised for procuring expensive electricity from coal power in the long term and passing on high fuel costs to customers (de Torres, 2020). When Meralco changed the energy mix of its baseload generation capacity in 2022, it procured 500 MW mid-merit capacity through scheduled bidding, 300 MW RES-E baseload capacity, and 600 MW conventional baseload capacity. The 500 MW mid-merit capacity was set to come from pumped hydro storage facilities (Velasco, 2022b). Notably, off-take from utility-scale solar is marginal (Meralco, 2022).

Nonetheless, NGCP has decided on the pricing and energy/event-triggered compensation systems for ancillary services by type of service without consideration for differences in the types of technology. This pricing makes the revenue of service suppliers uncertain and highly volatile, encouraging technologies with low fixed costs, such as heavy fuel oil, diesel, and fully depreciated coal power plants, to be employed as flexible dispatchable generation in the Ancillary Service Procurement Agreements (Barroco & Herrera, 2019). Meanwhile, incumbent generators and DUs have capitalised on the ESS framework to initiate large-scale front-of-the-meter (FTM) battery ESS projects, once solar photovoltaic combined with battery ESS proved to be competitive for baseloads below 11 MW in grid applications (Jose, 2022). The reactions of incumbent generators and DUs block the electricity system from moving towards the super-grid and distributed smart-grid paradigms.

6.5.3 *Transition to the Flexible Grid Paradigm or Fuel Shift*

Ongoing CREZ with sufficient grid connection capacity can reconcile the integration of several utility-scale RES-E projects with adequacy requirements with minimum additional grid investments to address congestion (NGCP, 2019), thus helping overcome the time differences between fast-growing RES-E and connecting transmission developments (NGCP, 2016). Moreover, the framework for battery ESS and the subsequent boost of FTM battery ESS investments requires relatively few changes in institutional and infrastructural elements, making it easier to redirect the electricity system towards the flexible paradigm. A future vision for hydrogen power may further persuade incumbent generators to invest in LNG power, which can be used as new power capacity in the short run but as flexible capacity in the long run (Flores, 2023).

However, using natural gas and LNG power as new capacity increases the risk of falling into a mere fuel shift and gas lock-in in the worst-case scenario. Given huge investment requirements in LNG assets and infrastructure, gas power for ancillary services tends to strand assets. The fact that energy oligarchs make large investments in LNG assets suggests that they will exercise their bargaining power to block the electricity system from transitioning towards an RES-based one, even the flexible grid paradigm, to avoid death spiralling and asset stranding.

Our arguments imply that incumbent power generators and distributors can affect the direction and speed of electricity system transitions even in a system with vertical unbundling and competitive markets. The underdevelopment of high-voltage backbone and interconnection transmission grids impedes the efficient operation of markets, prolonging the switch from long-term power purchase agreements with coal power generation to market procurement of RES-E, even if the institutions are already in place. The prevalence and strong bargaining power of incumbent power utilities block new organisations from emerging and supplying a variety of flexibility for grid stability. With the set of infrastructural, institutional, and organisational elements, the coal power moratorium is likely to induce a fuel switch rather than a transition to an RES-based electricity system.

6.6 CONCLUSIONS

Under electricity sector reform since the early 2000s, the Philippines' electricity regime has been dominated by conglomerate-energy-oligarch-generated coal power. The moratorium on new coal power in 2020 destabilised the regime, prompting oligarchs to reorganise their business portfolios. The government has encouraged LNG projects to increase LNG imports for power to ensure energy security, and the House of Representatives passed an act to use gas as a bridge fuel, rather than accelerating the transition to RES-based electricity systems.

Against this backdrop, we analysed the changes in complementary elements of the electricity system in the Philippines to elucidate the direction and speed of electricity system transition. We also explored the drivers and barriers that significantly affect transition. We conducted a document-based content analysis supplemented by semi-structured interviews.

Our findings show that delays in grid infrastructure development have critically affected the direction of transitions despite two decades of institutional reform consistent with the development of RES-based electricity systems. However, the delays make it difficult to overcome the vested interests of energy oligarchs. These energy oligarchs capitalise on new institutions to increase economic gains under the coal moratorium by supplying ancillary services from their old hydropower plants, fully depreciated coal power plants, large-scale battery ESS, and gas power.

We also found that such delays and restrictive RES-E policy affect the speed of transition. Uncertain grid access, tight FiT deadlines, low technology-specific capacity caps, and low supply requirements from RES-E in the RPS increase the revenue uncertainty of RES-E investments, making local banks hesitant to finance them. Long-term contracts and PPAs block distributors and consumers from changing procurement from coal to RES-E suppliers despite developing WESM and implementing merit order supply requirements. Furthermore, energy security concerns, such as the perceived growth of electricity demand and the depletion of domestic gas fields, motivate the government and politicians to use natural gas as an additional generation rather than a balancing power. Anticipating future renovation to hydrogen co-firing, incumbent power generators perceive low stranded costs for new gas assets. All these factors have directed the Philippines' electricity system towards a natural-gas-based system, combined with the flexible paradigm in the RES-based system with a few clean dispatchable capacities.

These findings indicate the need for further research on the tipping point separating the transition towards the flexible paradigm in the RES-based electricity system and lock-ins to gas power. Gas power will be locked in under the current intolerably high levelised cost of hydrogen power. By contrast, China's experience indicates that developments of high-voltage backbone and interconnection transmission networks and grids can overcome local protests seeking to protect vested interests (Mori, 2018), reduce renewable curtailment, and weaken the bargaining power of incumbent utility companies by widening conflicts of interest among them (Mori, 2021a). Thus, development in grid infrastructure can block gas lock-in and redirect the transition pathway towards the RES-based system.

Nonetheless, grid development has become a political controversy in the Philippines after the State Grid Corporation of China acquired a 40% stake in the NGCP and a 25-year concession on the latter's operation and development. Further research is needed on accelerating grid development under the ownership of and concessions to Chinese state companies.

7 How Has Global Net-Zero Finance Advanced Net-Zero Electricity System Transitions?

The Cases of ETM and JETP

7.1 INTRODUCTION

International climate finance is essential to accelerate energy transitions, particularly in emerging markets and developing economies (EMDEs) that rely heavily on fossil fuels. Despite the cost competitiveness of renewable-energy-sourced electricity (RES-E) technologies, EMDEs must bear significant transition costs associated with technological, infrastructural, institutional, and organisational changes, as shown in Chapters 3–6. Uncertainties in long-term planning, policies, and power market regulations, as well as a lack of technical capacity in infrastructure (e.g., grid integration constraints), have slowed RES-E adoption (GCF, 2022). These barriers vary across regions, making energy transitions dependent on specific contextual conditions; hence, different policy solutions and financing arrangements are required (Ehlers et al., 2023). However, climate finance flows primarily to the most bankable, lowest-risk, highest-return, and often largest-scale projects (Anantharajah & Setyowati, 2022), causing financial gaps for EMDEs in net-zero energy transitions.

Developed countries have been urged to provide financial resources to mitigate transition costs borne by EMDEs. In the Cancun Agreement, the parties committed to providing USD 100 billion annually to developing country parties in 2020 and set up the Green Climate Fund (GCF) to mobilise climate finance globally. Although these initiatives have mobilised climate finance, financial commitments have not yet been fulfilled (Colenbrander et al., 2022; Zagema et al., 2023).

The failure to meet the Cancun Agreement's financial promise and urgent calls for net-zero transition require a breakthrough in climate finance mechanisms. This is not limited to the quantity of climate funds but also involves the quality of climate finance to allow a just and equitable energy transition resulting in transformative impacts. At the 26th UN Climate Change Conference of the Parties (COP 26) in 2021, a more solid commitment to mobilising finance, mainly towards fossil fuel phase-out, was made, in which there were many notable new announcements and initiatives from various actors to limit global warming with a focus on the role of the financial sector (Gibbs et al., 2021). Governments from developed countries through the International Partners' Group (IPG),[1] in collaboration with private actors through the Glasgow Financial Alliance for Net Zero (GFANZ),[2] for instance, launched the Just Energy Transition Partnership (JETP) to transform economies in pursuit of net-zero emissions. JETP aims to accelerate energy transitions by focusing on emerging economies that rely heavily on fossil fuels while minimising negative implications. A similar programme on a regional scale was initiated by the Asian Development Bank (ADB), known as the Energy Transition Mechanism (ETM) and focusing on coal phase-out. This initiative aims to help countries in Asia and the Pacific boldly commit to reducing emissions from the power sector.

Both JETP and ETM offer opportunities to accelerate climate action towards net-zero ambitions by providing transition finance to support the early retirement of coal power, boost the development of renewables, and reduce transition costs borne by EMDEs. However, JETP, in particular, has been suspected of and criticised for undermining each country's ambitious energy transition plans

[1] IPG members include the European Union, the United Kingdom, the United States of America, Japan, Germany, France, Italy, Canada, Denmark, and Norway.

[2] GFANZ consists of over 675 financial institutions from more than 50 countries; the Working Group members include Bank of America, Citi, Deutsche Bank, HSBC, Macquarie Group, Mizuho, MUFG, Prudential PLC, Shinhan, SMBC, and Standard Chartered.

(Hauber, 2023), as it predominantly uses debts, burdening recipient countries and forcing them to sacrifice other development goals (Lenferna, 2023; Sharma et al., 2023).

Furthermore, understanding climate finance for energy transitions from the perspective of equity and justice is critical to ensuring that the need for diversity in climate mitigation is acknowledged. Equity in climate finance highlights the fair share of financial contribution to climate action. This includes financing phasing out of fossil fuels to share substantial costs in decommissioning, retirement, and social adjustments borne by poor and fossil-fuel-dependent countries (iGST, 2022; Ehlers et al., 2023). Thus, climate finance is expected to drive parties, particularly EMDEs, to take more ambitious climate actions if finance initiatives fulfil the criteria of equity and justice.

Besides equity and justice, transformative change is overlooked in climate finance for energy transitions. Indicators such as carbon reduction contribution, number of beneficiaries, changes in policy and behaviour, and innovation can be used to assess whether climate finance can drive substantial impacts (Ari & Isik, 2022; Puri et al., 2022). These are critical to emerging climate finance initiatives that are expected to help EMDEs advance energy transitions, mainly in phasing out fossil fuels and achieving the net-zero emissions target (NZE).

Against this backdrop, this chapter evaluates GCF, ETM, and JETP in view of criteria for equity and justice in fund allocation and for transformative change. Then, it discusses the role of mandates and requirements in finance and fund allocation, and scalability and replicability for future transformative changes, giving implications for the Glasgow financial regime.

The remainder of this chapter is organised as follows. Section 7.2 presents our viewpoints and evaluation criteria. Section 7.3 explains the research design. Section 7.4 provides the results of our evaluations. Section 7.5 interprets the results and discusses them to give implications. Finally, Section 7.6 concludes the chapter and discusses the remaining challenges.

7.2 ANALYTICAL VIEWPOINTS

7.2.1 *Equity and Justice*

Cost-effective mitigation investments in climate finance require acknowledging the differentiated responsibilities, capabilities (or capacities), and needs of parties following the principles of 'common but differentiated responsibility and respective capabilities' (CBDR-RC) to be realised with an equitable outcome (Pachauri et al., 2022; Dooley et al., 2021). This acknowledgement demonstrates a commitment to equitable and just climate finance to guarantee that no one is left behind in addressing climate change. In this case, distributive justice has been widely considered (Dorman & Ciplet, 2022; Islam, 2022; Pachauri et al., 2022), helping parties allocate and deliver climate finance fairly.

In terms of responsibility and capacity, developed countries are asked to provide a large share of climate finance to help developing countries fill the financing gap. Yet the mechanisms for fund allocation, delivery, and distribution remain challenging due to the lack of consistent rules, signifying the ineffectiveness and inefficiency of climate finance operations (Qi & Qian, 2023). Various factors, such as donors' self-interest (e.g., geopolitical considerations, economic benefits, path dependence, and international peer pressure) and recipients' conditions (e.g., CO_2 intensity, GDP per capita, quality of governance, investment readiness, and risks) undeniably influence funding allocation decisions (Qi & Qian, 2023; Halimanjaya, 2014; Islam, 2022; Dorman & Ciplet, 2022; Awuah, 2023).

Alongside distributive justice, procedural justice is critical in highlighting the fairness of procedures, practices, and agreements among donors and recipients in allocating fair outcomes to climate finance guarantees (O'Dwyer, 2023). Balancing top-down and bottom-up approaches to ascertain the amount of financial assistance, accounting for assessment based on needs, is one of the manifestations of procedural justice. Elements in procedural climate justice such as self-determination, transparency, equal participation, and voice help parties design climate finance to be more inclusive, gaining representations from a wide range of stakeholders (de Ridder et al., 2023). For example, fund allocation should enhance the public goods of local communities, particularly those that are historically marginalised, and provide equal opportunity to access resources, including co-benefits (Anantharajah & Setyowati, 2022; Dorman & Ciplet, 2022).

The choice of climate finance instruments also requires assessment from equity and climate justice viewpoints. The recipient country's macroeconomic situation and policy objectives determine the instruments (Belianska et al., 2022). Loans can be financed for projects that potentially generate returns or for borrowers with high creditworthiness. Concessional loans have higher impacts than grants, as they can mobilise more co-finance from the private sector (Bhattacharya et al., 2020). The repaid loans can be reinvested in new projects, overcoming the limitations of public climate finance (Pauw et al., 2022). However, a large proportion of loans in the climate finance portfolio can lead to unsustainable debt burdens for low-income countries (Zagema et al., 2023), contradicting the spirit of fairness in addressing climate change.

7.2.2 *Transformative Change*

The quality of climate finance holds significance in ensuring transformative outcomes. As climate finance has been considered an instrument to accelerate energy transitions, funds should be allocated to innovative, high-impact, and transformative investments (GCF, 2022). Poor-quality climate finance hinders developing countries from utilising resources effectively to deliver activities addressing climate change (Colenbrander et al., 2022). Transformative change is increasingly relevant to climate finance, as a shift or change in perspective on climate change is necessary to move towards low-emission and climate-resilient development pathways (Winkler & Dubash, 2015; Puri et al., 2022). Unlike incremental change, transformative change entails a significant shift, resulting in a fundamentally new system or process (Mapfumo et al., 2017) measured by depth, scope, and speed (Termeer et al., 2017).

However, transformative change in pursuing low-carbon objectives in developing countries may pose potential risks for other development agendas, such as economic growth, energy access, improved local environmental issues, and equal distribution (Winkler & Dubash, 2015). Thus, transformative change initiatives should balance between mitigation and development objectives and should acknowledge the independence of recipients to manage and control the use of finance so long as substantial impacts in reducing emissions align with their development agenda (Winkler, 2021).

Criteria to assess the performance of climate finance are essential to achieve transformative change. The Climate Investment Fund (CIF), Global Environment Facility, and Adaptation Fund use scale, behavioural change, replicability, sustainability, innovation, policy change, depth of change, and relevance as criteria for the assessment of transformative change. Puri et al. (2022) incorporate a prolonged process of transformation to propose a framework for transformative change for assessing GCF projects comprising eight components necessary for transformations to emerge: scale, depth of change, complementarity and coherence, permanence, demonstration ability, behavioural change, policy change, and innovation.

7.2.3 *Evaluation Criteria*

We combine the two viewpoints, equity and justice, in fund allocation and transformative change representing the quantity and quality of climate finance to delineate and assess climate finance mechanisms for GCF, ETM, and JETP (Table 7.1). The first viewpoint, focusing on the quantity of climate finance, helps identify whether funding allocation provided by the donors is sufficient. The equity and justice lens proposed by Dorman and Ciplet (2022), Pachauri et al. (2022), and de Ridder et al. (2023) help frame the assessment indicators, such as funding allocation, funding scope, the involvement of stakeholders in climate finance, and the choice of financial instruments.

Table 7.1 *Evaluation criteria for climate finance*

Aspect	Viewpoint	Variable	Indicator
Quantity	Equity and justice	Distributive justice	• Funding allocation • Funding scope
		Procedural justice	• Stakeholders' engagement in decision-making processes • Choice of financial instruments
Quality	Transformative change	Scale	• Number of beneficiaries • Potential emissions reductions
		Complementarity and coherence	• Alignment with other climate finance mechanisms
		Permanence	• Inclusion of stakeholder engagement
		Behavioural change	• Need for change
		Policy change	• Potential to catalyse policy change
		Demonstration ability	• Number of jobs created
		Innovation	• Whether climate finance triggers innovation or disruption

Source: Previous studies by the authors.

Meanwhile, the second viewpoint focuses on transformative change to represent the quality of climate finance. We refer to the framework proposed by Puri et al. (2022) for the criteria to analyse potential transformative change created by climate finance. The framework considers transformative change processes (*permanence*), starting with developing innovation, going on to demonstrating concepts, implementing, replicating, and scaling, and ending with paradigm shifts manifested in policy and behavioural changes. Along the way, projects funded by climate finance have the potential to be complemented by other financial mechanisms (*complementarity* and *coherence*).

7.3 RESEARCH DESIGN

7.3.1 *Methodology*

This study combines the previous literature and findings from three climate finance mechanisms: GCF, ETM, and JETP. A qualitative multi-case study approach was applied (Yin, 2018), and the cases were used to illustrate the role of emerging international climate and transition finance mechanisms, mainly ETM and JETP, in advancing energy transitions towards net-zero emissions targets. We dive deeply into potential transformative change created by climate finance mechanisms.

Data collection and analysis were conducted using the following steps. First, we reviewed written materials related to climate finance and its significance to energy transitions to gain an initial understanding of the topic and define the analytical lens. Second, we collected secondary data from various sources, including academic articles; reports; relevant documents related to climate finance published by donors, intermediaries, and recipient countries; and news articles. We obtained information on funding commitment from the GCF database and JETP partners' investment plans. Third, we analysed the findings based on our research objectives. In this step, we referred to the framework shown in Table 7.1 to assess the mechanisms.

7.3.2 *Case Overview*

7.3.2.1 *Green Climate Fund (GCF)*

GCF was established at the Durban COP in 2011 but became fully operational with its first projects approved by the end of 2015. GCF acts as an operating entity of both UNFCCC and the Paris Agreement financial mechanism, and its funds serve as a catalyst to attract investment from private actors. GCF commits to a 50:50 balanced finance allocation to climate mitigation and adaptation activities. The first round of funding mobilisation was worth USD 10 billion for 2020–2023, and in 2023, GCF received the second round of funding commitment worth USD 12.8 billion for the term 2024–2027. All developing country parties under the UNFCCC framework, mainly Least Developed Countries, Small Island Developing States, and African states, are eligible to access funding from GCF. Still, they must collaborate with multilateral development banks (MDBs), international commercial banks, UN agencies, and other accredited national, regional, and subnational implementing entities to access funding. In providing access to finance, GCF evaluates the project proposed by recipient countries using six investment criteria: impact potential, paradigm shift potential, sustainable development potential, recipient needs, country ownership, and efficiency and effectiveness (GCF, 2022).

7.3.2.2 *Energy Transition Mechanism (ETM)*

In 2021, the ADB initiated the ETM, a programme aimed at helping ADB's developing member countries confront the issue of climate change by reducing emissions and, in particular, accelerating the retirement of fossil fuel power plants, particularly coal, and replacing them with clean energy alternatives, using concessional and commercial capital. To achieve these goals, ETM uses two funding vehicles. First is the Carbon Reduction Fund, which is tasked with refinancing or purchasing coal assets. Second is the Clean Energy Fund, which facilitates investment in clean energy. The ETM programme began with three pilot countries, Indonesia, the Philippines, and Vietnam, and has extended to Pakistan and Kazakhstan. The ETM is a scalable model, meaning that it is expected to have the potential to be scaled up and replicated with different mechanisms by others, including a single country without ADB support.

To mobilise resources from donors and support activities related to ETM, the Energy Transition Mechanism Partnership Trust Fund (ETMPTF) was established. The ETMPTF adheres to the governance structure of the Clean Energy Financing Partnership Facility, which includes the Climate Change Steering Committee, comprising the Director General of ADB's Sustainable Development and Climate Change Department as the chair, the heads of relevant ADB operations departments, and ADB's Chief Economist (ADB, 2022a). Japan was the first country to provide seed funding worth USD 25 million through grants, followed by Germany in 2022 with a USD 26 million grant commitment, and New Zealand in 2024 with USD 25 million for ADB's energy transition mechanism (ADB, 2022b; Xinhua, 2024).

7.3.2.3 *Just Energy Transition Partnership (JETP)*

At COP 26 in 2021, the GFANZ and IPG members committed to mobilising international funds from their members to transform economies towards net-zero emissions through the JETP. This new climate finance mechanism has three ultimate goals: (i) facilitate the early retirement of fossil-fuel-based, particularly coal, power plants, (ii) mobilise private sector capital to fund decarbonisation activities, and (iii) deliver a 'just transition' for the society. Currently, there are four JETP pilot countries: South Africa, Indonesia, Vietnam, and Senegal, with a total funding commitment of around USD 49.7 billion. The funds from the public sector (IPG members) are channelled through multilateral and bilateral development financial institutions.

JETP is distinct from earlier financing mechanisms as it embraces the concept of 'just transition', showing JETP's willingness to incorporate the interests of affected groups in energy transitions. Additionally, the long-term vision of JETP involves ensuring just, equitable, and inclusive outcomes for all stakeholders and aspects, such as livelihoods, workers, and communities affected by energy transitions. To achieve this vision, the recipients submit their JETP Implementation Plan, consisting of wish-lists of programmes and estimated investment needs; that is, total investments required to decarbonise the energy system and achieve the NDC target. The process contrasts with the Just Transition Transaction (JTT) previously implemented in South Africa, which adopted a predominantly top-down approach (Jindal et al., 2024; Winkler et al., 2021).

7.4 RESULTS

7.4.1 Financial flows

7.4.1.1 GCF

By June 2024, the GCF had approved 254 projects from 128 countries, mainly from lower- and upper-middle economies, with a total project value of USD 14 billion (Figure 7.1). MDBs were the dominant accredited entities channelling funding from GCF (44.9%), followed by UN agencies (17.8%). By the number of projects, adaptation accounted for 43.3%, followed by cross-cutting (29.9%) and mitigation (26.8%). Energy access and power generation accounted for 28.7% of total approved projects, including mitigation and cross-cutting categories and ranging from micro to large scale.

Loans accounted for the largest share of financial instruments for energy access and power generation projects (43.8% on average), followed by equity and grants, 30.2% and 24.3% respectively (Figure 7.2). The ratio of GCF funding to the total project value was 24.6% on average, and the remaining value was supported by co-financing. The disbursement rate was around 41% on average, which was higher than the overall projects average (29.63%), not limited to energy access and power generation (i.e., all projects under adaptation, mitigation, and cross-cutting categories) in 2023 (GCF, 2023a). However, it took 21 months from the approval date for the energy access and power generation projects to receive their first disbursement (longer than the overall project average, 11 months in 2022) (GCF, 2023b).

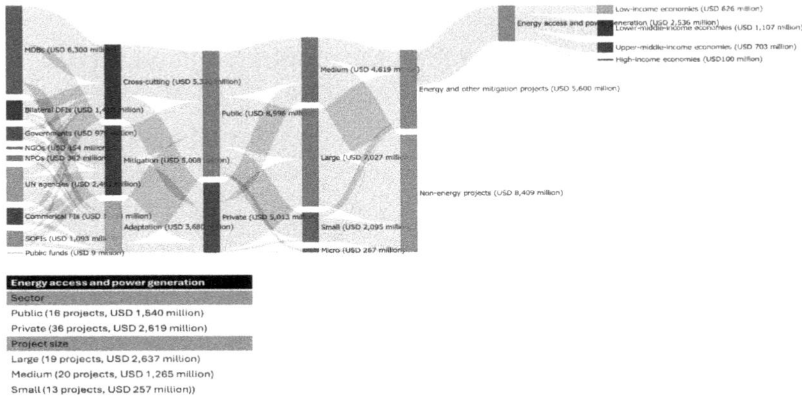

FIGURE 7.1 GCF financial flows based on approved projects.
Note: Non-energy-related projects include mitigation activities not related to energy and adaptation.
Source: Compiled by the authors based on data from GCF at June 2024.

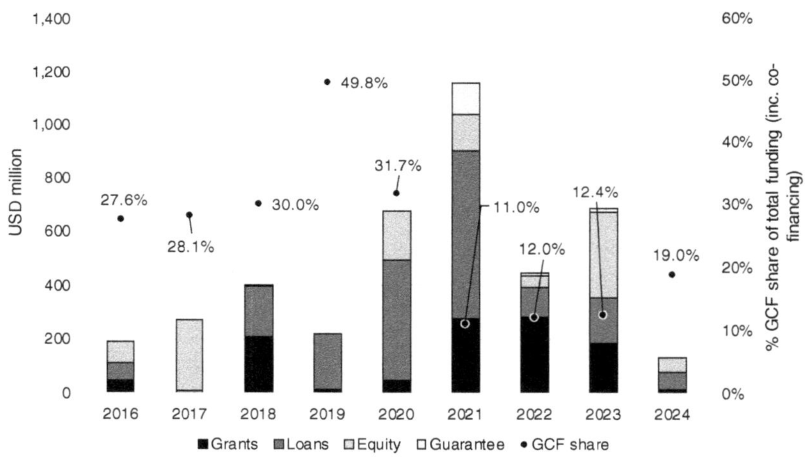

FIGURE 7.2 Financial instruments used for energy access and power generation projects; percentage of GCF funding in total project value (on average).
Source: Compiled by the authors based on data from GCF at June 2024.

7.4.1.2 *ETM*

By June 2024, ETM had accomplished significant advancements across multiple phases; however, financial commitment has only been made by ADB with Indonesia, Kazakhstan, Pakistan, and the Philippines (Figure 7.3). Indonesia received a financial commitment of USD 500 million from ADB and CIF-ACT, with co-financing support from MDBs of USD 2,059 million. Of the USD 2,559 million deal, 50% has been allocated to early retirement programmes of both state-owned and private coal power plants, followed by coal power plant repurposing (29.3%), just transitions (13.2%), and RES-E (7.4%). Although Kazakhstan and Pakistan received USD 0.225 million and USD 0.3 million, respectively, in technical assistance to conduct a pre-feasibility study, they had no further funding commitment as of June 2024. The Philippines received a funding allocation of USD 500 million endorsed by CIF-ACT, invested by ADB, World Bank Group, government, and private sectors through co-financing support of around USD 2.3 billion. The funding is allocated to retiring and repurposing coal power plants, implementing a just transition (36.4%), and scaling up RES-E generation (25.1%).

Funds for the ETM in the three pilot countries are provided by ADB (USD 1,665 million), CIF-ACT (USD 1,102 million), IFC

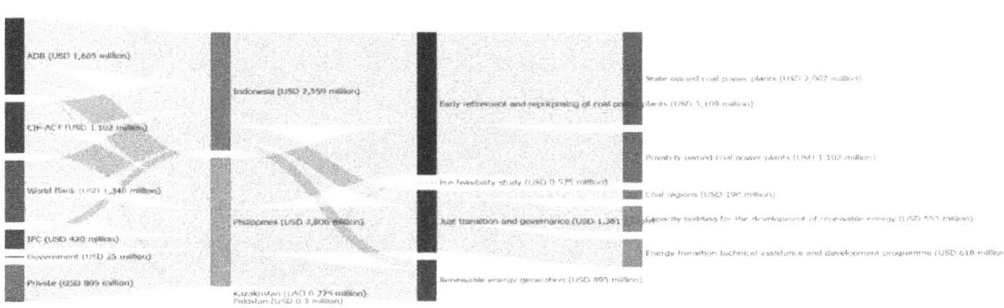

FIGURE 7.3 ETM flows based on commitment at June 2024.
Source: Compiled by the authors based on data from Indonesia's CIPP (2023), ADB (2023), and ADB, IFC, & World Bank (2024).

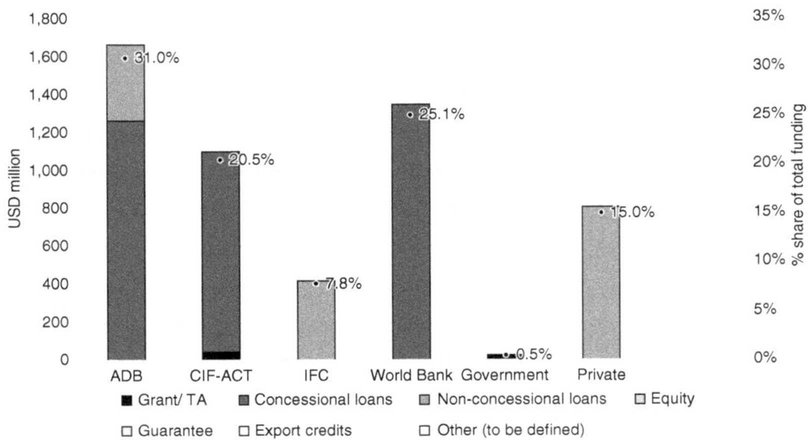

FIGURE 7.4 ETM funding breakdown at June 2024.
Source: Compiled by the authors based on data from Indonesia's CIPP (2023), ADB (2023), and ADB, IFC & World Bank (2024).

(USD 420 million), World Bank (USD 1,348 million), government (USD 25 million), and private sectors (USD 805 million) (Figure 7.4). The funding comprises concessional (68.4%) and commercial loans (30.3%). ADB Private, IFC, and private sectors mostly provide commercial loans for early retirement of privately owned coal power plants and RES-E generation. A relatively small portion of grants (1.3%) is used for early retirement of state-owned coal power plants and activities related to just transitions, such as capacity building (including R&D), incentives for coal regions, and energy transition governance.

7.4.1.3 *JETP*

As a collaborative framework, JETP focuses on mobilising funds from both public and private sources, including concessional loans, grants, and investments, to accelerate coal phase-out. Funding allocation is guided by tailored country-specific investment plans that prioritise projects delivering substantial emissions reductions and addressing equity concerns, such as reskilling workers and supporting communities that are dependent on fossil fuels. JETP countries, except Senegal, published their investment plans, covering their investment needs and potential designated funding allocations supported by JETP.

As the first JETP country, South Africa received a commitment of USD 8.5 billion for three to five years for three focus areas: electricity, new energy vehicles, and green hydrogen. In 2023 the country received additional funding commitments, bringing the total contribution from international partners to USD 11.7 billion, or 11.78% of total investment needs (USD 98.38 billion). As of June 2024, South Africa completed projects totalling only 2% (USD 16 million) of the disbursed funding (USD 697 million) (The Government of South Africa, 2024). Lack of transparency in donors' fund allocation and disbursement delayed recipients' actions towards the transition (Vanheukelom, 2023).

Indonesia, the second JETP country, received an initial commitment of USD 20 billion, of which half was from IPG members and another half in private financing from GFANZ. This funding accounts for 20.6% of the total estimated investment cost needed (USD 97.1 billion). It is allocated for five investment focus areas: transmission lines and grid deployment, early coal power plant retirement and managed phase-out, dispatchable RES-E, variable RES-E, and RES-E supply chain.

Vietnam became the third JETP partner and received a USD 15.5 billion commitment from the IPG countries and GFANZ with a 50:50 ratio. The JETP funding commitment contributes 11.5% of the total estimated investment cost needed until 2030 (USD 134.7 billion). The funding is allocated to enhancing the regulatory framework for energy transition, transforming coal power plants, developing RES-E generation and transmission and energy storage, improving energy efficiency, adopting electric vehicles, fostering innovation, and ensuring a just transition.

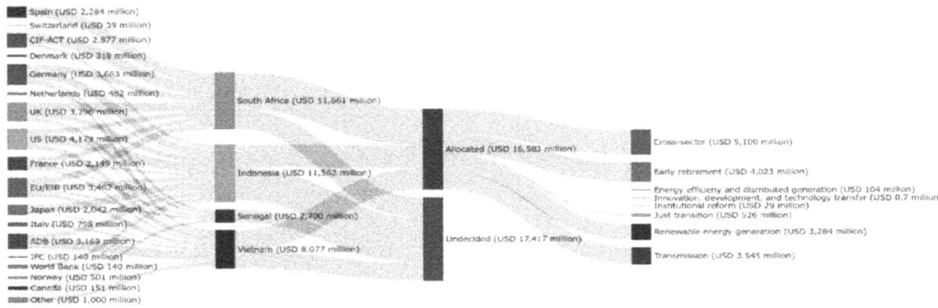

FIGURE 7.5 South Africa's, Indonesia's, Senegal's, and Vietnam's JETP flows as committed at June 2024.
Notes: 'Undecided' refers to all potential projects to be financed; 'Cross-sector' includes projects with more than one focus area (e.g., RE and transmission, RE and decommissioning); Senegal received USD 2.7 billion from France, Germany, the EU, the UK and Canada, but there is no detailed information available about the contribution of each donor (an equal share was assumed in creating the figure).
Source: Compiled by the authors based on data from South Africa's JET IP (2023), Indonesia's CIPP (2023), and Vietnam's RMP (The Government of Vietnam, 2023).

Senegal, the fourth JETP country, has not released its investment plan despite a commitment to USD 2.7 billion in funding. The country committed to launching its JETP investment plan within one year from the commencement of the JETP programme in 2023.

By June 2024, about half of the commitment amount among all JETP countries remained unassigned (undecided) to specific programmes (Figure 7.5). Some programmes are cross-sectoral, covering RES-E and transmission and RES-E and decommissioning under one financial package.

Loans are the main financial instruments in JETP. Concessional and non-concessional loans account for 50.7% and 27.5% of the total allocation, respectively (Figure 7.6). These instruments are mainly used to finance the development of electricity infrastructure. Meanwhile, grants contribute 4.4% of total JETP funding. They support capacity-building activities, including policy research, pilot projects, skills development, and reskilling and training workers in the renewable energy sector.

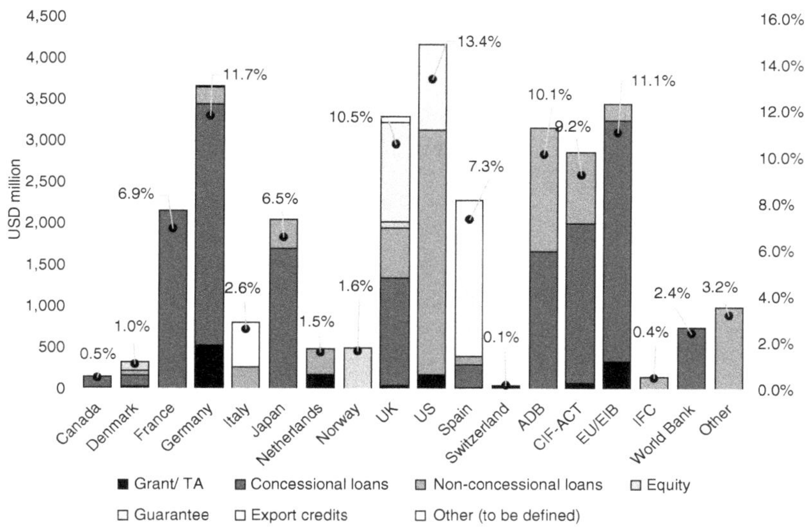

FIGURE 7.6 JETP public finance breakdown by country/entity and funding mechanism at June 2024.
Notes: funds from ACT IP-CIF exclude the amount of USD 330 million to be mobilised from local DFIs; UK guarantees to increase AfDB lending to South Africa through concessional loans; grants provided by the Netherlands include a USD 54 million initial grant contribution from Invest International to leverage USD 1,080 GH_2 Fund; USD 2.7 billion from Senegal is excluded as there is no detailed information available about the contribution of each donor or the types of financial instrument used.
Source: Compiled by the authors based on data from South Africa's JET IP (2023), Indonesia's CIPP (2023), and Vietnam's RMP (The Government of Vietnam, 2023).

7.4.2 *Equity and Justice Considerations*

7.4.2.1 *GCF*

GCF has not completely achieved distributional justice in the allocation of funds. Funding allocation was not significantly different between low-income and upper-middle-income countries, while their emissions were different (Table 7.2). Also, upper-middle-income countries received less funding, whereas their emissions were higher than those of lower-middle-income countries.

Table 7.2 *Funding allocation to energy-access and power-generation projects compared with emissions, by income classification*

Income classification[a]	Funding allocation (USD million)[b]	Emissions 1990–2020 ($GtCO_2$)[c]
Low income	625.6	1.49
Lower-middle income	1,106.79	70.49
Upper-middle income	703.21	74.96
High income	100.37	3.33

[a] World Bank (2024).
[b] Assuming all countries receive equal funds (Dorman & Ciplet, 2022).
[c] IPCC (2022a) and Minx et al. (2022).
Source: Compiled by the authors.

Historical emissions can reflect future emissions. Lower-middle-income and upper-middle-income countries are developing countries that consume substantial energy to fuel their economies, so their emissions will increase following their economic growth. These countries mostly rely on fossil fuels, so they are the potential targets for GCF to mitigate climate change by transforming their energy sectors. In other words, more funding is needed for these countries to phase out fossil fuels, mainly coal.

As for procedural justice, GCF is country-driven, so the initiative comes from the country proposing the project (GCF, 2022). Besides, GCF emphasises the inclusion of stakeholders in the project proposal to increase the scale of the impacts. This can be seen from the projects that are not proposed, not only for the public sector but also for the private sector.

7.4.2.2 ETM

ETM has not incorporated distributional justice in fund allocation, particularly for Indonesia, the first pilot country. Compared to the Philippines, while Indonesia has the potential to reduce substantial emissions from coal power plants, considering the share of coal in power generation, the country received less funding from the ETM scheme (Table 7.3). Meanwhile, it seems that the status of income and climate risk of the Philippines does not affect the choice of financial instruments, as the share of debts in funding composition is comparable with that of Indonesia.

Procedural justice has not been fully implemented. In Indonesia, ADB claims that civil society and communities were involved in a preliminary assessment to understand social and economic issues and gain their perceptions towards energy transitions (ADB, 2024a). Similarly, in the Philippines, the government, with UNDP, conducted the Multi-Stakeholder Consultation on Just Energy Transition with energy stakeholders, including IPPs, electric utilities, transmission and distribution entities, among others, to gather their views on just transition and discuss policy options; with ADB, they conducted a study to assess the impacts of the transition (ADB, IFC, & World Bank, 2024). However, stakeholder engagement was still limited, particularly with civil society and communities relying on coal (Sausmikat, 2024).

7.4.2.3 *JETP*

JETP's focus on coal does not fully ensure distributional justice in funding allocation, which is not in line with the condition of each country under three attributes related to equity and just transition. South Africa and Vietnam received only slightly different funding commitments, while the differences in their emissions from coal combustion are relatively significant (Table 7.4). The rationale behind the difference is early retirement costs. Aged coal power plants are prevalent in South Africa (PCC, 2023), claiming smaller expenses for early retirement than young ones that prevail in Vietnam. While its energy sector is fuelled by oil, Senegal faces energy poverty, with only 70% of the population having access to electricity (Gaba, 2023). The government of Senegal plans to switch to gas to power the economy.

Table 7.3 *Funding allocation and attributes related to equity and justice in ETM pilot countries*

	Indonesia	Kazakhstan	Pakistan	Philippines
Funding allocation	–	–	–	–
Funding commitment (USD billion)	2.6	0.000225	0.0003	2.8
Share of debt in funding (%)	99.2	n/a	n/a	98.2
Responsibility	–	–	–	–
Electricity generation from coal in 2022 (TWh)[a]	248.6	70	27.5	66.4
Emissions from power generation (coal) in 2022 ($GtCO_2$)[a]	0.26	0.099	0.031	0.069
Emissions 1990–2020 ($GtCO_2$)[b]	11.48	6.73	4.09	2.66
Capacity	–	–	–	–
Income classification[c]	Upper-middle income	Upper-middle income	Lower-middle income	Lower-middle income
Needs	–	–	–	–
Long-term climate risk index (rank)[d]	74 (72)	141.83 (154)	29 (8)	18.17 (4)
Living standard[e]	6.43	8.22	4.6	6.11

[a] IEA (2023a).
[b] IPCC (2022) and Minx et al. (2022).
[c] World Bank (2024).
[d] Global Climate Risk Index 2000–2019 (Eckstein et al., 2021).
[e] Huo et al. (2023).
Source: Compiled by the authors.

Table 7.4 *Funding allocation and attributes related to equity and justice in JETP pilot countries*

	South Africa	Indonesia	Vietnam	Senegal
Funding allocation				
Funding commitment (USD billion)	11.59	20	15.5	2.7
Investment needs (USD billion), 2023–2030	98.38	97.1	134.7	n/a
JETP as % of total investment needs	11.78	20.6	11.5	n/a
% of debt in funding – existing condition (excl. GFANZ)	77.18	73.83	85.94	n/a
Responsibility				
Electricity generation from coal in 2022 (TWh)[a]	197.4	248.6	111	0.59
Emissions from power generation (coal) in 2022 ($GtCO_2$)[a]	0.22	0.26	0.12	0.001
Emissions 1990–2020 ($GtCO_2$)[b]	12.43	11.48	3.63	0.18
Capacity				
Income classification[c]	Upper-middle income	Upper-middle income	Lower-middle income	Lower-middle income
Needs				
Long-term climate risk index (rank)[d]	92.67 (78)	74 (72)	35.67 (13)	123 (138)
Living standard[e]	5.69	6.43	6.62	3.82

a IEA (2023a).

b IPCC (2022) and Minx et al. (2022).

c World Bank (2023).

d Global Climate Risk Index 2000–2019 (Eckstein et al., 2021).

e Huo et al. (2023).

Source: Compiled by the authors.

JETP funding packages do not undergo a comprehensive and transparent process. The requirement to formulate investment plans appears perplexing, as declarations regarding IPG funding conveyed an impression of a consolidated support package to which recipient countries merely needed to agree (Hauber, 2023). To exemplify, Indonesia and Vietnam are tied to projects with preconditions, and most earmarked spending existed long before each country came up with its JETP investment plans. This indicates that JETP funding packages do not consider recipients' specific needs, an issue that threatens country ownership.

JETP countries must seek other financial sources to realise their investment plans because JETP provides a small portion of the funding needed for them (i.e., South Africa, 11.78%; Indonesia, 20.6%; and Vietnam, 11.5%: see Table 7.4). Additionally, debt-based instruments account for over 75% of the committed funding. This approach can increase recipients' public debts and adversely affect their economies. South Africa may face a serious economic problem, considering that its fiscal accounts were under pressure due to an unprecedented energy crisis and the COVID-19 pandemic (IMF, 2023).

Furthermore, procedural justice has been ensured to a varied degree. South Africa and Indonesia have conducted extensive stakeholder engagement through public consultations to improve their investment plans (see PCC, 2023; CIPP, 2023). South Africa's JETP has considered the voices of affected groups based on the Komati project to update its investment plan by including a social security programme, especially for communities in coal-mining areas (Krutham, 2023).[3] Indonesia's JETP secretariat conducted many public hearings to obtain input from various stakeholders, ensuring a just transition (JETP Indonesia, 2024a). Besides, a number of JETP programmes request Indonesia to address social and economic issues

[3] In November 2022, the World Bank Group approved a USD 497 million project to support the decommissioning of the Komati coal-fired power plant, repurpose the project area with RE and batteries, and create opportunities for workers and communities. This retirement plan pre-dates the JET IP, so it is not part of the JET IP pledges (PCC, 2023).

caused by energy transitions, such as energy access and employment, in the deliverables (JETP Indonesia, 2024b). In contrast, Vietnam lacks stakeholder engagement, mainly from civil society. This raises concerns about the delineation of justice (Behrens, 2023; International Rivers & Vietnam Climate Defenders Coalition, 2024; Wischermann, 2024).

7.4.3 *Transformative Change*

7.4.3.1 *GCF*

GCF's funding for energy transitions has been mainly used to increase RES-E capacity and provide capacity building, including technical assistance, to improve institutional readiness and smooth programme implementation.

Several GCF projects have created transformational change, such as (i) accelerating the transformational shift to a low-carbon economy in the Republic of Mauritius, (ii) Renewable Energy Program #1 – Solar, (ii) Line of Credit for Solar rooftop segment for commercial, industrial, and residential housing sectors, and (iv) Climate Investor One.[4] These projects successfully installed new solar power plants (including battery storage), improved grid capacity, created new job opportunities, and avoided significant emissions. Countries that relied heavily on fossil fuel imports were able to improve their trade balance.

Furthermore, GCF projects induced recipient countries to improve their institutions to align with renewable energy systems. In Mauritius, the government released regulations for RES-E standards and implemented various RES-E schemes for religious bodies and NGOs to adopt RES-E. In Mongolia, the GCF project enabled substantial knowledge and learning for financial institutions and country stakeholders and functions regarding the feasibility and viability of RES-E projects, thereby providing valuable insights to potential

[4] Most GCF projects are at implementation stage. Some of them were affected by the COVID-19 pandemic, delaying progress. Thus, we selected projects that have published Annual Performance Reports to trace their progress.

investors. In India, the GCF project sensitised people and created awareness about RES-E and its benefits.

7.4.3.2 *ETM*

ETM explicitly focuses on accelerating the transition from coal power plants to clean energy through retiring and repurposing coal power plants, increasing the share of clean energy, helping DMCs develop and enact policy and regulatory measures to accelerate the transition, and supporting a just transition. The first ETM project with a funding commitment was to retire a 660 MW coal power plant (Cirebon 1) commissioned in 2012 in Indonesia by shortening its lifetime until 2035, potentially avoiding over 15 years' worth of emissions (assuming 40 years' lifetime on average). Another ETM project is a 1,050 MW coal power plant (Pelabuhan Ratu) in Indonesia, which is expected to retire by 2035/2036.[5]

The early retirement of the Cirebon 1 coal power plant is expected to reduce emissions and improve the quality of life for communities living near the power plant (IPD, 2023). With the early retirement programme coupled with the development of RES-E, ETM potentially provides economic benefits, such as increased GDP, job creation, poverty reduction, and increased profits, particularly for industries highly correlated with the electricity sector (Adhinegara et al., 2024).

ADB funded an ETM project to retire and repurpose the 210 MW Mindanao coal power plant in the Philippines (ADB, IFC, & World Bank, 2024; Flores, 2024). The Philippines government has started technical discussions to find solutions and options for assets related to power replacement through a state-owned company managing power sector assets and liabilities. Although ETM funded by ADB has not shown significant progress, the ETM concept has been replicated by the private sector, resulting in the early retirement of the 246 MW coal plant (ACEN, 2022).

[5] Under the due diligence and transaction review process.

7.4.3.3 JETP

South Africa undertook institutional reforms in a package of debt relief measures for Eskom in 2023 (Government of South Africa, 2023). The JETP enabled South Africa to adopt strategies to address the electricity supply crisis and fiscal constraints, industrial development from renewables, inclusivity, and capacity building to accelerate energy transitions. It has also upgraded the skills of coal power plant ex-workers to get jobs in RES-E industries, such as solar PV installation and mounting (PCC, 2023).

Indonesia and Vietnam have shown slow progress in infrastructure development and in the decommissioning, repowering, and repurposing of coal power plants. They released their investment plans in 2023, indicating their JETP implementation was still nascent. In its investment plan, Indonesia focuses on institutional reform by improving the regulations related to the RES-E industry (e.g., local content requirements), adjusting supply-side incentives, enhancing RES-E procurement processes, making power purchase agreements more bankable, ensuring PLN financial sustainability, and strengthening financial policy (Government of Indonesia, 2023). Transformative change remains invisible because the disbursement started in the second quarter of 2024, and only feasibility studies (i.e., the retirement of coal power plants, project exploration, technical assistance, and capacity building) have been implemented (JETP Indonesia, 2024b, 2024c). Similarly, Vietnam assessed the energy transition scenarios to repurpose coal power plants for biomass, green hydrogen/ammonia, and bioenergy carbon capture and storage (BECCS) (Viet Nam Energy Partnership Group, 2024). In addition, under the Sustainable Energy Transition Budget Support Programme (SETP), the country organised training and workshops to enhance institutional capacities and legal and technical frameworks, support private sector activities, and increase awareness of the benefits of renewable energy and energy efficiency (e.g., EU-Vietnam SETP, 2024a, 2024b).

7.5 DISCUSSION

7.5.1 *Mandates and Requirements of the Fund Operation*

Our results suggest that funds' mandates and procedures critically influence the quantity and quality of overall fund and sectoral allocations. The project selection process, guided by clear and detailed criteria, directs GCF towards fund allocation to high-quality investments. This can ensure that the projects achieve their goals of making significant transformations. Accredited entities allow collaboration with host countries to design project ideas that have the potential to be funded. The GCF's commitment to country ownership also enables host countries to propose a project that aligns with its specific needs, thus ensuring procedural justice, resulting in the exclusive allocation to energy access and RES-E generation capacity in the energy sector.

However, the GCF's mandates and requirements impede host countries from taking more ambitious climate actions, as the decision-making process involving multiple stakeholders could delay the approval of projects. The mandate of a 50:50 allocation may restrict financial access for energy transitions. The requirement for allocation based on selective indicators determined by donors (Seo, 2019) also steers host countries towards bilateral agreements that frequently disadvantage them (Maffei, 2019; Achampong, 2022).

ETM and JETP ensure procedural justice in project selection. They are mandated to support transitions to low-carbon and resilient development pathways (OECD, 2022), emphasising early retirements of coal power and addressing the social consequences associated with the transitions. Both ETM and JETP are flexible in specifying funded projects in which host countries can customise the project to fit their conditions (tailor-made).

However, ETM's and JETP's focus on coal phase-out threatens country ownership. Host country governments must address longstanding challenges that commonly hold for developing countries, such as lack of capacity in RES-E development, low institutional quality, rigidity in conducting policy reforms, and regulatory uncertainty. Simultaneously addressing these multiple challenges raises capital costs and makes RES-E projects unattractive (Resosudarmo et al., 2023; World Economic Forum, 2023). They should attract private investors to fill the financing gap from other sources.

7.5.2 *Scaling and Replication*

Our results raise doubts about the scaling and replication of ETM and JETP for financing net-zero transitions. First, this could increase default risk, particularly in high-debt countries such as South Africa. Given that developed/industrialised countries (also known as Annex I countries) failed to fulfil their commitment to provide USD 100 billion annually, and the IPG has provided insufficient financial resources in JETP, EMDEs have needed to find other funding sources to fill the financing gap. Besides, the low proportion of GCF and JETP finance in the total investment value requires a large portion of co-financing, most of which is supposed to be debt finance from MDBs and commercial banks. The dominance of debts in the financing structure imposes an additional financial burden on host countries.

Second, attracting private financial actors in GFANZ is still challenging as they tend to finance 'bankable projects' and are concerned about investment risk–return profiles. Environment, social, and governance investment standards remain inadequately defined, which may deter potential investors from making investments. Besides, JETP countries are emerging economies where coal is still dominant in the energy mix, and the renewable energy market is yet to mature (Ehlers et al., 2023). India and IPG member countries, including the United States and Germany, discontinued talks about JETP in 2024 (Srivastrava & Wettengel, 2024).

Third, substantial time differences exist between current international climate finance and net-zero transitions. GCF provides finance on a project basis. ETM and JETP initiatives will last for three to five years. In contrast, net-zero transitions require more than a decade to complete the required reforms and overcome the adverse impacts of the reforms to make the transition just. Without donors' long-term firm financial commitment, political leaders in host countries hesitate to make serious commitments to net-zero transitions that demand substantial institutional and organisational changes (see Chapter 3) and thus can generate political risk and undermine their legitimacy.

Finally, replacing many young, large-scale coal power plants that satisfy the growing electricity demand with new RES-E capacity demands significant funding. Given that the proliferation of these plants reduces transition costs and finance, EMDEs will be funded from ETM and JETP and finance early retirements with their funding only if they perceive larger benefits from them than form proliferation. This holds particularly for EMDEs where private companies own a majority of coal power plants. Financial incentives or compensation for their losses are indispensable to attract private owners. Also, early retirement depends on owners' perceptions of benefits and stranded costs.

7.5.3 *Implications for the Paris–Glasgow Financial Regime*

The reservations about scaling and replicating financing net-zero transitions have two implications. First, financial allocation should be based on long-term integrated value that incorporates financial and decarbonisational values instead of short-termism. Collaborations with transparency will play a critical role in strengthening the long-term commitment of host countries to these partnerships and demonstrating potential economic benefits from a green transition (Seiler et al., 2023).

Second, stewardship should be fostered based on direct links between IPG members and private investors in GFANZ, on the one hand, and host country governments and electric utilities, on the other hand. Active stewardship can not only foster the spirit of burden-sharing that can mitigate the implications associated with generating winners and losers (Resosudarmo et al., 2023) but also help in navigating transition and changing the business models of electric utilities (Loorbach et al., 2020).

7.6 CONCLUSION

This chapter assessed what international climate finance has achieved in advancing energy transitions, ensuring equity and justice, and creating transformative change, taking ETM and JETP as cases and comparing them with GCF. Our analysis revealed that equity and justice were considered, but to a varied extent. Recipients' investment needs reflected in their investment plans have not been adequately met, as the quantity of funding from JETP is small. Besides, justice was marginally considered. Although South Africa and Indonesia performed public consultations in JETP, they hosted them to comply with procedural justice but did not disclose or monitor who would gain benefits. Consequently, this inadequacy put a substantial financial burden on host countries, especially those with low financial capacity. Besides, the considerable reliance on debt instruments in funding contradicted the spirit of justice.

Our analysis also showed ETM's and JETP's potential to create transformative change going beyond the phasing out of coal power. However, fund allocation is considered insufficient to cover all the investment programmes listed in the JETP Investment Plan. Besides, their specific focus on coal and their donor-driven approach threatens country ownership. This sharply contrasts with GCF, which adopts a country-driven approach and clear assessment guidelines so that host countries can innovate in energy transitions that can be adjusted to country-specific conditions.

Our case studies may be premature due to limited information and implementation periods, especially for ETM and JETP. More nuanced analyses are expected in tandem with the progress of these net-zero financial mechanisms.

8 Making Financial Systems Work for Net-Zero Transitions in Electricity Systems

8.1 REVISITING THE RESEARCH QUESTIONS

The IPCC's Sixth Assessment Report confirms that rapid and deep reductions in CO_2 emissions are necessary to limit temperature rise to 1.5°C. In response, OECD and G20 agreements officially supported export credit to end support for unabated coal power plants (OECD, 2021a). Some emerging markets and developing economies (EMDEs) have gone beyond their Nationally Determined Contributions (NDCs) to pledge future net-zero emissions (NZE).

To achieve NZE, the global energy mix must undergo a profound transformation with a dramatic increase in low-emissions sources and their replacement of unabated fossil-fuel-based energy sources across the whole energy sector. The transition to NZE requires a paradigm shift that entails multiple and simultaneous transitions of different sociotechnical systems and swift, radical, and active pushes by many vital societal actors. The commitments that have been made to NZE have reinforced the momentum for climate action and widened the sectors involved. In the electricity system, transportation and financial capital are regarded as complementary elements of the system that need to be co-evolved in the transition from fossil-fuel-based to renewable energy-sourced electricity (RES-E) systems (Mori, 2021b). The need for synchronised changes in multiple sectors and systems has increased attention on multi-system transitions or the creation of new multi-system interactions as drivers to accelerate net-zero transitions (Andersen & Geels, 2023).

However, abrupt divestment and reduction of fossil fuel investment ahead of a ramp-up of clean energy technologies will hike fossil fuel prices to satisfy growing energy demand. Russia's war in

Ukraine has spurred energy price hikes, raising energy security concerns in energy-importing countries and bringing windfalls for fossil fuel producers. The European Parliament decided to include gas and nuclear power as transitional activities in the EU Taxonomy for Sustainable Activities in 2022. All of these factors may attract international investors and EMDEs to natural gas investments as an alternative to coal power.

Natural gas has sparked controversy in arguments over sustainable energy transitions. On the one hand, it is argued to be a bridge between coal and renewable energy technologies in the short term, a means towards just global energy transition (IEA, 2011; Kemfert et al., 2022) and net-zero transitions (Bistline & Young, 2022). On the other hand, natural gas is criticised for causing lock-in, stranding gas assets, and delaying transitions to renewables for a substantial period (Brauers, 2022). The latter criticism, particularly the one-size-fits-all approach to the natural gas phase-down, raises another round of argument from the viewpoint of just energy transitions.

The Paris–Glasgow financial regime was formed to mobilise finance for NZE globally. The Paris Climate Agreement has enhanced the financial sector's concerns about climate-related risks and stranded assets for financial stability, institutionalising disclosure of climate-related risk exposures. The Glasgow COP 26 reinforced the momentum for climate action in the financial sector. The Glasgow Financial Alliance for Net Zero (GFANZ) was founded to mobilise the entire financial sector to achieve the investment levels required for a net-zero transition. It collaborated with the International Partners' Group to launch the Just Energy Transition Partnership (JETP) to mobilise finance NZE on top of the Green Climate Fund. The Asian Development Bank (ADB) launched the Energy Transition Mechanism (ETM) to provide grants and concessional finance for early coal retirement and clean energy investments. Sustainable investing assets and climate bonds have been boosted.

However, negotiation has been prolonged. While JETP agreed to finance South Africa, Indonesia, Senegal, and Vietnam, it has disbursed to concrete projects only in South Africa. ADB agreed to work with Indonesia, the Philippines, and Vietnam but had financed only a few projects by 2023. Few studies have been conducted on the relevance of fund allocation, not to mention its impacts on NZE.

Against this backdrop, the book raised two research questions:

(1) Why has the Paris–Glasgow financial regime and financing net zero been slow in progress?
(2) Why are highly coal-dependent small EMDEs attracted to the shift to natural-gas-based electricity systems instead of RES-based ones?

This chapter gives answers to these research questions. The remainder of the chapter is organised as follows. Section 8.2 describes the propagation of transition risks between the financial and real sectors based on the conventional risk–return management perspective that we presented in Chapter 2 and provides an integrated cost–benefit perspective as an alternative. Section 8.3 evaluates the costs and benefits of transitions to RES-based electricity systems, based on our findings in Chapters 3–6. Section 8.4 explores why JETP and ETM marginally increase the benefit of transition and how the benefits differ by host country. Section 8.5 discusses how financial system transitions address the underlying factors behind these marginal benefits. Lastly, Section 8.6 answers the book's main research questions and proposes future challenges worth investigating.

8.2 INTERACTIONS BETWEEN FINANCIAL AND ELECTRICITY SYSTEMS

8.2.1 Risk–Return Management Perspective

Previous research describes a propagation mechanism of climate-related transition risks between financial actors and their clients in the real sector from a risk reduction perspective. In essence, financial actors translate the climate-related transition risks generated by landscape developments, policy interventions, or changes in sentiment into the financial cost of capital and transfer this to their clients. Banks and bond underwriters change the terms of conditions. Investors change capital allocation, screen out companies based on their ESG practices, and adjust shareholder engagement to influence real-sector actors (Kölbel et al., 2020). These changes trigger changes within the real sector, which may in turn trigger repercussions in the financial sector and generate feedback effects in the end (as represented in Figures 2.1, 2.2, and 2.3).

However, financial and real-sector actors are not always economically rational. They may have different perceptions of the seriousness of commitments to NZE and climate-related transition risks and may fail to agree on changes in financial costs. Asymmetric power relations between financial- and real-sector actors make it difficult to add climate-related transition risks to the financial cost of capital. Changes in capital cost may not trigger behavioural changes in real-sector actors when incumbent actors dominate the market or when governments intervene in the market for political, social, security, and macroeconomic reasons.

In Vietnam and the Philippines, it was the OECD and G20 agreements, not the change in the financial cost associated with the propagation of climate-related transition risks, that stopped export credit to unabated coal power plants and redirected electricity production towards low-carbon systems.

8.2.2 Electricity System Transitions

Chapter 3 showed that the technological changes needed for transitioning towards RES-based electricity systems must be associated with synchronised changes in infrastructural, institutional, and organisational elements. The changes required in each element differ substantially according to the grid paradigm used. The flexible grid paradigm requires the least changes in all the elements, allowing vertical-integration utilities to remain intact and accept natural gas as flexible energy. By contrast, the super-grid paradigm demands significant investments in ultra-high-voltage transmission lines and changes of business models into system integrators, and the distributed smart-grid paradigm requires market transactions by unbundled utilities and distributed prosumers and investments in smart grids and behind-the-meter energy storage systems. (The changes associated with each of the three paradigms are outlined in Table 3.1). Transition costs can be intolerably high in countries where there are substantial gaps between the required elements in each paradigm and the current state of the art.

The need for these associated synchronised changes in infrastructural, institutional, and organisational elements explains why changes in the cost of capital are not so powerful in generating behavioural changes in electricity companies. Changes in the cost of capital may incentivise companies to take add-on measures such as investments in energy efficiency and RES-E. However, they induce organisational changes and business model innovations only when companies perceive potentially serious and permanent damage to business as usual and when they have knowledge, prior experience, organisational culture on sustainable practices, and sufficient assets to take advantage of innovation opportunities (Mori, 2021a). They may perceive that the transition cost is still higher than the benefits even after changes in the capital cost.

8.2.3 Integrated Cost–Benefit Perspective

Cost–benefit analysis at the national level helps explain government intervention, or lack of it, in the financial sector's potential to induce transformative changes in the real sector.

Figure 8.1 illustrates the total costs and benefits of electricity system transitions. The total costs include the stranded costs associated with early retirements of fossil fuel power plants, installation costs of new RES-E capacity, and transition costs associated with changes in the infrastructural, institutional, and organisational elements described in Chapter 3. The socioeconomic impacts of these transitions, such as loss of jobs and livelihoods, add to the cost schedule.

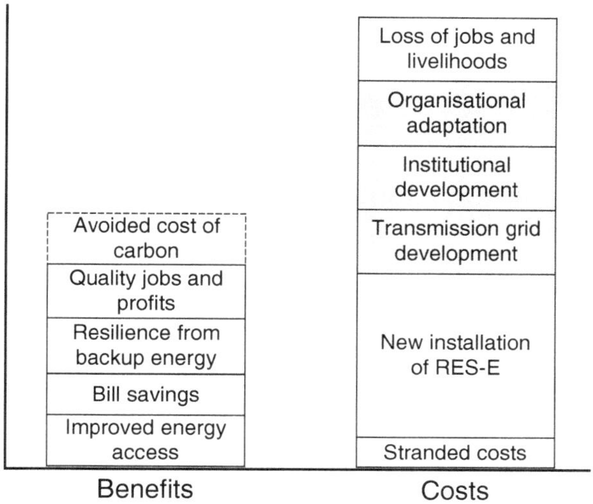

FIGURE 8.1 Cost and benefit schedules of the transition towards RES-based electricity systems.
Source: Authors.

The total benefits include improved energy access, electricity bill savings through the replacement of fossil fuel, and backup power that improves the system's resilience for end-users (Yamashiro & Mori, 2023). Added to the benefit schedule are quality jobs and profits from creating local value chains and new industries, and avoided cost of carbon.

These cost and benefit schedules are contingent on several factors. First is the current state of power shortage. The benefits of energy access are substantial where power outages are chronic and severe. Stable energy access enables businesses to increase productivity by supplying goods and services as planned, and it improves welfare for end-users through time-saving and loss reduction. It may also create new value by increasing access to irrigation water (Rahman et al., 2022).

The second factor is changes in infrastructural, institutional, and organisational elements (grey shading in Figure 8.1). Synchronised and prior changes in these elements can make investments in RES-E capacity bankable and profitable. As a result, their new installation costs will be smaller and can even be negative. By contrast, unsynchronised directions or rates of change may deter transitions and increase costs.

A third factor affecting costs and benefits is the impact of these transitions on trade patterns, balance, and dependency. Critical materials production and reserves for RES-E are geographically concentrated. In 2022, China produced 85% of the world's solar photovoltaic (PV) polysilicon, 97% of PV wafers, 84% of PV cells, and 78% of PV modules (IEA PVPS, 2023). It also had 60% of the world's wind turbine manufacturing capacity in 2023 (GWEC, 2023). China's dominance in production implies that countries depending on domestic coal for power will lose jobs, worsen the trade balance, and increase trade dependency on China, all of which add to the cost schedule. In contrast, countries that depend on importing coal for power will be less affected, and those that have capacity for component manufacturing, installation, and operation and maintenance (O&M) may increase benefits.

A fourth factor is the availability, affordability, and international and social acceptance of using natural gas as a bridge fuel. Countries with domestic natural gas fields can offset the higher upfront expenditure for new gas facilities and the loss of domestic coal production by reducing coal imports. Those who have domestic coal mining and do not have domestic natural gas fields will lose jobs and worsen the trade balance, while those who do not have either will need to install liquid natural gas facilities for imports. The impacts of natural gas use on the cost and benefit schedule are also contingent on international natural gas prices and the credibility of the global NZE pledge. High and unstable international natural gas prices and strong credibility add the stranded cost of natural gas assets to the transition cost (Miller, 2023). This discourages EMDEs from switching to natural gas and investing in power generation capacity for gas with carbon capture and storage (CCS) (as illustrated in Figures 4.6 and 4.10) and motivates them to proliferate coal power with installed CCS (Figures 4.7 and 4.11).

The fifth factor impacting the cost and benefit schedule is environmental value. Transitions of electricity systems can generate environmental co-benefits by reducing health and ecological damage from air and water pollution. They can also reduce the cost of CO_2 emissions imposed by carbon pricing and border carbon adjustment mechanisms, thus increasing the benefits.

8.3 COSTS AND BENEFITS OF ELECTRICITY SYSTEM TRANSITIONS

8.3.1 Changes in the Technological Element

Chapter 4 demonstrated that the Southeast Asian region would have to bear about four times larger costs for new installation of RES-E than stranded costs to attain the 2050 net-zero target. The installation costs of RES-E are estimated to be 7.9% of GDP per year in 2021–2050 if CCS technology is not commercially available, whereas stranded costs are around 1.5%. The technological transition costs peak at 13% in 2025–2035 and decrease after that. Our estimates revealed higher new installation costs than predicted in the literature summarising the latest available mitigation scenarios, such as Rogelj et al. (2018).

These higher costs accrue to the rapid increase in coal power since the early 2010s and the expected continuous high growth of electricity demand in the coming decades in this region. By the 1990s, the high-energy-consuming countries of Malaysia and Thailand had increased gas power capacities and were using domestically produced water resources and natural gas to satisfy the growing demand for electricity. The Philippines and Vietnam exploited their domestic natural gas fields to do the same in the 2010s (Mori, 2021b). However, the perceived depletion of domestic natural gas production makes it hard for these countries to satisfy the growing demand at an affordable price. The same holds for Cambodia and, to a lesser

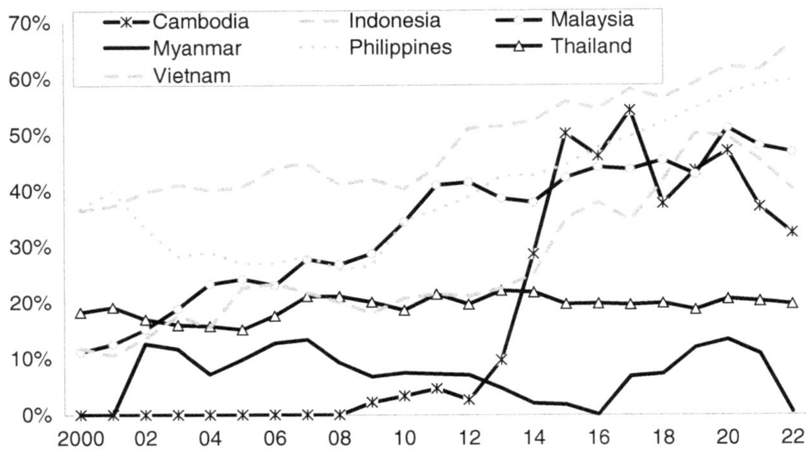

FIGURE 8.2 Percentage of coal in the energy mix of power generation in selected Southeast Asian countries, 2000–2022.
Source: Compiled by the authors based on IEA (2024c; 2024d; 2024e; 2024f; 2024a; 2024g; 2024b).

extent, Myanmar. The quest for energy security prompted several of these countries to increase coal power capacity and the amount of coal power generation in the 2010s (see Figure 8.2). In other words, countries in the Southeast Asian region have increased the number of young coal power plants that will accrue high stranded costs if these countries are to achieve NDC and net-zero emissions targets.

The amounts of stranded assets for Southeast Asian region are comparable to those of other emerging economies with heavy reliance on coal. Around 43.4 GW of coal power plants in Indonesia are stranded (Cui et al., 2022). In India, coal capacity stranding will be around 133–237 GW after 2030 if India pursues an ambitious climate policy (Malik et al., 2020). In China, over 1,000 GW of plants may be retired early during 2030–2050 to meet the requirements for a 2°C limit (Wang et al., 2020b). In regions less reliant on coal, stranded coal power capacity will be smaller: around 18.2 GW of coal power plants will be stranded in Latin America and the Caribbean (Binsted et al., 2020). However, the retired capacity of gas power plants will be more significant.

These comparisons imply that regions whose electricity systems are dominated by coal will suffer from significant stranded assets. For instance, China, India, and Indonesia have a substantial number of young coal fleets, so they are affected by decarbonisation.

The situation would be similar in regions relying on gas for electricity. While gas power discharges fewer CO_2 emissions than coal power and thus can play a role in bridging the transition, gas assets are not exempted from early retirement to achieve climate goals. The magnitude of asset stranding will depend on each region's climate policy stringency.

Nonetheless, these stranded costs do not necessarily motivate transitions towards RES-based electricity systems. First, switching to natural gas claims much lower transition costs than switching to RES-E. Gas power is less capital-intensive and has shorter operation periods than coal power. Our estimates suggest that stranded costs are less significant for gas power than for coal. Installation costs for new RES-E capacity are 8.7 times higher than stranded costs of fossil-fuel-based power capacity (as shown in Table 4.3) and become lower if CCS and nuclear power are available. High gas prices make the fuel switch to gas more economically attractive. Stranded costs from gas power decrease by 22–25%, and new installation costs of RES-E increase by 0.2–1.5% to compensate for lower investments in gas power capacity.

Second, policymakers in EMDEs perceive international pledges to NZE as probabilistic and negotiable rather than absolutely binding and completely achievable. They can reduce expected transition costs if they extend the deadline to achieve NZE and prolong the lifetime of existing young fossil fuel power. They perceive a marginal increase in transition costs if they perceive a higher probability of deadline extension.

These findings imply that switching to natural gas as a transition fuel and investing in CCS, nuclear power, and RES-E capacity are rational choices for Southeast Asian countries that aim to decarbonise their electricity systems.

8.3.2 Changes in Infrastructural, Institutional, and Organisational Elements

In response to the OECD and G20 agreements to end support for unabated coal power plants, Vietnam and the Philippines decided to discontinue investments in new coal power plants; Vietnam's pledge to net-zero emissions at the Glasgow COP meeting in 2021, and the Philippines' moratorium on new coal power projects, make it hard for them to invest in coal power that goes beyond what has been approved. Both countries implemented feed-in tariffs (FiT) for RES-E. However, they terminated them within a few years and decided to shift from coal to natural gas and RES-E simultaneously instead of transitioning to an RES-based electricity system.

Chapter 5 showed that, in Vietnam, uncertain, abrupt, and disorderly policy intervention, severe renewable curtailment, and slower institutional changes made RES-E projects less bankable despite the implementation of generous FiT for RES-E and the development of high-voltage backbone transmission lines. The vertically integrated electricity model, the dominance of state-owned electric companies, and the slow development of smart grids block the electricity system from adopting demand-side integration. Integration could help increase the capacity and productivity of distributed RES-E and thus can reduce new installation costs. Demand-side integration requires radical institutional and organisational changes that include unbundling of vertically integrated electricity models, competitive wholesale and ancillary service markets, retail competition, and network governance to ensure non-discriminative access to the grid. However, these changes raise conflicts with incumbents' interests. Perceiving the high political cost of institutional changes, in May 2023 Vietnam's cabinet decided to keep the existing electricity system intact, shifting from coal to natural gas and utility-scale RES-E in the approved Eighth Power Development Plan (PDP8) for 2021–2030. It plans to capitalise on additional hydropower capacity as front-of-meter energy storage systems (FOM-ESS) instead of

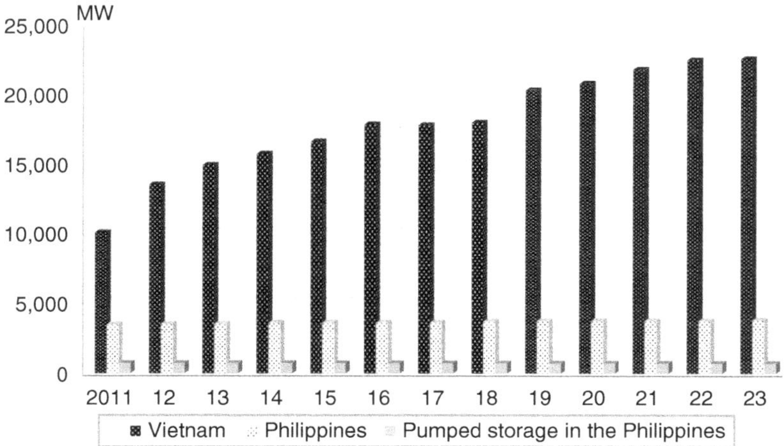

FIGURE 8.3 Installed capacity of hydropower in Vietnam and the Philippines and of pumped storage in the Philippines, 2011–2023. Source: Compiled by the authors based on data from IRENA (2021; 2024).

fostering ancillary and system-balancing services and capacity trade in the wholesale market and waiting for ammonia-biomass co-firing and hydrogen power to be commercially available on a large scale. However, ecological constraints have deterred developments in hydropower capacities (as shown in Figure 8.3). Continuous power outages in 2022–2024 destabilised the electricity regime. In response, the government implemented a full-fledged direct power purchase agreement to increase supply from rooftop solar. It is also reconsidering installing nuclear power, which was planned but abandoned in the past (Vu, 2024).

Chapter 6 showed that the Philippines has developed market-based institutions that can make the wholesale electricity spot market work effectively for large-scale integration of utility-scale RES-E. These include ancillary service markets, renewable energy markets, the Green Energy Option Programme, and a competitive selection process, as well as retail competition and open access. These institutional developments in the Philippines contrast sharply with those in Vietnam (see Table 8.1).

Table 8.1 *Institutions supporting electric flexibility trading related to RES-E, Vietnam and the Philippines*

Institution	Vietnam	Philippines
Institutions for electricity and flexibility trading		
Wholesale electricity spot market	2019 (full operation)	2010 (Luzon &Visayas); 2023 (nationwide)
Ancillary service markets/procurement agreements	No bidding mechanism for ancillary services	2019 (5-year, monthly-based firm contract)
Balancing service markets or mechanisms		
Capacity market/ payment contracts	No	
Renewable energy market	No	Launched interim commercial operation in 2022
Institutions for electric flexibility trading for demand-side integration		
Retail market	Scheduled to run (2023)	Retail Competition and Open Access (2004)
Direct power purchase agreements	Pilot (2021–2023)	No
Third-party access	Via Electric Power Trading Company	Off-grid areas (2019)
Time-based and location-based tariffs	Time-based tariff for industrial and commercial customers	No
Demand response	2019 (to reduce peak load)	No
Smart-grid policy	Smart Grid Roadmap (2012)	National Smart Grid Policy Framework (2020)

Source: Compiled by the authors based on the descriptions in Chapters 5 and 6 in this book.

However, ancillary service markets are designed to proliferate obsolete fossil fuel plants owned by incumbent utilities. Unfavourable revenue contracts failed to boost ancillary service supplies from pump-up hydro and battery energy storage systems (ESS) (Barroco, 2021) and pump-up hydro capacity. The Philippines has not increased installed capacity of pump-up hydro capacity, and Vietnam has not installed yet (see Figure 8.3). A lack of technical specifications in the competitive selection process is criticised for driving distribution utilities to choose long-term power purchase agreements with coal power in the context of the high-levelised cost of RES-E (de Torres, 2020). On top of the insufficiency of these institutions, grid connections for small-scale RES-E remain uncertain, rooftop solar is incentivised only through net metering, and development of high-voltage backbone transmission lines has been delayed. These obstacles would encourage an incumbent power utility to sell out its coal power plant for early retirement but to invest in international, not domestic, RES-E projects (AC Energy, 2019; ACEN, 2023a; Burgos, 2023) and battery ESS (Minh, 2023). Such obstacles have also driven other incumbent domestic power utilities and foreign investors to invest in battery ESS that can work as FOM-ESSs, and the government plans to operate a commercial nuclear station from the early 2030s (Inoue & Shiga, 2024).

8.3.3 Total Transition Costs and Benefits

The findings described in Sections 8.3.1 and 8.3.2 imply that the total benefits of such electricity system transitions hardly exceed the total costs in the Southeast Asian region, particularly in the coal-power-dependent countries of Vietnam and the Philippines. In addition to the four-times-larger cost for the new installation of RES-E than the benefit of avoiding the stranded cost of fossil-fuel-based electricity, the two countries must bear substantial transition costs associated with changes in infrastructural, institutional, and organisational elements.

Vietnam may offset these transition costs by switching from coal to natural gas. The country used to be a coal exporter but became an importer in the 2010s (Mori, 2021b; Vo & Ju, 2021). Switching from coal to gas will reduce coal imports and increase domestic natural gas consumption, thus improving trade balance and reducing energy dependency. However, the country has postponed exploitation of this possibility. The government perceives domestic natural gas production in the South China Sea as risky. All the approved gas power projects using domestically produced natural gas are in central and southern regions. The government also sees unlimited increases in liquid natural gas (LNG) imports as threatening national security. All the approved LNG power plants are owned and operated by foreign investors under standardised power purchase agreements, which require them to arrange project finance with USD-denominated, fixed-interest-rate loans to develop projects without compensation for the loss incurred by policy changes, including tariff changes and PPA termination (Hong et al., 2020). This is why Vietnam's cabinet-approved Eighth Power Development Plan treats natural gas and LNG as bridging technologies; they will be increased to satisfy growing electricity demand by 2030 but will be substituted by hydrogen by 2050. The Korean and Vietnamese owners of the Quang Tri thermal plant signed an agreement to convert it to LNG power (as mentioned in Table 5.2) and to explore opportunities in hydrogen production (Biogradlija, 2023).

The energy switch from coal to natural gas will not substantially impact jobs and trade balance in the Philippines, which imports both coal and LNG. The perceived insignificance of these impacts explains why the energy oligarchs in the country aimed to attract foreign investment in LNG facilities and to use LNG as bridge fuel soon after the moratorium on new coal power plants.

Transition costs associated with changes in the infrastructural, institutional, and organisational elements suggest that there will be a preference for transition from coal to natural-gas-based, hierarchical, and centrally controlled supply systems rather than for developing bridges towards a centrally controlled flexible grid RES-based electricity system (Figure 3.3). However, transition costs and benefits vary in the long run. They are affected by infrastructural, institutional, and organisational changes that may aim to propel narratives and policy goals other than net-zero transitions. The variability of cost and benefit schedules opens a window of opportunity for financing net-zero to induce EMDEs to accelerate net-zero transitions by changing their cost and benefit schedules.

8.4 HOW HAS THE JETP AFFECTED THE INTEGRATED COST–BENEFIT SCHEDULE?

ETM and JETP are both designed to carry out this function in the energy sector, although they have different scopes. ETM focuses on compensating sponsors for foregone dividends caused by the early retirement of coal power plants on a project basis. The ETM facility provides soft loans for refinancing existing debt, distributing a one-off special dividend to the sponsors, and supporting the creation of decent work and quality jobs (Asian Development Bank, 2024).

In contrast, JETP focuses on decarbonising state-owned electricity companies that monopolise electricity supply but cover the entire electricity sector and addressing the loss of jobs and livelihoods. It covers not only compensation to financiers and sponsors but also infrastructural and institutional development; this makes the new installation of RES-E capacity bankable and facilitates skill development and community development in affected areas (Semelane et al., 2021; World Bank, 2023). To encourage a common understanding, the International Partners' Group (IPG) defines the scope of JETP, articulates its priority areas and details in conceptual notes, and makes them available to potential counterparts (Socialist Republic of Vietnam, 2023).

The specification described in their Implementation Plan and Resource Mobilisation Plan makes the cost reduction components identical among the three JETP countries (see Table 8.2). They have neutralised the loss incurred by financiers and sponsors of coal power plants, new installation of RES-E capacity, transmission grid

Table 8.2 *Intended changes in cost and benefit schedules in the JETP Implementation Plan*

	Benefits	Costs
South Africa	Energy access for all Local value chains for RES-E and transmission Local value chains for BEV and battery Green hydrogen and its derivative industry Economic diversification Improvement of air quality	Decommission and repositioning of coal power plants New installation of RES-E generation capacity and battery storage Development of transmission grid Skill development Community development for affected people
Indonesia	Local value chain for RES-E	Early retirement of coal power plants New installation of dispatchable RES-E New installation of variable RES-E Development of transmission grid
Vietnam	Energy access for all Coal power flexibility Local value chain for RES-E Green hydrogen and its derivative industry	Early retirement of coal power plants New installation of RES-E generation capacity and battery storage Development of transmission grid Jobs and livelihoods for affected people

Source: Compiled by the authors based on the Just Energy Transition Partnership Indonesia (2023), The Presidency, Republic of South Africa (2023), and Socialist Republic of Vietnam (2023).

and energy storage system development, and mitigation of socioeconomic impacts. For Indonesia, they have added new installations of dispatchable RES-E such as bioenergy, geothermal, and hydropower.

In contrast, the benefit components are varied. While the development of the local value chain of RES-E is common, benefits for South Africa and Vietnam include energy access for all, and the development of green hydrogen and its derivative industry are priority areas. The provision for South Africa goes further to include the development of local value chains for battery electric vehicles (BEV), battery, transmission, economic diversification, and air quality improvement in the affected areas (The Presidency, Republic of South Africa, 2023). Vietnam counts on coal power flexibility as a benefit.

We can infer several reasons behind the planning of the different benefit components. First is the institutional setup in JETP countries. South Africa has facilitated coordination and alignment across relevant policy areas, diverse levels of government, and stakeholders. By contrast, Indonesia and Vietnam understand the JETP's aims as decarbonisation in the electricity sector and have not sought policy alignment or synergies between energy transition and ongoing transition in other sectors such as transport, trade, or finance (Seiler et al., 2023).

The second factor in the variance among countries is the seriousness of power outage problems. South Africa has suffered from severe load-shedding due to its chronic energy crisis. However, subsidised pricing and corruption have restricted the state-owned monopolised power company (Eskom) from developing generation and grid capacities and thus securing energy access (Tyler & Mgoduso, 2022). The deployment of new RES-E generation capacity, coupled with that of transmission grids, and institutional changes such as removing licensing thresholds for embedded generation are listed as generating co-benefits of decarbonisation and energy access for all.

Vietnam also suffers from seasonal power outages due to growing electricity demand and increasing fluctuations of hydropower water storage due to extreme weather and upstream hydropower developments in China and Laos (Chapter 5). In contrast, Indonesia does not suffer from such crises. Instead, the country has been experiencing an oversupply of electricity since 2020, especially in

Java, Bali, and Sumatra (Hamdi, 2021; PLN, 2021). PLN, the state-owned power company, has no grid capacity to accept additional generation from newly installed RES-E without upgrading or expanding existing systems or inter-island interconnection. Higher interest payments and a full guarantee to PLN credit risk from the Indonesian government were given to Chinese banks for installing coal power plants in the 2000s and 2010s (Mori, 2020).

The third factor affecting JETP outcomes in the different countries is the power of state-owned electricity companies and the embeddedness of the coal network. While the JETP neutralises the financial impacts of decommissioning and of the early phase-out of coal power on financiers, sponsors, and owners, it does not do so for the forgone revenue stream of state-owned electricity companies and the coal industry. These large adverse impacts require mitigation measures for adversely affected stakeholders who have not been sufficiently compensated.

South Africa has attempted to implement comprehensive energy reforms to address the crisis since the late 1990s. The reform package is identical to the policy reform proposed by the JETP: unbundling the state-owned monopolised power company (Eskom), opening up the electricity market, phasing out subsidised pricing, and encouraging private investment in RES-E. However, these reforms have been marginally implemented at best. Furious resistance by a powerful coal lobby around Eskom, big industrial consumers, trade unions, big business, those living off the extended coal value chain, and critical factions of the ruling political party (the ANC) or President Zuma have blocked the reforms, heightening the crisis (Vanheukelom, 2023). Opposition forced the government to postpone the decommission of Escom's Komati coal power plant, whose last remaining operating unit was to have been closed by October 2022 (World Bank, 2023). This strong opposition led to the revision of the electricity sector reform measures in the Just Energy Transition Implementation Plan, adding organisational changes in Eskom and a law-enforcement team addressing crime and corruption as components (Suharsono & Maulidia, 2023).

Indonesia has already gone through partial unbundling of its vertically integrated electricity supply system and allowed independent power producers (IPPs) to supply electricity to PLN. While the Cirebon coal power plant, operated by an IPP and jointly owned by domestic coal mines and international investors, accepted early retirement of the plant under the ETM scheme (ADB, 2024b), it is about to operate a new, larger, efficient, and low-emission coal power plant nearby. While PLN accepts deployment of RES-E in off-grid areas, it has worked with the government to block developing grid capacity in the already congested Java–Bali line to create space for IPPs to export RES-E (Mori, 2020). The lengthy planning and development of transmission grids is regarded as mismatched with the 3- to 5-year time window of JETP (Suharsono & Maulidia, 2023).

Vietnam has undergone phased electricity sector reform so that EVN, the dominant and state-owned electric company, can adapt to RES-based electricity systems. However, institutional reform and RES-E deployment policy have been slow and have oscillated, blocking a large-scale integration of RES-E and generating large-scale renewable curtailment (Chapter 5). EVN has exerted strong political influence to use coal as a flexibility power to proliferate them.

The fourth factor influencing JETP planning is the accessibility to GFANZ and alternative financial sources for new financial value creation. The financial investment needed for all the priority projects in the Implementation Plan amounts to USD 98 billion over 2023–2027 for South Africa (Suharsono & Maulidia, 2023), at least USD 97 billion between 2023 and 2030 and USD 580 billion between 2023 and 2050 for Indonesia, and, through the Eighth Power Development Plan, USD 135 billion by 2030 for Vietnam (Barnes, 2023). In contrast, IPG and GFANZ made an initial pledge of USD 8.5 billion for South Africa, USD 20 billion for Indonesia, and USD 15.5 billion for Vietnam. Whether the JETP countries can fill the financial gap and attract investments it is critically contingent on whether the initial pledge from IPG and GFANZ plays a catalyst role.

As for the RES-E value chain, South Africa and Vietnam have advantages. South Africa has a mature renewable energy industry due to a long history of deployment and procurement (Suharsono & Maulidia, 2023). Vietnam produces 6.1 GW or 2% of the world's PV wafers, 18.8 GW or 5% of PV cells, and 24.1 GW or 6% of PV modules, due to investments and production by major Chinese solar cell manufacturers (IEA PVPS, 2023: 48). Local production of components, installation, and O&M are estimated to generate more than 0.1 million jobs (IEA PVPS, 2023: 67).

By contrast, Indonesia's solar PV industry has failed to gain a competitive edge due to weak and temporary policy incentives for RES-E deployment, protectionist restrictions such as tariffs on imported solar panels, and high local content requirements (Burke et al., 2019). Utility-scale floating solar PV may be the only RES-E that arrives at grid parity (Christian et al., 2021).

As for the BEV and battery value chain, Indonesia has successfully attracted Chinese investments. An export ban on unprocessed raw minerals in 2014 and on unprocessed nickel ore, the main component for making steel and electric-vehicle batteries, in 2020, pressured Chinese companies to invest in nickel mining and smelting in Indonesia to maintain their access to nickel resources (Maulia, 2023). The Belt and Road Initiative also pushed them to establish large industrial parks near mining sites (Tritto, 2023). Indonesian coal-mining companies have partnered with Chinese companies to diversify their business to nickel mining and smelters for battery materials and manufacturing of commercial BEVs (Maulia & Daamyanti, 2023). The leading Chinese BEV manufacturer, BYD, and a BEV subsidiary of Indonesian coal conglomerate, Bakrie and Brothers, partnered to operate a public transport bus system in Jakarta (BYD, 2022) and assemble electric trucks and buses (Belinda, 2023).

Vietnamese conglomerate VinFast collaborated with China's Gotion High-Tech to start domestic production of BEV in 2021 and lithium batteries in 2022. Despite suffering a negative profit margin, the company enjoyed rapid delivery and strong revenue growth, exhibiting substantial profit improvements year by year (Finanz Nachrichten, 2024). Also, the Vietnamese government requested PowerChina, which won the engineering, procurement, and construction (EPC) contracts to build 600 MW wind power in Laos, to invest in energy storage, hydrogen, and ammonia (Hoang, 2024).

Meanwhile, the information available from the JETP for South Africa and Indonesia does not clearly show how technology transfer will be supported in these partnerships and to what extent. For example, financing for investments in new energy vehicles and the green hydrogen value chains included in the JETP Investment Plan for South Africa remains largely unidentified. This leaves questions about whether partners will support incentives for private-sector partnerships in manufacturing to deliver new scaled-up manufacturing value chains (Seiler et al., 2023).

These underlying factors suggest that JETP does not guarantee private finance for electricity system changes that go beyond bankable renewable energy projects. The attraction of private green finance is contingent on the industrial basis and on developments in infrastructural, institutional, and organisational elements of the electricity systems.

Besides, financing system transformation can generate negative social and environmental value, offsetting the benefits of new financial value. Chinese investors have developed captive coal power plants to supply electricity to energy-intensive nickel smelting plants. In the smelting process, nineteen tonnes of carbon are released for every tonne of smelted nickel, and toxic waste that is difficult to manage is produced due to the use of high-pressure acid leaching technology, which is indispensable to producing battery-grade nickel. While some refinery companies have been committed to installing RES-E capacity (Maulia, 2022), adverse impacts on local society and the environment will persist as long as the global boost in BEV continues (Adnas, 2022; Dinata et al., 2020).

8.5 PERSPECTIVES FOR NET-ZERO FINANCIAL AND ELECTRICITY SYSTEM TRANSITIONS

8.5.1 Transition Finance

Transition finance has emerged as a new financial instrument to direct the hard-to-abate and carbon-intensive sectors towards the net-zero emission pathway. A strict definition of 'green' makes it difficult for green finance to advance transitions to net-zero emissions for incumbent companies in high-carbon-intensive sectors. Transition finance can potentially overcome this difficulty, facilitating client engagement in decarbonisation, so long as clients have credible, feasible, and sufficiently ambitious transition plans, and transition finance meaningfully advances a client's net-zero journey, including managed phase-out projects. To effectively mainstream transition finance into general corporate finance, banks should prepare transition finance frameworks that reflect their business models and operating footprints or geographies (Net-Zero Banking Alliance, 2022).

So far, transition finance accounts for a tiny portion of total financing in this area. Sustainability-link bonds (SLBs) and transition bonds were boosted to exceed US$100 billion and US$3 billion in market size in 2021. Transition bonds were initially driven by Europe but were dominated by China and Japan in 2022. Following a pilot scheme of SLB issuance in 2021 and guidelines on transition bond products, China explored transition bonds for eight heavy industries in 2022 (Climate Bonds Initiative, 2023a). The Japanese government implemented national transition finance programmes and developed sectoral decarbonisation roadmaps, leading to transition bond insurance by electric companies, oil and gas companies, and steel industries (METI, 2023). However, these measures are far smaller than green bonds, whose market size exceeded US$580 billion in the same year (Climate Bonds Initiative, 2023b).

The scarcity of transition finance accrues to insufficient understanding of the need for financing carbon-intensive sectors. Unlike green finance, clearly defined targets and definitions or taxonomies can hardly be applied to transition finance because they can increase financed emissions in the short term. Most sustainability-linked bonds have been tied to weak, irrelevant, or already achieved climate targets (Zhao & Shi, 2023).

To make transition finance work better for the net-zero energy transition, it is indispensible to establish the credibility of an issuer's GHG emissions reduction strategy, commitments, and practices. Issuers are recommended to disclose their climate transition strategy and governance, business model environmental materiality, science-based climate targets, and implementation transparency (Climate Transition Finance & ICMA, 2023). Clear guidance must be given to help issuers create and document country-level and sector-level targets and pathways linked to the global target and to evaluate interim goals. Country-specific contexts, such as energy security and affordability for governments and their citizens, must be considered in addition to science-based targets (Asia Transition Finance Study Group, 2022).

These new requirements may call for a systemic transformation of the financial sector. Financial institutions and investors must change their business models to enhance deep engagement with clients through science-based transition strategies, governance, and key performance indicators. Some global investors have fostered stewardship and exercised constructive, behind-the-scenes engagement. These include informed dialogue with management and boards in executing fiduciary responsibilities, expressing views about environment, social, and governance (ESG) disclosure and practices, and monitoring corporate activities before exercising ownership rights such as shareholder proposals and proxy voting at public annual general meetings or expressing views through the press (Coronation, 2023; van Benthem et al., 2022).

Because climate-related risks affect the stability of financial institutions, central banks and financial regulatory authorities need to expand the scope of responsibility from traditional narrow mandates to incorporate climate-related risks into their policy frameworks to safeguard macro-financial stability (Dikau & Volz, 2019). Only 12% out of 135 central banks worldwide had explicit sustainability mandates as of 2017 (Dikau & Volz, 2021). They may devise policy interventions to foster green investments within Basel III, an internationally agreed set of measures developed by the Basel Committee on Banking Supervision in response to the financial crisis of 2007–2009. However, they may foster green investments in ways that will not destabilise the financial sector (D'Orazioa & Popoyan, 2019) or violate the neutrality of monetary policy.

8.5.2 Transformative Finance

Our findings reveal that financial system transitions lag behind net-zero transitions in electricity systems, slowing the latter. EMDEs have increasingly advanced net-zero transitions in the electricity system. Green finance and ESG investments have become no exception. JETP has stepped into early retirement of coal power plants, perceiving the importance of decarbonisation in the electricity sector. However, green finance and ESG investments are concentrated in the US, Europe, and China, as is the deployment of RES-E generation capacity. Several companies in EMDEs have attracted international finance and investments to create alternative financial value through electric battery and vehicle production. However, the financial sector is unfamiliar with financing early-stage technologies and is not good at matching the needs of niche projects (Geddes & Schmidt, 2020). Domestic financial institutions and investors tend to assess such projects as unbankable and provide insufficient finance even if these projects are likely to create long-term integrated value, including social and environmental value.

Transformative finance, or finance for transformative changes, is proposed as a means to accelerate financial system transitions. Transformative finance requires business model innovation at the actor level. It may include shifting capital allocation from the traditional financial risk–return thinking and optimal risk–return investments towards long-term sustainability investments and prioritising financial return from investing in system change; changing the performance evaluation of clients from financial value towards integrated value (Schoenmaker & Schramade, 2021); and fostering in-house skillsets and mindsets to map out unquantifiable systemic uncertainties and maximise system change impact focusing on long-term benefits (Loorbach et al., 2020). Enhancing engagement with clients aiming for long-term social value creation (Barko et al., 2022; Kölbel et al., 2020) and those in which investors have substantial stakes (Azar et al., 2021) can mitigate reputation risk and increase share prices.

At the industrial level, financial actors may organise alliances to collectively engage incumbent electric companies to identify environmental materiality, set science-based targets, develop scenario-based climate transition strategy and governance, disclose all of these inititatives, and steer progress.

However, these novel endeavours are not sufficiently powerful to overcome the short-termism that prevents long-term sustainable investments (Hafner et al., 2020). Delegated investment management also causes agency problems between the asset owner or principal and the delegated asset manager or agent responsible for making investment decisions (Schoenmaker & Schramade, 2021).

Further institutional changes can generate feedback effects for transformative changes. The change of laws and regulations defining the obligations of an investment fiduciary can direct financial actors to prioritise financial returns from system changes (Penna, 2023). Market-based institutions such as the carbon trading market, renewable energy certificate scheme and certification market, and non-fossil value trading market enable electric companies and financial actors to capture integrated values. Scope 3 carbon disclosure may incentivise the real sector to decarbonise its supply chain, stimulating demand for non-fossil-fuel-based electricity, carbon credit, and non-fossil value. These changes in the source of financial returns may incentivise the financial and real sectors to co-create new business models that produce and capture long-term sustainable value and drive electricity and financial systems towards net zero.

8.6 CONCLUSIONS

These findings bring us to the answers to the two research questions of this book:

(1) Why has the Paris–Glasgow financial regime and financing net zero been slow in progress?
(2) Why are highly coal-dependent small EMDEs attracted to the shift to natural-gas-based electricity systems instead of RES-based ones?

To address the first question, the Paris–Glasgow financial regime maintains traditional financial risk–return thinking and optimal risk–return investments and requires EMDEs to reform the electricity system. Policy uncertainty about net-zero transitions makes it difficult for the financial regime to persuade their regulators and asset owners, who are locked in short-termism, to accept the expanded understanding of fiduciary duty that attaches importance to long-term sustainability benefits. This short-termism results in capital allocation to bankable projects on a commercial basis, not on concessional terms of conditions. Traditional financial risk–return thinking, optimal risk–return investments, and short-termism have restricted green finance and ESG investments, not to mention conventional finance from creating and upscaling integrated value that will be captured as financial return in the future. Meanwhile, the necessary reform is hard for EMDEs to implement for political and social reasons. Most of the electricity systems in EMDEs are vertically integrated and dominated by state-owned utilities that offer many jobs. Such utilities are not motivated to function as energy service suppliers and thus to create integrated value that will be captured as financial return in the future.

As for the second research question, the cost of transition to an RES-based electricity system is tremendously higher than the cost of transition to a natural-gas-based system and may outweigh the benefits of transition. While our scenario analysis has focused on the Southeast Asian region except Indonesia and our case studies are two EMDEs in Southeast Asia, scenario analyses using the Global Change Analysis Model (GCAM) suggest that our results can hold for many EMDEs that have young coal power plants and can access natural gas for power at a reasonable price.

Our findings throughout the book indicate the need for further research on this topic. First, the temporal interaction between decarbonisation policy and lock-ins must be investigated. While an early implementation of a stringent decarbonisation policy increases system transformation costs in the near term, it can prevent coal and gas lock-ins from being further strengthened. Conversely, a late implementation may take advantage of declining costs of RES-E technologies, encouraging potential prosumers to install rooftop solar even in countries with low energy prices and thus producing bill savings and saving system transformation costs. However, a late implementation can strengthen lock-ins, claiming a higher transition cost in the end. Given that carbon lock-ins can be classified into technological, infrastructural, institutional, and behavioural (Seto et al., 2016), context-specific analyses might generate more productive findings than one-size-fits- all ones.

Second, it is worth investigating how recently developed technological options such as ammonia-coal and hydrogen-gas co-firing, direct air capture, and bioenergy carbon capture and storage can create and capture new financial and environmental value, and how such options can advance or retard net-zero electricity and financial system transitions. Ammonia and hydrogen co-firing can reduce stranded costs of coal and gas power plants and related infrastructure facilities, offsetting renovation costs. Most Japanese power utilities are developing and demonstrating these technological options (Trencher et al., 2024), and the Japanese government advertises them as a technological option for the Asian Zero Emission Community and Asia Energy Transition Initiative. Accordingly, Japanese major financial groups took the lead in organising an Asian transition financial study group with major commercial banks in Thailand, Indonesia, the United States, and the United Kingdom to publish a practical playbook that would help create pathways, technology roadmaps, and technology lists for transition finance assessment, and to assess whether ammonia-coal co-firing and exclusive firing can be justified for inclusion in transition finance (ATF Study Group, 2022). While the lack of available data on the availability, scalability, political and social acceptance, and costs prevented us from making a scenario analysis with GCAM, future studies are expected to assess whether these new technologies can reconcile net-zero transitions and integrated value creation and capture. Mitsubishi UFJ Financial Group (MUFG) has explored the bankability of these new technology application projects (MUFG, 2023).

Third, it is worth investigating under what contexts and market structures financial system transitions generate transformative changes that bring long-term sustainability benefits in the real sector. While stakeholder engagement proves to generate positive financial effects, it is contingent on clients' serious commitments to long-term social value creation and stakeholders' strong influences and has not generated and accelerated the required transformation of the economy (Busch et al., 2021). Investors' participation in climate-oriented coalitions generates mixed financial performance (Bolton & Kacperczyk, 2021a; McDonnell & Gupta, 2023). While this book suggests that market-based institutions and Scope 3 carbon disclosure are promising, their effectiveness has not been proven yet. It is not until the benefits of financial system transition become visible and certain that regulators and asset owners will shift short-termism towards long-term sustainability benefits, driving finance and electricity systems towards net zero.

References

Aboitiz. (2023). *Aboitiz Integrated Report 2022*. https://sustainability.aboitiz.com/app/uploads/2023/04/2022-Aboitiz-Integrated-Report.pdf/, [accessed 8 July 2023].

Abolitz Power. (2023). GNPower Dinginin. https://aboitizpower.com/about-us/our-businesses/power-generation/thermal/gnpower-dinginin/, [accessed 8 May 2023].

Abrishambaf, O., Lezama, F., Faria, P., Vale, Z. (2019). Towards transactive energy systems: An analysis on current trends. *Energy Strategy Rev.* 26, 100418. https://doi.org/10.1016/j.esr.2019.100418.

AC Energy. (2019). AC Energy and the blue circle start the construction of a 170 MW wind farm in Vietnam. Press Release (6 May 2019). www.acenrenewables.com/wp-content/uploads/2020/03/AC-Energy-and-The-Blue-Circle-to-develop-a-40-MW-Wind-Farm-in-Vietnam.pdf/, [accessed 29 June 2023].

ACEN. (2022). ACEN completes the world's first energy transition mechanism transaction for the 246 MW SLTEC coal plant. www.acenrenewables.com/2022/11/acen-completes-worlds-first-energy-transition-mechanism-etm-transaction-246-mw-sltec-coal-plant/, [accessed 17 February 2024].

ACEN. (2023a). ACEN continues to bolster renewable energy capacity in Vietnam. *Vietnam Investment Review* (18 January 2023). https://vir.com.vn/acen-continues-to-bolster-renewable-energy-capacity-in-vietnam-99323.html/, [accessed 29 June 2023].

ACEN. (2023b). Geographic presence. www.acenrenewables.com/our-businesses/?section=#presence/, [accessed 8 July 2023].

ACEN RES. (2023). Renewable energy solutions. https://acenres.com/what-we-offer/, [accessed 8 July 2023].

Achampong, L. (2022). How lessons from development finance can strengthen climate finance. In Cash, C., Swatuk, L. A. (eds.) *The Political Economy of Climate Finance: Lessons from International Development*, Palgrave Macmillan, 21–44. https://doi.org/10.1007/978-3-031-12619-2.

ADB (Asian Development Bank). (2015). Assessment of power sector reforms in Viet Nam: Country report. Manila. www.adb.org/sites/default/files/institutional-document/173769/vie-power-sector-reforms.pdf, [accessed 18 December 2022].

ADB. (2017). *Pathways to Low-carbon Development for the Philippines*. ADB, Manila. https://doi.org/10.22617/TCS179189-2.

ADB. (2018). *Philippines: Energy Sector Assessment Strategy, and Roadmap*. ADB, Manila. http://doi.org/10.22617/TCS189616.

ADB. (2021). *Power Transmission Investment Program – Tranche 1: Project Completion Report*. Manila. www.adb.org/projects/documents/vie-42039-034-pcr, [accessed 16 December 2022].

ADB. (2022a). *Establishment of the Energy Transition Mechanism Partnership Trust Fund under the Clean Energy Financing Partnership Facility*. Asian Development Bank (ADB). www.adb.org/sites/default/files/institutional-document/822601/establishment-energy-transition-mechanism-partnership-trust-fund.pdf, [accessed 21 December 2023].

ADB. (2022b). Germany commits €25 million to ADB's energy transition mechanism. *Asian Development Bank (ADB)* (17 November 2022). www.adb.org/news/germany-commits-25-million-adb-energy-transition-mechanism, [accessed 21 December 2023].

ADB. (2023). Update on ADB's energy transition mechanism. *Asian Development Bank (ADB)* (27 April 2023). www.adb.org/news/features/update-energy-transition-mechanism-april-2023, [accessed 21 December 2023].

ADB. (2024a). Environmental and social compliance audit report: Indonesia: Cirebon energy transition mechanism pilot project. Asian Development Bank (ADB). www.adb.org/sites/default/files/project-documents/56294/56294-001-escar-en.pdf, [accessed 4 April 2024].

ADB. (2024b). Indonesia: Cirebon energy transition mechanism pilot project. www.adb.org/projects/documents/ino-56294-001-dpta/, [accessed 29 February 2024].

ADB. (n.d.). Viet Nam: Power transmission investment program (MFF): Sovereign project 42039-033. www.adb.org/projects/42039-033/main, [accessed 16 December 2022].

ADB, IFC, World Bank. (2024). Climate investment fund-accelerating coal transition program: Investment plan for the republic of the Philippines. www.adb.org/sites/default/files/page/752686/CIF-ACT-IP-Philippines-Feb2024-tracked.pdf, [accessed 25 September 2024].

Adhinegara, B. Y., Saleh, M., Huda, N., Monica, L. (2024). Antisipasi Dampak Ekonomi Pensiun Dini PLTU Batu Bara: Studi Kasus pada PLTU Cirebon-1, PLTU Pelabuhan Ratu dan PLTU Suralaya. CELIOS & Yayasan Indonesia CERAH. https://celios.co.id/2024/dampak-pensiun-dini-pltu-batu-bara-terhadap-ekonomi/, [accessed 21 December 2023, Indonesian language].

Adnas, T. P. (2022). Rescaling politics of nickel: A case study of recentralization impact for environment sustainability, governance quality and community livelihoods in Indonesia. MSc thesis of Environmental Policy (ENP-80436), Wageningen. Wageningen University and Research. https://edepot.wur.nl/568831/, [accessed 27 February 2024].

Ahmed, S. J. (2018). Unlocking rooftop solar in the Philippines: Energy-supply security and lower electricity costs. *IEEFA update* (1 August 2018). https://ieefa.org/wp-content/uploads/2018/08/IEEFA_Unlocking-Rooftop-Solar-in-the-Philippines_August-2018.pdf /, [accessed 14 May 2023].

Ahmed, S. J. (2020a). China's state grid group triggers oversight controversy in the Philippines. *IEEFA update* (18 February 2020). https://ieefa.org/resources/ieefa-update-chinas-state-grid-group-triggers-oversight-controversy-philippines/, [accessed 6 May 2023].

Ahmed, S. J. (2020b). Paying less for more – How auctions can transform the Philippines power sector. *IEEFA update* (1 February 2020). https://ieefa.org/media/253/download?attachment/, [accessed 9 May 2023].

Alfsen, K. H., Alnes, K., Berg, A. O., Clapp, C., Dejonckheere, S., Lund, H. F., Schiessl, B., Torvanger, A. (2018). *CICERO MILESTONES 2018. A Practitioner's Perspective on the Green Bond Market*. CICERO Center for International Climate and Environmental Research, Oslo. https://pub.cicero.oslo.no/cicero-xmlui/handle/11250/2561603 [accessed 27 September 2023].

Alova, G. (2020). A global analysis of the progress and failure of electric utilities to adapt their portfolios of power-generation assets to the energy transition. *Nat. Energy* 5, 920–992. https://doi.org/10.1038/s41560-020-00686-5.

Anantharajah, K., Setyowati, A. B. (2022). Beyond promises: Realities of climate finance justice and energy transitions in Asia and the Pacific. *Energy Res. Social Sci.* 89, 102550. https://doi.org/10.1016/j.erss.2022.102550.

Anbumozhi, V., Kalirajan, K., Kimura, F. (eds.). (2018). *Financing for Low-carbon Energy Transition*. Springer Nature Singapore. https://doi.org/10.1007.978-981-10-8582-6.

Anbumozhi, V., Kalirajan, K., Kimura, F., Yao, X. (eds.). (2016). *Investing on Low-Carbon Energy Systems*. Springer Nature Singapore. https://doi.org/10.1007.978-981-10-0761-3.

Andersen, A. D., Geels, F. W. (2023). Multi-system dynamics and the speed of net-zero transitions: Identifying causal processes related to technologies, actors, and institutions. *Energy Res. Soc. Sci.* 102, 103178. https://doi.org/10.1016/j.erss.2023.103178.

Andersen, A. D., Gulbrandsen, M. (2020). The innovation and industry dynamics of technology phase-out in sustainability transitions: Insights from diversifying petroleum technology suppliers in Norway. *Energy Res. Soc. Sci.* 64, 101447. https://doi.org/10.1016/j.erss.2020.101447.

Andres, P., Mealy, P., Handler, N., Fankhauser, S. (2023). Stranded nations? Transition risks and opportunities towards a clean economy. *Environ. Res. Lett.* 18, 045004. https://doi.org/10.1088/1748-9326/acc347.

Ansari, D., Holz, F. (2020). Between stranded assets and green transformation: Fossil-fuel-producing developing countries towards 2055. *World Dev.* 130, 104947. https://doi.org/10.1016/j.worlddev.2020.104947.

Antikainen, J., Gebertm, R., Moller, U. (2011). Review of the greater Mekong sub-region regional power trade: Final report. https://cdn.sida.se/publications/files/sida61461en-review-of-the-greater-mekong-sub-region-regional-power-trade.pdf, [accessed 15 July 2022].

Ari, I., Isik, M. (2022). Assessing the performance of the developing countries for the utilization of the green climate fund. *Front. Clim.* 4, 813406. https://doi.org/10.3389/fclim.2022.813406

ASEAN Taxonomy Board. (2021). ASEAN Taxonomy for Sustainable Finance Version 1. https://asean.org/book/asean-taxonomy-for-sustainable-finance/ [assessed 28 September 2023].

ASEAN Taxonomy Board. (2023). ASEAN Taxonomy for Sustainable Finance Version 2. https://asean.org/wp-content/uploads/2023/03/ASEAN-Taxonomy-Version-2.pdf/, [accessed 28 September 2023].

Asia Transition Finance (ATF) Study Group. (2022). *Asia Transition Finance Guidelines 1st Edition.* www.enecho.meti.go.jp/category/others/aggpm/downloads/ATF_Guidelines_1st_Edition.pdf, [accessed 25 September 2023].

Asian Power. (2023). Meralco breaks into the Philippines' solar industry with Spectrum. *Asian Power* (2 June 2023). https://asian-power.com/ipp/exclusive/meralco-breaks-philippines-solar-industry-spectrum/, [accessed 7 June 2023].

Auger, T., Trüby, J., Balcombe, P., Staffell, I. (2021). The future of coal investment, trade, and stranded assets. *Joule* 5(6), 1462–1484. https://doi.org/10.1016/j.joule.2021.05.008

Awuah, G. B. (2023). Do all African countries need just transition partnership deals? *Daily Maverick* (6 February 2023). www.dailymaverick.co.za/article/2023-02-06-do-all-african-countries-need-just-transition-partnership-deals/, [accessed 10 October 2023].

Azar, J., Duro, M., Kadach, I., Ormazabal, G. (2021). The big three and corporate carbon emissions around the world. *J. Financ. Econ.* 142(2), 674–696. https://doi.org/10.1016/j.jfineco.2021.05.007.

Bacon, R. (2019). *Learning from Power Sector Reform: The Case of The Philippines.* http://documents.worldbank.org/curated/en/385061557771818564/Learning-from-Power-Sector-Reform-The-Case-of-The-Philippines/, [accessed 6 June 2023].

Baldwin, E., Cai, Y., Kuralbayeva, K. (2020). To build or not to build? Capital stocks and climate policy. *J. Environ. Econ. Manag.* 100, 102235. https://doi.org/10.1016/j.jeem.2019.05.001.

Bang, L. (2023). EVN sends messages about electricity outages, raising concerns. *Vietnamnet Global* (23 May 2023). https://vietnamnet.vn/en/evn-sends-messages-about-electricity-outages-raising-concerns-2143649.html/, [accessed 9 June 2023].

Banpu Power. (2021). Banpu power invests in the IGCC power plant in Japan. Press Release (2 April 2021). www.banpupower.com/wp-content/uploads/2021/04/BPP_Press-Release_2021_Nakoso_EN.pdf/, [accessed 9 August 2023].

Barko, T., Cremers, M., Renneboog, L. (2022). Shareholder engagement on environmental, social, and governance performance. *J. Bus. Ethics* 180, 777–812. https://doi.org/10.1007/s10551-021-04850-z.

Barnes, M. (2023). Vietnam's just energy transition partnership resource mobilization plan: Unpacked. Vietnam Briefing (5 December 2023). www.vietnam-briefing.com/news/vietnams-just-energy-transition-partnership-resource-mobilization-plan-unpacked.html/, [accessed 28 February 2024].

Barroco, J. (2021). Designing financeable ancillary services revenue contracts in developing economies: Learnings from the Philippines. *Energy Policy* 152, 112218. https://doi.org/10.1016/j.enpol.2021.112218.

Barroco, J., Herrera, M. (2019). Clearing barriers to project finance for renewable energy in developing countries: A Philippines case study. *Energy Policy* 135, 111008. https://doi.org/10.1016/j.enpol.2019.111008.

Bassen, A., Kaspereit, T., Buchholz, D. (2021). The capital market impact of Blackrock's thermal coal divestment announcement. *Finance Res. Lett.* 41, 101874. https://doi.org/10.1016/j.frl.2020.101874.

Battiston, S., Jakubik, P., Monasterolo, I., Riahi, K., van Ruijven, B. (2019). Climate risk assessment of the sovereign bond portfolio of European insurers. In: European Insurance and Occupational Pension Fund (ed.) *Financial Stability Report*. EIOPA, Luxembourg, 69–89. www.eiopa.europa.eu/publications/climate-risk-assessment-sovereign-bond-portfolio-european-insurers_en/, [accessed 14 August 2023].

Battiston, S., Mandel, A., Monasterolo, I., Schütze, F., Visentin, G. (2017). A climate stress test of the financial system. *Nat. Clim. Change* 7, 283–288. https://doi.org/10.1038/NCLIMATE3255.

Behrens, J. (2023). Vietnam's JETP agreement: Accelerating the energy transition in a just way? *ISEAS Perspective*, 2. www.iseas.edu.sg/wp-content/uploads/2023/06/ISEAS_Perspective_2023_62.pdf, [accessed 3 November 2024].

Belianska, A., Bohme, N., Cai, K., et al. (2022). Climate change and select financial instruments: An overview of opportunities and challenges for Sub-Saharan Africa. *Staff Clim. Notes* 2022(009), A001. Retrieved 31 January 2024, from https://doi.org/10.5089/9798400225208.066.A001.

Belinda, Y. (2023). VKTR to build electric bus, truck assembly plant next year after IPO. Jakarta Post (14 June 2023). www.thejakartapost.com/business/2023/06/14/vktr-to-build-electric-bus-truck-assembly-plant-next-year-after-ipo.html, [accessed 19 September 2023].

Bellini, E. (2021). Vsun to build 4 GW panel factory in Vietnam. *pv magazine* (4 January 2021). www.pv-magazine.com/2021/01/04/vsun-to-build-4-gw-panel-factory-in-vietnam/, [accessed 28 June 2023].

Bellini, E. (2022). Philippines increases net-metering size limit for renewables to 1 MW PV Magazine (29 November 2022). www.pv-magazine.com/2022/11/29/philippines-increases-net-metering-size-limit-for-renewables-to-1-mw/, [accessed 9 May 2023].

Bellini, E. (2023). AD Green commissions 3 GW solar module factory in Vietnam. *pv magazine* (20 June 2023). www.pv-magazine.com/2023/06/20/ad-green-commissions-3-gw-solar-module-factory-in-vietnam/, [accessed 28 June 2023].

Bellini, E. (2024a). Vietnam opens energy market to bilateral PPAs (5 July 2024). *pv magazine.* www.pv-magazine.com/2024/07/05/vietnam-opens-energy-market-to-bilateral-ppas/, [accessed 9 November 2024].

Bellini, E. (2024b). Vietnam to launch new net-metering scheme for rooftop solar (26 September 2024). www.pv-magazine.com/2024/09/26/vietnam-to-launch-new-net-metering-scheme-for-rooftop-solar/, [accessed 9 November 2024].

Benz, L., Paulus, S., Scherer, J., Syryca, J., Trück, S. (2021). Investors' carbon risk exposure and their potential for shareholder engagement. *Bus Strat Env.* 30, 282–301. https://doi.org/10.1002/bse.2621.

Berggren, C., Magnusson, T., Sushandoyo, D. (2015). Transition pathways revisited: Established firms as multi-level actors in the heavy vehicle industry. *Res. Policy* 44, 1017–1028. http://doi.org/10.1016/j.respol.2014.

Bessi, A., Guidolin, M., Manfredi, P. (2021). The role of gas on future perspectives of renewable energy diffusion: Bridging technology or lock-in? *Renew. Sustain. Energy Rev.* 152, 111673. https://doi.org/10.1016/j.rser.2021.111673.

Bhattacharya, A., Calland, R., Averchenkova, A., Gonzalez, L., Martinez-Diazand, L., van Rooij, J. (2020). Delivering on the $100 billion climate finance commitment and transforming climate finance. Independent Group on Climate Finance. www.un.org/sites/un2.un.org/files/2020/12/100_billion_climate_finance_report.pdf, [accessed 17 February 2024].

Bhutta, U. S., Tariq, A., Farrukh, M., Raza, A., Iqbal, M. K. (2022). Green bonds for sustainable development: Review of literature on development and impact of green bonds. *Technol. Forecast. Soc. Change* 175, 121378. https://doi.org/10.1016/j.techfore.2021.121378.

Binsted, M. et al. (2020). Stranded asset implications of the Paris Agreement in Latin America and the Caribbean. *Environ. Res. Lett.* 15, 044026. https://doi.org/10.1088/1748-9326/ab506.

Binsted, M., Iyer, G., Edmonds, J., Vogt-Schilb, A., Arguello, R., Cadena, A., Delgado, R., Feijoo, F., Lucena, A. F. P., McJeon, H., Miralles-Wilhelm, F., Sharma, A. (2020). Stranded asset implications of the Paris Agreement in Latin America and the Caribbean. *Environ. Res. Lett.* 15(4). https://doi.org/10.1088/1748-9326/ab506d.

Biogradlija, A. (2023). Vietnam and Korea collaborate to advance LNG and hydrogen projects. *Energy News* (26 June 2023). https://energynews.biz/vietnam-and-korea-collaborate-to-advance-lng-and-hydrogen-projects/, [accessed 1 July 2023].

Bistline, J. E. T., Young, D. T. (2022). The role of natural gas in reaching net-zero emissions in the electric sector. *Nat. Commun.* 13(1), 4743, 1–11. https://doi.org/10.1038/s41467-022-32468-w.

Bjørn, A., Lloyd, S. M., Brander, M., et al. (2022). Renewable energy certificates threaten the integrity of corporate science-based targets. *Nat. Clim. Chang.* 12, 539–546. https://doi.org/10.1038/s41558-022-01379-5.

Blondeel, M., Colgan, J., Van de Graaf, T. (2019). What drives norm success? Evidence from anti-fossil fuel campaigns. *Glob. Environ. Polit.* 19(4), 63–84. https://doi.org/10.1162/glep_a_00528.

Bogmans, C., Pescatori, A., Prifti, E. (2023). The impact of climate policy on oil and gas investment: Evidence from firm-level data. *IMF Working Paper* WP/23/140. www.imf.org/en/Publications/WP/Issues/2023/06/30/The-Impact-of-Climate-Policy-on-Oil-and-Gas-Investment-Evidence-from-Firm-Level-Data-535491/, [accessed 28 September 2023].

Bolton, P., Kacperczyk, M. (2021a). Carbon Disclosure and the cost of capital. Working Paper, Imperial College London.

Bolton, P., Kacperczyk, M. (2021b). Do investors care about carbon risk? *J. Financ. Econ.* 142(2), 517–549. https://doi.org/10.1016/j.jfineco.2021.05.008.

Bos, K., Gupta, J. (2018). Climate change: The risks of stranded fossil fuel assets and resources to the developing world. *Third World Q.* 39(3), 436–453. https://doi.org/10.1080/01436597.2017.1387477.

Bos, K., Gupta, J. (2019). Stranded assets and stranded resources: Implications for climate change mitigation and global sustainable development. *Energy Res. Social Sci.* 56(June 2018), 101215. https://doi.org/10.1016/j.erss.2019.05.025.

Bousso, R., Meijer, B., Nasralla, S. (2021). Shell ordered to deepen carbon cuts in landmark Dutch climate case. *Reuters* (27 May 2021). www.reuters.com/business/sustainable-business/dutch-court-orders-shell-set-tougher-climate-targets-2021-05-26/, [accessed 27 September 2023].

Brauers, H. (2022). Natural gas as a barrier to sustainability transitions? A systematic mapping of the risks and challenges. *Energy Res. Soc. Sci.* 89, 102538. https://doi.org/10.1016/j.erss.2022.102538.

Brauers, H., Braunger, I., Jewell, J. (2021). Liquefied natural gas expansion plans in Germany: The risk of gas lock-in under energy transitions, *Energy Res. Soc. Sci.* 76, 102059. https://doi.org/10.1016/j.erss.2021.102059.

Bretschger, L., Soretz, S. (2022). Stranded assets: How policy uncertainty affects capital, growth, and the environment. *Environ. Resource Econ.* 83, 261–288. https://doi.org/10.1007/s10640-021-00632-3.

Bryant, S. T., Straker, K., Wrigley, C. (2018). The typologies of power: Energy utility business models in an increasingly renewable sector. *J. Clean. Prod.* 195, 1032–1046. https://doi.org/10.1016/j.jclepro.2018.05.233.

Budinis, S., Krevor, S., Dowell, N. M., Brandon, N., Hawkes, A. (2018). An assessment of CCS costs, barriers and potential. *Energy Strat. Rev.* 22, 61–81. https://doi.org/10.1016/j.esr.2018.08.003.

Bugaje, A.-A. B., Dioha, M. O., Abraham-Dukuma, M. C., Wakil, M. (2022). Rethinking the position of natural gas in a low-carbon energy transition. *Energy Res. Soc. Sci.* 90, 102604. https://doi.org/10.1016/j.erss.2022.102604.

Bunda, N., Sunio, V., Palmero, S. S., Tabañag, I. D. F., Reyes, D. J., Ligot, E. (2023). Stage model of the process of solar photovoltaic adoption by residential households in the Philippines. *Clean. Responsible Consum.* 9, 100114. https://doi.org/10.1016/j.clrc.2023.100114.

Burger, S., Chaves-Ávila, J. P., Batlle, C., Pérez-Arriaga, I. J. (2017). A review of the value of aggregators in electricity systems. *Renew. Sustain. Energy Rev.* 77, 395–405. https://doi.org/10.1016/j.rser.2017.04.014.

Burgholzer, B., Auer, H. (2016). Cost/benefit analysis of transmission grid expansion to enable further integration of renewable electricity generation in Austria. *Renew. Energy* 97, 189–196. https://doi.org/10.1016/j.renene.2016.05.073.

Burgos, H. (2023). Philippines' Ayala Corp. continues regional expansion with $165 million investment in Vietnam solar firm. *Forbes* (3 February 2022). www.forbes.com/sites/jonathanburgos/2022/02/03/philippines-ayala-corp-continues-regional-expansion-with-165-million-investment-in-vietnam-solar-firm/?sh=5f2923821cde/, [accessed 29 June 2023].

Burke, F., Nguyen, T. H. (2021). Vietnam: Key highlights of new draft of national power development plan (Draft PDP8). *Baker McKenzie* (4 March 2021).

https://insightplus.bakermckenzie.com/bm/energy-mining-infrastructure_1/vietnam-key-highlights-of-new-draft-of-national-power-development-plan-draft-pdp8/, [accessed 7 September 2023].

Burke, P. J., Widnyana, J., Anjum, Z., Aisbett, E., Resosudarmo, B., Baldwin, K. G. H. (2019). Overcoming barriers to solar and wind energy adoption in two Asian giants: India and Indonesia. *Energy Policy* 132, 1216–1228. https://doi.org/10.1016/j.enpol.2019.05.055.

Busch, T., Bruce-Clark, O., ... Weber, O. (2021). Impact investments: A call for (re)orientation. *SN Bus Econ* 1(2021), 33. https://doi.org/10.1007/s43546-020-00033-6.

Business World. (2020). Meralco targets to install smart meters for 3.3M customers (27 May 2020). www.bworldonline.com/corporate/2020/05/27/296418/meralco-targets-to-install-smart-meters-for-3-3m-customers/, [accessed 17 May 2023].

BYD. (2022). BYD and Bakrie & Brothers group cooperate with local Indonesian body builder group, Tri Sakti, to initiate electric bus industrialization. News release (14 March 2022). www.bydglobal.com/en/news/2022-03-14/BYD-and-Bakrie-%2526-Brothers-Group-Cooperate-with-Local-Indonesian-Body-Builder-Group%2C-Tri-Sakti%2C-to-Initiate-Electric-Bus-Industrialization, [accessed 19 September 2023].

Cabico, G. K. (2022). Fossil gas expansion seen to threaten Philippine marine corridor, coastal folk. Climate Tracker (4 May 2022). https://climatetracker.org/fossil-gas-expansion-seen-to-threaten-philippine-marine-corridor-coastal-folk/, [accessed 12 September 2023].

Cahen-Fourot, L., Campiglio, E., Godin, A., Kemp-Benedict, E., Trsek S. (2021). Capital stranding cascades: The impact of decarbonisation on productive asset utilization. *Energy Econ.* 103, 105581. https://doi.org/10.1016/j.eneco.2021.105581.

Caldecott, B. (2017). Introduction to special issue: Stranded assets and the environment. *J. Sustain. Finance Invest.* 7(1), 1–13. https://doi.org/10.1080/20430795.2016.1266748.

Caldecott, B. (2018). Introduction: Stranded assets and the environment. In: Caldecott, B. (ed.) *Stranded Assets and the Environment: Risk, Resilience and Opportunity*. Routledge, Abingdon, 1–22.

Caldecott, B., Clark, A., Koskelo, K., Mulholland, E., Hickey, C. (2021). Stranded assets: Environmental drivers, societal challenges, and supervisory responses. *Annu. Rev. Environ. Resour.* 46, 417–447. https://doi.org/10.1146/annurev-environ-012220-101430.

Caldecott, B., Dericks, G., Mitchell, J. (2015). *Subcritical Coal in Australia: Risks to Investors and Implications for Policymakers*. Accessed from www.smithschool.ox.ac.uk/sites/default/files/2022-04/Subcritical-Coal-in-Australia_Investors-Policymakers.pdf

Caldecott, B., Dericks, G., Tulloch, D. J., Kruitwagen, L., Kok, I. (2016). *Stranded Assets and Thermal Coal in Japan: An Analysis of Environment-related Risk Exposure.* Smith School of Enterprise and Environment, Oxford Accessed from www.smithschool.ox.ac.uk/research/sustainable-finance/publications/satc-japan.pdf

Caldecott, B., Dericks, G., Tulloch, D. J., Liao, X., Kruitwagen, L., Bouveret, G., Mitchell, J. (2017). *Stranded Assets and Thermal Coal in China: An Analysis of Environment-related Risk Exposure.* Accessed from www.smithschool.ox.ac.uk/sites/default/files/2022-04/Stranded-Assets-and-Thermal-Coal-in-China-Working-Paper-February2017.pdf

Caldecott, B., McDaniels, J. (2014). *Stranded Generation Assets: Implications for European Capacity Mechanisms, Energy Markets and Climate Policy.* Smith School of Enterprise and the Environment, Oxford.

Caldecott, B., Tilbury, J., Ma, Y. (2013). *Stranded Down Under? Environment-related Factors Changing China's Demand for Coal and What This Means for Australian Coal Assets.* Accessed from www.smithschool.ox.ac.uk/sites/default/files/2022-03/stranded-down-under-report.pdf

Caldecott, B., Tulloch, D., Liao, X., Kruitwagen, L., Bouveret, G., Mitchell, J. (2017). *Stranded Assets and Thermal Coal in China: An Analysis of Environment-Related Risk Exposure.* Smith School of Enterprise and the Environment, Oxford.

Calvin, K., Bond-Lamberty, B., Clarke, L., Edmonds, J., Eom, J., Hartin, C., Kim, S., Kyle, P., Link, R., Moss, R., McJeon, H., Patel, P., Smith, S., Waldhoff, S., Wise, M. (2017). The SSP4: A world of deepening inequality. *Global Environ. Change* 42, 284–296. https://doi.org/10.1016/j.gloenvcha.2016.06.010.

Calvin, K., Patel, P., Clarke, L., Asrar, G., Bond-Lamberty, B., Cui, R. Y., Di Vittorio, A., Dorheim, K., Edmonds, J., Hartin, C., Hejazi, M., Horowitz, R., Iyer, G., Kyle, P., Kim, S., Link, R., McJeon, H., Smith, S. J., Snyder, A., ... Wise, M. (2019). GCAM v5.1: Representing the linkages between energy, water, land, climate, and economic systems. *Geosci. Model Dev.* 12(2), 677–698. https://doi.org/10.5194/gmd-12-677-2019.

Campiglio, E., Daumas, L., Monnin, P., von Jagow, A. (2022). Climate-related risks in financial assets. *J. Econ. Surv.* 37, 950–992. https://doi.org/10.1111/joes.12525.

Canelas, J., Carvalho, A. (2023). The dark side of the energy transition: Extractivist violence, energy (in)justice and lithium mining in Portugal. *Energy Res. Soc. Sci.* 100, 103096. https://doi.org/10.1016/j.erss.2023.103096.

Capasso, G., Gianfrate, G., Spinelli, M. (2020). Climate change and credit risk. *J. Clean. Prod.* 266, 121634. https://doi.org/10.1016/j.jclepro.2020.121634.

Capongcol, M. C., Gutierrez, L. L., Lawson, S., Watson, A. (2020). Ready for renewables – Grid planning and competitive renewable energy zones (CREZ) in the Philippines. NREL/TP-7A40-76235. www.nrel.gov/docs/fy20osti/76235.pdf/, [accessed 17 May 2023].

Carbon Tracker. (2011). Unburnable Carbon: Are the World's Financial Markets Carrying a Carbon Bubble? https://carbontracker.org/reports/carbon-bubble/, [accessed 28 September 2023].

Carl, J. (2015). The causes and implications of India's coal production shortfall. In: Thurber, M. C., Morse, R. K. (eds.) *The Global Coal Market: Supplying the Major Fuel for Emerging Economies*. Cambridge University Press, Cambridge, 294–373.

Carney, M. (2015). *Breaking the tragedy of the horizon – climate change and financial stability*. Speech. Bank Engl., London. www.bankofengland.co.uk/speech/2015/breaking-the-tragedy-of-the-horizon-climate-change-and-financial-stability/, [accessed 24 September 2023].

Castaneda, M., Jimenez, M., Zapata, S., Franco, C. J., Dyner, I. (2017). Myths and facts of the utility death spiral. *Energy Policy* 110, 105–116. https://doi.org/10.1016/j.enpol.2017.07.063.

Cato, M. S. (2022). *Sustainable Finance: Using the Power of Money to Change the World*. Palgrave MacMillan. https://doi.org/10.1007/978-3-030-91578-0.

Cavcic, M. (2025). Boost for Germany's energy security comes with third LNG terminal up and running. *Offshore Energy Today* (27 May). www.offshore-energy.biz/boost-for-germanys-energy-security-comes-with-third-lng-terminal-up-and-running/, [accessed 3 September 2025].

CDP (Carbon Disclosure Project). (2023). How companies can take action. www.cdp.net/en/companies/, [accessed 24 September 2023].

CEED Office. (2020). Think-tank: unambitious NDC fails to align with 1.5°C global target, just transition imperatives (23 December 2020). https://ceedphilippines.com/think-tank-unambitious-ndc-fails-to-align-with-1-5c-global-target-just-transition-imperatives/, [accessed 6 May 2023].

CEED Office. (2021). Comments/Recommendations on the draft department circular 'Amending certain provisions of and supplementing department circular No. DC2018-02-0003 on the competitive selection process in the procurement by the distribution utilities of power supply agreement for the captive market'. (August 2021). https://ceedphilippines.com/wp-content/uploads/2021/08/Comments-on-the-draft-Supplementary-CSP-Policy.pdf/, [accessed 4 July 2023].

CEED Office. (2023). Gas development bills to burn holes in people's pockets. https://ceedphilippines.com/gas-development-bills-to-burn-holes-in-peoples-pockets/, [accessed 13 September 2023].

Central Electricity Authority. (2022). *Growth of Electricity Sector in India (1947–2022).* https://cea.nic.in/wp-content/uploads/pdm/2023/02/Growth_Book_2022_PDF.pdf/, [accessed 10 October 2023].

Central Electricity Authority. (2023). *All India Electricity Statistics: General Review 2023.* https://cea.nic.in/general-review-report/?lang=en/, [accessed 10 October 2023].

Chan, H.-Y., Merdekawati, M., Suryadi, B. (2022). Bank climate actions and their implications for the coal power sector. *Energy Strategy Rev.* 39, 100799. https://doi.org/10.1016/j.esr.2021.100799.

Chan, M., De Torres, A., Andres, B. I. (2020). RePower negros: A scoping study of negros Island's power sector transformation. https://ceedphilippines.com/wp-content/uploads/2020/09/REPower_Negros.pdf/, [accessed 13 September 2023].

Chen, X., Mauzerall, D. L. (2021). The expanding coal power fleet in Southeast Asia: Implications for future CO_2 emissions and electricity generation. *Earth's Future* 9(12), 1–17. https://doi.org/10.1029/2021ef002257.

Chevallier, J., Goutte, S., Ji, Q., Guesmi, K. (2021). Green finance and the restructuring of the oil-gas-coal business model under carbon asset stranding constraints. *Energy Policy* 149, 112055. https://doi.org/10.1016/j.enpol.2020.112055.

Christian, J., Prasojo, H., Tampubolon, A. P., et al. (2021). *Indonesia Energy Transition Outlook (IETO) 2021.* Institute for Essential Services Reform. https://iesr.or.id/en/pustaka/indonesia-energy-transitionoutlook-ieto-2021/, [accessed 26 March 2024].

Christophers, B. (2019). Environmental beta or how institutional investors think about climate change and fossil fuel risk. *Ann. Assoc. Am. Geogr.* 109(3), 754–774. https://doi.org/10.1080/24694452.2018.1489213.

Claeys, G., Le Mouel, M., Tagliapietra, S., Wolff, G. B., Zachmann, G. (2024). *The Macroeconomics of Decarbonisation: Implications and Policies.* Cambridge University Press, Cambridge.

Clark, R., Zucker, N., Urpelainen, J. (2020). The future of coal-fired power generation in Southeast Asia. *Renew. Sustain. Energy Rev.* 121. https://doi.org/10.1016/j.rser.2019.109650.

Clarke, L., Jiang, K., Akimoto, K., Babiker, M., Blanford, G., Fisher-Vanden, K., Hourcade, J. C., Krey, V., Kriegler, E., Löschel, A., McCollum, D., Paltsev, S., Rose, S., Shukla, P. R., Tavoni, M., van der Zwaan, B. C. C., van Vuuren, D. P.

(2014). Assessing transformation pathways. In: Edenhofer, O., Pichs-Madruga, R., Sokona, Y., Farahani, E., Kadner, S., Seyboth, K., Adler, A., Baum, I., Brunner, S., Eickemeier, P., Kriemann, B., Savolainen, J., Schlömer, S., von Stechow, C., Zwickel, T., Minx, J. C. (eds.) *Climate Change 2014: Mitigation of Climate Change. Contribution of Working Group III to the Fifth Assessment Report of the Intergovernmental Panel on Climate Change.* Cambridge University Press, Cambridge and New York.

Clayton, T., Spinardi, G., Williams, R. (1999). *Policies for Cleaner Technology: A New Agenda for Government and Industry.* Routledge, Abingdon.

Climate Action Tracker. (2022). CAT net zero target evaluations (last updated 10 November 2022). https://climateactiontracker.org/global/cat-net-zero-target-evaluations/, [accessed 11 October 2023].

Climate Bonds Initiative. (2023a). China sustainable debt state of the market report 2022. www.climatebonds.net/resources/reports/china-sustainable-debt-state-market-report-2022/, [accessed 6 October 2023].

Climate Bonds Initiative. (2023b). Sustainable debt, global state of the market 2022. www.climatebonds.net/resources/reports/global-state-market-report-2022/, [accessed 27 September 2023].

Climate Bonds Initiative. (2023c). Interactive data platform as of the end of 2022. www.climatebonds.net/market/data/ [accessed 27 September 2023].

Climate Bonds Initiative. (2023d). Sustainable debt, global state of the market 2022. www.climatebonds.net/resources/reports/global-state-market-report-2022/ [accessed 27 September 2023].

Climate Transition Finance & ICMA. (2023). Climate transition finance handbook guidance for issuers. www.icmagroup.org/assets/documents/Sustainable-finance/2023-updates/Climate-Transition-Finance-Handbook-CTFH-June-2023-220623v2.pdf/, [accessed 28 September 2023].

Colenbrander, S., Pettinotti, L., Cao, Y. (2022). *A Fair Share of Climate Finance? An Appraisal of Past Performance, Future Pledges and Prospective Constributors.* ODI Working Paper. ODI, London. https://odi.org/en/publications/a-fairshare-of-climate-finance-an-appraisal-of-past-performance-future-pledges-andprospective-contributors/, [accessed 10 October 2023].

Colenbrander, S., Vaze, P., Vikas, C., Ayer, S., Kumar, N., Vikas, N., Burge, L. (2023). Low-carbon transition risks for India's financial system. *Glob. Environ. Change* 78, 102634. https://doi.org/10.1016/j.gloenvcha.2022.102634.

Colthorpe, A. (2021). Vietnam battery storage pilot project gets US$3 million grant from US. *Energy Storage News* (18 October 2021). www.energy-storage.news/vietnam-battery-storage-pilot-project-gets-us3-million-grant-from-us/, [accessed 8 September 2023].

Comerford, D., Spiganti, A. (2022). The Carbon Bubble: Climate policy in a fire-sale model of deleveraging. *Scand. J. Econ.* 125(3), 655–687. https://doi.org/10.1111/sjoe.12519.

Comins, L. (2023). Eskom unbundling 'milestone' announced. *The Mail & Guardian* (30 July 2023). https://mg.co.za/environment/2023-07-30-eskom-unbundling-milestone-announced/ [accessed 2 October 2023].

Coronation. (2023). Stewardship and sustainable investing policy. www.coronation.com/globalassets/asset-library/regulatory-documents/sustainability-related-disclosures/stewardship-and-sustainable-investing-policy.pdf/, [accessed 3 October 2023].

CTI. (2011). *Unburnable Carbon – Are the World's Financial Markets Carrying a Carbon Bubble?* Carbon Tracker Initiative. Accessed from https://carbontracker.org/reports/carbon-bubble/

CTI. (2013). *Unburnable Carbon 2013: Wasted Capital and Stranded Assets.* Carbon Tracker Initiative. Accessed from http://carbontracker.live.kiln.digital/Unburnable-Carbon-2-Web-Version.pdf

Cui, R. Y., Hultman, N., Edwards, M. R., et al. (2019). Quantifying operational lifetimes for coal power plants under the Paris goals. *Nat. Commun.* 10(1), 4759, 1–9. https://doi.org/10.1038/s41467-019-12618-3.

Cui, R. Y., Tumiwa, F., Zhao, A., Arinaldo, D., Wiranegara, R., Cui, D., Dahl, C., Myllyvitra, L., Squire, C., Simamora, P., Hultman, N. E. (2022). *Financing Indonesia's Coal Phase-Out: A Just and Accelerated Retirement Pathway to Net-Zero.* Accessed from https://cgs.umd.edu/sites/default/files/2022-08/UMD%20Indo%20Report%20Final_0.pdf; https://cgs.umd.edu/research-impact/publications/financing-indonesias-coal-phase-out-just-and-accelerated-retirement/, [accessed 13 March 2024].

Curtin, J., McInerney, C., Gallachóir, B. Ó., Hickey, C., Deane, P., Deeney, P. (2019). Quantifying stranding risk for fossil fuel assets and implications for renewable energy investment: A review of the literature. *Renew. Sustain. Energy Rev.* 116, 109402. https://doi.org/10.1016/j.rser.2019.109402.

D'Orazioa, P., Popoyan, L. (2019). Fostering green investments and tackling climate-related financial risks: Which role for macroprudential policies? *Ecol. Econ.* 160, 25–37. https://doi.org/10.1016/j.ecolecon.2019.01.029.

Daumas, L. (2023). Financial stability, stranded assets and the low-carbon transition: A critical review of the theoretical and applied literature. *J. Econ. Surv.* 38, 601–716. https://doi.org/10.1111/joes.12551.

Davidson, M. R., Gao, X., Busby, J., Shearer, C., Eisenman J. (2023). Hard to say goodbye: South Korea, Japan, and China as the last lenders for coal. *Env. Polit.* 32(7), 1186–1207. https://doi.org/10.1080/09644016.2023.2211488.

Dawkins, C. (2018). Elevating the role of divestment in socially responsible investing. *J. Bus. Ethics* 153(2), 465–478. https://doi.org/10.1007/s10551-016-3356-7.

DCCEEW. (2023). Options for electricity generation and storage capacity: Impact analysis. https://oia.pmc.gov.au/published-impact-analyses-and-reports/capacity-investment-scheme/, [accessed 15 November 2024].

DCCEEW. (2024a). Background paper: Options for electricity generation and storage capacity. https://oia.pmc.gov.au/sites/default/files/posts/2024/07/Addendum%20-%20superseded%202024-07-05.pdf/, [accessed 15 November 2024].

DCCEEW. (2024b). Implementation design paper: Capacity investment scheme. https://storage.googleapis.com/files-au-climate/climate-au/p/prj2c881026ae734a70e1030/survey/Capacity%20Investment%20Scheme%20-%20Implementation%20Design%20Paper.pdf/, [accessed 15 November 2024].

de la Cruz, E. (2013). Power crisis fears unnerve industry in booming Philippines. *Reuters* (18 June 2013). www.reuters.com/article/us-philippines-power-idUSBRE95G13L20130617/, [accessed 13 May 2023].

de la Cruz, E. (2014). Philippines' Aquino seeks more power for government to avert electricity crisis. *Reuters* (11 September 2014). www.reuters.com/article/uk-philippines-electricity-aquino-idUKKBN0H60FR20140911/, [accessed 13 May 2023].

de la Cruz, E. (2023). Philippines greenlights seventh LNG project, gears up for gas imports. *Reuters* (27 January 2023). www.reuters.com/business/energy/philippines-greenlights-seventh-lng-project-gears-up-gas-imports-2023-01-27/, [accessed 30 May 2023].

de Ridder, K., Schultz, F. C., Pies, I. (2023). Procedural climate justice: Conceptualizing a polycentric solution to a global problem. *Ecol. Econ.* 214, 107998. https://doi.org/10.1016/j.ecolecon.2023.107998.

de Torres, A. (2020). Preventing another 20 years of coal: Lessons from Meralco's electricity procurement practices. CEED, Malina. https://ceedphilippines.com/wp-content/uploads/2021/08/Policy-Brief-Preventing-Another-20-Years-of-Coal-Dec-2020.pdf/, [accessed 6 June 2023].

Delina, L. (2021). Promises and pitfalls of China-Southeast Asia energy connectivity. *Energy Strategy Rev.* 33, 100574. https://doi.org/10.1016/j.esr.2020.100574.

Delmas, M. A., Burbano, V. C. (2011). The drivers of greenwashing. *Calif. Manage. Rev.* 54, 64–87. https://doi.org/10.1525/cmr.2011.54.1.64.

Denholm, P., Clark, K., O'Connell, M. (2016). *On the Path to SunShot: Emerging Issues and Challenges in Integrating High Levels of Solar into the Electrical Generation and Transmission System.* National Renewable Energy Laboratory,

Cambridge, USA. www.nrel.gov/docs/fy16osti/65800.pdf, [accessed 15 December 2022].

Dezan Shira & Associates. (2021). COP 26 and climate change: Vietnam's commitment to reducing emissions. *Vietnam Briefing* (5 November 2021). www.vietnam-briefing.com/news/cop26-climate-change-vietnams-commitment-reducing-emissions.html, [accessed 22 November 2022].

Dickel, R. (2020). Blue hydrogen as an enabler of green hydrogen: the case of Germany. OIES Paper: NG 159, Oxford Institute for Energy Studies. https://doi.org/10.26889/9781784671594.

Dikau, S., Volz, U. (2019). Central banking, climate change, and green finance. In: Sachs, J. D., Woo, W. T., Yoshino, N., Taghizadeh-Hesary, F. (eds.) *Handbook of Green Finance: Energy Security and Sustainable Development*. Springer, 81–102. https://doi.org/10.1007/978-981-13-0227-5_17.

Dikau, S., Volz, U. (2021). Central bank mandates, sustainability objectives, and the promotion of green finance. *Ecol. Econ.* 184, 107022. https://doi.org/10.1016/j.ecolecon.2021.107022.

Dinata, S., Ikhsan, M., Silaban, M., Umam, A. K. (2020). The outcome of China's investment in Indonesia: Lessons from the nickel industry. Paramadina Public Policy Institute. https://policy.paramadina.ac.id/the-outcome-of-chinas-investment-in-indonesia-lessons-from-the-nickel-industry, [accessed 27 February 2024].

Do, B., Tran, T., Nguyen, N. (2021). Renewable energy integration in Vietnam's power system: Generation adequacy assessment and strategic implications. *Energies* 14, 3541. https://doi.org/10.3390/en14123541.

Do, T. K. T., Nguyen, T. K. C., Nguyen, D. D. (2021). Factors affecting renewable energy supply chain link: A case of solar power in Vietnam. *Uncertain Supply Chain Manage.* 9, 989–994. https://doi.org/10.5267/j.uscm.2021.7.001.

Do, T. N., Burke, P. J. (2023). Phasing out coal power in a developing country context: Insights from Vietnam. *Energy Policy* 176, 113512. https://doi.org/10.1016/j.enpol.2023.113512.

Do, T. N., Burke, P. J., Baldwin, K. G. H., Nguyen, C. T. (2020). Underlying drivers and barriers for solar photovoltaics diffusion: The case of Vietnam. *Energy Policy* 144, 111561. https://doi.org/10.1016/j.enpol.2020.111561.

Do, T. N., Burke, P. J., Hughes, L., Thi, T. D. (2022). Policy options for offshore wind power in Vietnam. *Mar. Policy* 141, 105080. https://doi.org/10.1016/j.marpol.2022.105080.

Do, T. N., Burke, P. J., Nguyen, H. N., Overland, I., Suryadi, B., Swandaru, A., Yurnaidi, Z. (2021). Vietnam's solar and wind power success: Policy implications for the other ASEAN countries. *Energy Sustain. Dev.* 65, 1–11. https://doi.org/10.1016/j.esd.2021.09.002.

Donovan, C. W. (ed.). (2020). *Renewable Energy Finance: Funding the Future of Energy*. World Scientific, Singapore.

Dooley, K., Holz, C., Kartha, S., et al. (2021). Ethical choices behind quantifications of fair contributions under the Paris Agreement. *Nat. Clim. Change* 11(4), 300–305. https://doi.org/10.1038/s41558-021-01015-8.

Dorman, D. R., Ciplet, D. (2022). Sustainable energy for all? Assessing global distributive justice in the green climate fund's energy finance. *Global Environ. Polit.* 22(1), 94–116. https://doi.org/10.1162/glep_a_00621.

Dorsman, A., Arslan-Ayaydin, Ö., Karan, M. B. (eds.). (2016). *Energy and Finance: Sustainability in the Energy Industry*. Springer. https://doi.org/10.1007/978-3-319-32268-1.

Dubash, N. K., Kale, S. S., Bharvirkar, R. (2018). Conclusion: Mapping power in comparative state context. In: Dubash, N. K., Kale, S. S., Bharvirkar, R. (eds.) *Mapping Power: The Political Economy of Electricity in India's States*. Oxford University Press, Oxford, 340–363.

Duc, T. (2023). State utility to halt payment for rooftop solar projects with incomplete legal documents. *The Investor* (16 February 2023). https://theinvestor.vn/state-utility-to-halt-payment-for-rooftop-solar-projects-with-incomplete-legal-documents-d3721.html/, [accessed 4 July 2023].

Dunz, N., Naqvi, A., Monasterolo, I. (2021). Climate sentiments, transition risk, and financial stability in a stock-flow consistent model. *J. Financ. Stab.* 54, 100872. https://doi.org/10.1016/j.jfs.2021.100872.

Dutt, D., Ranjan, A. (2022). Towards a just energy transition in Delhi: Addressing the bias in the rooftop solar market. *Energy Policy* 160, 112667. https://doi.org/10.1016/j.enpol.2021.112667.

Eberhard, A., Shkaratan, M. (2012). Powering Africa: Meeting the financing and reform challenges. *Energy Policy* 42, 9–18. https://doi.org/10.1016/j.enpol.2011.10.033.

Eckstein, D., Künzel, V., Schäfer, L. (2021). Global climate risk index 2021: Who suffers most from extreme weather events? Weather-related loss events in 2019 and 2000–2019. *Briefing Paper*. Germanwatch. www.germanwatch.org/sites/default/files/Global%20Climate%20Risk%20Index%202021_2.pdf, [accessed 12 December 2023].

Edenhofer, O., Kalkuhl, M., Requate, T., Steckel, J. C. (2020). How assets get stranded: The impact of climate policy on capital and fossil fuel owners. Introduction to the JEEM special section on climate policy and political economy. *J. Environ. Econ. Manag.* 100, 102300. https://doi.org/10.1016/j.jeem.2020.102300.

Edwards, M. R., Cui, R., Bindl, M., Hultman, N., Mathur, K., McJeon, H., Iyer, G., Song, J., Zhao, A. (2022). Quantifying the regional stranded asset risks from new coal plants under 1.5°C. *Environ. Res. Lett.* 17(2). https://doi.org/10.1088/1748-9326/ac4ec2.

Ehlers, T., Gardes-Landolfini, C., Gratcheva, E., Sing, S., Tabarraei, H., Xiao, Y. (2023). Chapter 3. Financial sector policies to unlock private climate finance in emerging market and developing economies. In Global Financial Stability Report, October 2023, International Monetary Fund (IMF), USA. https://doi.org/10.5089/9798400249686.082.CH003.

Eid, C., Hakvoort, R., de Jong, M. (2017). Global trends in the political economy of smart grids. In: Arent, D., Arndt, C., Miller, M., Tarp, F., Zinaman, O. (eds.) *The Political Economy of Clean Energy Transitions.* Oxford University Press, Oxford, 329–348.

Eklund, J., Kapoor, R. (2019). Pursuing the new while sustaining the current: Incumbent strategies and firm value during the nascent period of industry change. *Organ. Sci.* 30(2), 383–404. https://doi.org/10.1287/orsc.2018.1229.

El Gohary, F., Nordin, M., Juslin, P., Bartusch, C. (2022). Evaluating user understanding and exposure effects of demand-based tariffs. *Renew. Sustain. Energy Rev.* 155, 111956. https://doi.org/10.1016/j.rser.2021.111956.

El Gohary, F., Nordin, M., Juslin, P., Bartusch, C. (2023). Getting the signal – Do electricity users meet the preconditions for making informed decisions on demand response? *Energy Res. Soc. Sci.* 100, 103119. https://doi.org/10.1016/j.erss.2023.103119.

Employee Benefits Security Administration. (2015). Interpretive bulletin relating to the fiduciary standard under ERISA in considering economically targeted investments. *Fed. Regist.* 80(206), 65135–65137. www.govinfo.gov/content/pkg/FR-2015-10-26/pdf/2015-27146.pdf/ [accessed 12 October 2023].

Energy Regulatory Commission (ERC) of the Philippines. (2019). ERC adopts amendments to the net-metering rules (21 October 2019). www.erc.gov.ph/ContentPage/61857/, [accessed 9 May 2023].

Erdiwansyah, M., Mamat, R., Sani, M. S. M., Khoerunnisa, F., Kadarohman, A. (2019a). Target and demand for renewable energy across 10 ASEAN countries by 2040. *Electr. J.* 32(10), 106670. https://doi.org/https://doi.org/10.1016/j.tej.2019.106670.

Erdiwansyah, Mamat, R., Sani, M. S. M., Sudhakar, K. (2019b). Renewable energy in Southeast Asia: Policies and recommendations. *Sci. Total Environ.* 670, 1095–1102. https://doi.org/10.1016/j.scitotenv.2019.03.273.

European Commission. (2022). EU Taxonomy: Commission welcomes the result of today's vote by the European parliament on the complementary delegated Act. Press Release (6 July 2022). https://ec.europa.eu/commission/presscorner/detail/en/ip_22_4349 [accessed 7 January 2023].

European Union. (2022). Directive (EU) 2019/944 of the European parliament and of the council of 5 June 2019 on common rules for the internal market for electricity and amending Directive 2012/27/EU (recast). http://data.europa.eu/eli/dir/2019/944/2022-06-23/, [accessed 12 September 2023].

EU-Vietnam SETP. (2024a). Accelerating energy efficiency in enterprises through industrial Save energy in businesses through industrial steam system optimisation . *IEEP, SETP News* (22 March 2024). https://setp.vn/eu_news/accelerating-energy-efficiency-in-enterprises-through-industrial-save-energy-in-businesses-through-industrial-steam-system-optimisation/, [accessed 22 November 2023].

EU-Vietnam SETP. (2024b). Awareness workshop on energy management systems and system optimisation adoption. *IEEP, SETP News* (17 April 2024). https://setp.vn/eu_news/awareness-workshop-on-energy-management-systems-and-system-optimisation-adoption-3/, [accessed 22 November 2023].

EVN. (2016). Time-of-use electricity charge. https://en.evn.com.vn/d6/news/TIME-OF-USE-ELECTRICITY-CHARGE-9-28-264.aspx, [accessed 18 December 2022].

EVN. (2017). Development history. https://en.evn.com.vn/d6/news/Development-history-2-34-391.aspx, [accessed 17 December 2022].

EVN. (2018). Milestones in the development the power system in Vietnam. https://en.evn.com.vn/d6/news/Milestones-in-the-development-the-power-system-in-Vietnam-2-34-392.aspx, [accessed 17 December 2022].

EVN. (2019). Overview of hydropower in Vietnam. https://en.evn.com.vn/d6/news/Overview-of-hydropower-in-Vietnam-66-163-1514.aspx, [accessed 15 May 2023].

EVN. (2020). Development of 500 kV transmission network in the future – A questionable issue. (22 October 2020). https://en.evn.com.vn/d6/news/Development-of-500-kV-transmission-network-in-the-future-a-questionable-issue-66-163-2065.asp, [accessed 12 January 2023].

EVN. (2021). Power transmission grid interconnection in the region: 'A proper solution to ensure national energy security' (12 October 2021). https://en.evn.com.vn/d6/news/Power-transmission-grid-interconnection-in-the-region-A-proper-solution-to-ensure-national-energy-security-66-163-2626.aspx, [accessed 18 December 2022].

EVN. (2022a). 10 years of operating a competitive electricity market. *EVN's Activities* (6 July 2022). https://en.evn.com.vn/d6/news/10-years-of-operating-a-competitive-electricity-market-66-163-2965.aspx, [accessed 11 July 2023].

EVN. (2022b). Ministry not putting 6,800 MW of coal-fired power in draft power plan. *EVN's Activities* (14 October 2022). https://en.evn.com.vn/d6/news/Ministry-not-putting-6800-MW-of-coal-fired-power-in-draft-power-plan-66-163-3112.aspx, [accessed 14 October 2022].

EVN. (2022c). The conclusions of the standing government on power development planning VIII. (9 September 2022). https://vietnamenergy.vn/the-conclusions-of-the-standing-government-on-power-development-planning-viii-29378.html, [accessed 23 November 2022].

EVN. (2022d). There are 108 power plants participating in offering in the competitive electricity market in Vietnam (30 December 2022). https://vietnamenergy.vn/there-are-108-power-plants-participating-in-offering-in-the-competitive-electricity-market-in-vietnam-30091.html, [accessed 11 June 2023].

EVN. (2023). Electricity regulatory authority of Vietnam works with EVN on electricity market operation. Press Release (5 April 2023). https://en.evn.com.vn/d6/news/Electricity-Regulatory-Authority-of-Vietnam-works-with-EVN-on-electricity-market-operation-66-163-3410.aspx/ [accessed 2 October 2023].

Faccini, R., Matin, R., Skiadopoulos, G. (2023). Dissecting climate risks: Are they reflected in stock prices? *J. Bank Financ.* 155, 106948. https://doi.org/10.1016/j.jbankfin.2023.106948.

Fagiani, R., Hakvoort, R. (2014). The role of regulatory uncertainty in certificate markets: A case study of the Swedish/Norwegian market. *Energy Policy* 65, 608–618. https://doi.org/10.1016/j.enpol.2013.10.076.

Farand, C. (2023). Can 'just transition partnerships' usher in the end of coal? For the partnerships to support developing nations to move towards clean energy, the criteria for receiving finance need streamlining. *China Dialogue* (14 September 2023). https://chinadialogue.net/en/climate/can-jetp-usher-in-the-end-of-coal/ [accessed 21 September 2023].

Farfan, J., Breyer, C. (2017). Structural changes of global power generation capacity towards sustainability and the risk of stranded investments supported by a sustainability indicator. *J. Clean. Prod.* 141, 370–384. https://doi.org/10.1016/j.jclepro.2016.09.068.

Farias-Rocha, A. P., Hassan, K. M. K., Malimata, J. R. R., Sánchez-Cubedo, G. A., Rojas-Solórzano, L. R. (2019). Solar photovoltaic policy review and economic analysis for on-grid residential installations in the Philippines. *J. Clean. Prod.* 223, 45–56. https://doi.org/10.1016/j.jclepro.2019.03.085.

Finanz, N. (2024). VinFast Reports Unaudited Fourth Quarter and Full Year 2023 Financial Results. PR Newswire (22 February 2024). www.finanznachrichten.de/nachrichten-2024-02/61481103-vinfast-auto-ltd-vinfast-reports-unaudited-fourth-quarter-and-full-year-2023-financial-results-008.htm/, [accessed 29 February 2024].

Finstad, J., Andersen, A. D. (2023). Multi-sector technology diffusion in urgent net-zero transitions: Niche splintering in carbon capture technology. *Technol.*

Forecast. Soc. Change 194, 122696. https://doi.org/10.1016/j.techfore.2023.122696.

Firdaus, N., Mori, A. (2023). Stranded assets and sustainable energy transition: A systematic and critical review of incumbents' response. *Energy Sustain. Dev.* 73, 76–86. https://doi.org/10.1016/j.esd.2023.01.014.

First Gen. (2020). Locate our clean energy facilities. www.firstgen.com.ph/our-business/energy-facilities-locations/, [accessed 7 May 2023].

Flammer, C. (2021). Corporate green bonds. *J. Financ. Econ.* 142(2), 499–516. https://doi.org/10.1016/j.jfineco.2021.01.010.

Flores, A. M. S. (2023). The P60-billion Batangas power plant set to start construction in August. *Manila Standard Net* (8 January 2023). www.manilastandard.net/business/power-technology/314294464/p60-billion-batangas-power-plant-set-to-start-construction-in-august.html, [accessed 4 July 2023].

Flores, A. M. S. (2024). PSALM begins Mindanao coal plant's retirement, repurposing. *Manila Standard* (26 July 2024). https://manilastandard.net/business/314476714/psalm-begins-mindanao-coal-plants-retirement-repurposing.html, [accessed 3 November 2024].

Fofrich, R., Tong, D., Calvin, K., De Boer, H. S., Emmerling, J., Fricko, O., Fujimori, S., Luderer, G., Rogelj, J., Davis, S. J. (2020). Early retirement of power plants in climate mitigation scenarios. *Environ. Res. Lett.* 15(9). https://doi.org/10.1088/1748-9326/ab96d3.

Fornillo, B., Lampis, A. (2023). From the lithium triangle to the Latin American quarry: The shifting geographies of de-fossilisation. *Extr. Ind. Soc.* 15, 101326. https://doi.org/10.1016/j.exis.2023.101326.

Foster, V., Witte, S., Banerjee, S. G., Moreno, A. (2017). Charting the diffusion of power sector reforms across the developing world. Policy Research Working Paper 8235. World Bank, Washington, DC. http://hdl.handle.net/10986/28853.

Fox-Penner, P. (2020). *Power after Carbon: Building a Clean, Resilient Grid.* Harvard University Press, Cambridge, MA.

Franta, B. (2017). Litigation in the fossil fuel divestment movement. *Law Policy* 39(4), 393–411. https://doi.org/10.1111/lapo.12086.

Freedom of Information Philippines. (2022). Latest Status of Smart Distribution Utility Roadmap (14 December 2022). www.foi.gov.ph/requests/aglzfmVmb2ktcGhyHQsSB0NvbnRlbnQiEERPRS01MjMyNDgxMzE1MDQM/, [accessed 1 June 2023].

Frei, F., Sinsel, S. R., Hanafy, A., Hoppmann, J. (2018). Leaders or laggards? The evolution of electric utilities' business portfolios during the energy transition. *Energy Policy* 120, 655–665. https://doi.org/10.1016/j.enpol.2018.04.043.

French, D., Resnick-ault, J. (2021). Shell exits Permian with $9.5 bln Texas shale sale to ConocoPhillips. *Reuters* (21 September 2021). www.reuters.com/business/shell-nears-deal-sell-texas-shale-assets-conocophillips-95-bln-wsj-2021-09-20/, [accessed 15 August 2023].

Fujimori, S., Oshiro, K., Hasegawa, T., Takakura, J., Ueda, K. (2023). Climate change mitigation costs reduction caused by socioeconomic-technological transitions. *npj Climate Action* 2, 9. https://doi.org/10.1038/s44168-023-00041-w.

Gaba, M. (2023). For an equitable energy transition: The just energy transition partnership (JETP) in Senegal – Explanations, challenges and courses of action. *Policy Brief*. Heinrich-Böll-Stiftung. https://sn.boell.org/sites/default/files/2024-02/ev_policy-brief-jetp_en.pdf, [accessed 3 November 2024].

Gantchev, N., Giannetti, M., Li, R. (2022). Does money talk? Divestitures and corporate environmental and social policies. *Rev. Financ.* 26(6), 1469–1508. https://doi.org/10.1093/rof/rfac029.

Gao, X., Davidson, M., Busby, J., Shearer, C., Eisenman, J. (2021). The challenges of coal phaseout: Coal plant development and foreign finance in Indonesia and Vietnam. *Global Environ. Polit.* 21, 110–133. https://doi.org/10.1162/glep_a_00630.

Gawel, E., Lehmann, P., Purkus, A., et al. (2022). Security of supply as a political bargaining issue: Why Germany opted against capacity markets. *Energy Res. Soc. Sci.* 86, 102321. https://doi.org/10.1016/j.erss.2021.102321.

GCF. (2022). *Sectoral Guide Consultation Version 1: Energy Access and Power Generation*. Global Climate Fund (GCF), Incheon, Korea. www.greenclimate.fund/sites/default/files/document/gcf-energy-access-power-generation-sectoral-guide-consultation-version-1.pdf, [accessed 15 November 2023].

GCF. (2023a). *Annual Report 2023*. Global Climate Fund (GCF), Incheon, Korea. www.greenclimate.fund/sites/default/files/document/gcf-annual-report-2023-040919.pdf, [accessed 15 November 2023].

GCF. (2023b). *Progress Report: GCF's First Replenishment Period 2020–2023*. Global Climate Fund (GCF), Incheon, Korea. www.greenclimate.fund/sites/default/files/document/20230501-gcf-1-progress-report.pdf, [accessed 15 November 2023].

GCR Staff. (2021). Vietnam seals deal with South Korean contractor to build $3bn LNG power station in long an. *Global Construction Review* (1 April 2021). www.globalconstructionreview.com/vietnam-seals-deal-south-korean-contractor-build-3, [accessed 23 April 2022].

Geddes, A., Bridle, R., Mostafa, M., Roth, J., Sanchez, L., Garg, V., Scholtz, L., Saliem Fakir, S. (2020). *Rethinking Eskom: Lessons from Electricity Sector Reform in India and Mexico*. International Institute for Sustainable

Development and Global Subsidy Initiative. www.iisd.org/publications/report/rethinking-eskom-lessons-electricity-sector-reform-india-and-mexico/ [accessed 2 October 2023].

Geddes, A., Schmidt, T. S. (2020). Integrating finance into the multi-level perspective: Technology niche finance regime interactions and financial policy interventions. *Res. Policy* 49, 103985. https://doi.org/10.1016/j.respol.2020.103985.

General Electric. (2019). Vietnam electricity awards GE battery energy storage feasibility study funded by U.S. Trade and development agency. *Press Release* (12 April 2019). www.ge.com/news/press-releases/vietnam-electricity-awards-ge-battery-energy-storage-feasibility-study-funded-us, [accessed 20 December 2022].

Generation Foundation. (2013). *Stranded Carbon Assets: Why and How Carbon Risk Should Be Incorporated in Investment Analysis*. Accessed from http://genfound.org/media/pdf-generation-foundation-stranded-carbon-assets-v1.pdf

GFANZ. (2022a). 2022 progress report. https://assets.bbhub.io/company/sites/63/2022/10/GFANZ-2022-Progress-Report.pdf/ [accessed 4 October 2023].

GFANZ. (2022b). Financial institution net-zero transition plans: Fundamentals, recommendations, and guidance. www.gfanzero.com/our-work/financial-institution-net-zero-transition-plans/ [accessed 4 October 2023].

Gibbs, S., McDaniels, J., Palmer, M. (2021). COP26: Outcomes and implications for the global financial sector. *IIF Briefing Note*. Institute of International Finance (IIF).

Giglio, S., Kelly, B., Stroebel, J. (2021). Climate finance. *Annu. Rev. Financ. Econ.* 13, 15–36. https://doi.org/10.1146/annurev-financial-102620-103311.

Global Energy Interconnection Development and Cooperation Organization. (2019). *Research and outlook on Global Energy Interconnection*. China Electric Power Press, Beijing.

Global Energy Monitor and Centre for Research on Energy and Clean Air. (2021). China Dominates 2020 Coal Plant Development. Briefing, February 2021. https://globalenergymonitor.org/wp-content/uploads/2021/02/China-Dominates-2020-Coal-Development.pdf/, [accessed 27 August 2023].

Global Energy Monitor. (2023). Construction starts on new coal plants on track to hit a record low outside of China since yearly data collection began in 2015. Accessed from https://globalenergymonitor.org/wp-content/uploads/2023/11/GEM_Coal_Construction_StartsQ32023.pdf

Global Sustainable Investment Alliance. (2021). Global sustainable investment review 2020. www.gsi-alliance.org/wp-content/uploads/2021/08/GSIR-20201.pdf/ [accessed 5 October 2023].

Godin, A., Hadji-Lazaro, P. (2020). Demand-induced transition risks: A systemic approach applied to South Africa. Research Papers 199, Agence Francaise de

Developpement. www.afd.fr/en/ressources/demand-induced-transition-risks-south-africa/, [accessed 19 August 2023].

Gratwick, K. N., Eberhard, A. (2008). Demise of the standard model for power sector reform and the emergence of hybrid power markets. *Energy Policy* 36, 3948–3960. https://doi.org/10.1016/j.enpol.2008.07.021.

Green Climate Fund. (2023). Project portfolio. www.greenclimate.fund/projects/dashboard/ [accessed 7 October 2023].

Green, J., Newman, P. (2017). Disruptive innovation, stranded assets and forecasting: The rise and rise of renewable energy. *J. Sustain. Finance Invest.* 7, 169–187. https://doi.org/10.1080/20430795.2016.1265410.

Guidolin, M., Alpcan, T. (2019). Transition to sustainable energy generation in Australia: Interplay between coal, gas and renewables. *Renew. Energy* 139, 359–367. https://doi.org/10.1016/j.renene.2019.02.045.

Guild, J. (2019). Feed-in-tariffs and the politics of renewable energy in Indonesia and the Philippines. *Asia Pac Policy Stud.* 6, 417–431. https://doi.org/10.1002/app5.288.

Gulagi, A., Alcanzare, M., Bogdanov, D., Esparcia, E., Jr., Ocon, J., Breyer, C. (2021). Transition pathway towards 100% renewable energy across the sectors of power, heat, transport, and desalination for the Philippines. *Renew. Sustain. Energy Rev.* 144, 110934. https://doi.org/10.1016/j.rser.2021.110934.

Gulagi, A., Bogdanov, D., Breyer, C. (2018). The role of storage technologies in energy transition pathways towards achieving a fully sustainable energy system for India. *J. Energy Storage* 17, 525–539. https://doi.org/10.1016/j.est.2017.11.012.

Gunningham, N. (2017). Building norms from the grassroots up: Divestment, expressive politics, and climate change. *Law Policy* 39(4), 372–392. https://doi.org/10.1111/lapo.12083.

Gupta, J., Rempel, A., Verrest, H. (2020). Access and allocation: The role of large Shareholders and Investors in leaving fossil fuels underground. *Int. Environ. Agreem-P.* 20, 303–322. https://doi.org/10.1007/s10784-020-09478-4.

Gürsan, C., de Gooyert, V. (2021). The systemic impact of a transition fuel: Does natural gas help or hinder the energy transition? *Renew. Sustain. Energy Rev.* 138, 110552. https://doi.org/10.1016/j.rser.2020.110552.

GWEC. (2021). *Vietnam's Future Transition to Offshore Wind Auctions.* Global Wind Energy Council. https://gwec.net/vietnams-future-transition-to-offshore-wind-auctions-international-best-practices-and-lessons-learned/, [accessed 29 June 2023].

GWEC. (2022). *Global Offshore Wind Report 2022.* Global Wind Energy Council. https://gwec.net/wp-content/uploads/2022/06/GWEC-Global-Offshore-Wind-Report-2022.pdf/, [accessed 29 June 2023].

GWEC. (2023). *Global Wind Report 2023*. https://gwec.net/globalwindreport2023, [accessed 16 June 2023].

Hafner, S., Jones, A., Anger-Kraavi, A., Pohl, J. (2020). Closing the green finance gap: A systems perspective. *Environ. Innov. Soc. Transit.* 34, 26–60. https://doi.org/10.1016/j.eist.2019.11.007.

Halimanjaya, A. (2014). Climate mitigation finance across developing countries: What are the major determinants. *Clim. Policy* 15(2), 223–252. https://doi.org/10.1080/14693062.2014.912978.

Hamdi, E. (2021). Indonesia wants to go greener, but PLN is stuck with excess capacity from coal-fired power plants. Institute for Energy Economics and Financial Analysis. https://ieefa.org/wp-content/uploads/2021/11/Indonesia-Wants-to-Go-Greener-but-PLN-Is-Stuck-With-Excess-Capacity_November-2021.pdf/, [accessed 26 March 2024].

Hansen, T. A. (2022). Stranded assets and reduced profits: Analyzing the economic underpinnings of the fossil fuel industry's resistance to climate stabilization. *Renew. Sustain. Energy Rev.* 158, 112144. https://doi.org/10.1016/j.rser.2022.112144.

Hauber, G. (2023). Financing the JETP: Making sense of the packages. Institute for Energy Economic and Financial Analysis (IEEFA). https://ieefa.org/resources/financing-jetp-making-sense-packages, [accessed 29 January 2024].

Hauenstein, C. (2023). Stranded assets and early closures in global coal mining under 1.5°C. *Environ. Res. Lett.* 18, 024021. https://doi.org/10.1088/1748-9326/acb0e5.

Hawkins, K. (2022). Vietnam: Changes to the law on electricity. *DFDL* (1 April 2022). www.dfdl.com/resources/legal-and-tax-updates/vietnam-changes-to-the-law-on-electricity, [accessed 25 August 2022].

Heede, R., Oreskes, N. (2016). Potential emissions of CO_2 and methane from proved reserves of fossil fuels: An alternative analysis. *Glob. Environ. Chang.* 36, 12–20. https://doi.org/10.1016/j.gloenvcha.2015.10.005.

Helms, T. (2016). Asset transformation and the challenges to servitize a utility business model. *Energy Policy* 91, 98–112. https://doi.org/10.1016/j.enpol.2015.12.046.

Herzog-Hawelka, J., Gupta, J. (2023). The role of (multi)national oil and gas companies in leaving fossil fuels underground: A systematic literature review. *Energy Res. Soc. Sci.* 103, 103194. https://doi.org/10.1016/j.erss.2023.103194.

Hess, D. J. (2014). Sustainability transitions. A political coalition perspective. *Res. Policy* 43(2), 278–283. https://doi.org/10.1016/j.respol.2013.10.008.

Hickey, C., O'Brien, J., Caldecott, B., McInerney, C., Gallachóir, B. Ó. (2021). Can European electric utilities manage asset impairments arising from net zero carbon targets? *J. Corp. Finance* 70, 102075. https://doi.org/10.1016/j.jcorpfin.2021.102075.

Ho, K., Wong, A. (2023). Effect of climate-related risk on the costs of bank loans: Evidence from syndicated loan markets in emerging economies. *Emerg. Mark. Rev.* 55, 100977. https://doi.org/10.1016/j.ememar.2022.100977.

Hoang, L. (2024). Vietnam seeks tech transfer from Chinese energy giant. *Nikkei Asia* (29 February 2024). https://asia.nikkei.com/Business/Energy/Vietnam-seeks-tech-transfer-from-Chinese-energy-giant/, [accessed 1 March 2024].

Hong, W. M., Knowles, T., Alebi, C., Moncrieff, A., Huynh, T., Ross, A. (2020). Banking Solar in Vietnam: A look at the next wave of renewable power projects in Vietnam. *Allen&Overy* (13 May 2020). www.allenovery.com/en-gb/global/news-and-insights/publications/banking-solar-in-vietnam--a-look-at-the-next-wave-of-renewable-power-projects-in-vietnam, [accessed 7 June 2023].

Huang, H. H., Kerstein, J., Wang, C., Wu, F.(H.) (2022). Firm climate risk, risk management, and bank loan financing. *Strateg. Manag. J.* 43(13), 2849–2880. https://doi.org/10.1002/smj.3437.

Hung, L. M. (2016). Integration strategy in refining and petrochemical complex. 34th JCCP International Symposium. www.jccp.or.jp/international/conference/docs/LP-5%20Dr.%20Le%20Manh%20Hung%20-%2034th%20JCCP%20Int%20Symposium.pdf.

Hunt, C., Weber, O. (2019). Fossil fuel divestment strategies: Financial and carbon-related consequences. *Organ. Environ.* 32(1), 41–61. https://doi.org/10.1177/1086026618773985.

Huo, J., Meng, J., Zheng, H., Parikh, P., Guan, D. (2023). Achieving decent living standards in emerging economies challenges national mitigation goals for CO_2 emissions. *Nat. Commun.* 14, 6342. https://doi.org/10.1038/s41467-023-42079-8.

ICLEI. (2023). How four Philippine cities are cutting down emissions under the Cities Race to Zero. News (5 September 2023). https://icleiseas.org/index.php/2023/09/05/how-four-philippine-cities-are-cutting-down-emissions-under-the-cities-race-to-zero/, [accessed 24 October 2023].

ICMA. (2022). Green bond principles: Voluntary process guidelines for issuing green bonds. June 2021 (with June 2022 Appendix 1). www.icmagroup.org/assets/documents/Sustainable-finance/2022-updates/Green-Bond-Principles-June-2022-060623.pdf/ [accessed 3 October 2023].

IEA. (2011). IEA special report explores potential for 'golden age' of natural gas, www.iea.org/news/iea-special-report-explores-potential-for-golden-age-of-natural-gas, [accessed 26 December 2022].

IEA. (2013). *Redrawing the Energy-Climate Map: World Energy Outlook Special Report*. International Energy Agency. Accessed from www.iea.org/

publications/freepublications/publication/WEO_Special_Report_2013_Redrawing_the_Energy_Climate_Map.pdf%5Cn; www.iea.org/publications/freepublications/publication/name,38764,en.html

IEA. (2016). *Re-powering Markets: Market Design and Regulation during the Transition to Low-carbon Power Systems*. International Energy Agency, Paris.

IEA. (2022). *World Energy Outlook 2022*. Paris. www.iea.org/reports/world-energy-outlook-2022 [accessed 14 January 2023].

IEA. (2023a). Countries and regions. www.iea.org/countries/, [accessed 17 February 2024].

IEA. (2023b). *The State of Clean Technology Manufacturing*. IEA, Paris. https://iea.blob.core.windows.net/assets/0a421001-6157-436d-893c-c37eeab54967/TheStateofCleanTechnologyManufacturing.pdf/, [accessed 28 June 2023].

IEA. (2024a). Philippines. www.iea.org/countries/philippines/electricity, [accessed 2 November 2024].

IEA. (2024b). Viet Nam. www.iea.org/countries/viet-nam/electricity/, [accessed 2 November 2024].

IEA. (2024c). Cambodia. www.iea.org/countries/cambodia/electricity/, [accessed 7 November 2024].

IEA. (2024d). Indonesia. www.iea.org/countries/Indonesia/electricity/, [accessed 2 November 2024].

IEA. (2024e). Malaysia. www.iea.org/countries/malaysia/electricity/, [accessed 7 November 2024].

IEA. (2024f). Myanmar. www.iea.org/countries/myanmar/electricity/, [accessed 2 November 2024].

IEA. (2024g). Thailand. www.iea.org/countries/thailand/electricity, [accessed 2 November 2024].

IEA. (2024h). China. www.iea.org/countries/china/electricity/ [accessed 2 November 2024].

IEA. (2024i). India. www.iea.org/countries/india/electricity/ [accessed 2 November 2024].

IEA. (2024j). South Africa. www.iea.org/countries/south-africa/electricity [accessed 2 November 2024].

IEA. (2024k). *World Energy Investment 2023 Datafile*. www.iea.org/data-and-statistics/data-product/world-energy-investment-2023-datafile-2/ [accessed 1 November 2024].

IEA PVPS. (2023). *Trends in Photovoltaic Application 2023*. https://iea-pvps.org/trends_reports/trends-2023, [accessed 25 February 2024].

IEG Review Team. (2022). Vietnam – transmission efficiency project (TEP). World Bank Group, Washington, DC. http://documents.worldbank.org/curated/

en/099530012062229427/P1315580fe65690e2092c3082fb08a71ab3, [Accessed 17 December 2022].

IFRS Foundation. (2023). About the international sustainability standards board. www.ifrs.org/groups/international-sustainability-standards-board/ [accessed 28 September 2023].

iGST Equity Working Group. (2022). The equity landscape. Equity Working Group of the independent Global Stocktake. www.climateworks.org/wp-content/uploads/2023/07/The-Equity-Landscape_independent-Global-Stocktake-Equity-Working-Group_2022_v2.pdf, [accessed 10 October 2023].

Ilhan, E., Krueger, P., Sautner, Z., Starks, L. T. (2023). Climate risk disclosure and institutional investors. *Rev. Financ. Stud.* 36(7), 2617–2650. https://doi.org/10.1093/rfs/hhad002.

Inoue, K., Shiga, Y. (2024). Thailand, Philippines embrace nuclear power to cut emissions. *Nikkei Asia* (26 March 2024). https://asia.nikkei.com/Business/Energy/Thailand-Philippines-embrace-nuclear-power-to-cut-emissions/, [accessed 26 March 2024].

Institute for Policy Development [IPD]. (2023). Persepsi Masyrakat atas Kebijakan Pemensiunan Dini PLTU Batubara dalam Transisi Energi. Institute for Policy Development & Yayasan Indonesia CERAH. www.cerah.or.id/publications/report/detail/public-perception-of-pltu-early-retirement-policy, [accessed 21 December 2023, Indonesian language].

International Monetary Finance [IMF]. (2023). South Africa: Staff concluding statement of the 2023 Article IV Mission. www.imf.org/en/News/Articles/2023/03/21/mcs032223-south-africa-2023-article-iv-mission, [accessed 1 December 2023].

International Rivers & Vietnam Climate Defenders Coalition. (2024). The missing 'Just' in Vietnam's just energy transition partnership. www.internationalrivers.org/wp-content/uploads/sites/86/2024/06/Vietnam-JETP-Report-English.pdf, [accessed 3 November 2024].

International Trade Administration, U.S. Department of Commerce (n.d.). Vietnam – power generation, transmission, and distribution. www.trade.gov/country-commercial-guides/vietnam-power-generation-transmission-and-distribution, [accessed 1 December 2022].

IPCC. (2007). *Climate Change 2007 Mitigation. Contribution of Working Group III to the Fourth Assessment Report of the Intergovernmental Panel on Climate Change* (Metz, B., Davidson, O., Bosch, P., Dave, R., Meyer, L. (eds.)). Intergovernmental Panel on Climate Change (IPCC): Cambridge University Press. https://doi.org/10.1017/CBO9780511546013.

IPCC. (2014). *Climate Change 2014 Mitigation of Climate Change. Contribution of Working Group III to the Fifth Assessment Report of the Intergovernmental*

Panel on Climate Change (Edenhofer, O., Pichs-Madruga, R., Sokona, Y., Minx, J. C., Farahani, E., Kadner, S., Seyboth, K., Adler, A., Baum, I., Brunner, S., Eickemeier, P., Kriemann, B., Savolainen, J., Schlömer, S., von Stechow, C., Zwickel, T. (eds.)). Intergovernmental Panel on Climate Change (IPCC): Cambridge University Press. https://doi.org/10.1017/cbo9781107415416.

IPCC. (2018). *Special Report: Global Warming of 1.5°C.* www.ipcc.ch/site/assets/uploads/sites/2/2022/06/SR15_Full_Report_LR.pdf [accessed 14 May 2022].

IPCC. (2021). *Climate Change 2021: The Physical Science Basis. Contribution of Working Group I to the Sixth Assessment Report of the Intergovernmental Panel on Climate Change.* www.ipcc.ch/report/ar6/wg1/downloads/report/IPCC_AR6_WGI_FullReport.pdf [accessed 14 May 2022].

IPCC. (2022a). Climate change 2022: Mitigation of climate change. In: Shukla, J. M. P. R., Skea, J., Slade, R., Al Khourdajie, A., van Diemen, R., McCollum, D., Pathak, M., Some, S., Vyas, P., Fradera, R., Belkacemi, M., Hasija, A., Lisboa, G., Luz, S. (eds.) *Contribution of Working Group III to the Sixth Assessment Report of the Intergovernmental Panel on Climate Change.* Cambridge University Press, Cambridge.

IPCC. (2022b). Summary for policymakers. In: *Climate Change 2022: Mitigation of Climate Change. Contribution of Working Group III to the Sixth Assessment Report of the Intergovernmental Panel on Climate Change.* www.ipcc.ch/report/sixth-assessment-report-working-group-3 [accessed 14 May 2022].

IRENA. (2017). Stranded Assets and Renewables: How the Energy Transition Affects the Value of Energy Reserves, Buildings and Capital Stock. International Renewable Energy Agency. Accessed from www.irena.org/-/media/Files/IRENA/Agency/Publication/2017/Jul/IRENA_REmap_Stranded_assets_and_renewables_2017.pdf

IRENA. (2018). Global Energy Transformation: A Roadmap to 2050. https://abeeolica.org.br/wp-content/uploads/2018/05/IRENA_Report_GlobalEnergyTransformation_A-Roadmapto2050_2018.pdf/, [accessed 8 November 2025].

IRENA. (2020). *Renewable Power Generation Costs in 2019.* International Renewable Energy Agency, Abu Dhabi, www.irena.org/-/media/Files/IRENA/Agency/Publication/2020/Jun/IRENA_Power_Generation_Costs_2019.pdf/, [accessed 14 January 2021].

IRENA. (2021). *Renewable Energy Statistics 2021.* www.irena.org/-/media/Files/IRENA/Agency/Publication/2021/Apr/IRENA_RE_Capacity_Statistics_2021.pdf, [accessed 4 July 2023].

IRENA. (2022). *Renewable Energy Outlook for ASEAN: Towards a Regional Energy Transition.* 2nd Edition. International Renewable Energy Agency. Accessed from www.irena.org/publications/2022/Sep/Renewable-Energy-Outlook-for-ASEAN-2nd-edition

IRENA. (2023). *Renewable Energy Statistics 2023*. www.irena.org/Publications/2023/Mar/Renewable-capacity-statistics-2023, [accessed 4 July 2023].

IRENA. (2024). *Renewable Energy Statistics 2024*. www.irena.org/-/media/Files/IRENA/Agency/Publication/2024/Jul/IRENA_Renewable_Energy_Statistics_2024.pdf/, [accessed 2 November 2024].

Islam, M. M. (2022). Distributive justice in global climate finance: Recipients' climate vulnerability and the allocation of climate funds. *Global Environ. Change* 73, 102475. https://doi.org/10.1016/j.gloenvcha.2022.102475.

IUCN. (2022a). Grid integration of renewables. www.iucn.org/news/viet-nam/202205/grid-integration-renewables, [accessed 21 August 2022].

IUCN. (2022b). Opportunities and challenges in expanding wind in Vietnam's electricity mix. www.iucn.org/news/viet-nam/202205/grid-integration-renewables, [accessed 21 August 2022].

Iychettira, K. K. (2021). Lessons for renewable integration in developing countries: The importance of cost recovery and distributional justice. *Energy Res. Soc. Sci.* 77, 102069. https://doi.org/10.1016/j.erss.2021.102069.

Iyer, G. C., Edmonds, J. A., Fawcettet, A. A., et al. (2015). The contribution of Paris to limit global warming to 2°C. *Environ. Res. Lett.* 10, 125002. https://doi.org/10.1088/1748-9326/10/12/125002.

Iyer, G., Ledna, C., Clarke, L., Edmonds, J., McJeon, H., Kyle, P., Williams, J. H. (2017). Measuring progress from nationally determined contributions to mid-century strategies. *Nat. Clim. Change* 7(12), 871–874. https://doi.org/10.1038/s41558-017-0005-9.

Jackson, A. (2018). A Stock-Flow Consistent Framework for the Analysis of Stranded Assets and the Transition to a Low Carbon Economy. PhD dissertation, University of Surrey.

Jaffe, A. M. (2020a). Financial herding must be checked to avert climate crashes. *Nat Energy* 5, 101–103. https://doi.org/10.1038/s41560-020-0551-7.

Jaffe, A. M. (2020b). Stranded assets and sovereign states. *Natl. Inst. Econ. Rev.* 251, R25–R36. https://doi.org/10.1017/nie.2020.4.

Janzwood, A., Millar, H. (2022). Bridge fuel feuds: The competing interpretive politics of natural gas in Canada. *Energy Res. Soc. Sci.* 88, 102526. https://doi.org/10.1016/j.erss.2022.102526.

Javadi, S., Masum, A.-A. (2021). The impact of climate change on the cost of bank loans. *J. Corp. Finance* 69, 102019. https://doi.org/10.1016/j.jcorpfin.2021.102019.

Jenkins, J. D., Luke, M., Thernstrom, S. (2018). Getting to zero carbon emissions in the electric power sector. *Joule* 2, 2487–2510. https://doi.org/10.1016/j.joule.2018.11.013.

JETP Indonesia. (2024a). JETP: A look back at 2023 and a glimpse of what is to come in 2024. https://jetp-id.org/news/a-look-back-at-2023-and-a-glimpse-of-what-is-to-come-in-2024, [accessed 12 March 2024].

JETP Indonesia. (2024b). JETP grant mapping. https://jetp-id.org/news/jetp-grant-mapping, [accessed 3 November 2024].

JETP Indonesia. (2024c). Norwegian and British investment in Indonesian start up marks first equity milestone in JETP disbursement. https://jetp-id.org/news/norwegian-and-british-investment-in-indonesian-start-up-marks-first-equity-milestone-in-jetp-disbursement, [accessed 3 November 2024].

JGCRI. (2023). GCAM Documentation (Version 6.0). https://github.com/JGCRI/gcam-doc. Joint Global Change Research Institute. https://doi.org/10.5281/zenodo.6619287.

Johnson, N., Krey, V., McCollum, D. L., Rao, S., Riahi, K., Rogelj, J. (2015). Stranded on a low-carbon planet: Implications of climate policy for the phase-out of coal-based power plants. *Technol. Forecasting Social Change* 90(PA), 89–102. https://doi.org/10.1016/j.techfore.2014.02.028.

Johnstone, P., Hielscher, S. (2017). Phasing out coal, sustaining coal communities? Living with technological decline in sustainability pathways. *Extr. Ind. Soc.* 4, 457–461. https://doi.org/10.1016/j.exis.2017.06.002.

Jose, A. E. O. (2022). Battery tech seen sufficiently mature to support PHL's renewables push. *Business World* (10 November 2022). www.bworldonline.com/economy/2022/11/10/486489/battery-tech-seen-sufficiently-mature-to-support-phls-renewables-push/, [accessed 20 January 2023].

Just Energy Transition Partnership Indonesia. (2023). Comprehensive investment and policy plan. https://jetp-id.org/cipp, [accessed 27 February 2024].

Kalkuhl, M., Steckel, J. C., Edenhofer, O. (2020). All or nothing: Climate policy when assets can become stranded. *J. Environ. Econ. Manag.* 100, 102214. https://doi.org/10.1016/j.jeem.2019.01.012.

Keck, F., Lenzen, M., Vassallo, V., Li, M. (2019). The impact of battery energy storage for renewable energy power grids in Australia. *Energy* 173, 647–657. https://doi.org/10.1016/j.energy.2019.02.053.

Kefford, B. M., Ballinger, B., Schmeda-Lopez, D. R., Greig, C., Smart, S. (2018). The early retirement challenge for fossil fuel power plants in deep decarbonization scenarios. *Energy Policy* 119, 294–306. https://doi.org/10.1016/j.enpol.2018.04.018.

Kemfert, C., Präger, F., Braunger, I., et al. (2022). The expansion of natural gas infrastructure puts energy transitions at risk. *Nat Energy* 7, 582–587. https://doi.org/10.1038/s41560-022-01060-3.

Khoa, T. D. (2018). Market efficiency and market power in Vietnam competitive generation market. *Int. J. Energy Econ. Policy* 8(1), 181–189. www.econjournals.com/index.php/ijeep/article/view/5828.

Köberle, A. C., Vandyck, T., Guivarch, C., Macaluso, N., Bosetti, V., Gambhir, A., Tavoni, M., Rogelj, J. (2021). The cost of mitigation revisited. *Nat. Clim. Change* 11(12), 1035–1045. https://doi.org/10.1038/s41558-021-01203-6.

Kölbel, J. F., Heeb, F., Paetzold, F., Busch, T. (2020). Can sustainable investing save the world? Reviewing the mechanisms of investor impact. *Organ. Environ.* 33(4), 554–574. https://doi.org/10.1177/1086026620919202.

Koty, A. C. (2022). Vietnam electricity reforms spark opportunities for foreign investment. ASEAN Briefing (26 May 2022). www.aseanbriefing.com/news/vietnam-s-amended-electricity-law-sparks-new-opportunities-for-foreign-investment, [accessed 25 August 2022].

Kraan, O., Kramer, G. J., Nikolic, I., Chappin, E., Koning, V. (2019). Why fully liberalised electricity markets will fail to meet deep decarbonisation targets even with strong carbon pricing. *Energy Policy* 131, 99–110. https://doi.org/10.1016/j.enpol.2019.04.016.

Krueger, P., Sautner, Z., Starks, L. T. (2020). The importance of climate risks for institutional investors. *Rev. Financ. Stud.* 33(3), 1067–1111. https://doi.org/10.1093/rfs/hhz137.

Krutham. (2023). JET issues in public finance: A focus on mobilising funding for Mpumalanga. *Research Report*, September 2023. www.krutham.com/projects/just-energy-transition/, [accessed 29 December 2023].

Kuchler, M., Höök, M. (2020). Fractured visions: Anticipating (un)conventional natural gas in Poland. *Resour. Policy* 68, 101760. https://doi.org/10.1016/j.resourpol.2020.101760.

Kumar, A., Chatterjee, S. (2012). *Electricity Sector in India: Policy and Regulation*. Oxford University Press, New Delhi. https://doi.org/10.1093/acprof:oso/9780198082279.001.0001.

Lagac, J. M. P., Yap, J. T. (2020). Evaluating the feed-in tariff policy in the Philippines. ASOG working paper 20-004. Ateneo School of Government. https://ssrn.com/abstract=3520401/, [accessed 13 May 2023].

Lam, L. H., Bach, D. X. (2023). Uniform purchasing price approach for Vietnam wholesale electricity market: modeling and discussing. *Int. J. Electr.* 148, 109012. https://doi.org/10.1016/j.ijepes.2023.109012.

Lamperti, F., Bosetti, V., Roventini, A., Tavoni, M. (2019). The public costs of climate-induced financial instability. *Nat. Clim. Chang.* 9, 829–833. https://doi.org/10.1038/s41558-019-0607-5.

Le, T.-H., Han, P., Le, H.-C. (2022). Electricity market development in Viet Nam: Historical trends and future perspectives. In: Phoumin, H., et al. (eds.) *Revisiting Electricity Market Reforms*. Springer Open, 45–74. https://doi.org/10.1007/978-981-19-4266-2_3.

Le, T.-H., Han, P., Le, H.-C., Bui M.-T. (2023). Electricity market development in Vietnam: Historical trends and future outlooks. *Util. Policy*. 81, 101510. https://doi.org/10.1016/j.jup.2023.101510.

Lee, A. D., Gerner, F. (2020). Learning from power sector reform experiences: The case of Vietnam. Policy Research Working Paper 9169, World Bank, Washington, DC. https://openknowledge.worldbank.org/handle/10986/33412, [accessed 4 December 2022].

Lehr, R. L. (2013). New utility business models: Utility and regulatory models for the modern era. *Electr. J.* 26(8), 35–53. https://doi.org/10.1016/j.tej.2013.09.004.

Lenferna, A. (2023). South Africa's unjust climate reparations: A critique of the just energy transition partnership. *Rev. Afr. Polit. Econ.* 50(177–178), 491–501. https://doi.org/10.1080/03056244.2023.2278953.

Li, S., Wu, X. (2023). How does climate risk affect bank loan supply? Empirical evidence from China. *Econ. Change Restruct* 56, 2169–2204. https://doi.org/10.1007/s10644-023-09505-9.

Li, Y., Yang, Z., Dong, X. (2025). Green bond and greenwashing: New insights from Chinese firms. *Finance Res. Lett.* 85, Part A, 107847. https://doi.org/10.1016/j.frl.2025.107847.

Liebman, A., Reynolds, A., Robertson, D., Nolan, S., Argyriou, M., Sargent, B. (2019). Green finance in Indonesia: Barriers and solutions. In: Sachs, J. D., Woo, W. T., Yoshino, N., Taghizadeh-Hesary, F. (eds.), *Handbook of Green Finance: Energy Security and Sustainable Development*. Springer, 557–586. https://doi.org/10.1007/978-981-13-0227-5_5.

Lin, J., Kahrl, F., Yuan, J., Liu, X., Zhang, W. (2019). Challenges and strategies for electricity market transition in China. *Energy Policy* 133, 110899. https://doi.org/10.1016/j.enpol.2019.110899.

Linseed Field Power Corporation. (2021). Environmental impact statement summary for the public –Ilijan LNG import facility project. https://eia.emb.gov.ph/wp-content/uploads/2021/02/Ilijan-LNG-Project_ESP-English.pdf/ [accessed 13 September 2023].

Lipari, G., Rosario, G. D., Corchero, C., Ponci, F., Monti, A. (2018). A real-time commercial aggregator for distributed energy resources flexibility management. *Sustain. Energy, Grids Netw.* 15, 63–75. https://doi.org/10.1016/j.segan.2017.07.002.

Löffler, K., Burand, T., Hainsch, K., Oei, P.-Y. (2019). Modeling the low-carbon transition of the European energy system: A quantitative assessment of the stranded assets problem. *Energy Strategy Rev.* 26, 100422. https://doi.org/10.1016/j.esr.2019.100422.

Loorbach, D., Schoenmaker, D., Schramade, W. (2020). Finance in transition: Principles for a positive finance future. Rotterdam School of Management

Report, Erasmus University, Rotterdam. www.rsm.nl/fileadmin/Corporate/About_RSM/Positive_Change/2020_Finance_in_Transition.pdf/, [accessed 2 January 2024].

Lu, Y., Cohen, F., Smith, S. M., et al. (2022). Plant conversions and abatement technologies cannot prevent stranding of power plant assets in 2°C scenarios. *Nat. Commun.* 13, 806. https://doi.org/10.1038/s41467-022-28458-7.

Madrigal, M., Stoft, S. (2012). *Transmission Expansion for Renewable Energy Scale-Up: Emerging Lessons and Recommendations*, A World Bank Study. World Bank: Washington, DC. http://hdl.handle.net/10986/9375/, [accessed 14 January 2021].

Maffei, L. (2019). Blended finance in development—Chile: A shift from people's needs to business demands in country cases: Blended finance in development. International Trade Union Confederation. www.ituc-csi.org/country-cases-blended-finance-in-development, [accessed 10 November 2023].

Maguire, G. (2023). Philippines set to go from renewable laggard to leader in SE Asia. *Reuters* (14 March 2023). www.reuters.com/markets/commodities/philippines-set-go-renewable-laggard-leader-se-asia-2023-03-14/, [accessed 10 May 2023].

Mah, D. N.-Y., Wu, M. Y.-Y., Hills, P. R. (2017). Explaining the role of incumbent utilities in sustainable energy transitions: A case study of the smart grid development in China. *Energy Policy* 109, 794–806. https://doi.org/10.1016/j.enpol.2017.06.059.

Malik, A., Bertram, C., Despres, J., et al. (2020). Reducing stranded assets through early action in the Indian power sector. *Environ. Res. Lett.* 15(9), 094091. https://doi.org/10.1088/1748-9326/ab8033.

Maltais, A., Nykvist, B. (2020). Understanding the role of green bonds in advancing sustainability. *J. Sustain. Finance Invest.* https://doi.org/10.1080/20430795.2020.1724864.

Mapfumo, P., Onyango, M., Honkponou, S. K., et al. (2017). Pathways to transformational change in the face of climate impacts: An analytical framework. *Clim. Dev.* 9(5), 439–451. https://doi.org/10.1080/17565529.2015.104036.

Markard, J. (2018). The next phase of the energy transition and its implications for research and policy. *Nat. Energy* 3, 628–633. https://doi.org/10.1038/s41560-018-0171-7.

Markard, J., Hoffmann, V. H. (2016). Analysis of complementarities: Framework and examples from the energy transition. *Technol. Forecast. Soc. Change* 111, 63–75. http://doi.org/10.1016/j.techfore.2016.06.008.

Markard, J., Rosenbloom, D. (2023). Phases of the net-zero energy transition and strategies to achieve it. In: Araújo, K. (ed.) *Routledge Handbook of*

Energy Transitions. Routledge, New York, 102–123. https://doi.org/10.4324/9781003183020-8.

Markard, J., Wirth, S., Truffer, B. (2016). Institutional dynamics and technology legitimacy – A framework and a case study on biogas technology. *Res. Policy* 45, 330–344. https://doi.org/10.1016/j.respol.2015.10.009.

Marollano, E. M. C. P. (2020). Luzon Power Situation and Outlook. *Energy Investment Briefing in Region III*, Fontana Leisure Park and Hotel, Clark, Pampanga (4 March 2020). www.doe.gov.ph/sites/default/files/pdf/e_ipo/02_03-2020_doe_luzon_power_outlook.pdf/, [accessed 8 May 2023].

Masinloc Power Partners Co Ltd (n.d.). Overview. https://mppcl.com.ph/, [accessed 8 May 2023].

Massmann, O., Nguyen, T. L. (2022). Vietnam – energy – LNG and power development plan 8 – pdp 8 – latest updates. *Duane Morris Vietnam* (26 September 2022). https://blogs.duanemorris.com/vietnam/2022/09/26/vietnam-energy-lng-and-power-development-plan-8-pdp-8-latest-updates/#page=1, [accessed 15 October 2022].

Maulia, E. (2022). Dirty metals for clean cars: Indonesian nickel could be key to EV battery industry. *Nikkei Asia* (19 October 2022). https://asia.nikkei.com/Spotlight/The-Big-Story/Dirty-metals-for-clean-cars-Indonesian-nickel-could-be-key-to-EV-battery-industry/ [accessed 17 February 2024].

Maulia, E. (2023). Indonesia bets on critical mineral export bans as deadline nears. *Nikkei Asia* (23 May 2023). https://asia.nikkei.com/Spotlight/Asia-Insight/Indonesia-bets-on-critical-mineral-export-bans-as-deadline-nears, [accessed 27 February 2024].

Maulia, E., Daamyanti, I. (2023). Indonesia's nickel riches spur local company EV, battery ambition: Old economy conglomerates, businesses pounce as government pushes industry takeoff. *Nikkei Asia* (3 February 2023). https://asia.nikkei.com/Business/Business-Spotlight/Indonesia-s-nickel-riches-spur-local-company-EV-battery-ambition, [accessed 12 February 2023].

McDonnell, C., Gupta J. (2023). Beyond divest vs. engage: A review of the role of institutional investors in an inclusive fossil fuel phase-out. *Clim. Policy* 23(3), 314–331. https://doi.org/10.1080/14693062.2023.2261900.

McDonnell, C., Rempel, A., Gupta, J. (2022). Climate action or distraction? Exploring investor initiatives and implications for unextractable fossil fuels. *Energy Res. Soc. Sci.* 92, 102769. https://doi.org/10.1016/j.erss.2022.102769.

McGlade, C., Ekins, P. (2015). The geographical distribution of fossil fuels unused when limiting global warming to 2°C. *Nature* 517(7533), 187–190. https://doi.org/10.1038/nature14016.

McKibben, B. (2012). Global warming's terrifying new math: Three simple numbers that add up to global catastrophe – and that make clear who the real enemy is. *Rolling Stone* (19 July 2012). www.rollingstone.com/politics/news/global-warmings-terrifying-new-math-20120719?print=true/ [accessed 28 September 2023].

Meadowcroft, J., Layzell, D., Mousseau, N. (2019). The transition accelerator: Building pathways to a sustainable future. *Transition Accel. Rep.* 1(1), 1–65. www.transitionaccelerator.ca.

Meralco. (2022). *Power Supply Procurement Plan 2022*. https://meralcomain.s3.ap-southeast-1.amazonaws.com/images/ckeditor-documents/MERALCOs-2022-Power-Supply-Procurement-Plan-MERALCO.pdf/, [accessed 25 June 2023].

Mercure, J. F., Pollitt, H., Viñuales, J. E., et al. (2018). Macroeconomic impact of stranded fossil fuel assets. *Nat. Clim. Change* 8, 588–593. https://doi.org/10.1038/s41558-018-0182-1.

Mercure, J.-F., Pollitt, H., Viñuales, J. E. (2018). Macroeconomic impact of stranded fossil fuel assets. *Nat. Clim. Chang.* 8, 588–593. https://doi.org/10.1038/s41558-018-0182-1.

Mercure, J.-F., Salas, P., Vercoulen, P., et al. (2021). Reframing incentives for climate policy action. *Nat. Energy* 6, 1133–1143. https://doi.org/10.1038/s41560-021-00934-2.

Mercurio, R. (2023a). LNG infrastructure buildup still slow in Philippines, says Fitch. *The Philippine Star* (19 February 2023). www.philstar.com/business/2023/02/19/2245937/lng-infrastructure-buildup-still-slow-philippines-says-fitch/, [accessed 30 May 2023].

Mercurio, R. (2023b). SMC Ilijan to resume operations soon. *The Philippine Star* (3 April 2023). www.philstar.com/business/2023/04/03/2256341/smc-ilijan-resume-operations-soon/, [accessed 4 July 2023].

METI (Japanese Ministry of Economy, Trade and Industry). (2023). Transition finance. www.meti.go.jp/english/policy/energy_environment/transition_finance/index.html/, [accessed 28 September 2023].

Miller, S. (2023). Global gas realities. Energy Intelligence (10 November 2023). www.energyintel.com/0000018b-b884-dbb5-a5ef-fcf75cb40000/, [accessed 30 December 2023].

Minh. (2021). Limit the construction of more inter-regional transmission lines. *VN Express* (23 December 2021). https://vnexpress.net/han-che-xay-them-duong-day-truyen-tai-lien-mien-4406710.html, [accessed 22 November 2022] (in Vietnamese).

Minh, H.-D. (2020). Stranded assets risk derails Vietnam's plan for new coal power plants. *IAEE Energy Forum* First Quarter 2020, 27–29. www.iaee.org/en/publications/newsletterdl.aspx?id=853, [accessed 24 August 2022].

Minh, V. (2023). Vietnam's latest power plan opens door to foreign investment: US energy firm. *The Investor* (23 May 2023). https://theinvestor.vn/vietnams-latest-power-plan-opens-door-to-foreign-investment-us-energy-firm-d5074.html/, [accessed 1 July 2023].

Ministry of Industry and Trade (MOIT). (2021). 84 wind power projects in time for commercial operation with a total capacity of more than 3,980MW. *Press Release* (3 November 2021). https://moit.gov.vn/tin-tuc/phat-trien-nang-luong/84-du-an-dien-gio-kip-van-hanh-thuong-mai-voi-tong-cong-suat-hon-3.980-mw.html, [accessed 30 June 2023] (in Vietnamese).

Minx, J. C., Lamb, W. F., Andrew, R. M., et al. (2022). A comprehensive and synthetic dataset for global, regional and national greenhouse gas emissions by sector 1970–2018 with an extension to 2019 [Data set]. Zenodo. https://doi.org/10.5281/zenodo.6483002.

MOIT. (2022). Reviewing the 8th electricity planning. https://thuvienphapluat.vn/cong-van/EN/Dau-tu/Official-Dispatch-3787-BCT-DL-2022-reviewing-the-8th-Electricity-Planning/523359/tieng-anh.aspx, [accessed 25 August 2022].

Monasterolo, I. (2020). Climate change and the financial system. *Annu. Rev. Resour. Econ.* 12, 299–320. https://doi.org/10.1146/annurev-resource-110119-031134.

Monasterolo, I., Battiston, S., Janetos, A. C., Zheng, Z. (2017). Vulnerable yet relevant: The two dimensions of climate-related financial disclosure. *Clim. Change* 145(3–4), 495–507. https://doi.org/10.1007/s10584-017-2095-9.

Monasterolo, I., Zheng, J. I., Battiston, S. (2018). Climate transition risk and development finance: A carbon risk assessment of China's overseas energy portfolios. *China World Econ.* 26(6), 116–142. https://doi.org/10.1111/cwe.12264.

Morales-España, G., Martínez-Gordón, R., Sijm, J. (2022). Classifying and modelling demand response in power systems. *Energy* 242, 122544. https://doi.org/10.1016/j.energy.2021.122544.

Mori, A. (2003). Kingdom of Thailand. In: Japan Environmental Council (ed.) *The State of the Environment in Asia 2002/2003*. Springer, Tokyo, 183–188.

Mori, A. (2018). Sociotechnical and political economy perspectives in the Chinese energy transition. *Energy Res. Soc. Sci.* 35, 29–36. https://doi.org/10.1016/j.erss.2017.10.043.

Mori, A. (2020). Foreign actors, faster transitions? Co-evolution of complementarities, perspectives and sociotechnical systems in the case of Indonesia's electricity supply system. *Energy Res. Soc. Sci.* 69, 101594. https://doi.org/10.1016/j.erss.2020.101594.

Mori, A. (2021a). How do incumbent companies' heterogeneous responses affect sustainability transitions? Insights from China's major incumbent power generators. *Environ. Innov. Soc. Transit.* 39, 55–72. https://doi.org/10.1016/j.eist.2021.02.003.

Mori, A. (2021b). Struggles for energy transition in the electricity system in Asian countries: A complementarity perspective. In: Mori, A. (ed.) *China's Carbon-Energy Policy and Asia's Energy Transitions: Carbon Leakage, Relocation and Halos*. Routledge, Abingdon, 23–54. https://doi.org/10.4324/9781003190905-3.

Mori, A. (2022). Do Chinese power companies employ investments in foreign power projects as a geographical diversification strategy? In: Mori, A. (ed.) *China's Carbon-Energy Policy and Asia's Energy Transition: Carbon Leakage, Relocation and Halos*. Routledge, Abingdon, 92–126. https://doi.org/10.4324/9781003190905-7.

Mori, A. (2024). Fiscal regime transitions in Asia: Toward strong and green fiscal regime? In: Ekins, P., Kim, C. J., Kacaribu, F., et al. (eds.) *Fiscal Policy Instruments and Green Development*. Edward Elgar, Cheltenham.

Mori, A., Dong, L. (2018). Impact of the resource boom in the 2000s on Asian-Pacific energy exporting countries. In: Mori, A. (ed.) *China's Climate-Energy Policy: Domestic and International Impacts*. Routledge, Abingdon, 123–153. https://doi.org/10.4324/9781351037587-8.

Mori, A., Rahman, S. M., Uddin, Md. N. (2019). Climate financing through the adaptation fund: What determines fund allocation? *J. Environ. Dev.* 28(4), 366–385. https://doi.org//10.1177/1070496519877483 5.

MUFG. (2023). *MUFG Asia Transition White Paper 2023*. www.mufg.jp/english/csr/report/transition/index.html/, [accessed 13 March 2024].

Müller, S., de Sisternes, F., Patriarca, E., Portellano, A., Goeritz, A., Moller, J. D., Peter, J., Holttinen, H. (2014). *The Power of Transformation: Wind, Sun, and the Economics of Flexible Power Systems*. International Energy Agency, Paris. https://iea.blob.core.windows.net/assets/b6a02e69-35c6-4367-b342-2acf14fc9b77/The_power_of_Transformation.pdf/, [accessed 11 July 2022].

Muratori, M., Ledna, C., McJeon, H., Kyle, P., Patel, P., Kim, S. H., Wise, M., Kheshgi, H. S., Clarke, L. E., Edmonds, J. (2017). Cost of power or power of cost: A U.S. modeling perspective. *Renew. Sustain. Energy Rev.* 77(April), 861–874. https://doi.org/10.1016/j.rser.2017.04.055.

Murtaugh, D., Ding, L. (2022). The World's biggest source of clean energy is evaporating fast: from California to Germany and china, climate change-fueled heatwaves and droughts have shrunk rivers that feed giant hydropower plants. *Bloomberg News* (26 October 2022). www.bloomberg.com/news/features/2022-10-26/drought-from-china-to-us-hits-hydro-dams-slashing-the-top-clean-energy-source#xj4y7vzkg/ [accessed 28 September 2023].

Nam, P. (2022). VN banks boost retail lending for solar energy. *Vietnam Global* (25 June 2019). https://vietnamnet.vn/en/vn-banks-boost-retail-lending-for-solar-energy-544604.html/, [accessed 7 June 2023].

National Grid Corporation of the Philippines (NGCP). (2016). *Transmission Development Plan 2014–2015 Final Report Volume I: Major Network Development*. www.doe.gov.ph/sites/default/files/pdf/electric_power/tdp_2014-2015_volume_1_final_report.pdf/, [accessed 9 July 2023].

Neely, J. (2021). Vietnam approves new $2.3 bln LNG project. *Reuters* (8 October 2021). www.reuters.com/article/vietnam-energy-lng-idUKL1N2R40OH, [accessed 23 April 2022].

Net-Zero Banking Alliance. (2022). *NZBA Transition Finance Guide*. www.unepfi.org/industries/banking/net-zero-banking-alliance-transition-finance-guide/, [accessed 2 October 2023].

Neville, K. J. (2020). Shadows of divestment: The complications of diverting fossil fuel finance, *Glob. Environ. Politics*. 20(2), 3–11. https://doi.org/10.1162/glep_a_00555.

Newbery, D., Pollitt, M. G., Ritz, R. A., Strielkowski, W. (2018). Market design for a high-renewables European electricity system. *Renew. Sustain. Energy Rev.* 91, 695–707. https://doi.org/10.1016/j.rser.2018.04.025.

Newell, P. (2021). *Power Shift: The Global Political Economy of Energy Transitions*. Cambridge University Press, Cambridge.

Newell, R., Pizer, W. (2001). *Discounting the Benefits of Climate Change Mitigation: How Much Do Uncertain Rates Increase Valuations?* The Pew Center on Global Climate Change, Washington, DC.

NGCP. (2019). *Transmission Development Plan 2016–2040 Final Report Volume I: Major Network Development*. www.ngcp.ph/Attachment-Uploads/TDP%202016-2040%20Final%20Report%20Volume%201%20Major%20Network%20Development-2019-05-14-16-43-41.pdf/, [accessed 9 July 2023].

NGCP. (2020a). NGCP interconnection projects aimed at One Grid Philippines. Press Release (3 May 2023). www.ngcp.ph/article?cid=16137/, [accessed 7 May 2023].

NGCP. (2020b). Transmission development plan 2022–2040. www.ngcp.ph/Attachment-Uploads/Transmission%20Development%20Plan%202022-2040%20Consultation%20Draft_Web_Final-2022-03-04-10-02-48.pdf/, [accessed 9 July 2023].

NGCP. (2021). List of existing ancillary service providers. *Customer Bulletin 2021–2031*. https://ngcp.ph/Attachment-Uploads/Customer%20Bulletin%202021-31-2021-11-11-11-05-09.pdf/, [accessed 16 May 2023].

NGCP. (2022). Transmission development plan 2022–2040. www.ngcp.ph/Attachment-Uploads/Transmission%20Development%20Plan%202022-2040%20Consultation%20Draft_Web_Final-2022-03-04-10-02-48.pdf/, [accessed 9 July 2023].

NGCP. (2023). NGCP energizes Mindanao-Visayas interconnection. Press Release (3 May 2023). www.ngcp.ph/article?cid=16636/, [accessed 7 May 2023].

NGFS (Network of Central Banks and Supervisors for Greening the Financial System). (2019). A call for action: Climate change as a source of financial risk. Paris: Network for Greening the Financial System. www.ngfs.net/en/first-comprehensive-report-call-action/, [accessed 22 August 2023].

NGFS. (2019). *A Call for Action: Climate Change as a Source of Financial Risk*. NGFS, Paris. www.ngfs.net/en/liste-chronologique/ngfs-publications?year=2019/ [accessed 24 September 2023].

NGFS. (2023). Stocktake on financial institutions' transition plans and their relevance to micro-prudential authorities. www.ngfs.net/en/stocktake-financial-institutions-transition-plans-and-their-relevance-micro-prudential-authorities/ [accessed 5 October 2023].

Nguyen, L. D. (2022). Vietnam's renewable energy policies and opportunities for the private sector. The National Bureau of Asian Research (May 2022). www.nbr.org/wp-content/uploads/pdfs/publications/clean_edge_asia_dan_may22.pdf, [accessed 22 November 2022].

Nguyen, N. H. (2021). Renewable energy development in Vietnam. *ACCEPT* (16 July 2021). https://accept.aseanenergy.org/renewable-energy-development-in-vietnam/, [accessed 29 November 2022].

Nguyen, O., Nguyen, T. H. (2021). Vietnam: October 2021 updates to the Draft PDP8. Baker & McKenzie, [accessed 14 August 2022].

Nguyen, T. C., Chuc, A. T., Dang, L. N. (2019). Green finance in Viet Nam: Barriers and solutions. In: Sachs, J. D., Woo, W. T., Yoshino, N., Taghizadeh-Hesary, F. (eds.) *Handbook of Green Finance: Energy Security and Sustainable Development*. Springer, 675–705. https://doi.org/10.1007/978-981-13-0227-5_35.

Nhede, N. (2016). Energy conservation and grid status in the Philippines. *Smart Energy* (13 September 2016). www.smart-energy.com/features-analysis/energy-conservation-philippines-analysis/, [accessed 17 May 2023].

Nillessen, P., Pollitt, M. (2016). New business models for utilities to meet the challenge of the energy transition. In: Sioshansi, F. P. (ed.) *Future of Utilities, Utilities of the Future*. Elsevier, Walnut Creek, CA, 283–301. https://doi.org/10.1016/B978-0-12-804249-6.00015-4.

Nitta, Y., Shiga, Y. (2023). Vietnam, Philippines heat up LNG demand in Southeast Asia: With renewables lagging, countries seek more accessible alternative to coal. Nikkei Asia (14 July 2023). https://asia.nikkei.com/Business/Energy/Vietnam-Philippines-heat-up-LNG-demand-in-Southeast-Asia/ [accessed 3 October 2023].

Norman, W. (2023a). Chinese companies commit US$13.7 billion for renewables in Philippines. *pv tech* (9 January 2023). www.pv-tech.org/chinese-companies-commit-us13-7-billion-for-renewables-in-philippines/, [accessed 10 May 2023].

Norman, W. (2023b). Trina's 6.5GW Vietnamese wafer factory to be online this year, targeting US market. *pv tech* (13 January 2023). www.pv-tech.org/trinas-6-5gw-vietnamese-wafer-factory-to-be-online-this-year-targeting-us-market/, [accessed 28 June 2023].

O'Connell, N., Pinson, P., Madsen, H., O'Malley, M. (2014). Benefits and challenges of electrical demand response: A critical review. *Renew. Sustain. Energy Rev.* 39, 686–699. https://doi.org/10.1016/j.rser.2014.07.098.

O'Dwyer, C. (2023). The green climate fund lacks procedural justice. *SPI's Climate Finance (CLiFin) Series*. https://sevenpillarsinstitute.org/green-climate-fund-lacks-procedural-justice/, [accessed 12 December 2023].

O'Neill, B. C., Kriegler, E., Ebi, K. L., Kemp-Benedict, E., Riahi, K., Rothman, D. S., van Ruijven, B. J., van Vuuren, D. P., Birkmann, J., Kok, K., Levy, M., Solecki, W. (2017). The roads ahead: Narratives for shared socioeconomic pathways describing world futures in the 21st century. *Global Environ. Change* 42, 169–180. https://doi.org/10.1016/j.gloenvcha.2015.01.004.

Oanh, K. (2022). JA Solar to develop $189-million facility in Vietnam. *Vietnam Investment Review* (19 February 2022). https://vir.com.vn/ja-solar-to-develop-189-million-facility-in-vietnam-91379.html/, [accessed 28 June 2023].

Ode, K. A., Wadin, J. L. (2019). Business model translation – The case of spreading a business model for solar energy. *Renew. Energy* 133, 23–31. https://doi.org/10.1016/j.renene.2018.09.036.

OECD. (2021a). Arrangement on officially supported export credits. www.oecd.org/trade/topics/export-credits/arrangement-and-sector-understandings/, [accessed 14 October 2022].

OECD. (2021b). *Mobilising Institutional Investors for Financing Sustainable Development in Developing Countries: Emerging Evidence of Opportunities and Challenges*. OECD Publishing, Paris.

OECD. (2022). *OECD Guidance on Transition Finance: Ensuring Credibility of Corporate Climate Transition Plans*. Green Finance and Investment, OECD Publishing, Paris, https://doi.org/10.1787/7c68a1ee-en.

Ohlendorf, N., Löhr, M., Markard, J. (2023). Actors in multi-sector transitions: Discourse analysis on hydrogen in Germany. *Environ. Innov. Soc. Transit.* 47, 100692. https://doi.org/10.1016/j.eist.2023.100692.

Olawuyi, D. S. (2022). The role of natural gas in a just and equitable energy transition. In: Olawuyi, D. S., Pereira, E. G. (eds.). *The Palgrave Handbook of Natural Gas and Global Energy Transitions*. Palgrave MacMillan, Cham, 73–95. https://doi.org/10.1007/978-3-030-91566-7_3.

Oshiro, K., Fujimori, S. (2021). Stranded investment associated with rapid energy system changes under the mid-century strategy in Japan. *Sustainability Sc.* https://doi.org/10.1007/s11625-020-00862-2.

Oxford Business Group. (2021). The Philippine government's new priorities for energy. In: Oxford Business Group (ed.) *The Philippines 2021*. https://oxfordbusinessgroup.com/reports/philippines/2021-report/economy/powerful-shift-a-year-of-disruption-allows-the-government-to-re-evaluate-priorities-and-chart-a-new-path-for-the-future-of-the-sector/, [accessed 5 June 2023].

Pachauri, S., Pelz, S., Bertram, C., et al. (2022). Fairness consideration in global mitigation investment. *Science* 378(6624), 1057–1059. https://doi.org/10.1126/science.adf006.

Papandreou, A. A. (2021). Stranded assets and the financial system. In: Tsani, S., Overland, I. (eds.) *Handbook of Sustainable Politics and Economics of Natural Resources*. Edward Elgar, 320–333. https://doi.org/10.4337/9781789908770.00031.

Pauw, W. P., Moslener, U., Zamarioli, L. H., et al. (2022). Post-2025 climate finance target: How much more and how much better? *Clim. Policy* 22(9–10), 1241–1251. https://doi.org/10.1080/14693062.2022.2114985.

PCC. (2023). *Early Lessons and Recommendations from Komati's Decommissioning and Repurposing Project*. The Presidential Climate Commission (PCC). https://pccommissionflo.imgix.net/uploads/documents/PCC-Komati-Power-Station-Recommendations-Report.pdf, [accessed 21 December 2023].

Pekic, S. (2022). First Gen looking for suppliers for Batangas LNG terminal. Offshore Energy (20 May 2022). www.offshore-energy.biz/first-gen-looking-for-suppliers-for-batangas-lng-terminal/, [accessed 17 May 2023].

Penna, C. C. R., et al. (2023). Transformative investment: New rules for investing in sustainability transitions. *Environ. Innovation Societal Transitions* 49, 100782. https://doi.org/10.1016/j.eist.2023.100782.

Pereira, E. G., Olawuyi, D. S. (2022). The future of natural gas: Synthesis and summary for policy makers. In: Olawuyi, D. S., Pereira, E. G. (eds.) *The Palgrave Handbook of Natural Gas and Global Energy Transitions*. Palgrave MacMillan, Cham, 595–610. https://doi.org/10.1007/978-3-030-91566-7_25.

Pereira, G. I., Niesten, E., Pinkse, J. (2022). Sustainable energy systems in the making: A study on business model adaptation in incumbent utilities. *Technol. Forecast. Soc. Change* 174, 121207. https://doi.org/10.1016/j.techfore.2021.121207.

Pfeiffer, A. (2018). The 'decarbonization identity': Stranded assets in the power generation sector. In: Caldecott, B. (ed.) *Stranded Assets and the Environment: Risk, Resilience and Opportunity*. Routledge, Abingdon, 55–86.

Pfeiffer, A., Hepburn, C., Vogt-Schilb, A., Caldecott, B. (2018). Committed emissions from existing and planned power plants and asset stranding required to meet the Paris Agreement. *Environ. Res. Lett.* 13(5). https://doi.org/10.1088/1748-9326/aabc5f.

Pfeiffer, A., Millar, R., Hepburn, C., Beinhocker, E. (2016). The '2°C capital stock' for electricity generation: Committed cumulative carbon emissions from the electricity generation sector and the transition to a green economy. *Appl. Energy* 179, 1395–1408. https://doi.org/10.1016/j.apenergy.2016.02.093.

Pham, L. (2022). Vietnam targets net zero, but struggles to break coal dependence. *China Dialogue* (31 January 2022). https://chinadialogue.net/en/climate/vietnam-targets-net-zero-but-struggles-to-break-coal-dependence/, [accessed 14 October 2022].

Philippines Department of Energy. (2016). *Power Development Plan 2016–2040*. www.doe.gov.ph/sites/default/files/pdf/electric_power/development_plans/pdp_2016-2040.pdf/, [accessed 9 July 2023].

Philippines Department of Energy. (2019a). Philippine Energy Plan 2018–2040. https://policy.asiapacificenergy.org/sites/default/files/Philippine%20Energy%20Plan%202018-2040.pdf, [accessed 10 January 2023].

Philippines Department of Energy. (2019b). Providing a framework for energy storage system in the electric power industry. www.doe.gov.ph/sites/default/files/pdf/issuances/dc2019-08-0012.pdf/, [accessed 3 June 2023].

Philippines Department of Energy. (2020). Providing a national smart grid policy framework for Philippine electric power industry and roadmap for distribution utilities. www.doe.gov.ph/sites/default/files/pdf/issuances/dc2020-02-0003.pdf/, [accessed 3 June 2023].

Philippines Department of Energy. (2021a). *Philippine Energy Plan 2020–2040: Towards a Sustainable and Clean Energy Future*. www.doe.gov.ph/sites/default/files/pdf/pep/PEP_2020-2040_signed_01102022.pdf/, [accessed 10 January 2023].

Philippines Department of Energy. (2021b). *Power Development Plan 2020–2040*. www.doe.gov.ph/sites/default/files/pdf/electric_power/pdp-2020-2040.pdf/, [accessed 30 May 2023].

Philippines Department of Energy. (2022a). *National Renewable Energy Program 2020–2040*. www.doe.gov.ph/sites/default/files/pdf/renewable_energy/nrep_2020-2040_0.pdf/, [accessed 13 May 2023].

Philippines Department of Energy. (2022b). *Net-Metering Guidebook*. www.doe.gov.ph/sites/default/files/pdf/renewable_energy/Net-Metering-Guidebook-2022.pdf.

Philippines Department of Energy. (2022c). *Philippines Energy Situationer 2021*. www.doe.gov.ph/sites/default/files/pdf/energy_statistics/doe-pes-kes-2021.pdf/, [accessed 15 May 2023].

Philippines Department of Energy. (2022d). *40th Electric Power Industry Reform Act (EPIRA) Implementation Status Report*. www.doe.gov.ph/sites/default/files/pdf/electric_power/40th-EPIRA-Status_Report-FINAL.pdf/, [accessed 16 July 2023].

Philippines Department of Energy. (2023a). *2022 Renewable Energy Act Implementation Status Report*. www.doe.gov.ph/renewable-energy/renewable-energy-act-implementation-status-report-2022?q=renewable-energy/renewable-energy-act-implementation-status-report-2022/, [accessed 6 July 2023].

Philippines Department of Energy. (2023b). GEOP (Green Energy Option Program). www.doe.gov.ph/national-renewable-energy-program?q=/renewable-energy/geop/, [accessed 6 May 2023].

Philippines Department of Energy. (2023c). Private Sector-Initiated Power Projects as of April 30, 2023. www.doe.gov.ph/list-existing-power-plants?q=private-sector-initiated-power-projects/, [accessed 4 July 2023].

Philippines Department of Energy. (2024a). Gross generation per grid and per technology. https://doe.gov.ph/sites/default/files/pdf/energy_statistics/03_2023_Gross_Generation_per_Grid_and_per_technology_rev2.pdf, [accessed 4 November 2024].

Philippines Department of Energy. (2024b). Summary of 2023 power statistics. https://doe.gov.ph/sites/default/files/pdf/energy_statistics/01_Summary_of_2023_Power_Statistics.pdf/, [accessed 3 November 2024].

Philippines Department of Energy. (2024c). *Private Sector-Initiated Power Projects as of October 31, 2024*. https://doe.gov.ph/electric-power/private-sector-initiated-power-projects-october-31-2024/, [accessed 24 November 2024].

Phoumin, H., Taghizadeh-Hesary, F., Kimura, F., Nepal, R. (eds.). (2023). *Electricity Market Reforms in the ASEAN, China, India, and Japan*. World Scientific, Singapore.

Planko, J., Chappin, M. M. H., Cramer, J., Hekkert, M. P. (2019). Coping with coopetition—Facing dilemmas in cooperation for sustainable development: The case of the Dutch smart grid industry. *Bus. Strat. Env.* 28, 665–674. https://doi.org/10.1002/bse.2271.

Planko, J., Cramer, J. M. (2021). The networked business model for systems change: Integrating a systems perspective in business model development for sustainability transitions. In: Aagaard, A., et al. (eds.) *Business Models for Sustainability Transitions*. Springer Nature, 59–88. https://doi.org/10.1007/978-3-030-77580-3_3.

Plantinga, A., Scholtens, B. (2021). The financial impact of fossil fuel divestment. *Clim. Policy* 21(1), 107–119. https://doi.org/10.1080/14693062.2020.1806020.

PLN. (2021). PLN's electricity business plan 2021–2030. https://web.pln.co.id/statics/uploads/2021/10/ruptl-2021-2030.pdf/, [accessed 26 March 2024].

Power Philippines News. (2020). AC Energy dropping coal (24 November 2020). https://powerphilippines.com/ac-energy-dropping-coal/, [accessed 8 July 2023].

Power Philippines News. (2021). 8 more power projects endorsed to NGCP for system impact study. (18 May 2021). https://powerphilippines.com/8-more-power-projects-endorsed-to-ngcp-for-system-impact-study/, [accessed 8 July 2023].

Power Philippines News. (2022). First Gen LNG to be completed by 2023 (18 October 2022). https://powerphilippines.com/first-gen-lng-to-be-completed-by-2023/, [accessed 12 May 2023].

Power Philippines News. (2023a). DOE: 'Inadequacies' in transmission lines caused red, yellow alerts (9 May 2023). https://powerphilippines.com/doe-inadequacies-in-transmission-lines-caused-red-yellow-alerts/, [accessed 17 May 2023].

Power Philippines News. (2023b). Gathalian wants senate inquiry on delays of NGCP transmission projects (23 May 2023). https://powerphilippines.com/gathalian-wants-senate-inquiry-on-delays-of-ngcp-transmission-projects/, [accessed 24 May 2023].

Power Philippines News. (2023c). Power interruptions hit Luzon as NGCP declares red alert (8 May 2023). https://powerphilippines.com/luzon-grid-on-red-alert-ngcp/, [accessed 23 May 2023].

Proka, A., Hisschemöller, M., Loorbach, D. (2020). When top-down meets bottom-up: Is there a collaborative business model for local energy storage? *Energy Res. Soc. Sci.* 69, 101606. https://doi.org/10.1016/j.erss.2020.101606.

Prudential Regulation Authority. (2015). *The Impact of Climate Change on the UK Insurance Sector: A Climate Change Adaptation Report by the Prudential Regulation Authority*. Rep., Prudent. Regul. Auth., Bank Engl., London. www.bankofengland.co.uk/prudential-regulation/publication/2015/the-impact-of-climate-change-on-the-uk-insurance-sector/ [accessed 24 September 2023].

Puri, J., Prowse, M., Roy, E. D., Huang, D. (2022). Assessing the likelihood for transformational change at the green climate fund: An analysis using self-reported project data. *Clim. Risk Manage.* 35, 100398. https://doi.org/10.1016/j.crm.2022.100398.

PwC. (2018). *Power in Indonesia: Investment and Taxation Guide, November 2018, 6th edition*, www.pwc.com/id/en/publications/assets/eumpublications/utilities/power-guide-2018.pdf/, [accessed 6 April 2019].

Qi, J., Qian, H. (2023). Climate finance at a crossroads: It is high time to use the global solution for global problems. *Carbon Neutrality* 2, 31. https://doi.org/10.1007/s43979-023-00071-7.

Quang, B. (2022) Draft national power plan sidelines ExxonMobil's LNG-fueled project. *The Investor* (19 March 2022). https://theinvestor.vn/draft-national-power-plan-sidelines-exxonmobils-lng-fueled-project-d71.html/, [accessed 1 July 2023].

Rahman, S. M., Mori, A., Rahman, S. M. (2022). How does climate adaptation co-benefits help scale-up solar-powered irrigation? A case of the Barind Tract, Bangladesh. *Renew. Energy* 182, 1039–1048. https://doi.org/10.1016/j.renene.2021.11.012.

Rahul, K. (2021). Project Information Document – Vietnam Renewable Energy Accelerating Change (REACH) – P174460. Washington, DC, World Bank Group. http://documents.worldbank.org/curated/en/108161626148803011/Project-Information-Document-Vietnam-Renewable-Energy-Accelerating-Change-REACH-P174460, [accessed 17 December 2022].

Raikar, S., Adamson, S. (2019). *Renewable Energy Finance: Theory and Practice*. Academic Press, Cambridge, MA.

Reghezza, A., Altunbas, Y., Marques-Ibanez, D., d'Acri, C. R., Spaggiari, M. (2022). Do banks fuel climate change? *J. Financ. Stab.* 62, 101049. https://doi.org/10.1016/j.jfs.2022.101049.

Rempel, A., Gupta, J. (2020). Conflicting commitments? Examining pension funds, fossil fuel assets and climate policy in the organisation for economic co-operation and development (OECD). *Energy Res. Soc. Sci.* 69, 101736. https://doi.org/10.1016/j.erss.2020.101736.

Republic of the Philippines. (2015). Intended nationally determined contributions. www4.unfccc.int/sites/submissions/INDC/Published%20Documents/Philippines/1/Philippines%20-%20Final%20INDC%20submission.pdf/, [accessed 6 May 2023].

Republic of the Philippines. (2021). Nationally determined contribution. https://unfccc.int/sites/default/files/NDC/2022-06/Philippines%20-%20NDC.pdf/, [accessed 6 May 2023].

Resosudarmo, B. P., Effendi, Y. (2022). Implications of East Asia electricity market integration on Southeast Asian economies and CO_2 emissions. In: Mori, A. (ed.) *China's Carbon-Energy Policy and Asia's Energy Transition: Carbon Leakage, Relocation and Halos*. Routledge, Abingdon, 255–278.

Resosudarmo, B. P., Rezki, J. F., Effendi, Y. (2023) Prospects of energy transition in Indonesia. *Bull. Indones. Econ. Stud.* 59(2), 149–177. https://doi.org/10.1080/00074918.2023.2238336.

Ricardo Energy & Environment. (2018). *TA 8851: Establishing the Vietnam Wholesale Electricity Market (VWEM). Final Report (2 of 4)*. ADB. www.adb.org/sites/default/files/project-documents/48328/48328-001-tacr-en_0.pdf, [accessed 26 August 2022].

Rivera, D. (2021). More firms to build LNG terminals. *The Philippine Star* (14 January 2021). www.philstar.com/business/2021/01/14/2070197/more-firms-build-lng-terminals/, [accessed 30 May 2023].

Rivera, D. (2022). NGCP's Negros-Panay subsea cable completion seen by June. *The Philippine Star* (10 May 2022). www.philstar.com/business/2022/05/10/2179883/ngcps-negros-panay-subsea-cable-completion-seen-june/, [accessed 16 May 2023].

Rochlin, C. (2016). Distributed renewable resources and the utility business model. *Electr. J.* 29, 7–12. http://dx.doi.org/10.1016/j.tej.2015.12.001.

Rode, D. C., Fischbeck, P. S., Páez, A. R. (2017). The retirement cliff: Power plant lives and their policy implications. *Energy Policy* 106, 222–232. https://doi.org/10.1016/j.enpol.2017.03.058.

Rogelj, J. et al. (2018). Scenarios towards limiting global mean temperature increase below 1.5°C. *Nat. Clim. Change* 8(4), 325–332. https://doi:10.1038/s41558-018-0091-3.

Romero, A. (2016). Mindanao on power red alert due to bombed towers. *Philipp. Star.* (4 January 2016). www.philstar.com/headlines/2016/01/04/1539369/mindanao-power-red-alert-due-bombed-towers/, [accessed 7 May 2023].

Roncoroni, A., Battiston, S., Escobar-Farfán, L. O. L., Martinez-Jaramillo, S. (2021). Climate risk and financial stability in the network of banks and investment funds. *J. Financ. Stab.* 54, 100870. https://doi.org/10.1016/j.jfs.2021.100870.

Rose, A., Stoner, R., Pérez-Arriaga, I. (2016). Integrating market and bilateral power trading in the South African power. WIDER Working Paper 132/2016, UNU-WIDER. https://doi.org/10.35188/UNU-WIDER/2016/176-5.

Rosenbloom, D., Rinscheid, A. (2020). Deliberate decline: An emerging frontier for the study and practice of decarbonization. *WIREs Clim. Change* 11, e669. https://doi.org/10.1002/wcc.669.

Rossi, J., Srivastava, A., Hoang, T. T., Tran, Q. T., Warneryd, M. (2022). Pathways for the development of future intelligent distribution grids. *Energy Policy*, 169, 113140. https://doi.org/10.1016/j.enpol.2022.113140.

Rotmans, J., van Asselt, M. (2001). Uncertainty in integrated assessment modelling: A labyrinthic path. *Integr. Assess.* 2(2), 43–55. https://doi.org/10.1023/A:1011588816469.

Rozenberg, J., Vogt-Schilb, A., Hallegatte, S. (2020). Instrument choice and stranded assets in the transition to clean capital. *J. Environ. Econ. Manag.* 100, 102183. https://doi.org/10.1016/j.jeem.2018.10.005.

Ruggiero, S., Kangas, H.-L., Annala, S., Lazarevic, D. (2021). Business model innovation in demand response firms: Beyond the niche-regime dichotomy. *Environ. Innov. Soc. Transit.* 39, 1–17. https://doi.org/10.1016/j.eist.2021.02.002.

Saigon Times. (2023). Shortage, but abundance. *Vietnamnet Global* (22 May 2023). https://vietnamnet.vn/en/shortage-but-abundance-2145693.html/, [accessed 9 June 2023].

San Miguel Global Power. (n.d.), Ilijan power plant. https://smcglobalpower.com.ph/our-business-power-generation?slug=ilijan-power-plant&p=4/, [accessed 7 May 2023].

Sangiorgi, I., Schopohl, L. (2021). Why do institutional investors buy green bonds: Evidence from a survey of European asset managers. *Int. Rev. Financial Anal.* 75, 101738. https://doi.org/10.1016/j.irfa.2021.101738.

Santos, B. (2022a). Pumped hydro storage takes shape in the Philippines. *PV Magazine* (13 September 2022). www.pv-magazine.com/2022/09/13/pumped-hydro-storage-takes-shape-in-the-philippines/, [accessed 14 May 2023].

Santos, B. (2022b). Vietnam set to open renewable energy market to PPAs. PV Magazine (27 October 2022). www.pv-magazine.com/2022/10/27/vietnam-set-to-open-renewable-energy-market-to-ppas/, [accessed 8 June 2023].

Sarangi, G. K. (2019). Green finance in India: Barriers and solutions. In: Sachs, J. D., Woo, W. T., Yoshino, N., Taghizadeh-Hesary, F. (eds.) *Handbook of Green Finance: Energy Security and Sustainable Development*. Springer, 539–556. https://doi.org/10.1007/978-981-13-0227-5_4.

Sauer, J. M. T., Anadón, L. D., Kirchherr, J., Braeckman, J. P., Schulhof, V. (2022). Chinese and multilateral development finance in the power sector. *Glob. Environ. Change* 75, 102553. https://doi.org/10.1016/j.gloenvcha.2022.102553.

Sausmikat, N. (2024). *Polluters Getting Paid: The ADB's Energy Transition Mechanism (ETM)*. Urgewald e.V., Sassenberg, Germany. www.urgewald.org/sites/default/files/media-files/urgewald_ADB_ETM_Paper.pdf, [accessed 3 November 2024].

Saygin, D., Rigter, J., Caldecott, B., Wagner, N., Gielen, D. (2019). Power sector asset stranding effects of climate policies. *Energy Sources Part B: Econ. Plan. Policy* 14(4), 99–124. https://doi.org/10.1080/15567249.2019.1618421.

Schmidt, O., Melchior, S., Hawkes, A., Staffell, I. (2019). Projecting the future levelized cost of electricity storage technologies. *Joule* 3, 81–100. https://doi.org/10.1016/j.joule.2018.12.008.

Schmidt, T. S., Matuo, T., Michaelowa, A. (2017). Renewable energy policy as an enabler of fossil fuel subsidy reform? Applying a socio-technical perspective to the cases of South Africa and Tunisia. *Global Environ. Change* 45, 99–110. http://doi.org/10.1016/j.gloenvcha.2017.05.004.

Schoenmaker, D., Schramade, W. (2021). Investing for long-term value creation. *J. Sustain. Finance Invest.* 9(4), 356–377. https://doi.org/10.1080/20430795.2019.1625012.

Scholten, D., Bazilian, M., Overland, I., Westphal, K. (2020). The geopolitics of renewables: New board, new game. *Energy Policy* 138, 111059. https://doi.org/10.1016/j.enpol.2019.111059.

Seiler, A., Brown, H., Matthews, S. (2023). The JETPs of South Africa and Indonesia: A blueprint for the move away from coal? *Policy Paper No. 302.* Center for Global Development. www.cgdev.org/publication/jetps-south-africa-and-indonesia-blueprint-move-away-coal/, [accessed 27 February 2024].

Seltzer, L., Starks, L., Zhu, Q. (2022). Climate regulatory risk and corporate bonds. NBER Working Paper 29994. www.nber.org/papers/w29994.

Semelane, S., Nwulu, N., Kambule, N., Tazvinga, H. (2021). Evaluating available solar photovoltaic business opportunities in coal phase-out regions – An energy transition case of Steve Tshwete local municipality in South Africa. *Energy Policy* 155. https://doi.org/10.1016/j.enpol.2021.112333.

Semieniuk, G., Campiglio, E., Mercure, J.-F., Volz, U., Edwards, N. R. (2021). Low-carbon transition risks for finance. *WIREs Clim. Change* 12, e678. https://doi.org/10.1002/wcc.678.

Semieniuk, G., Holden, P. B., Mercure, J. F., et al. (2022). Stranded fossil-fuel assets translate to major losses for investors in advanced economies. *Nat. Clim. Change* 12(6), 532–538. https://doi.org/10.1038/s41558-022-01356-y.

Sen, S., von Schickfus, M.-T. (2020). Climate policy, stranded assets, and investors' expectations. *J. Environ. Econ. Manag.* 100, 102277. https://doi.org/10.1016/j.jeem.2019.102277.

Senlen, O., Roberts, L., Littlecott, C., et al. (2023). Diverging pathways: China's new coal boom takes it on a detour. *E3G briefing.* www.e3g.org/publications/world-drives-forward-on-no-new-coal-but-china-takes-a-detour/, [accessed 27 August 2023].

Seo, N. S. (2019). *The Economics of Global Allocations of the Green Climate Fund: An Assessment from Four Scientific Traditions of Modeling Adaptation Strategies.* Springer, Cham, Switzerland. https://doi.org/10.1007/978-3-030-18274-8.

Seto, K. C., Davis, S. J., Mitchell, R. B., Stokes, E. C., Unruh, I. G., Urge-Vorsatz, D. (2016). Carbon lock-in: Types, causes, and policy implications. *Annu. Rev. Environ. Resour.* 41, 425–452. https://doi.org/10.1146/annurev-environ-110615-085934.

SGGP. (2023). Vietnam faces power shortage despite excess of renewable energy. *Vietnamnet Global* (25 May 2023). https://vietnamnet.vn/en/vietnam-faces-power-shortage-despite-excess-of-renewable-energy-2146679.html/, [accessed 9 June 2023].

Sharma, A., Johnstone, I., Firdaus, N. (2023). Equity in Climate Financing: Spotlight on the Energy Transition. Working Paper. Center for Global Sustainability, School of Public Policy, University of Maryland, College Park, MD. https://cgs.umd.edu/sites/default/files/2023-12/Team%201_iGST%20Working%20Paper.pdf, [accessed 21 December 2023].

Shepherd, C. (2023). China's coal plant approvals highest in seven years, research finds. *The Washington Post* (26 February 2023). www.washingtonpost.com/world/2023/02/26/china-coal-plant-fossil-fuel-pollution/, [accessed 27 August 2023].

Shimbar, A. (2021a). Environment-related stranded assets: An agenda for research into value destruction within carbon-intensive sectors in response to environmental concerns. *Renew. Sustain. Energy Rev.* 144, 111010. https://doi.org/10.1016/j.rser.2021.111010.

Shimbar, A. (2021b). Environment-related stranded assets: What does the market think about the impact of collective climate action on the value of fossil fuel stocks? *Energy Econ.* 103, 105579. https://doi.org/10.1016/j.eneco.2021.105579.

Shoji, T. (2020). Positive economic growth in Vietnam in 2020 under COVID-19: A perspective for Ca Voi Xanh (CVX)/Blue Whale gas field project. JOGMEC (in Japanese). https://oilgas-info.jogmec.go.jp/_res/projects/default_project/_page_/001/008/932/2101_em_vn_development_of_gas_in_vietnam_r.pdf, [accessed 19 August 2022].

Socialist Republic of Vietnam. (2023). Resource Mobilisation Plan. https://climate.ec.europa.eu/system/files/2023-12/RMP_Viet%20Nam_Eng_%28Final%20to%20publication%29.pdf/, [accessed 27 February 2024].

Sorote, R. (2022). The irony of Negros Island's abundant renewable energy. *ClimateTracker* (6 May 2022), https://climatetracker.org/the-irony-of-negros-islands-abundant-renewable-energy/, [accessed 6 May 2023].

Sovacool, B. K., Axsen, J., Sorrell S. (2018). Promoting novelty, rigor, and style in energy social science: Towards codes of practice for appropriate methods and research design. *Energy Res. Soc. Sci.* 45, 12–42. https://doi.org/10.1016/j.erss.2018.07.007.

Sovacool, B. K., Geels, F. W. (2016). Further reflections on the temporality of energy transitions: A response to critics. *Energy Res. Soc. Sci.* 22, 232–237. http:/doi.org/10.1016/j.erss.2016.08.013.

Sovacool, B. K., Hook, A., Sareen, S., Geels, F. W. (2021). Global sustainability, innovation and governance dynamics of national smart electricity meter transitions. *Glob. Environ. Change* 68, 102272. https://doi.org/10.1016/j.gloenvcha.2021.102272.

Srivastrava, R., Wettengel, J. (2024). India, donor countries give up on just energy transition partnership – German official. *Clean Energy Wire* (20 November

2024). www.cleanenergywire.org/news/india-donor-countries-give-just-energy-transition-partnership-german-official/, [accessed 29 November 2024].

Steen, M., Weaver, T. (2017). Incumbents' diversification and cross-sectorial energy industry dynamics. *Res. Policy* 46, 1071–1086. https://doi.org/10.1016/j.respol.2017.04.001.

Steffen, B., Matsuo, T., Steinemann, D., Schmidt, T. S. (2018). Opening new markets for clean energy: The role of project developers in the global diffusion of renewable energy technologies. *Bus. Polit.* 20(4), 553–587. https://doi.org/10.1017/bap.2018.17.

Stern, Z. (2023). Retirement plan fiduciaries can now consider ESG factors. The Regulatory Review (26 January 2023). www.theregreview.org/2023/01/26/stern-retirement-plan-fiduciaries-can-now-consider-esg-factors/ [accessed 12 October 2023].

Strambach, S., Pflitsch, G. (2020). Transition topology: Capturing institutional dynamics in regional development paths to sustainability. *Res. Policy* 49, 104006. https://doi.org/10.1016/j.respol.2020.104006.

Suarez, I. (2022). China's no overseas coal pledge: 15 projects cancelled so far, but grey areas remain. *China Dialogue* (27 May 2022). https://chinadialogue.net/en/energy/chinas-no-overseas-coal-power-pledge-15-projects-cancelled/, [accessed 27 August 2023].

Suharsono, A., Maulidia, M. (2023). What can Indonesia learn from South Africa's experience of the just energy transition process? In: *Policy Brief*. International Institute for Sustainable Development. www.iisd.org/publications/brief/indonesia-south-africa-jetp-lessons/, [accessed 26 February 2024].

Tachev, V. (2022). Vietnam's Block B Gas Project – the Potential impact on the involved parties. *Energy Tracker Asia* (11 August 2022). https://energytracker.asia/vietnam-block-b-gas-project-potential-impact, [accessed 19 August 2022].

Taghizadeh-Hesary, F., Rasoulinezhad, E., Shahbaz, M., Vo, X. V. (2021). How energy transition and power consumption are related in Asian economies with different income levels? *Energy* 237, 121595. https://doi.org/10.1016/j.energy.2021.121595.

Takahashi, T. (2024). Will Vietnam face another power crisis this year? *Nikkei Asia* (25 May 2024). https://asia.nikkei.com/Spotlight/Comment/Will-Vietnam-face-another-power-crisis-this-year/, [accessed 25 May 2024].

Take, S. (2023). Philippines, Vietnam to import LNG, but long-term doubts loom: Competition from renewables raises fears new terminals will be 'underutilized'. Nikkei Asia (7 March 2023). https://asia.nikkei.com/Business/Energy/Philippines-Vietnam-to-import-LNG-but-long-term-doubts-loom/ [accessed 3 October 2023].

Tan, X., Lin, S., Liu, Y.-L., Xie, B.-C. (2022). Has the inter-regional transmission expansion promoted the low-carbon transition of China's power sector? *Comput. Ind. Eng.* 168, 108059. https://doi.org/10.1016/j.cie.2022.108059.

TCFD. (2017). *Recommendations of the Task Force on Climate-related Financial Disclosures*. www.fsb-tcfd.org/recommendations/, [accessed 24 August 2023].

ten Heuvelhof, E., Weijnen, M. (2013). Investing in smart grids within the market paradigm: The case of the Netherlands and its relevance for China. *Policy Soc.* 32(2), 163–174. https://doi.org/10.1016/j.polsoc.2013.05.002.

Termeer, C. J. A. M., Dewulf, A., Biesbroek, R. (2017). Transformational change: governance interventions for climate change adaptation from a continuous change perspective. *J. Environ. Plann. Man.* 60(4), 558–576. https://doi.org/10.1080/09640568.2016.1168288.

The Government of Indonesia. (2023). Just energy transition partnership Indonesia: Comprehensive investment and policy plan (CIPP) 2023. https://jetp-id.org/storage/official-jetp-cipp-2023-vshare_f_en-1700532655.pdf, [accessed 21 December 2023].

The Government of South Africa. (2023). Just energy transition implementation plan (JET IP) 2023–2027. www.stateofthenation.gov.za/assets/downloads/JET%20Implementation%20Plan%202023-2027.pdf, [accessed 21 December 2023].

The Government of South Africa. (2024). JET grants register. www.stateofthenation.gov.za/priorities/growing-the-economy-and-jobs/just-transition-to-a-low-carbon-economy, [accessed 3 November 2024].

The Government of Vietnam. (2023). Resource mobilisation plan (RMP): Implementing Vietnam's just energy transition partnership (JETP). www.stateofthenation.gov.za/priorities/growing-the-economy-and-jobs/just-transition-to-a-low-carbon-economy, [accessed 15 February 2024].

The Presidency, Republic of South Africa. (2023). *Just Energy Transition Implementation Plan 2023–2027*. www.stateofthenation.gov.za/assets/downloads/JET%20Implementation%20Plan%202023-2027.pdf/, [accessed 26 February 2024].

The Socialist Republic of Viet Nam. (2023). Decision approving national power development Plan 8. Government News (14 June 2023). https://en.baochinhphu.vn/decision-approving-national-power-development-plan-8-111230614195813455.htm/, [accessed 1 July 2023].

The Socialist Republic of Vietnam. (2016). *Intended Nationally Determined Contribution of Viet Nam*. https://unfccc.int/documents/498031, [accessed 22 November 2022].

The Socialist Republic of Vietnam. (2020). *Updated Nationally Determined Contribution (NDC)*. https://unfccc.int/sites/default/files/NDC/2022-06/Viet%20Nam_NDC_2020_Eng.pdf, [accessed 14 October 2022].

The Socialist Republic of Vietnam. (2022). *Nationally Determined Contribution (NDC) (Updated in 2022)*. https://unfccc.int/documents/622541, [accessed 22 November 2022].

Thompson, B., Harrison, D., Chow, M. B., Haberfield, D. (2022). Vietnam's Direct PPA pilot scheme. Energy Market Update June 2022. *Mayer Brown*. www.mayerbrown.com/en/perspectives-events/publications/2022/06/vietnams-direct-ppa-pilot-scheme-energy-market-update-june-2022, [accessed 25 August 2022].

Thompson, B., Harrison, D., Chow, M. B., Nguyen, H. T. (2023). Vietnam's PDP8 Released. Mayer/Brown (18 May 2023). www.mayerbrown.com/en/perspectives-events/publications/2023/05/vietnams-pdp8-released/, [accessed 8 June 2023].

Thomsen, J., Weber, C. (2021). Getting prices for prosumers right? Incentivizing investment and operation of small-scale PV-battery storage systems through prices, charges and levies. *Z Energiewirtsch* 45, 35–59. https://doi.org/10.1007/s12398-020-00295-5.

Thomson, A. M., Calvin, K. V., Smith, S. J., Kyle, G. P., Volke, A., Patel, P., Delgado-Arias, S., Bond-Lamberty, B., Wise, M. A., Clarke, L. E., Edmonds, J. A. (2011). RCP4.5: A pathway for stabilization of radiative forcing by 2100. *Clim. Change* 109(1), 77–94. https://doi.org/10.1007/s10584-011-0151-4

Tordoir, P. (2022). Is natural gas the next coal? A framework for utilities and governments to think about the place of natural gas in the energy mix. *Electr. J.* 35(2), 107077. https://doi.org/10.1016/j.tej.2022.107077.

Tran, N. (2022). Vietnam – Power Generation, Transmission, and Distribution. International Trade Administration of the United States (Last Publication 15 December 2022). www.trade.gov/country-commercial-guides/vietnam-power-generation-transmission-and-distribution, [accessed 17 December 2022].

Trencher, G., Okubo, Y., Mori, A. (2024). Phasing out carbon not coal? Identifying coal lock-in sources in Japan's power utilities. *Clim. Policy* 24(6), 766–784. https://doi.org/10.1080/14693062.2024.2302324.

Tritto, A. (2023). How Indonesia used Chinese industrial investments to Turn Nickel into the new gold. Carnegie Endowment for International Peace. https://carnegieendowment.org/files/Tritto_Indonesia_Nickel.pdf, [accessed 27 February 2024].

Trivedi, S., Srivastava, S. (2023). 200 and counting: Global financial institutions are exiting coal. The Institute for Energy Economics and Financial Analysis (IEEFA). https://ieefa.org/resources/200-and-counting-global-financial-institutions-are-exiting-coal/ [accessed 30 September 2023].

Tuhkanen, H., Vulturius, G. (2022). Are green bonds funding the transition? Investigating the link between companies' climate targets and green debt financing. *J. Sustain. Finance Invest.* 12(4), 1194–1216. https://doi.org/10.1080/20430795.2020.1857634.

Tushman, M. L., Rosenkopf, L. (1992). Organizational determinants of technological change: Toward a sociology of technological evolution. *Res. Organ. Behav.* 14, 311–347.

Tyler, E., Mgoduso, L. (2022). *Just Energy Transitions and Partnerships in Africa: A South African Case Study*. Meridian Economics. www.iddri.org/en/publications-and-events/report/just-energy-transitions-and-partnerships-africa-south-african-case/, [accessed 26 March 2024].

U.S. Mission in Vietnam. (2023). AMI AC renewables and Honeywell to collaborate on battery energy storage system project. Press Release (12 May 2023). https://vn.usembassy.gov/ami-ac-renewables-and-honeywell-to-collaborate-on-battery-energy-storage-system-pilot-project-co-funded-by-u-s-mission-vietnam/, [accessed 8 September 2023].

Uhde, H., Malima, G. C. (2020). Experimenting with local electricity markets in China – multilevel drivers and barriers in the sociotechnical regime. *Energy Res. Soc. Sci.* 69, 101577. https://doi.org/10.1016/j.erss.2020.101577.

UK Department for Business, Energy & Industrial Strategy. (2021). *Energy Retail Market Strategy for the 2020s: Helping Consumers on their Net Zero Journey*. https://assets.publishing.service.gov.uk/government/uploads/system/uploads/attachment_data/file/1005307/energy-retail-strategy.pdf, [accessed 12 May 2023].

UN Climate Change Conference UK 2021. (2021). Global coal to clean power transition statement. https://webarchive.nationalarchives.gov.uk/ukgwa/20230313120149/, [accessed 1 July 2023].

UNDP Philippines. (2022). Making REM possible: The launch of the Philippine renewable energy (RE) market interim commercial operations. Press Release (3 August 2022). www.undp.org/philippines/press-releases/making-rempossible/, [accessed 10 May 2023].

UNEP FI. (2005). A legal framework for the integration of environmental, social and governance issues into institutional investment. www.unepfi.org/industries/investment/a-legal-framework-for-the-integration-of-environmental-social-and-governance-issues-into-institutional-investment/ [accessed 25 September 2023].

UNEP FI. (2009). Fiduciary responsibility: Legal and practical aspects of integrating environmental, social and governance issues into institutional investment. www.unepfi.org/industries/investment/fiduciary-responsibility-legal-and-practical-aspects-of-integrating-environmental-social-and-governance-issues-into-institutional-investment/ [accessed 25 September 2023].

UNEP FI. (2015). Fiduciary duty: Global statement on investor obligations and duties. www.unepfi.org/industries/investment/fiduciary-duty-global-statement-on-investor-obligations-and-duties-2/ [accessed 25 September 2023].

UNEP FI. (2021). Guidelines for climate target setting for banks. www.unepfi.org/wordpress/wp-content/uploads/2021/04/UNEP-FI-Guidelines-for-Climate-Change-Target-Setting.pdf/ [accessed 5 October 2023].

UNFCCC. (2021). The Glasgow climate pact – Key outcomes from COP 26. https://unfccc.int/process-and-meetings/the-paris-agreement/the-glasgow-climate-pact-key-outcomes-from-cop26, [accessed 15 January 2023].

Uribe-Pérez, N., Hernández, L., de la Vega, D., Angulo, I. (2016). State of the art and trends review of smart metering in electricity grids. *Appl. Sci.* 6(3), 68. https://doi.org/10.3390/app6030068.

Urpelainen, J., Yang, J. (2019). Global patterns of power sector reform, 1982–2013. *Energy Strategy Rev.* 23(2019), 152–162. https://doi.org/10.1016/j.esr.2018.12.001.

USAID. (2021). USAID vietnam low emission energy program (V-LEEP) technical report: Impact analysis of integrating significant renewable energy in Vietnam's power sector: A PLEXOS-based analysis of long-term power development planning. https://pdf.usaid.gov/pdf_docs/PA00XGQH.pdf, [accessed 7 January 2023].

van Benthem, A. A., Crooks, E., Giglio, S., et al. (2022). The effect of climate risks on the interactions between financial markets and energy companies. *Nat. Energy* 7, 690–697. https://doi.org/10.1038/s41560-022-01070-1.

Van de Graaf, T. (2018). Battling for a shrinking market: Oil producers, the renewables revolution, and the risk of stranded assets. In: Scholten, D. (eds.) *The Geopolitics of Renewables*. Springer Cham, 97–121.

van der Ploeg, F. (2020). Race to burn the last ton of carbon and the risk of stranded assets. *Eur. J. Political Econ.* 64, 101915. https://doi.org/10.1016/j.ejpoleco.2020.101915.

van der Ploeg, F., Rezai, A. (2020). Stranded assets in the transition to a carbon-free economy. *Annu. Rev. Resour. Econ.* 12, 281–298. https://doi.org/10.1146/annurev-resource-110519-040938.

Vanheukelom, J. (2023). Two years into South Africa's just energy transition partnership: How real is the deal? *Briefing Note*, No. 174. ecdpm. https://ecdpm.org/work/two-years-south-africas-just-energy-transition-partnership-how-real-deal, [accessed 21 December 2023].

Vanheukelom, J. (2023). Two years into South Africa's just energy transition partnership: How real is the deal? ECDPM (27 November 2023). https://ecdpm.org/work/two-years-south-africas-just-energy-transition-partnership-how-real-deal, [accessed 26 February 2024].

Velasco, M. M. (2022a). ERC firming up regulation on smart meters. *Manila Bulletin* (24 May 2022). https://mb.com.ph/2022/05/23/erc-firming-up-regulation-on-smart-meters/, [accessed 17 May 2023].

Velasco, M. M. (2022b). Meralco lines up 1,400MW supply procurement. *Manila Bulletin* (6 August 2022). https://mb.com.ph/2022/08/06/meralco-lines-up-1400mw-supply-procurement/, [accessed 25 June 2023].

Velasco, M. M. (2023). NGCP files MR for ancillary services contracts. *Manila Bulletin* (31 March 2023). https://mb.com.ph/2023/3/31/ngcp-files-mr-for-ancillary-services-contracts/, [accessed 16 May 2023].

Vera, M. S., Manrique, L. G., Peña, I. R., De la Vega-Navarro, A. (2023). Drivers of electricity GHG emissions and the role of natural gas in Mexican energy transition. *Energy Policy* 173, 113316. https://doi.org/10.1016/j.enpol.2022.113316.

Vermeulen, R., Schets, E., Lohuis, M., Kölbl, B., Jansen, D.-J., Heeringa, W. (2021). The heat is on: A framework for measuring financial stress under disruptive energy transition scenarios. *Ecol. Econ.* 190, 107205. https://doi.org/10.1016/j.ecolecon.2021.107205.

Viet Nam Energy Partnership Group. (2020). Factsheet on rooftop solar development. https://vepg.vn/wp-content/uploads/2021/02/VEPG_RTS_Factfile_Dec_2020_EN_fin.pdf/, [accessed 9 November 2024].

Viet Nam Energy Partnership Group. (2024). UNDP's Technical meeting on Assessment of scenarios of taking coalthermal power generation in Viet Nam to net-zero GHG emissions by 2050. *Viet Nam Energy Partnership Group News*, 17 April 2024. https://vepg.vn/2024/04/17/undps-technical-meeting-on-assessment-of-scenarios-of-taking-coalthermal-power-generation-in-viet-nam-to-net-zero-ghg-emissions-by-2050/, [accessed 22 November 2024].

Viet Nam News. (2020). EVNHCMC to complete installation of electronic meters for all customers next year (5 October 2020). https://vietnamnews.vn/society/793097/evnhcmc-to-complete-installation-of-electronic-meters-for-all-customers-next-year.html, [accessed 18 December 2022].

VietBiz. (2021). The recent development of the renewable energy market in Vietnam and its future prospective. https://vietbiz.jp/renewable-energy-vietnam/, [accessed 15 May 2023] (in Japanese).

VietBiz. (2023). Hydropower in Vietnam: Why is hydropower attracting attention? https://vietbiz.jp/en/hydro-power-vn-en/, [accessed 15 May 2023].

Vietnam Electricity. (2021). *Annual Report 2021*. https://en.evn.com.vn/userfile/User/huongBTT/files/2021/10/EVNAnnualReport2021%20final%2022_10_2021.pdf, [accessed 18 December 2022].

Vietnam Initiative for Energy Transition (VIET). (2021a). Energy storage system in Vietnam: Recommendation on technology, financial and legal mechanism support. PN/08VIET08.2021/ENG. https://vietse.vn/en/publication/energy-storage-system-in-vietnam-recommendation-on-technology-financial-and-legal-mechanism-support, [accessed 18 December 2022].

Vietnam Initiative for Energy Transition (VIET). (2021b). Virtual power plant: Digital utility technology in the Vietnam's competitive electricity market. RR/10-VIET06.2021/EN. https://vietse.vn/en/publication/virtual-power-plant-digital-utility-technology-in-the-vietnams-competitive-electricity-market, [accessed 18 December 2022].

Viola, H. (2019). The real deal behind the Philippines' power crisis. *Philstar.com* (13 April 2019). www.philstar.com/news-commentary/2019/04/13/1909737/commentary-real-deal-behind-philippines-power-crisis/, [accessed 13 May 2023].

Vo, L. T., Ju, Y. (2021). Generating or receiving carbon leakages? An examination of China's CO_2 emissions in Asia. In: Mori, A. (ed.) *China's Carbon-Energy Policy and Asia's Energy Transition: Carbon Leakage, Relocation and Halos.* Routledge, 231–251. https://doi.org/10.4324/9781003190905-14.

Vu, K. (2024). Vietnam to amend national power plan to include nuclear energy. *Reuters* (21 October 2024). www.reuters.com/business/energy/vietnam-amend-national-power-plan-include-nuclear-energy-2024-10-21/, [accessed 27 November 2024].

Vu, K., Guarascio, F. (2023). Vietnam's power blackouts hit multinationals' manufacturing hubs. *Reuters* (5 June 2023). www.reuters.com/markets/asia/vietnams-power-blackouts-hit-multinationals-manufacturing-hubs-2023-06-05/, [accessed 9 June 2023].

Vu, M. (2022). Vietnam urged to update smart grid for network reliability, *Hanoi Times* (27 March 2022). https://m.hanoitimes.vn/vietnam-urged-to-update-smart-grid-for-network-reliability-320357.html, [accessed 18 December 2022].

Vu, T. (2021). Vietnam's EVN stands out with a strong 2020 financial performance, institute for energy economics and financial analysis. https://ieefa.org/wp-content/uploads/2021/07/Vietnams-EVN-Stands-Out-With-a-Strong-2020-Financial-Performance_July-2021.pdf, [accessed 3 December 2022].

Wagas, E., Andres, B. I. (2022). Marine ecology assessment along the coast of a fossil gas-fired power plant and LNG terminal within the Verde Island passage, Northern Philippines. CEED and Caritas Philippines. https://ceedphilippines.com/wp-content/uploads/2022/06/Marine-Ecology.pdf [accessed 12 September 2023].

Wang, H., Chen, W., Bertram, C., et al. (2020a). Early transformation of the Chinese power sector to avoid additional coal lock-in. *Environ. Res. Lett.* 15, 024007. https://doi.org/10.1088/1748-9326/ab5d99.

Wang, H., Chen, W., Zhang, H., Li, N. (2020b). Modeling of power sector decarbonization in China: Comparisons of early and delayed mitigation towards the 2-degree target. *Climatic Change* 162(4), 1843–1856. https://doi.org/10.1007/s10584-019-02485-8.

Way, R., Mealy, P., Farmer, J. D. (2020). Estimating the costs of energy transition scenarios using probabilistic forecasting methods. INET Oxford Working Paper No. 2021–01. Accessed from www.inet.ox.ac.uk/files/energy_transition_cost_INET_working_paper_with_SI1.pdf

Weber, C., Möst, D., Fichtner, W. (2022). *Economics of Power Systems: Fundamentals for Sustainable Energy*. Springer Nature, Switzerland.

Winkler, H., Dubash, N. K. (2015). Who determines transformational change in development and climate finance? *Clim. Policy* 16(6), 783–791. https://doi.org/10.1080/14693062.2015.1033674.

Winkler, H., Tyler, E., Keen, S., Marquard, A. (2021). Just transition transaction in South Africa: An innovative way to finance accelerated phase out of coal and fund social justice. *J. Sustainable Finance Investment* 13(3), 1228–1251. https://doi.org/10.1080/20430795.2021.1972678.

Wischermann, J. (2024). Vietnam: The just energy transition partnership (JETP) has high political costs. Heinrich-Böll-Stiftung. www.boell.de/en/2024/03/10/just-energy-transition-partnership-vietnam-jetp-has-high-political-costs, [accessed 25 September 2024].

World Bank. (2018). *Vietnam: Achieving 12 GW of Solar PV Deployment by 2030; An Action Plan*. http://documents1.worldbank.org/curated/en/225381584425186495/pdf/Vietnam-Achieving-12-GW-of-Solar-PV-Deployment-by-2030-An-Action-Plan.pdf, [accessed 15 December 2022].

World Bank. (2022). *Vietnam: Country Climate and Development Report*. https://openknowledge.worldbank.org/bitstream/handle/10986/37618/Vietnam%20REVISED.pdf?sequence=18, [accessed 14 October 2022].

World Bank. (2023). Eskom just energy transition project in South Africa. *Factsheet* (June 5, 2023). www.worldbank.org/en/news/factsheet/2023/06/05/factsheet-eskom-just-energy-transition-project-in-afe-south-africa, [accessed 26 February 2024].

World Bank. (2024). World bank group country classifications by income level. https://datahelpdesk.worldbank.org/knowledgebase/articles/378834-how-does-the-world-bank-classify-countries, [accessed 12 March 2024].

World Bank Group. (2016). *Smart Grid to Enhance Power Transmission in Vietnam*. https://openknowledge.worldbank.org/handle/10986/24027, [accessed 12 January 2023].

World Bank Group. (2022). *Philippines Country Climate and Development Report*. World Bank, Washington, DC. http://hdl.handle.net/10986/38280/, [accessed 6 May 2023].

World Economic Forum. (2023). Here are 3 innovative ways to manage the challenge of financing the energy transition in developing economies. www.weforum.org/

stories/2023/08/financing-energy-transition-developing-economies/, [accessed 3 November 2024].

Wright, B. (2022). Vietnam's first LNG-Fired power plants in the works: The plants are expected to be put into operation no later than 2024. J. Pet. Technol. (15 March 2022). https://jpt.spe.org/vietnams-first-lng-fired-power-plants-in-the-works, [accessed 23 April 2022].

Xinhua. (2024). New Zealand commits 25 mln USD for ADB's energy transition mechanism. *Xinhua* (19 April 2024). https://english.news.cn/asiapacific/20240419/d2ec07e23a9c47cea02dfeafce4120f2/c.html, [accessed 25 September 2024].

Xu, Q., Kim, T. (2022). Financial constraints and corporate environmental policies. *Rev. Financ. Stud.* 35(2), 576–635. https://doi.org/10.1093/rfs/hhab056.

Yamashiro, R., Mori, A. (2023). Combined third-party ownership and aggregation business model for the adoption of rooftop solar PV–battery systems: Implications from the case of Miyakojima Island, Japan. *Energy Policy* 173, 13392. https://doi.org/10.1016/j.enpol.2022.113392.

Yao, X., Huang, R., Du, K. (2019). The impacts of market power on power grid efficiency: Evidence from China. *China Econ. Rev.* 55, 99–110. https://doi.org/10.1016/j.chieco.2019.02.006.

Yergin, D. (2020). *The New Map: Energy, Climate, and the Clash of Nations.* Penguin Books, New York.

Yin, R. K. (2018). *Case Study Research and Applications: Design and Method.* 6th Edition. SAGE Publications, Los Angeles.

Yip, A. W. H., Bocken, N. M. P. (2018). Sustainable business model archetypes for the banking industry. *J. Clean. Prod.* 174, 150–169. https://doi.org/10.1016/j.jclepro.2017.10.190.

Zagema, B., Kowalzig, J., Walsh, L., Hattle, A., Roy, C., Dejgaard, H. P. (2023). *Climate Finance Shadow Report 2023: Assessing the Delivery of the $100 Billion Commitment.* Oxfam International. https://policy-practice.oxfam.org/resources/climate-finance-shadow-report-2023-621500/, [accessed 1 August 2023].

Zenghelis, D., Fouquet, R., Hippe, R. (2018). Stranded assets: Then and now. In: Caldecott, B. (ed.) *Stranded Assets and the Environment: Risk, Resilience and Opportunity.* Routledge, Abingdon. 23–54.

Zhao, X., Shi, Z. (2023). What's holding back transition finance in China? *China Dialogue* (11 April 2023). https://chinadialogue.net/en/energy/whats-holding-back-transition-finance-in-china/, [accessed 6 October 2023].

Zhou, H. (2018). Preface. In: Zhou, H., Qiu, W., Sun, K., … Yu, J. (eds.) *Ultra-high Voltage AC/DC Power Transmission.* Zhejiang University Press and Springer, Beijing. v–viii.

Zissler, R. (2023). *Renewable Energy: The Top-Priority for Southeast Asia to Fully Blossom*. Renewable Energy Institute, Tokyo. www.renewable-ei.org/en/activities/reports/20230905.php/ [accessed 5 September 2023].

Zott, C., Amit, R., Massa, L. (2011). The business model: Recent developments and future research. *J. Manage*. 37, 1019–1042. https://doi.org/10.1177/0149206311406265.

Index

For EU product safety concerns, contact us at Calle de José Abascal, 56–1°,
28003 Madrid, Spain or eugpsr@cambridge.org.

www.ingramcontent.com/pod-product-compliance
Ingram Content Group UK Ltd.
Pitfield, Milton Keynes, MK11 3LW, UK
UKHW022005220926
475880UK00004B/253
* 9 7 8 1 0 0 9 6 8 9 4 2 7 *